DK Communication

Lisa A. Ford-Brown
Columbia College

PEARSON

Boston Columbus Indianapolis New York San Francisco
Amsterdam Cape Town Dubai London Madrid Milan
Munich Paris Montréal Toronto Delhi Mexico City
São Paulo Sydney Hong Kong Seoul Singapore
Taipei Tokyo

Text design, page layout, and cover design: Stuart Jackman

PEARSON

Publisher, Communication: Karon Bowers
Editorial Assistant: Nikki Toner
Director of Development: Brita Nordin
Associate Creative Director: Blair Brown
Program Team Lead: Maureen Richardson
Program Manager: Anne Ricigliano
Project Team Lead: Melissa Feimer
Project Manager: Raegan Heerema
Product Marketer: Becky Rowland
Digital Project Lead: Peggy Bliss
Digital Media Project Manager: Sean Silver
Project Coordination and Electronic Page Makeup:
 Integra Software Services, Pvt. Ltd.
Cover Creative Director: Maria Lange
Cover Credits: Mint Images - Tim Robbins/Getty Images,
 Hero Images/Getty Images, Elena11/Shutterstock
Permissions Specialist: Peggy Davis
Text Permissions Project Manager: Jen Roach,
 Lumina Datamatics, Inc.
Printer/Binder: RR Donnelley/Crawfordsville
Cover Printer: Phoenix Color/Hagerstown

Acknowledgments of third party content appear on page 496, which constitutes an extension of this copyright page.

Library of Congress Cataloging-in-Publication Data

Names: Ford-Brown, Lisa A., author.
Title: DK Communication/Lisa Ford-Brown, Ph.D.
Description: Hoboken, NJ: Pearson Education, Inc., [2015] | Includes bibliographical references and index.
Identifiers: LCCN 2015038113 | ISBN 9780205956579 (student edition)
Subjects: LCSH: Communication.
Classification: LCC P91.2 .F67 2015 | DDC 302.2—dc23
LC record available at http://lccn.loc.gov/2015038113

Revel Edition ISBN 13: 978-0-13-396889-7
ISBN 10: 0-13-396889-8

Student Edition: ISBN 13: 978-0-205-95657-9
ISBN 10: 0-205-95657-2

Annotated Instructor's Edition: ISBN 13: 978-0-13-447578-3
ISBN 10: 0-13-447578-X

PEARSON

www.pearsonhighered.com

Contents

Part One: Understand Communication

Chapter 5:
Listening

Part Three: Connect with Others

Interpersonal Communication

Chapter 6:
Interpersonal Relationships

Public Communication

Chapter 11:
Creating a Speech

Chapter 12:
Presenting a Speech

Preface

Communication is dynamic, interactive, and engaging—so why not learn it that way? *DK Communication* combines a powerfully visual Dorling Kindersley (DK) design and strategically chunked information for a compelling new approach to the introduction to communication course. Concepts and theory come to life through visual examples and graphics that allow students to better understand ideas and make connections at a glance.

DK Communication features the straightforward descriptions, examples, and practical information that students seek and is supported with the foundational content instructors know their students need to succeed. Learning objectives are fully integrated with chapter contents, text, and review sections to consistently reinforce important content and help students improve their communication skills. In addition, headings utilize a question-and-answer format to address common student questions with clear answers.

Combining these elements with its comprehensive yet concise coverage, *DK Communication* offers an easy-to-navigate resource that equips students with the tools and confidence to be effective communicators in the classroom and beyond.

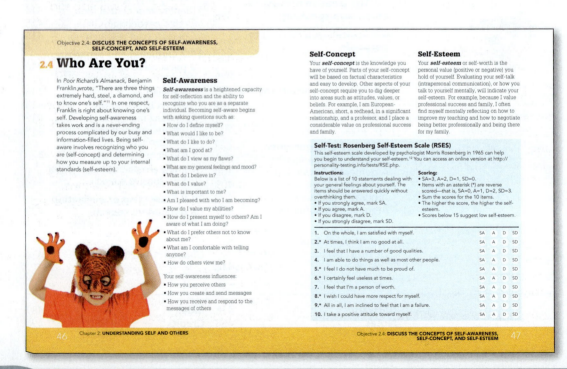

2.4 Who Are You?

In *Poor Richard's Almanack*, Benjamin Franklin wrote, "There are three things extremely hard, steel, a diamond, and to know one's self."[11] In one respect, Franklin is right about knowing one's self. Developing self-awareness takes work and is a never-ending process complicated by our busy and information-filled lives. Being self-aware involves recognizing who you are (self-concept) and determining how you measure up to your internal standards (self-esteem).

Self-Awareness

Self-awareness is a heightened capacity for self-reflection and the ability to recognize who you are as a separate individual. Becoming self-aware begins with asking questions such as:

- How do I define myself?
- What would I like to be?
- What do I like to do?
- What am I good at?
- What do I view as my flaws?
- What are my general feelings and mood?
- What do I believe in?
- What do I value?
- What is important to me?
- Am I pleased with who I am becoming?
- How do I value my abilities?
- How do I present myself to others? Am I aware of what I am doing?
- What do I prefer others not to know about me?
- What am I comfortable with telling anyone?
- How do others view me?

Your self-awareness influences:

- How you perceive others
- How you create and send messages
- How you receive and respond to the messages of others

Self-Concept

Your *self-concept* is the knowledge you have of yourself. Parts of your self-concept will be based on factual characteristics and easy to develop. Other aspects of your self-concept require you to dig deeper into areas such as attitudes, values, or beliefs. For example, I am European-American, short, a redhead, in a significant relationship, and a professor, and I place a considerable value on professional success and family.

Self-Test: Rosenberg Self-Esteem Scale (RSES)

This self-esteem scale developed by psychologist Morris Rosenberg in 1965 can help you begin to understand your self-esteem.[12] You can access an online version at http://personality-testing.info/tests/RSE.php.

Instructions:
Below is a list of 10 statements dealing with your general feelings about yourself. The items should be answered quickly without overthinking them.
- If you strongly agree, mark SA.
- If you agree, mark A.
- If you disagree, mark D.
- If you strongly disagree, mark SD.

Self-Esteem

Your *self-esteem* or self-worth is the personal value (positive or negative) you hold of yourself. Evaluating your self-talk (intrapersonal communication), or how you talk to yourself mentally, will indicate your self-esteem. For example, because I value professional success and family, I often find myself mentally reflecting on how to improve my teaching and how to negotiate being better professionally and being there for my family.

Scoring:
- SA=3, A=2, D=1, SD=0.
- Items with an asterisk (*) are reverse scored—that is, SA=0, A=1, D=2, SD=3.
- Sum the scores for the 10 items.
- The higher the score, the higher the self-esteem.
- Scores below 15 suggest low self-esteem.

	SA	A	D	SD
1. On the whole, I am satisfied with myself.	SA	A	D	SD
2.* At times, I think I am no good at all.	SA	A	D	SD
3. I feel that I have a number of good qualities.	SA	A	D	SD
4. I am able to do things as well as most other people.	SA	A	D	SD
5.* I feel I do not have much to be proud of.	SA	A	D	SD
6.* I certainly feel useless at times.	SA	A	D	SD
7. I feel that I'm a person of worth.	SA	A	D	SD
8.* I wish I could have more respect for myself.	SA	A	D	SD
9.* All in all, I am inclined to feel that I am a failure.	SA	A	D	SD
10. I take a positive attitude toward myself.	SA	A	D	SD

Features

REVEL™

Educational technology designed for the way today's students read, think, and learn

When students are engaged deeply, they learn more effectively and perform better in their courses. This simple fact inspired the creation of REVEL: an immersive learning experience designed for the way today's students read, think, and learn. Built in collaboration with educators and students nationwide, REVEL is the newest, fully digital way to deliver respected Pearson content. REVEL enlivens course content with media interactives and assessments—integrated directly within the author's narrative—that provide opportunities for students to read about and practice course material in tandem. This immersive educational technology boosts student engagement, which leads to better understanding of concepts and improved performance throughout the course.

Learn more about REVEL
http://www.pearsonhighered.com/REVEL/

In every chapter, interactive features promote comprehension and mastery of core concepts in ways that will engage students. These features include:

- **Videos with Accompanying Video Self-Checks** – Videos bring to life additional examples, scenarios, and explanations of communication principles across interpersonal, group, and public speaking situations. Sample speeches allow students to see speeches being delivered and provide extra help for students in developing and delivering their own speeches. Many videos are accompanied by video self-checks that allow students to test their knowledge of the content and information in the videos.

- **Self-Assessments** – Self-assessment instruments allow students to analyze their own communication styles, enabling them to learn and grow over the duration of the course.

- **Interactive Figures** – Figures and illustrations in the text (such as the Johari Window, Gottman's Negative Conflict Behaviors, and Maslow's Hierarchy of Needs) have been animated to make complex concepts easier to understand through interactivity.

- **Integrated Writing Opportunities** – Questions for review and reflection are integrated into the text, giving students an opportunity to stop and think about the content presented and to respond in a written format. These writing opportunities take the form of Journal prompts for individual student response and Shared Writing prompts that allow students to respond to and discuss the same questions as their classmates.

- **Audio Excerpts** – In-line audio allows students to hear short excerpts of dialogue, language use, and speeches as they read, giving them a better appreciation of these examples than can be gained from a printed text. These excerpts are identified in color both in print and in REVEL and are identified by red audio buttons in REVEL.

- **Full-Length Speech Outlines with Annotations** – Three complete preparation outlines of student speeches (two informative, one persuasive) are accompanied by audio annotations that highlight good outlining form and explain some of the choices the speakers made while preparing their outlines and speeches.

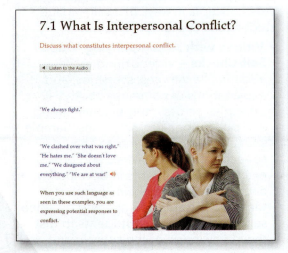

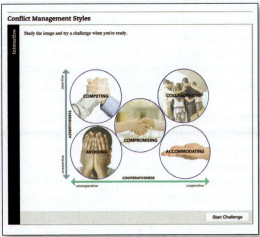

For more information about all the tools and resources in REVEL and access to your own REVEL account for *DK Communication*, go to www.pearsonhighered.com/REVEL

Additional Features

Designed for easy navigation and use: Color-coded chapters, chunked content, and question-and-answer heading formats help students quickly find the information they need. REVEL includes links between the table of contents, chapter contents, and modules to help students navigate the text.

Presents concepts visually, supported by text: The pairing of visuals and detailed explanations allows students to get an overview at a glance and read on for specifics. In REVEL, many visuals are animated to further help students understand concepts.

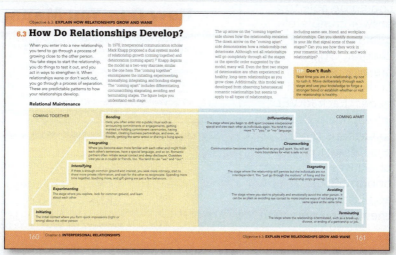

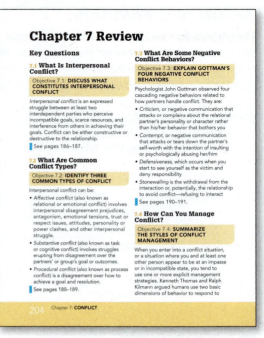

Chapter 7 Review

Key Questions

7.1 What Is Interpersonal Conflict?

Objective 7.1: DISCUSS WHAT CONSTITUTES INTERPERSONAL CONFLICT

Interpersonal conflict is an expressed struggle between at least two interdependent parties who perceive incompatible goals, scarce resources, and interference from others in achieving their goals. Conflict can be either constructive or destructive to the relationship.

See pages 186–187.

7.2 What Are Common Conflict Types?

Objective 7.2: IDENTIFY THREE COMMON TYPES OF CONFLICT

Interpersonal conflict can be:

* *Affective conflict* (also known as relational or emotional conflict) involves interpersonal disagreement prejudices, antagonism, emotional tensions, trust or respect issues, attitudes, personality or power clashes, and other interpersonal struggle.
* *Substantive conflict* (also known as task or cognitive conflict) involves struggles erupting from disagreement over the partners' or group's goal or outcomes.
* *Procedural conflict* (also known as process conflict) is a disagreement over how to achieve a goal and resolution.

See pages 188–189.

7.3 What Are Some Negative Conflict Behaviors?

Objective 7.3: EXPLAIN GOTTMAN'S FOUR NEGATIVE CONFLICT BEHAVIORS

Psychologist John Gottman observed four cascading negative behaviors related to how partners handle conflict. They are:

* *Criticism*, or negative communication that attacks or complains about the relational partner's personality or character rather than his/her behavior that bothers you
* *Contempt*, or negative communication that attacks or tears down the partner's self-worth with the intention of insulting or psychologically abusing her/him
* *Defensiveness*, which occurs when you start to see yourself as the victim and deny responsibility
* *Stonewalling* is the withdrawal from the interaction or, potentially, the relationship to avoid conflict—refusing to interact

See pages 190–191.

7.4 How Can You Manage Conflict?

Objective 7.4: SUMMARIZE THE STYLES OF CONFLICT MANAGEMENT

When you enter into a *conflict situation*, or a situation where you and at least one other person appear to be at an impasse or in incompatible state, you tend to use one or more explicit management strategies. Kenneth Thomas and Ralph Kilmann argued humans use two basic dimensions of behavior to respond to

Incorporates learning objectives in multiple ways: Learning objectives are emphasized throughout. Each chapter's table of contents and review section pair the objectives with their corresponding headings. Reinforcing the objectives, each chapter module starts with a question that students should be able to answer completely after reading the chapter. Objectives are also repeated at the bottoms of pages. Each REVEL interactive is designed to further support chapter learning objectives, providing opportunities for application, self-checks, and reflection.

Objective 7.4: **SUMMARIZE THE STYLES OF CONFLICT MANAGEMENT**

7.4 How Can You Manage Conflict?

When you enter into a ***conflict situation***, or a situation in which you and at least one other person appear to be at an impasse or in an incompatible state, you tend to use one or more explicit management styles. ***Conflict management*** is the

For more than 35 years, the Thomas-Kilmann Conflict Mode Instrument (TKI) has been the leading measure of conflict behavior strategies. Drawing from the work of Robert Blake and Jane Mouton, management researchers Kenneth Thomas and Ralph Kilmann argued humans use two basic dimensions of behavior to

Style	Corresponding Statements	Total
Accommodating	1, 10, 15	___ + ___ + ___ = ___
Avoiding	2, 6, 13	___ + ___ + ___ = ___
Collaborating	4, 7, 12	___ + ___ + ___ = ___
Competing	5, 8, 14	___ + ___ + ___ = ___
Compromising	3, 9, 11	___ + ___ + ___ = ___

Objective 7.4: **SUMMARIZE THE STYLES OF CONFLICT MANAGEMENT**   195

Emphasizes the big picture: Students are shown how to view any act of communication from a wider perspective, beginning with (1) understanding communication foundations, (2) using this knowledge to shape messages, and (3) building on both of these areas to connect with others in interpersonal relationships, small group interactions, and public speeches. An Understand–Shape–Connect graphic is used in each of the interpersonal, small group, and public speaking sections to emphasize their connections. REVEL features an interactive version of the graphic for more student engagement.

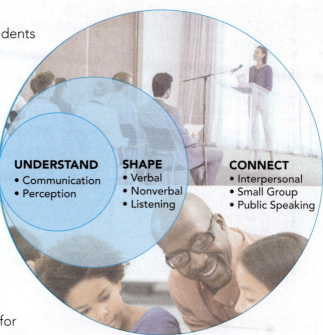

UNDERSTAND
- Communication
- Perception

SHAPE
- Verbal
- Nonverbal
- Listening

CONNECT
- Interpersonal
- Small Group
- Public Speaking

Practicing Ethics: Responsible Decisions

It is important for groups to make good, ethical decisions. Members should ask:

- Are we accomplishing the most important goal?
- Are there potential unintended or undesirable results? Is there a less harmful solution? If we were the ones influenced, would we still support it?
- What are the short- and long-term effects? What are the risks?
- Can we live with taking our decision public, or would we feel the need to hide behind the decision?

Emphasizes ethics in every communication situation: Building on the Chapter 1 discussion of ethics, *Practicing Ethics* sections are integrated into each chapter. To further draw attention to the importance of ethics, many of these sections in REVEL are paired with a Journal prompt or other writing exercise.

Practicing Ethics: Don't Fake It

Faking an impression or identity out of deceit, whether in person or in a mediated context, is unethical and even illegal in some situations. Strive to never construct an identity that is for personal gain only, designed to hurt others, or fraudulent.

Self-Test: Assess Your Conflict Management Style

Pinpointing exactly what conflict management style you will use in a given situation is a bit complex for a simple quiz. However, being cognizant of what behaviors you tend to rely on will help you understand your tendencies and can potentially help you change your behavior if needed.

As you read the following 15 statements, rate each with the following scale. Think about which ones seem the most reasonable or comfortable.

3 = Agree   2 = Somewhat Agree   1 = Disagree   0 = No opinion

___ **1.** "We should all get along. That is what is important."

___ **2.** "I just keep quiet when others disagree with me."

___ **3.** "You have to win some and you have to lose some."

___ **4.** "I need to make a decision about this issue but I want to hear what you think we should do."

___ **5.** "I love a good argument."

___ **6.** "You really can't do anything about most serious issues."

___ **7.** "I like working with others on problems."

___ **8.** "I often tell others how it is or what is right."

___ **9.** "Let's meet halfway on this."

___ **10.** "If this will make you happy, I will back off."

___ **11.** "If you get that, I want this."

___ **12.** "Let's consider everyone's feelings and concerns."

___ **13.** "I prefer to avoid people who don't have the same opinions as I do."

___ **14.** "I love the hunt for the right answer and the exhilaration of achievement."

___ **15.** "I worry about what others need. I can back off of my point of view."

Now, place the ranking you gave each corresponding statement in the equation under the "Total" column. Add the equations to determine which style or styles you relate to the most.

Style	Corresponding Statements	Total
Accommodating	1, 10, 15	___ + ___ + ___ = ___
Avoiding	2, 6, 13	___ + ___ + ___ = ___
Collaborating	4, 7, 12	
Competing	5, 8, 14	
Compromising	3, 9, 11	

TIP: Length
- Your introduction should be less than 15 percent of your total speech time.
- Your conclusion should be less than 5 percent of your total speech time.

Features self-checks, self-tests, and tips for practical application: Self-checks or self-tests in every chapter give students practical tools to assess their abilities. Boxed tips provide useful information and advice along the way. Many of these items in REVEL include interactive self-assessments or writing prompts.

Highlights examples: Diverse examples and scenarios are used throughout, with items such as dialogue, language techniques, and speech excerpts highlighted in an easy-to-find blue font. In REVEL, many examples include audio clips so students can hear as well as see examples of effective communication.

Main point I

The City of Jackson needs to institute a plan to decrease the number of pigeons because each year, thousands of pigeons flock to the city.

Subpoint A

Includes thorough coverage of public speaking: The public speaking chapters provide step-by-step practical guidance for creating and presenting a speech. Coverage includes numerous examples, many of them annotated, and emphasizes how to evaluate sources and how to cite them orally and in written form. REVEL provides videos of a variety of speeches as well as outlines with audio annotations.

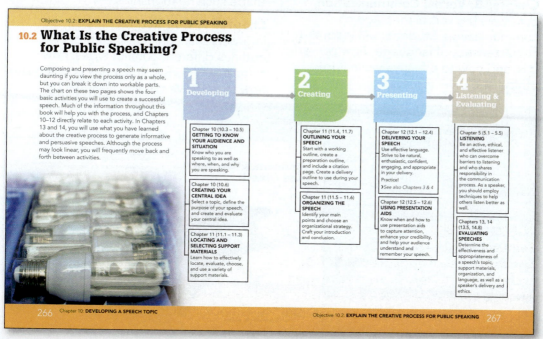

Objective 10.2: EXPLAIN THE CREATIVE PROCESS FOR PUBLIC SPEAKING

10.2 What Is the Creative Process for Public Speaking?

Composing and presenting a speech may seem daunting if you view the process only as a whole, but you can break it down into workable parts. The chart on these two pages shows the four basic activities you will use to create a successful speech. Much of the information throughout this book will help you with the process, and Chapters 10–12 directly relate to each activity. In Chapters 13 and 14, you will use what you have learned about the creative process to generate informative and persuasive speeches. Although the process may look linear, you will frequently move back and forth between activities.

1 Developing

2 Creating

3 Presenting

4 Listening & Evaluating

Chapter 10 (10.3 – 10.5)
GETTING TO KNOW YOUR AUDIENCE AND SITUATION
Know who you are speaking to as well as where, when, and why you are speaking.

Chapter 10 (10.6)
CREATING YOUR CENTRAL IDEA
Select a topic, define the purpose of your speech, and create and evaluate your central idea.

Chapter 11 (11.1 – 11.3)
LOCATING AND SELECTING SUPPORT MATERIALS
Learn how to effectively locate, evaluate, choose, and use a variety of support materials.

Chapter 11 (11.4, 11.7)
OUTLINING YOUR SPEECH
Start with a working outline, create a preparation outline, and include a citation page. Create a delivery outline to use during your speech.

Chapter 11 (11.5 – 11.6)
ORGANIZING THE SPEECH
Identify your main points and choose an organizational strategy. Craft your introduction and conclusion.

Chapter 12 (12.1 – 12.4)
DELIVERING YOUR SPEECH
Use effective language. Strive to be natural, enthusiastic, confident, engaging, and appropriate in your delivery. Practice!
› See also Chapters 3 & 4

Chapter 12 (12.5 – 12.6)
USING PRESENTATION AIDS
Know when and how to use presentation aids to capture attention, enhance your credibility, and help your audience understand and remember your speech.

Chapter 5 (5.1 – 5.5)
LISTENING
Be an active, ethical, and effective listener who can overcome barriers to listening and who shares responsibility in the communication process. As a speaker, you should employ techniques to help others listen better as well.

Chapters 13, 14 (13.5, 14.8)
EVALUATING SPEECHES
Determine the effectiveness and appropriateness of a speech's topic, support materials, organization, and language, as well as a speaker's delivery and ethics.

266   Chapter 10: DEVELOPING A SPEECH TOPIC

Objective 10.2: EXPLAIN THE CREATIVE PROCESS FOR PUBLIC SPEAKING   267

Chapter Overview

Chapter 1, Defining Human Communication, investigates why we communicate, what constitutes communication, and how to be a successful, ethical communicator. Students will learn the communication process, types of communication, and specific methods for communicating across cultures. This chapter frames the rest of the book.

Chapter 2, Understanding Self and Others, explores perception of self and others through examining perception as a process, influences on perception, and how to manage self-perception. The chapter's goal is to increase perception awareness and to help develop perception skills.

Chapter 3, Verbal Communication, considers the verbal message of communication. Students will learn the characteristics of language, how powerful it is, and how to effectively use it in ethical and diverse ways.

Chapter 4, Nonverbal Communication, examines specific characteristics of nonverbal communication, how it functions, and the channels used to convey nonverbal messages. Students will learn how to be better nonverbal communicators.

Chapter 5, Listening, discusses the listening process, important listening skills, and the different types of listening. Students will investigate barriers to effective listening and strategies for improvement.

Chapter 6, Interpersonal Relationships, explores what interpersonal relationships are, how they develop, and how to improve them. Students will consider how self-disclosure, culture, and gender shape such relationships.

Chapter 7, Conflict, focuses on interpersonal conflict. The chapter outlines different conflict types, how culture and gender influence conflict, and how to improve conflict negotiation.

Chapter 8, Group Communication and Leadership, investigates what constitutes a small group, how groups develop, and how to improve small group skills. Students will study small group networks, leadership and membership roles, and how culture and gender influence small group development.

Chapter 9, Groups at Work, focuses on group decision making and problem solving. Students will discuss how to generate ideas, how groups come to an ultimate decision or solution, how diversity influences group work, and how to communicate in a meeting.

Chapter 10, Developing a Speech Topic, starts the process of composing and presenting a speech. Students will learn the importance of audience/situation analysis, how to conduct an analysis, and how to create a central idea.

Chapter 11, Creating a Speech, guides students through researching and outlining a speech. Students will learn how to effectively locate, evaluate, and choose support materials and how to employ various organizational strategies.

Chapter 12, Presenting a Speech, offers advice on delivering a speech and using presentation aids. Students will explore effective language use and delivery techniques and find guidance on when and how to use presentation aids.

Chapter 13, Informative Speaking, explores the creative process for informative speaking. Students will learn what constitutes informative speaking and what is specific to developing, organizing, presenting, and evaluating an informative speech.

Chapter 14, Persuasive Speaking, explores the creative process for persuasive speaking. Students will learn what constitutes persuasive speaking and what is specific to developing, organizing, presenting, and evaluating a persuasive speech. Discussion includes exploring an argument, the types of arguments, and some common fallacies.

Instructor and Student Resources

Pearson MediaShare

Pearson's comprehensive media upload tool allows students to post video, images, audio, or documents for instructor and peer viewing, time-stamped commenting, and assessment. MediaShare is an easy, mobile way for students and professors to interact and engage with speeches, presentation aids, group projects, and other files. MediaShare gives professors the tools to provide contextual feedback to demonstrate how students can improve their skills.

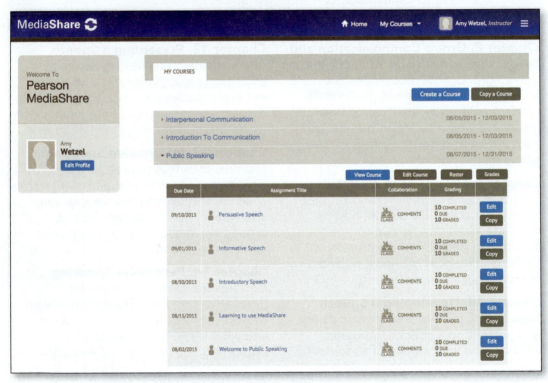

Structured like a social networking site, MediaShare helps promote a sense of community among students. In both online and in-seat course settings, MediaShare saves instructors valuable time and enriches the student learning experience by providing contextual feedback.

- Use MediaShare to assign or view speeches, outlines, presentation aids, video-based assignments, role plays, group projects, and more in a variety of formats, including video, Word, PowerPoint, and Excel.
- Assess students using customizable, Pearson-provided rubrics or create your own around classroom goals, learning outcomes, or department initiatives.
- Set up assignments for students with options for full-class viewing and commenting, private comments between you and the student, peer groups for reviewing, or as collaborative group assignments.
- Record video directly from a tablet, phone, or other webcam (including a batch upload option for instructors) and tag submissions to a specific student or assignment.
- Set up Learning Objectives tied to specific assignments, rubrics, or quiz questions to track student progress.

- Embed video from YouTube to incorporate current events into the classroom experience.
- Set up quiz questions on video assignments to ensure students master concepts and interact and engage with the media.
- Sync slides to media submissions for more robust presentation options.
- Import grades into most learning management systems.
- Ensure a secure learning environment for instructors and students through robust privacy settings.
- Upload videos, comment on submissions, and grade directly from our new MediaShare app, available as a free download from the iTunes store and GooglePlay; search for Pearson MediaShare.

Pearson MediaShare is available as a standalone product, as part of MyCommunicationLab, or in a package with REVEL.

Additional Resources

Key instructor resources include an Instructor's Manual (ISBN 978-0-205-89777-3), Test Bank (ISBN 978-0-205-94052-3), and PowerPoint Presentation Package (ISBN 978-0-205-94050-9). These supplements are available at www.pearsonhighered.com/irc (instructor login required). MyTest online test-generating software (ISBN 978-0-205-94051-6) is available at www.pearsonmytest.com (instructor login required).

For a complete listing of the instructor and student resources available with this text, please visit the Pearson Communication catalog at www.pearsonhighered.com/communication.

Acknowledgments

When I was a college student, many aspects about human communication caught my attention. This book is a culmination of that attraction as well as years of working with outstanding mentors, colleagues, and students. Thanks go to everyone whose work, input, and contributions are reflected in this book, including: at Pearson and Dorling Kindersley, Karon Bowers (Publisher, Communication), Brenda Hadenfeldt (Development Editor), Stuart Jackman (Design Director for DK Education), Sophie Mitchell (Publishing Director for DK Education), Raegan Heerema (Project Manager, Communication), Anne Ricigliano (Program Manager, Communication/The Arts), Blair Tuckman (Senior Marketing Manager), Becky Rowland (Product Marketing Manager), and Veronica Grupico (Editorial Assistant); the reviewers (listed on the opposite page); research assistants Karissa (Scott) King, Lauren Jaeger; Steven Dotson, Crystaldawn Howell, and Jared Reichel; current and former Columbia College students Michelle E. Arnold, Jeff Barringer, Caitlin Jenkins Campbell, Andria Caruthers, Desiree Chong, Rachel Coleman, Kelly Feisel, Tori Gehlert, Ashley Hardy, Brianna Hickman, Charity J. Hunter, Candace Johnson, Megan Kelly, Katherine Mancuso, Milos Milosavljevic, Logan Park, Shakeera Schneller, Kylie E. Stephenson, Jessica Ucci, Christopher Vietti, Mike Long, Klarissa McAuley, Rachel Wester, Morgan Wilde, Jamie Smith, and Ali Alnasser.

Throughout this project, I have been fortunate to enjoy the support and assistance of many colleagues on the Columbia College campus. I wish to thank President Scott Dalrymple, David Starrett, Terry Smith, David Roebuck, Peter Monacell, Mara Roberts, Janet Caruthers, Lucia D'Agostino, Mary Batterson, Peter Neely, Johanna Denzin, Tonia Compton, Gretchen Hendrickson, Amy Darnell, Laura Smith, the Humanities Department, and the entire Columbia College Technology Services group (specifically Gary Stanowski, Stefanie McCollum, B.J. Donaldson, Matt Meininger, Jennifer Tice, and Michael Van Duser).

I would like to thank several exceptional educators who have influenced me both professionally and personally: Sheron J. Dailey, C. Sue Davis, Mary Carol Harris, Harriet McNeal, Dan P. Millar, Ron Pelias, and Elyse Pineau.

I am extremely grateful to the Ford, Camp, and Brown families for all their support and understanding. Most importantly, I must recognize my life partner, Bruce Brown. Your devotion, patience, insight, and willingness to pick up extra duties are great examples of unconditional love.

Alone we can do so little.
Together we can do so much.
Helen Keller[1]

I thank you all!

Lisa A. Ford-Brown

Reviewers

Jennifer Adams, DePauw University; Martha Antolik, Wright State University; Joseph Bailey, Hardin-Simmons University; Kris Barton, Dalton State College; Tanya Biami, Cochise College; Pete Bicak, Rockhurst University; Myra Bozeman, Sinclair Community College; Ellen Bremen, Highline Community College; Luke Brenneman, Arizona State University; Amy Bryant, Nashville State Community College; Rod Carveth, Morgan State University; Tasha Davis, Austin Community College; Web Drake, Union University; Norman Earls, Jr., Valdosta State University; Brandy Fair, Grayson College; Diane Ferrero-Paluzzi, Iona College; Jodi Gaete, Suffolk County Community College; Angela Gibson, Shelton State Community College; Steven Ginley, Morton College; Justin Guild, Ivy Tech Community College; Heather Heritage, Cedarville University; Tracey Holley, Tarleton State College; Jason Hough, Hartnell College; Ladori Lara, Austin Community College; Gordana Lazic, University of Colorado, Denver; Joe Lock, Kirkwood Community College; Tami Martinez, Indiana University South Bend; Naomi Mathews, Seminole State College; Elizabeth McLaughlin, Valencia Community College; Laurie Metcalf, Blinn College; John Nash, Moraine Valley Community College; Kim Nyman, Collin College; Kate Pantinas, Ivy Tech Community College; John Parrish, Tarrant County College; Carol Paulnock, Saint Paul College; Daniel Paulnock, Saint Paul College; Sandy Pensoneau-Conway, Southern Illinois University; Owen Pillion, College of Southern Nevada; Brandi Quesenberry, Virginia Polytechnic Institute and State University; Richelle F. Rogers, Loyola University, Chicago; David Rosteck, University of Arizona; Tracy Routsong, Washburn University; Jessica Samens, Bethel University; Sheldon Smart, Tarrant County College; Tanika Smith, Prince George's Community College; Charlotte Toguchi, University of Hawaii; Lori Trumbo, Greenville Technical College; Becca Turner, Abraham Baldwin Agricultural College; John Weaver, Binghamton University; Denise Woolsey, Yavapai College; Elizabeth Word, Highline Community College

DK Communication

Chapter 1
Defining Human Communication

1.1 Why Do We Communicate?

Because much of how we communicate is usually something we learn as we go about our lives, it may seem unnecessary to study communication. However, as you will discover in this text, we can all learn better and new ways of interacting. Improving our communication skills is critical because those skills help us fulfill specific needs that are practical, professional, public, and personal.

Practical Needs

What would your day be like if you didn't have language or the ability to gesture or use facial expressions? You couldn't order your lunch, give directions, ask where you can find a particular bolt at the hardware store, or show your dentist how your tooth pain feels. It may seem like this type of communication is easy or natural, but it takes skill. Remember the last time you asked someone for directions and the person giving the directions was too detailed in his or her description. Or, recall the last time your boss gave you a new assignment with little detail on how to carry it out. Ineffective interaction even in these everyday communicative activities can cause major misunderstandings and problems. You have a practical need to communicate as you go about your daily life.

Professional Needs

When looking for a job, you will find that most employers place a high emphasis on good written and oral communication skills as they are hiring and evaluating their employees. (See the Tip box below.) The basic job interview is quite possibly the most difficult persuasive communication you will undertake. There are very few classes or jobs where you will not need to give a presentation or speech of some sort. Individuals who develop effective communication skills get better grades, more promotions, and higher pay, and they have more overall success in their educational and professional careers. No matter what major you select or what profession you end up working in, you will need to be able to interact effectively with colleagues, clients, customers, employees, and managers.

Public Needs

You will likely find a time in your life when you need to give a public speech in your community, develop close relationships with members of the public, or participate in civic groups. You may find yourself the president of a local historical society or a spokesperson for a special group. You may find yourself moved to run for political office or to speak out against or for a new law or policy. You will encounter numerous times throughout your life when you will need or feel the responsibility to take a stand, speak up, and influence others. Indeed, communication (especially public speaking) becomes a social force linking you to others, community, and country. Doing it well is one of your most powerful civic duties.

TIP: Unleash Your Potential

Research consistently demonstrates the importance of communication skills to your ability to get and keep a job. Here are the skills researchers suggest you must have.

1. Ability to communicate well in writing and verbally, including the ability to listen
2. Ability to analyze, organize, and plan
3. Ability to think creatively and willingness to be a lifelong learner
4. Ability to make decisions and solve problems
5. Ability to evoke team spirit and be cooperative
6. Ability to obtain and process information
7. Technical job-related knowledge
8. Computer, reading, and math proficiency
9. Ability to persuade
10. Good work attitude, manners, ethics, integrity, confidence, and control

Each of these is either directly or indirectly related to your communication skills. Developing and honing your communication competence will benefit you in every aspect of your life.[1]

Personal Needs

Most human beings spend their entire lives trying to connect personally with others, and for good reasons. We connect and communicate to build relationships, develop our identity, and maintain our health.

Relationships

Social interaction is any relationship based on communicative interaction between you and others. Effective communication offers you the means to create and maintain those relationships. Imagine how unhappy you would be if you didn't have the means to interact with others for enjoyment or to create an intimate relationship. Even when you experience conflict within a relationship, it is often communication that leads to an effective resolution. We are constantly looking for new technologies—such as FaceTime, Skype, texting, and email—to help us reach out to those we care about.

▌**Chapters 6 and 7** offer details on communicating within relationships.

Identity

Intertwined with our relationships is our need to understand who we are. It is through your interaction with others that you develop a sense of self, by comparing your understanding of self to others, by observing their reactions to you, and by seeing how they define you.

▌**Chapter 2** explores understanding the self and others.

Health

When denied social interaction, our physical and mental health suffers; even death can ensue. Scholars often cite the extremely unethical language deprivation experiment of German emperor Frederick II in the 13th century. The emperor allegedly placed 50 newborns in isolation to see what language they would develop on their own. Nurses caring for the babies could feed and bathe the babies but not hold or talk to them. As Salimbene di Adam, the Italian monk who recorded Frederick II's experiments, wrote, "[Fredrick] labored in vain, for the children could not live without clapping of hands, and gestures, and gladness of countenance, and blandishment." All of the children died.[2]

Current research on the benefits of touch for premature infants has led to changes in some hospitals such as staff using "kangaroo care," bundling an infant close to the body with skin-to-skin contact, for an hour or more.[3] For adults, researchers suggest that social interaction adds 7.5 years to the human lifespan.[4] Therefore, greater socialization is as beneficial as not smoking or consuming alcohol and seems to be slightly more beneficial than increased physical activity or weight reduction. Still other research suggests that strong social interaction can prevent illnesses like heart disease, high blood pressure, and even the common cold.

Communication Helps You Meet Your Needs

Practical
- Allows you to carry out necessary daily tasks
- Prevents major misunderstandings and problems in everyday life

Professional
- Assists you in getting a job
- Gives you the means to carry out professional tasks and to interact with colleagues or customers
- If effective, can lead to professional success

Public
- Allows you to fulfill your civic duty
- Gives you the means to stand up for rights
- Permits the transmission of knowledge in a public context

Personal
- Helps you build and maintain relationships
- Leads to a better understanding and development of self
- Helps maintain your physical and mental health

I believe that every right implies a responsibility; every opportunity, an obligation; every possession, a duty.[5]

John D. Rockefeller, Jr.

1.2 What Is Human Communication?

Think about all the times you interact with someone else. You yell at your sister to wake up as you head to breakfast. You text your best friend about when you will pick him up. You call your boss to see when you need to work, while you email an event coordinator the text of the speech you will give. On your way out the door, you hug your mom and wish her a happy birthday. All of these actions are communication.

Communication is the intentional or unintentional process of using verbal and nonverbal interaction to share information and construct meaning. Although this definition might seem simplistic, it is in the elements that make up the definition where you discover how complex and encompassing human communication is. Let's examine each part of the definition.

Communication is a process.

A process is defined as a method for doing something, generally involving a number of procedures and parts that interact and influence each other to produce change or create a specific result. A process is energetic and forceful. Outside influences can stop, change, or manipulate a process. Unlike most mechanical processes, communication is inevitable and can be intentional or unintentional, which adds to the complexity. Later in this chapter, you will discover models designed to help you understand communication as a process.

Communication uses verbal and nonverbal interaction.

When you engage in communication, you use two code systems to facilitate interaction. You express yourself through verbal messages (words, numbers, visual images) and nonverbal messages (vocal cues, facial expressions, body movement, space usage, clothing, and so on).

Because you are creating meaning with arbitrary, abstract, and often culturally specific codes, this process is much more complicated than mere transmission of a set of codes or data that don't have room for interpretation or misinterpretation.

Communication shares information and constructs meaning.

You use communication to share your experiences and knowledge. This type of information sharing is a big part of our daily activity. For example, you use communication to tell someone else what it was like to stand at the base of a giant tree in the Sequoia National Park or how to locate your house for a party.

Communication is...

Inescapable	Intentional or not, any type of human interaction makes communication unpreventable.
Irreversible	Once you say something or send a message and it is received, you can't erase it. There are no "do-overs" that wipe the process clean or allow you to undo what you have communicated. You might be able to reduce the effect or consequences.
Structured	For a process to function properly, it has to have a structural system of interrelated parts working for an outcome.
Contextual	When you communicate, what you say and do does not take place in a vacuum or a space empty of outside influences. The elements related to when, where, to whom, and how will always impact the communication process.
Relational	The relational history you have with the person or persons you are interacting with will shape your communication. Likewise, communication is how you develop your relationships.
Cultural	Your shared cultural beliefs, customs, practices, and social behavior will mold what and how you communicate.
Ever-changing	Because of all the previous features and the complexity of the parts, it is impossible for communication to be static or repeatable. The communication process grows, progresses, develops, and transforms with every interaction.

1.3 How Do We Visualize the Communication Process?

With any theory or process, it is often helpful to represent visually its complexities in a model. Modeling a process will help you clarify what parts are essential, establish how it works or not, and predict potential solutions when the process fails. The communication model has significantly evolved over the past 60 years, demonstrating how our knowledge of what we do when we communicate has improved. At times, these evolutions can still help us understand certain interactions or our own thoughts about our interactions with others. There are three main communication models: linear, interactional, and transactional.

Let's take a look at how the linear and interactional models evolved as we move to viewing communication as a transaction.

As a Linear Process

Developed by Claude Shannon and Warren Weaver in 1949, the **linear model** (also called the action model) is the earliest and most simplistic, representing communication as a process that injects or inoculates the message from the sender into the receiver.[6]

As you can see in the figure on the next page, the linear model highlights **sender, receiver, noise, message,** and **channel** as essential parts in the process.

This model represents communication closest to what happens over the radio or television. However, with radio and television, there is the potential for delayed interaction. Listeners will write or call in when they hear or see something they like or dislike. As you will see, Shannon and Weaver's model, even in its simplicity, highlights many of the major parts of the communication process as we view it today.

The Linear Model

The *sender* (sometimes called the source) is the person who initiates and is responsible for the feelings, idea, or thought conveyed via a message.

Noise is anything that can interfere with the message being sent or received. Noise can be outward and literal, such as a siren going off, or from within, such as hunger or sexism.

The *receiver* is the person or persons receiving the message.

SENDER
(encodes)

NOISE

NOISE   NOISE

CHANNEL   MESSAGE

RECEIVER
(decodes)

NOISE

NOISE

NOISE

The *channel* is the pathway or conduit for getting the message across. Speaking face-to-face, Skyping, writing a text message, and hearing a voice over the airwaves are all possible channels.

The *message* is the verbal and nonverbal elements encoded (conveyed) and decoded (interpreted), which creates the meaning.

Limitations of the Linear Model

- It doesn't recognize the back-and-forth interaction between the sender and the receiver other than the inoculation or transfer of an exact message in one direction, like data or an electronic signal.
- It gives the sender most of the power over message creation and meaning.
- It places importance on the quality and technical aspects of the channel (means of relaying the message), prevention of noise, and the content of the message. It is as if the sender has only one chance and must get it right the first time.

As an Interactional Process

Most scholars specify Wilber Schramm, in 1954, as the developer of the **interactional model,** which strengthened our understanding of communication by adding a **feedback** loop highlighting interaction and a setting, or **context,** for the interaction.[7] The table below explains types of contexts.

Feedback and the movement back and forth from sender to receiver create the interaction quality or loop in this model. See the figure on the next page.

By focusing on how people interpret messages within a context and emphasizing that feedback occurs, the interactional model demonstrates the complexity of human communication. It is not a simple one-shot process that can be encoded and decoded. Outside forces within the context, other than noise, can and do influence how the sender and receiver interpret messages and feedback. This model closely resembles the communicative activity you engage in when communicating on FaceTime or texting.

Contexts

Type of Environment	What Is It?	Examples of Influence
Physical environment	Literally where the communication takes place and any elements related to that, such as how many people are present, the time of day, and the ambiance	A conversation with your best friend sitting beside a lake at sunset will be different from a conversation between you, that same friend, and your boss in a large auditorium before you give a speech.
Relational environment	Relates to the relationship between the sender and receiver and anyone present in the physical context	Silence can be uncomfortable as you sit across from someone on a first date. But sitting in silences with that same person after you have been in a relationship for 10 years can be comfortable and special.
Psychological environment	Relates to context issues going on in the minds of the people communicating, such as state of mind, the emotions involved, or levels of confidence or privacy	Situations such as telling a friend about the death of a loved one or informing an employee that he is terminated are both highly intense psychological interactions.

The Interactional Model

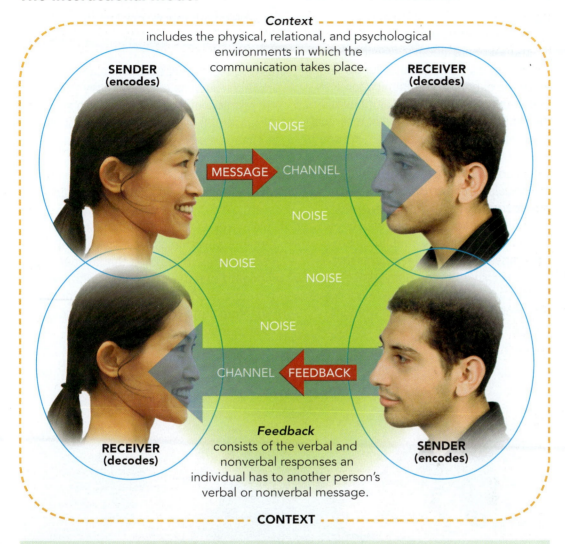

Context includes the physical, relational, and psychological environments in which the communication takes place.

SENDER (encodes)

RECEIVER (decodes)

NOISE

MESSAGE   CHANNEL

NOISE

NOISE

NOISE

NOISE

CHANNEL   FEEDBACK

RECEIVER (decodes)

SENDER (encodes)

Feedback consists of the verbal and nonverbal responses an individual has to another person's verbal or nonverbal message.

CONTEXT

Limitations of the Interactional Model

- It treats interaction as a discrete single act going on between the two individuals.
- It allows the individual to be sender and receiver but not simultaneously.
- It supports the notion that message and feedback do not simultaneously influence each other (a two-way street with separate lanes).

As a Transactional Process

Devised in 1967 by Paul Watzlawick, Janet Beavin Bavelas, and Don D. Jackson, the transactional model is considered a more representative and accurate depiction of human communication.[8] The **transactional model** emphasizes the simultaneous negotiation of meaning between communicators as they respond to each other and the context. This model adds an emphasis on viewing the individuals as **communicators** with a **background** and **common ground**. You no longer act solely as a sender or a receiver. You are a communicator simultaneously sending and receiving messages of verbal and nonverbal elements. You are a communicator bringing a personal perspective to the encounter, which is grounded in commonality. See the figure on the next page.

To understand this model, first focus on the word "transaction." We often define it as an instance of doing business or moving something from one place to another—such as moving money from a savings account into checking. This notion of transaction implies energetic motion or change evolving from negotiation, interaction between components, collaboration, and/or influence. It means you are *doing* or *completing* something.

This is true of the transactional model of communication as well. The model represents an interaction that is energetic, changing, negotiated, and collaborative. It is completed by communicators doing and being equally responsible for the understanding.

The Transactional Model

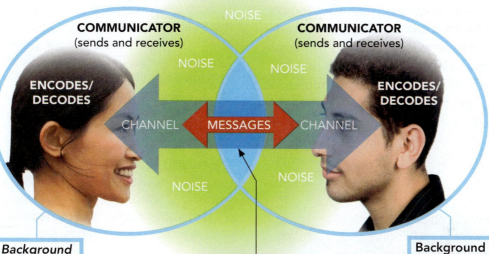

Communicators are individuals equally responsible for creating meaning through simultaneous messages.

CONTEXT

NOISE

COMMUNICATOR (sends and receives)

COMMUNICATOR (sends and receives)

NOISE

NOISE

ENCODES/ DECODES

ENCODES/ DECODES

CHANNEL

MESSAGES

CHANNEL

NOISE

NOISE

Background

Common ground

Background

CONTEXT

Background
refers to the communicator's identity and life experiences. The communication process does not reside in a vacuum. It is influenced by who you are; past, present, or future experiences; emotions; and cultural histories.

Common ground
refers to the overlap within the communicators' identities and life experiences. If both communicators are 19 years old, students, and from the Midwest, they will more likely have things in common that can help them connect, interact, and collaborate better. For example, current slang or texting language will likely be more common between these communicators.

Advantages of the Transactional Model

- It stresses the interdependence of the parts of the process.
- It captures the influence of more contextual factors.
- It views each individual as a communicator who simultaneously plays the roles of sender and receiver.
- It stresses the co-creation of meaning, which, in turn, disperses power more equally between the communicators.
- It regards communication as a vigorous, dynamic, energetic, ever-changing process.

1.4 What Are the Types of Communication?

You may be familiar with Sheldon on the hit TV show *The Big Bang Theory*. One of the reasons we find this wacky Caltech physicist so funny is that he never adapts his communication style from person to person or context to context. He doesn't understand the nuances of the different types of communication.

Sheldon is always formal, academic, and somewhat sterile, even in the comic book store or with his girlfriend, Amy. Early in their relationship, Sheldon draws up a 31-page "Relationship Agreement" that "enumerates, iterates, and codifies" the rules for his relationship with Amy—who is a scientist and finds this incredibly romantic. Fast-forward to the 2015 season finale, and Sheldon still misses the interpersonal communication mark when he fails to convey the same level of relationship commitment as Amy at a critical point in their relationship.

Like most multifaceted human activities, communication requires the ability to adapt; one type or style of communication doesn't work for all situations. You will determine a type of communication and what is important about that interaction based on the relationship environment aspect of the context. Specifically, the number of individuals engaging in the interaction determines the type of communication. The table on the following page summarizes each type and offers brief examples of when you are participating in each. This text will mainly focus on interpersonal communication, small group communication, and public speaking.

Type of Communication		What Is It?	When Do You Engage in This Type?
Intrapersonal communication		Communicating with yourself	Talking to yourself, whether in your mind or aloud
Interpersonal communication		Communicating with one other person with whom you have some sort of significant relationship	Communicating with a boyfriend or girlfriend, your boss, a coworker/classmate, or an individual family member
Small group communication		Communicating with 3 to 12 other people united over time for a common purpose	Communicating with your family as a group, a study group, a work group, or an athletic team
Public speaking		Communicating as an individual speaker to a large audience	Giving a graduation speech, a wedding toast, or a speech on how to install software
Mass communication		Communicating with a mass of people via electronic or print media	Delivering an instructional TED Talk, speaking on the radio or television, or creating a blog

1.5 How Can You Be a Successful Communicator?

Psychologist Abraham Maslow wrote, "I suppose it is tempting, if the only tool you have is a hammer, to treat everything as if it were a nail."[9] This applies to communication as well. If you only use one basic tool or method, you will limit your ability to communicate effectively.

Be Attentive to Sense of Self and Others

When engaging in any type of communication, it is important to identify and acknowledge the unique characteristics and viewpoints of those you interact with and of yourself. Don't mindlessly plow through your interactions. Pay attention to your communication style. Your communication style is what you say and how you say it (e.g., Are you aggressive or passive in your word choice and delivery?). Note how others react and communicate.

See Chapter 2 for more on understanding self and others.

Use and Interpret Verbal and Nonverbal Messages

It takes numerous tools to communicate. The common statement "There are no words to express what I am feeling" highlights the inadequacy of language to express our entire messages. The same could be said for nonverbal codes. Using or paying attention to only one or the other will often cause confusion or misinterpretation.

Chapters 3 and 4 will offer you guidance on effective verbal and nonverbal communication.

Listen Effectively

As you learned earlier in this chapter, one element that makes communication transactional is the fact that good communicators actively engage in the process even as listeners. You are not a passive vessel simply ready to be filled with the message. You must accept responsibility for helping in the completion and understanding of the message. Being an effective listener requires you to learn how to give your full attention, how to select and attend to what is important, how to assign meaning to a message, what to remember, and how to respond.

| **Chapter 5** will help you develop your listening skills.

Manage Your Apprehension

Communication apprehension is a term scholars give to the fears and anxiety you may have when engaging in communicative interactions with one or more persons. Communication apprehension can happen in any communication situation, such as on a date, during a meeting, or when giving a speech. Some common symptoms of anxiety include:

- Tight throat, producing a high pitch
- Dry mouth
- Trembling lips, hands, or legs
- Nausea
- Skin changes (perspiration, paleness, red patches)
- Cold, clammy, or sweaty hands
- Fast pulse and breathing rate
- Avoiding eye contact
- Adding vocal pauses and fillers ("ah," "um," "like," "you know")
- Memory issues or inability to concentrate
- Overwhelming feeling of anxiousness

You might experience one or more of these symptoms. You can turn any of these symptoms into a positive reaction if you realize what your body and mind are trying to tell you. Preparing for extraordinary life events, being familiar with the different types of communication, and practicing your skills will help reduce your anxiety. Learn to control the situation rather than letting your anxiety control you. Nervousness is normal—even important to extraordinary events—and can energize you. See the Improve Your Communication section at the end of this chapter and some Tip boxes for ways to control your fears.

Practice

In the first century BCE, Roman author Publilius Syrus wrote, "Practice is the best of all instructors."[10] Most of us don't think of practicing our communication for most situations and, if we do, it is likely when we are planning to give a formal speech. But practice can help you with any interaction. If you practice how you want to ask your parents for a new car, or how to ask that special someone out on a date, you are likely to be better at it—and more successful than if you don't practice. Have you ever said something to a family member, friend, coworker, or boss and almost immediately wanted to take it back or say it differently? Taking the time to gather facts, create the best messages, and practice will help with this.

One of the most common mistakes committed by beginning public speakers, for instance, is that they often do not practice enough or exactly as they plan to give their speeches. Bad habits (such as putting off writing a speech until the last minute, just reading over the speech instead of practicing it, or practicing it only once) can cause many problems. Practicing helps you hone all your skills, identify issues that are not working within your messages, and develop confidence. Let your mind and body become familiar with what you plan to say. Practicing will boost your confidence and make you a better communicator. You will begin to actually enjoy interacting with a wider range of others and giving speeches (Yes, you will!) if you work on your abilities and how you feel about them.

See the Big Picture

As the previous discussion reveals, taking a step back to view the act of communication from a wider perspective can be helpful. What you learn about interpersonal communication can benefit your small group skills or public speaking skills and vice versa. All communication, whether it is two people talking or a public speech in front of 200 people, requires you to understand, shape, and connect.

- **Understand Communication**: All communication begins with understanding communication and how you perceive yourself and others as you interact.

- **Shape Messages**: Use your foundation of understanding to guide your decisions in shaping your messages through verbal and nonverbal communication as well as listening.

- **Connect with Others**: Your abilities to understand communication and shape messages are the tools you use to make connections—whether in person or through mediated technology—in your interpersonal relationships, when you engage others in small groups, and when you take the stage as a public speaker.

Keep in mind that what you are learning applies to and is adaptable across all communication situations. All communication is understanding, shaping, and connecting.

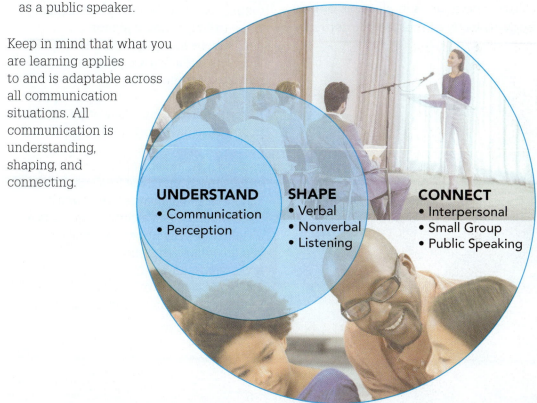

UNDERSTAND
- Communication
- Perception

SHAPE
- Verbal
- Nonverbal
- Listening

CONNECT
- Interpersonal
- Small Group
- Public Speaking

1.6 How Can You Be an Ethical Communicator?

Your **ethics**, or a set of standards that guide you to good and honorable behavior, helps others see you in a positive manner. Accepting ethical responsibility with your communication behavior is a crucial endeavor as a respectable citizen. An **ethical communicator** is a person who sets and follows a high moral standard of norms, beliefs, behaviors, attitudes, values, and actions in all of his or her body-to-body or mediated interactions.

Body-to-body communication occurs when the individuals participating in the interaction are co-present (physically in the same space).[11] The use of this term rather than face-to-face communication more accurately stresses use of the entire body as a channel for sending a message. **Mediated communication** takes place across time and space via some sort of media or technological channel to facilitate the interaction. Letter writing, texting, phoning, blogging, messaging, video calling, sending photos via applications like Snapchat, and web or video conferencing are all examples of mediated communication.

Almost everything you say or do has the potential to have positive or negative effects on the lives of others and even your own. As noted earlier in this chapter, what you say and do is irreversible, which can make the effects potent. If you need to communicate in a certain way or take a stance that might be risky, make sure you are willing to stand by your words and actions, now and in the future. The following sections offer further advice on nurturing ethics in your communication.

Practicing Ethics features, such as the one below, appear throughout the text to help you keep your ethical responsibility center stage as you enter into various communicative acts. The feature below contains a credo created and approved by the National Communication Association (NCA). Founded in 1914, NCA is a not-for-profit scholarly society devoted to the advancement of communication as a discipline. NCA is dedicated to promoting free and ethical communication.

Practicing Ethics: The NCA Ethics Credo

The National Communication Association Credo for Ethical Communication (approved by the NCA Legislative Council, November 1999)[12]

Questions of right and wrong arise whenever people communicate. Ethical communication is fundamental to responsible thinking, decision making, and the development of relationships and communities within and across contexts, cultures, channels, and media.

Moreover, ethical communication enhances human worth and dignity by fostering truthfulness, fairness, responsibility, personal integrity, and respect for self and others.

We believe that unethical communication threatens the quality of all communication and consequently the well-being of individuals and the society in which we live. Therefore we, the members of the National Communication Association, endorse and are committed to practicing the following principles of ethical communication:

- We advocate truthfulness, accuracy, honesty, and reason as essential to the integrity of communication.
- We endorse freedom of expression, diversity of perspective, and tolerance of dissent to achieve the informed and responsible decision making fundamental to a civil society.
- We strive to understand and respect other communicators before evaluating and responding to their messages.
- We promote access to communication resources and opportunities as necessary to fulfill human potential and contribute to the well-being of families, communities, and society.
- We promote communication climates of caring and mutual understanding that respect the unique needs and characteristics of individual communicators.
- We condemn communication that degrades individuals and humanity through distortion, intimidation, coercion, and violence and through the expression of intolerance and hatred.
- We are committed to the courageous expression of personal convictions in pursuit of fairness and justice.
- We advocate sharing information, opinions, and feelings when facing significant choices while also respecting privacy and confidentiality.
- We accept responsibility for the short- and long-term consequences for our own communication and expect the same of others.

Here is some general advice for being ethical in any situation.

Be Self-Monitoring

Pay attention to what you say and how you say it, as well as the behavior you display. Question any negative assumptions you have about another person or group. Reflect on how you view yourself and culture related to others. Be willing to change inappropriate behavior.

Be Knowledgeable

While you are in school, learning and gaining knowledge is an everyday activity. Once you graduate, ongoing learning and studying may not seem as necessary. But because communication is inherently the act of making and sharing meaning and sense, continuing your education and experience is imperative. Effective and ethical communicators are *lifelong learners,* or self-motivated individuals that never stop pursuing knowledge and skills. To actively be a lifelong learner:

- Surround yourself with experienced and creative people
- Read and then read some more
- Stay current on news and events
- Seek out information that contradicts your current or popular beliefs
- Learn new skills and use them
- Get involved in your community
- Teach others

Be Truthful

Being an ethical communicator demands telling the truth. Being truthful includes:

- Seeking out correct information
- Not omitting information or skewing it for your own benefit
- Allowing those you communicate with to see options and to have differing opinions
- Creating strong logical messages built on strong information and sound emotions
- Being willing to admit and fix errors

Be Caring

Consumed by the pressure to achieve individual success, we can often forget to practice concern for others. Given the relationship aspect of communication and the power of verbal and nonverbal codes, it is essential that you employ an "ethic of care" in your interactions.[13] As the Buddhist monk Maha Ghosananda suggests, "The thought manifests as the word. The word manifests as the deed. The deed develops into the habit. The habit hardens into the character. The character gives birth to the destiny. So, watch your thoughts with care and let them spring from love born out of respect for all beings."[14] You have a responsibility to promote the well-being of yourself and others.

Be Responsible Across All Situations and Channels

After the previous ethics discussion, this may seem repetitive. However, it is often easier to understand being responsible in some situations than others. For some, being responsible in intimate relationships or at work is obvious, but not so for others. For some, being responsible and kind in a body-to-body interaction is obvious, but not so much if mediated. You need to be willing to work at doing the right thing in your personal, professional, or public lives—regardless of the channel.

Recognize and Embrace Diversity

The ability to recognize differences and the willingness to embrace diversity as a positive—rather than undesirable, confusing, offensive, or daunting—is crucial to the communication process and to being truly ethical. The next sections are dedicated to helping you begin recognizing and embracing diversity.

Practicing Ethics: Digital Etiquette (also known as Netiquette)

- Don't use digital devices while driving.
- Don't use digital devices in places where it is inappropriate or would disturb others—for example, bookstores, libraries, cinemas, theaters, non-public places in hospitals, or places of worship.
- In some cultures, using a digital device during any group interaction is considered highly inappropriate.
- Obey copyright laws.
- If you can meet in person, do so.
- Don't say things online that you wouldn't say in person.
- Save your emotional interactions for body-to-body encounters.
- Don't engage in pornographic or sexual interaction online.

- Use emoticons, emoji, and digital-specific language only when in informal interactions. Be aware that they allow for a wide range of misinterpretation.
- Do not deliberately flame. Flaming is the creation of a hostile and insulting interaction just to incite extreme emotions and feelings. Help control flaming when you see it.
- Consider most private digital interactions, such as email and texts, as private until you ask for permission to share. Conversely, never assume mediated communication is completely private from the rest of the world. It has a digital record, is hard to erase completely, and can be widely disseminated.
- Don't exaggerate to make yourself into something you are not.[15]

1.7 How Can You Value Diversity?

Picture how we greet good friends. Men tend to greet male friends with a firm handshake or a pat on the shoulder. Women tend to greet female friends with a hug. However, in Japan, bowing is an extremely important and complex greeting. As a rule, the longer and deeper the bow, the more intensity it has, suggesting a stronger expression of respect. These examples highlight the complexity of our cultural backgrounds and their potential for influencing our interactions.

Culture is the system or learned patterns of knowledge, beliefs, values, attitudes, norms, and behaviors shared by a large group of people and handed down from generation to generation. Cultural members use symbols, language, rituals, visual art, music, cinema, and story to learn, perpetuate, document, and communicate their culture.

Cultural differences have always existed, but more sophisticated and widely available methods of communication and transportation, migration of peoples for various reasons, and a developing world marketplace are making us increasingly connected and interdependent. Your towns, neighborhoods, schools, offices, and digital lives are more diverse than ever, and it is important for you to understand and respond appropriately to those differences. Doing so begins with recognizing the value of difference and how culture influences communication.

Recognize the Value of Difference

"In diversity there is beauty and there is strength."[16] As this quotation by author and activist Maya Angelou suggests, diversity has a positive influence on our lives. Understanding how diversity can help you become a better communicator in your personal, professional, and public lives will assist you in accessing these positive influences. Sure, there will be times when you feel unprepared, uncomfortable, and uneasy. However, when we value diversity by recognizing differences, educating ourselves about others, and embracing the power that evolves from unique individuals coming together, we will benefit from the beauty and strength diversity has to offer. Being a better intercultural communicator will give you interpersonal and public advantages.

Interpersonal Advantages

This constructive intermingling of diverse people helps us understand who we are and what we are not. For example, my sister is an avid quilter and I love to fish. She will spend hours cutting patterns and placing the right stitch. I will drive hours and sit for days in a boat. Until I reflected on our respective hobbies, I used to think I was impatient compared to her. Now, I see we are similar yet different. Likewise, good intercultural communication can build confidence and self-value in both you and the people you interact with, by increasing sensitivity and respect. Consider how insensitive it is, and how it hinders effective communication, to say "that's so gay" in front of a gay man or lesbian or to point out how "articulate" an African American young man is as though it were unexpected. Think about some of the things you read on Facebook—pause and wonder who might be hurt by what is said. Realize how keeping the "peace" or negotiating conflict with your neighbors requires you to understand their perspective. Recognizing that everyone is an individual with different perspectives, experiences, and feelings will make you a better communicator—and family member, friend, lover, and neighbor.

Public Advantages

Effective intercultural communication is also a necessity in your community, workplace, and mediated interactions. It is more likely today than during your parents' generation that you will not live near where you grew up or, if you do, that the area will not be as homogeneous as in the past. Social media and the Internet bring you closer to other cultures at the push of a key or a click of a mouse. Businesses are hiring more diverse employees to access stronger knowledge bases, creativity, and problem-solving results. You could be European American and telework with a group in India. Or, what if you were asked to speak to a multicultural children's group about your travels abroad? Successful communication across cultures can help you get a job or promotion, win a major client, resolve a clash in your community, or run for a political or organizational office.

Recognize Cultural Differences

Numerous scholars have tried to create cultural behavior classifications to help intercultural communicators. Geert Hofstede and Edward T. Hall developed two of the most widely cited methods of classifying differences. Hofstede and Hall recognize seven variable cultural differences within organizations (see the table below and on the next page).[17]

These are cultural tendencies observed in organizations and not necessarily an individual's inclination or always true for the overall culture. However, they do offer valuable insight into possible cultural tendencies and might help you adapt your interactions appropriately—especially in the workplace or a public speaking forum.

Dimensions of Culture

Dimension	Explanation	Example Countries
High Power vs. Low Power	**High-power cultures** have clear, defined lines of authority and responsibility.	**High-power countries** Guatemala, Mexico, Venezuela, Arab countries
	Low-power cultures blur these lines.	**Low-power countries** Germany, Costa Rica, Great Britain, Denmark, U.S.
Individualist vs. Collectivist	**Individualist cultures** stand for self.	**Individualist countries** U.S., Australia, Great Britain, Canada, Netherlands, Italy
	Collectivist cultures stand for the group.	**Collectivist countries** Venezuela, Pakistan, Costa Rica, Taiwan, South Korea
Competitive vs. Nurturing	**Competitive cultures** stress competitiveness, assertiveness, ambition, wealth, and material possessions.	**Competitive countries** Japan, Austria, Venezuela, Italy, Ireland, Greece, U.S., Mexico, Great Britain
	Nurturing cultures stress relationships, quality of life, sexual equality, and care of the environment.	**Nurturing countries** Sweden, Norway, Chile, Costa Rica, Netherlands, South Korea, Denmark, Finland

Dimension	Explanation	Example Countries
High-Uncertainty Avoidance vs. Low-Uncertainty Avoidance	**High-uncertainty cultures** strive to avoid uncertainty and ambiguity through stability.	**High-uncertainty countries** Greece, Portugal, Japan, Costa Rica, Mexico, Israel
	Low-uncertainty cultures are tolerant of the unusual, new ideas, and other people.	**Low-uncertainty countries** Singapore, Jamaica, Denmark, Ireland, U.S., India
Long-Term Orientation vs. Short-Term Orientation	**Long-term cultures** value persistence, thriftiness, future, a strong work ethic, structure, and status.	**Long-term countries** China, Taiwan, Japan, South Korea, Brazil
	Short-term cultures emphasize time and immediate results, try to "cheat" old age, seek quick gratification, and deemphasize status.	**Short-term countries** Great Britain, Canada, the Philippines, U.S.
High Context vs. Low Context	**High-context cultures** emphasize indirect, inexplicit messages related to interpersonal relationships, harmony, and consensus.	**High-context countries** Africa, Brazil, China, France
	Low-context cultures stress direct, explicit messages that are logical, linear, and action-oriented.	**Low-context countries** Australia, Ireland, Switzerland, Germany, U.S.
Indulgence vs. Restraint	**Indulgent cultures** allow for free gratification such as having fun and indulging in food, drink, and social and sexual pleasures.	**Indulgent countries** Columbia, El Salvador, Mexico, New Zealand, Sweden, Venezuela
	Restraint cultures value restraint or self-discipline and believe in willpower, modesty, and moderation.	**Restraint countries** Bulgaria, Italy, Morocco, Russia, Pakistan

Recognize Co-cultural Differences

Co-cultures are diverse smaller groups within a culture, distinguished by, but not limited to, such factors as age, gender, sexual orientation, race, mental or physical abilities, religion, political affiliation, education, occupation, economic status, and even gang affiliation or Twitter usage (e.g., Tweeps). These groups often have beliefs, values, attitudes, norms, language, and behaviors different from the larger culture. For example, tweets can only use up to 140 characters per message, which makes using word shortcuts, dropping vowels or pronouns, and using keyboard symbols for words common or the norm. Like the larger culture, co-culture members learn, perpetuate, document, and communicate their co-culture through symbols, language, rituals, visual art, music, cinema, and story.

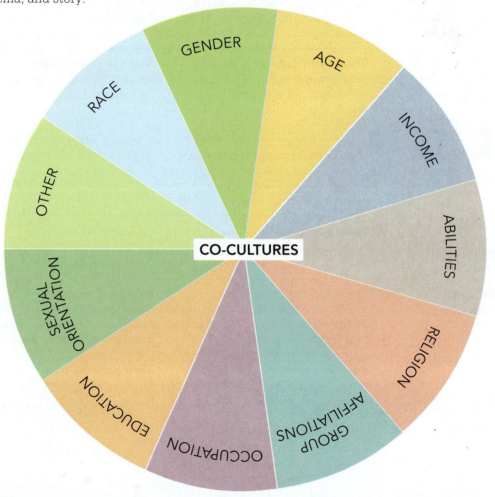

As the figure demonstrates, numerous types of co-cultures are common within most cultures. Even the activities you choose to participate in constitute co-cultures. For example, if you are a video game or CrossFit fanatic, you may identify with that co-culture.

Co-cultures are often marginalized by a dominant culture or those who have access to power, making it difficult to recognize or respond to the co-culture's needs, voice, and potential. This can range from your aunt thinking your frequent video game playing is a waste of time to societal issues such as the current immigration conflict in the United States.

Recognizing, embracing, and adapting to diversity will help you deal with the stress of the intercultural unknown, make you better at creating diverse interpersonal relationships, and improve your overall ability to communicate. This is only the beginning of our cultural discussion. As with ethics, you will return to diversity discussions often throughout the book, keeping it center stage in all communicative acts. Although it would be impossible to cover all cultures and co-cultures, we will focus on some overall cultural differences and gender. When appropriate, we will discuss other co-cultures—but this is just the tip of the cultural iceberg. Learn to be aware of the many different cultures and co-cultures around you.

Practicing Ethics: Beware of Ethnocentrism

Ethnocentrism is the assumption that your own cultural or co-cultural group is superior. Do not judge others by your own cultural standards. It leads to poor communication, misperceptions, prejudice, and, in extreme cases, genocide. When evaluating and responding to others from different cultures or co-cultures, strive to understand their points of view, needs, and behavior. Create a caring and mutual learning environment when responding to a message. For example, when you may disagree with someone's message or find their perspective foreign to yours, listen carefully to the entire message before you judge it.

Self-Check: You May Be Ethnocentric If...

Being self-reflexive about our expectations of others is hard work, and sometimes our own biases are hard to see. Here are just a few thoughts to provoke your cultural introspection.

❏ Do you unfriend, dislike, or find it rude if someone posts on Facebook in another language?

❏ Do you feel a need to persuade others to believe what you believe because you think their beliefs are behind the times or unfavorable?

❏ If someone is hesitant to make a decision without group consensus or defers to the person in charge, do you find that person weak and lacking ambition?

❏ Do you think that people who are not direct or ask a lot of questions are wasting time?

Chapter 1 Review

Key Questions

1.1 Why Do We Communicate?

Objective 1.1: EXPLAIN WHY WE COMMUNICATE

Improving your communication skills will help you fulfill specific needs that are:

- practical
- professional
- public
- personal

See pages 4–7.

1.2 What Is Human Communication?

Objective 1.2: DEFINE HUMAN COMMUNICATION

Communication is the intentional or unintentional process of using verbal and nonverbal interaction to share information and construct meaning. Communication is:

- inescapable
- irreversible
- structured
- contextual
- relational
- cultural
- ever-changing

See pages 8–9.

1.3 How Do We Visualize the Communication Process?

Objective 1.3: EXPLAIN COMMUNICATION AS A PROCESS

The communication model has significantly evolved over the past 60 years. Three main models have been used to visualize the communication process.

- As a linear process: The linear model represents communication as a process that injects or inoculates the message from the sender to the receiver. It emphasizes several parts of the process, including sender, receiver, message, channel, and noise.

- As an interactional process: The interactional model adds a feedback loop highlighting interaction and setting or context for the interaction.

- As a transactional process: The transactional model adds an emphasis on viewing the individuals as communicators with a background and common ground.

See pages 10–15.

1.4 What Are the Types of Communication?

The number of individuals engaging in the interaction determines the type of communication. The major types are:

• Intrapersonal communication
• Interpersonal communication
• Small group communication
• Public speaking
• Mass communication

See pages 16–17.

1.5 How Can You Be a Successful Communicator?

To be an effective communicator, you should:

• Be attentive to sense of self and others
• Use and interpret both verbal and nonverbal messages
• Listen effectively
• Practice
• See the big picture

See pages 18–21.

1.6 How Can You Be an Ethical Communicator?

To be an ethical communicator, you should:

• Be self-monitoring
• Be knowledgeable
• Be truthful
• Be caring
• Be responsible across all situations and channels
• Recognize and embrace diversity

See pages 22–25.

1.7 How Can You Value Diversity?

Valuing diversity begins with recognizing that culture is a system or learned patterns of beliefs, values, norms, and behaviors shared by a large group of people and handed down from generation to generation. To understand and value how culture influences communication, you should:

• Recognize the value of difference and the interpersonal and public advantages of successful intercultural communication
• Recognize cultural differences, such as those identified by Hofstede and Hall
• Recognize co-cultural differences, such as race, gender, age, income, abilities, religion, group affiliations, occupation, education, sexual orientation, and others

See pages 26–31.

Key Terms

social interaction (6)
communication (8)
linear model (10)
sender (10)
receiver (10)
noise (10)
message (10)
channel (10)
interactional model (12)
feedback (12)
context (12)
transactional model (14)
communicators (14)
background (14)
common ground (14)
intrapersonal communication (17)
interpersonal communication (17)
small group communication (17)
public speaking (17)
mass communication (17)
communication apprehension (19)
ethics (22)
ethical communicator (22)
body-to-body communication (22)
mediated communication (22)
culture (26)
co-cultures (30)
ethnocentrism (31)

Improve Your Communication

Controlling your communication apprehension or anxiety is an individual process. What works for one person may not for someone else, and the situation may call for a different method. Here are a few suggestions.

Techniques for Controlling Anxiety

- Put yourself in situations where you have to communicate.
- Prepare for your Interactions that trouble you the most.
- Make a list of why you are fearful. Are the fears reasonable? Is there a simple solution for any?
- Ask one or two people you can trust to give you advice.
- Anticipate problems or issues and try to work them out.
- Exercise to lower physical stress.
- Meditate or do stretching exercises.
- Concentrate on how good you are.
- Close your eyes and imagine the positive and enjoyable situation.
- Remember happy moments from your past.
- Listen to calming music before the interaction.
- Breathe deeply and slowly.
- Gesture, move, or redistribute your weight if your hands or legs are trembling.
- Remember that your nervous symptoms are more pronounced to you. Often, the other person or audience doesn't notice.

Apply Your Knowledge

1. Identify specific instances where you have communicated for practical, professional, public, and personal reasons. Which communication model best describes the process of communication you employed in each instance? How successful were you in each instance? Can you attribute the success or lack of success to the presence or absence of a particular attribute? (See Objective 1.5 for a list of effective attributes.) How did your background influence your communication in these instances?

2. Do you agree that communication is inescapable? Explain.

3. Explain a situation in which your cultural beliefs, customs, practices, or social behavior influenced how you communicated or interpreted the message of others.

4. Describe examples of how your culture or co-culture tends to support Hofstede's and Hall's cultural tendencies.

5. Watch your favorite film and analyze how effective your favorite characters are at communicating. How do they adapt to different situations? Explain how they are ethical or not.

Other Resources

Consult the following sources for more information.

Ethics

Babicki, Paul, Serkan Gecmen, and Laurie Babicki. *Netiquette IQ: A Comprehensive Guide to Improve, Enhance, and Add Power to Your Email.* North Charleston: CreateSpace, 2013. Print.

Bugeja, Michael. *Living Ethics: Across Media Platforms.* New York: Oxford UP, 2007. Print.

Kidder, Rushworth M. *Moral Courage.* New York: Harper, 2005. Print.

Tompkins, Paula S. *Practicing Communication Ethics.* Boston: Allyn, 2001. Print.

Communication Across Cultures

- www.pbs.org/ampu/crosscult.html
- www.geerthofstede.nl/dimensions-of-national-cultures
- www.kwintessential.co.uk/cultural-services/articles/tips-intercultural-leadership.html
- www.kwintessential.co.uk/cultural-services/articles/cross-cultural-dining-etiquette.html

Chapter 2
Understanding Self and Others

2.1 What Is Perception?

The minute you encounter a person, place, event, or object you begin forming mental observations known as your *first impressions*. Our first impressions tend to focus only on certain attributes. For example, is this person approachable, friendly, trustworthy, competent, confident, or likable? Traditionally, nonverbal cues—such as physical appearance, posture, smiling and other facial gestures, eye contact, use of space, or hand gestures, for example—have heavily influenced first impressions. You form first impressions as part of a process known as perception.

Perception is the ability to translate information into insight or awareness about something, usually people, places, events, or objects. When you encounter something, you use sensation to create meaning or understanding. Sensation is the neurological process that makes us aware of our environments through traditional senses such as sight, hearing, touch, smell, or taste. You also have the ability to process sensations related to temperature, pain, balance, time, and movement. Perception is the cognitive process that makes sense of those sensations. For example, how does your brain make sense of the images below? What do you see first?

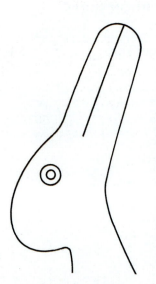

1. Do you see a rabbit or a duck?

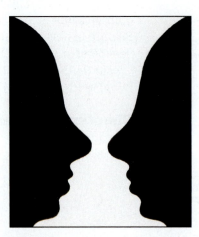

2. Do you see a vase or two people?

3. Do you see an old woman or a young woman?

The perception of self and other is fundamental to communication with others. See the table below for several characteristics of perception.

Perception is . . .

Learned	You must discover and refine your perception skills. As you will discover later in this chapter, perception is a process with interdependent actions that result in a particular aim to understand something. To do it well, you must move beyond an intuitive level.
Subjective	No two people will completely perceive something the same way. Each of us has a multitude of senses and varying degrees of sensitivity or sensory ability. Likewise, what you tend to value as important will influence what senses you are willing to attend to. Even your position within an environment or context can influence your perception. For example, sitting in a chair versus standing could change what you see.
Instinctive	Much of the perception process is quick and subconscious, giving you a sense that your perceptions are always true. You must question the perceptions you hold and why you interpret them the way you do.
Cultural	Cultural values (often conveyed nonverbally) will influence your perception, especially your first impressions. For example, tall, large (non-obese) men and tall, thin women tend to earn higher wages than others in the United States.[1] ▌**See Chapter 4** for more on nonverbal communication.
Influential	Perception impacts our communication and communication impacts our perceptions. You construct meaning when you perceive something (e.g., a tall, thin woman as intelligent and self-disciplined). That meaning impacts how you will interact with the thing perceived (treating a tall, thin woman with respect and admiration). If the thing being perceived interacts or communicates with you (the woman responds positively to your treatment of her), that can influence your perceptions.

2.2 What Is the Process of Perception?

The next time you walk down a street or hall, note what grabs your attention. What movements, sounds, and smells do you notice? What colors do you see? What judgments are you making about things you sense around you? How do you change your behavior based on those judgments? Your answers to these questions stem from your engaging in the process of perception.

The **process of perception** consists of three phases: selecting, organizing, and interpreting. These phases can be conscious or unconscious and seem to occur in a linear fashion. However, they interact and influence each other more than steps in a series. For example, how you tend to interpret interactions will influence what you selectively attend to.

Selecting

Selecting is the moment when some factor grabs your attention and forces you to focus on certain stimuli and ignore others. Because of the usual volume of stimuli, you tend to notice those that are useful, familiar, interesting, repeated, changing, unexpected, or intense.

Organizing
How does it relate?

Selecting
What am I sensing?

Interpreting
What does it mean?

Organizing

Organizing is where you mentally arrange your sensory information into more manageable patterns. You tend to organize by principles (rules),[2] schemas (patterns),[3] and scripts,[4] such as those identified in the table to the right.

Organizing by Principles

Proximity principle	People, places, events, or objects that are close together tend to be grouped together (e.g., two people sitting together must be like-minded).
Similarity principle	People, places, events, or objects that look similar tend to be grouped together (e.g., people dressed alike belong together).
Closure principle	Incomplete characteristics of people, places, events, or objects tend to be closed or filled in to complete the perception.
Contrast principle	People, places, events, or objects that are too different should not be together (e.g., people who are not of the same religion or age don't belong together).

Organizing by Schemas

Physical constructs	Classifying people according to appearance factors such as height, age, ethnicity, or body shape (e.g., young/old, heavy/thin)
Role constructs	Classifying people by social or professional position (e.g., student, professor, spouse, parent)
Interaction constructs	Classifying people by social behavior (e.g., helpful/unhelpful, shy/outgoing)
Psychological constructs	Classifying by a person's feelings, thoughts, and nature (e.g., angry/calm, confident/insecure)

Organizing by Scripts

A sequence of acceptable behaviors, events, or procedures for a given situation or how an event should unfold (e.g., you have a script for the first day of class or for texting)

Interpreting

Interpreting is where you attach meaning to what you have learned in the first two phases about a person, place, event, or object. As you will learn in the next section, several factors can influence your subjective interpretations. Likewise, some aspects can aid in creating your perceptions of individuals with whom you have a developed relationship, such as a friend or significant other. When you have a relational history or intimacy with someone, you will more likely interpret their behavior correctly and may be able to anticipate behavior. Plus, the degree to which you feel comfortable in the relationship assists you in perceiving behavior correctly.

2.3 What Factors Influence Perception?

When you perceive yourself or others, numerous factors can influence your understanding. Those factors can help or hinder your ability to form effective perceptions and therefore should be something you reflect on as you create and respond to your perceptions. Later in this chapter, you will explore barriers specific to the perception of others. Those barriers often lead to misperceptions or false perceptions.

For now, it is important to examine the factors that can influence any act of perception. They are physical, emotional, environmental, intellectual, experiential, cultural, and mediated factors.

Physical Factors

Your physical capabilities will influence individual perceptions. Individuals with limited eyesight often rely on touch, smell, and sounds to make interpretations. Some people can hear higher pitches than others, and some studies suggest that sensory differences exist between men and women. For example, women tend to have a heightened sense of smell and more taste buds, which can make them more sensitive to flavors. Women also experience pain differently.

Emotional Factors

Your emotional state at the time you form a perception can have a strong influence. For example, you select and remember positive traits more when you are happy or positively excited and negative traits more when sad, angry, or depressed. Your own personality will influence your perceptions of things. For example, if you are insecure, you will tend to perceive others as better than you or out to harm you. How others treat you can influence your emotional state and therefore your perception of self. This is one of the serious side effects of bullying and cyberbullying, which often occur while a child or young adult is developing self-perception. According to the National Center for Education, 21.5 percent of students ages 12–18 have reported being bullied; 6.9 percent have reported cyberbullying. Nearly 33 percent of those bullied/cyberbullied said it occurred at least once or twice a month—with 5.7 percent saying it happens almost every day.[5]

Environmental Factors

The time of day or the environmental context can influence your perceptions. For example, you might perceive someone eating a hamburger and drinking a beer at 8:00 a.m. as strange and dangerous if you didn't know she worked the night shift and morning is her "evening." Or, you might perceive a joke told in the workplace as inappropriate but okay in a social setting. The lack of body-to-body interaction in mediated contexts can cause misperceptions to form as well—or allow you to form significant relationships without superficial perceptions derailing the relationship development.

Intellectual Factors

The more you know about what you are perceiving, the more cognitively complex and potentially correct your perception could be. For example, if your roommate is Jewish, the more you know about his religious beliefs, the better and more complex your perceptions will be.

Experiential Factors

Past experiences and interactions influence how you perceive something. For example, you win four tickets to a major league baseball game and a coworker you barely know starts being friendly. Because of your past experience with others, you perceive the friendliness as trying to get close to you in hopes of being asked to go to the game with you.

Cultural Factors

Many of the stimuli we receive are culturally influenced. When you are a member of a cultural group or co-culture, you learn and share the perceptions valued by those groups and you tend to focus on what is important to your culture and/or co-culture. Therefore, culture influences the creation of your perceptions and can distort them.

For example, Beth might perceive her boyfriend's communication as cold or uncaring when they are trying to resolve a fight. Beth's boyfriend, Joe, perceives Beth as too emotional and focusing too much on feelings. He just wants to figure out the best way to resolve the conflict. In Western culture, most boys are taught to engage in task-solving talk and most girls are taught to engage in relationship talk.[6] Beth and Joe have learned behavior for what it means to be female or male, and this learned behavior influences their perceptions of each other. The cultures and co-cultures you belong to act as lenses tinting and shaping your perceptions.

Mediated Factors

Technology allows you to create and maintain perceptions that transcend time and space. You no longer need body-to-body interaction to form some sort of impression. Your online tools allow you to create, support, and maintain these impressions through **asynchronous engagements** or **synchronous engagements** (see the table to the right). Communication scholar Nancy K. Baym, in *Personal Connections in the Digital Age*, notes the benefits these communication tools offer us, and these are summarized in the last column of the table.[7]

Many scholars are even referring to the technological methods for staying connected offered via technology (e.g., Facebook, FaceTime, LinkedIn, Twitter, YouTube, or Instagram) as the new "first impressions." In the past, the lack of nonverbal communication—and a somewhat common misunderstanding that online communication is more dishonest[8]—allowed many to doubt the effectiveness of mediated perceptions. However, the more synchronous and richer media have become, the more effectively individuals are able to perceive.

TIP: Pressure to Conform to a Social Networking Site

Research suggests that even when you know your family, friends, colleagues, or bosses are watching, you will most likely conform to the norms of the social networking site (SNS) you are using. Your behavior may support a positive perception on the SNS but not outside of that network. This is particularly true for women, who are held to a different standard.[9] Beware of giving into the SNS pressure to be perceived as part of the in-group when individual perception is rooted in the larger cultural standards.

Mediated Interactions

Engagement Styles	Examples	Baym's Perception Benefits
Asynchronous engagements (also known as lean media[10]) occur when individual interactions occur with a time delay or are not in real time.	Interactions via email, voicemail, and sometimes texting when reaction times are not instant	Allow more members to engage effectively in the communication, longer time to craft a message

Engagement Styles	Examples	Baym's Perception Benefits
Synchronous engagements (also known as rich media) occur when individuals interact in real time.	Interactions via FaceTime, Skype, phone calls, and instant messaging or chat features	Better for intimate interpersonal interactions, response time is short, more information (verbal and nonverbal) transfers, and an enhanced sense of placelessness or closeness

Mediated factors can have their downsides, of course. As drastically demonstrated in the viral YouTube video "Time Lapse Video Shows Model's Photoshop Transformation," showing a woman who becomes "stunning" in 37 seconds, technology can negatively influence what we view as beautiful, sexy, male, female, and easily attainable.

2.4 Who Are You?

In *Poor Richard's Almanack*, Benjamin Franklin wrote, "There are three things extremely hard, steel, a diamond, and to know one's self."[11] In one respect, Franklin is right about knowing one's self. Developing self-awareness takes work and is a never-ending process complicated by our busy and information-filled lives. Being self-aware involves recognizing who you are (self-concept) and determining how you measure up to your internal standards (self-esteem).

Self-Awareness

Self-awareness is a heightened capacity for self-reflection and the ability to recognize who you are as a separate individual. Becoming self-aware begins with asking questions such as:

- How do I define myself?
- What would I like to be?
- What do I like to do?
- What am I good at?
- What do I view as my flaws?
- What are my general feelings and mood?
- What do I believe in?
- What do I value?
- What is important to me?
- Am I pleased with who I am becoming?
- How do I value my abilities?
- How do I present myself to others? Am I aware of what I am doing?
- What do I prefer others not to know about me?
- What am I comfortable with telling anyone?
- How do others view me?

Your self-awareness influences:
- How you perceive others
- How you create and send messages
- How you receive and respond to the messages of others

Self-Concept

Your **self-concept** is the knowledge you have of yourself. Parts of your self-concept will be based on factual characteristics and easy to develop. Other aspects of your self-concept require you to dig deeper into areas such as attitudes, values, or beliefs. For example, I am European-American, short, a redhead, in a significant relationship, and a professor, and I place a considerable value on professional success and family.

Self-Esteem

Your **self-esteem** or self-worth is the personal value (positive or negative) you hold of yourself. Evaluating your self-talk (intrapersonal communication), or how you talk to yourself mentally, will indicate your self-esteem. For example, because I value professional success and family, I often find myself mentally reflecting on how to improve my teaching and how to negotiate being better professionally and being there for my family.

Self-Test: Rosenberg Self-Esteem Scale (RSES)

This self-esteem scale developed by psychologist Morris Rosenberg in 1965 can help you begin to understand your self-esteem.[12] You can access an online version at http://personality-testing.info/tests/RSE.php.

Instructions:
Below is a list of 10 statements dealing with your general feelings about yourself. The items should be answered quickly without overthinking them.
- If you strongly agree, mark SA.
- If you agree, mark A.
- If you disagree, mark D.
- If you strongly disagree, mark SD.

Scoring:
- SA=3, A=2, D=1, SD=0.
- Items with an asterisk (*) are reverse scored—that is, SA=0, A=1, D=2, SD=3.
- Sum the scores for the 10 items.
- The higher the score, the higher the self-esteem.
- Scores below 15 suggest low self-esteem.

1. On the whole, I am satisfied with myself.	SA	A	D	SD
2.* At times, I think I am no good at all.	SA	A	D	SD
3. I feel that I have a number of good qualities.	SA	A	D	SD
4. I am able to do things as well as most other people.	SA	A	D	SD
5.* I feel I do not have much to be proud of.	SA	A	D	SD
6.* I certainly feel useless at times.	SA	A	D	SD
7. I feel that I'm a person of worth.	SA	A	D	SD
8.* I wish I could have more respect for myself.	SA	A	D	SD
9.* All in all, I am inclined to feel that I am a failure.	SA	A	D	SD
10. I take a positive attitude toward myself.	SA	A	D	SD

2.5 How Do You Create a Perception of Self?

So far, your perception of self may sound internal and void of outside influences, though of course that's not the case. For example, list all the people, life events, or cultural influences that have shaped who you are. Your list might include your grandfather, first-grade teacher, best friend during junior high, favorite college teacher, parents, the summer you worked at a camp for special needs children, or your favorite books, shows, and magazines.

As you grapple with defining who you are and giving value to yourself, you interact with others in your family, peer groups, significant relationships, and culture (see the images below). Through your interactions with these people, you learn:

- How others perceive you
- How to view yourself compared to others
- How to understand and regulate who you are from a cultural and co-cultural perspective
- How to view your own thoughts and actions
- How to ultimately value who you are

| How mom and dad see me | How my girlfriend sees me | How my older brother sees me | How my ex-girlfriend sees me |

Use Reflected Appraisal

This process of understanding self through symbolic interaction is known as **reflected appraisal** or the *looking glass self*.[13] Like mirrors reflecting your image back at you, the perceptions and evaluations from your parents, siblings, friends, peers, and mentors continually shape your concept of who you are.

Understand Social Comparison

First discussed by psychologist Leon Festinger in 1954, **social comparison theory** suggests that you are driven to evaluate your self by comparing your looks, attitudes, values, beliefs, and abilities to others in your social group or those you see as being similar to you.[14] You might ask, "Are these elements of my *self* OK compared to my social group or family?" You may do *downward comparisons* as a protective measure when you compare yourself to those worse off to make yourself feel better. Or, you might do an *upward comparison* to those better off, which lowers your self-esteem or motivates you to strive harder.[15]

Cultivate and Protect Who You Really Are

A strong self-concept is vital to your communication effectiveness and your overall mental and physical health.

1. Be kind to yourself.

Boost your confidence by thinking positive thoughts and acknowledging your successes. View dissatisfactions and frustrations with yourself as opportunities to improve, not as failures. Don't overly attack yourself.

2. Be willing to change and accept responsibility for negative as well as positive traits or behaviors.

According to psychologists Thomas Duval and Paul Silvia, a **self-serving bias** (also known as self-serving attribution) is the tendency to attribute your successes internally while attributing failures externally. **Attribution** is how we explain the cause of our or others' behavior.[16] For example, when you fail a test, don't immediately blame the instructor. Instead, evaluate your behavior before the test and how you studied.

See Objective 2.7 for how attribution inhibits impressions of others' behaviors.

3. Surround yourself with people who are healthy for you.

Surround yourself with people who nurture, inspire, love, and protect you. Take all steps possible to end abusive body-to-body and mediated relationships (e.g., cyberbullying and cyberstalking).

4. Beware of negative self-fulfilling prophecies created by you or others around you.

A **self-fulfilling prophecy** is a prediction you or someone else makes that directly or indirectly causes the prediction to come true. Some self-fulfilling prophecies can have a positive influence and others can be negative. For example, if you predict that you will be horrible at public speaking and so you fail to prepare or practice, you will make the prediction come true.

Set constructive goals that still challenge you but are attainable. Setting unrealistic or destructive goals is the first step toward a negative self-fulfilling prophecy.

2.6 How Do You Manage the "Self" You Present to Others?

Sociologist Erving Goffman wrote, "The self … is not an organic thing that has a specific location, whose fundamental fate is to be born, to mature, to die; it is a dramatic effect arising diffusely from a scene that is present."[17] As Goffman suggests, when you interact with others, like an actor on stage, you attempt to control or guide the impression others have of you by altering things like the environment, your appearance, or your behavior. In essence, you manage your impression on others.

Impression management (also known as self-presentation or identity management) is the process of controlling the impression you wish to make on others. When you manage your impression, you select which aspects of yourself to disclose, hide, or fake in order to create an impression on those you interact with. You do this by negotiating what you let others perceive of you (your public identity) and what you keep hidden (your private identity).

Other communication elements that can and should influence how you negotiate your identity can be the length of your relationship with others, the reason for the encounter, and the specific situation or context. All of these converging influences can make managing your impression complex. For example, it can be confusing to call everyone you give access to view your Facebook a "friend." If you define your Facebook "friends" as you do in your non-mediated interaction (someone you can trust with aspects of your private identity), you might give the wrong impression on Facebook to people who are really just acquaintances, bosses, potential employers, or family, especially if you "friend" just about anyone.

The table on the next page offers some advice on managing the "self" you present to others.

Practicing Ethics: Don't Fake It

Faking an impression or identity out of deceit, whether in person or in a mediated context, is unethical and even illegal in some situations. Strive to never construct an identity that is for personal gain only, designed to hurt others, or fraudulent.

Impression management . . .

. . . is often conveyed via verbal and nonverbal messages.

As with most messages you wish to send, you often use verbal and nonverbal codes to create an impression. However, the people you associate with can influence the impression others have of you. For example, if all of your college friends are athletes, people meeting you for the first time might assume you are too.

. . . requires you to manage multiple roles.

Consider all the roles you play in a given day. You may interact with someone as a sibling, a child, a parent, a lover, a face-to-face friend, a Facebook friend, a student, a patient, a cancer survivor, an employee, a coworker, or a customer. Each of these roles has certain expectations. How well you construct different roles and different nuances within those roles (e.g., a little sister and not just a sibling) will influence how well you communicate.

. . . is a collaborative act.

The roles you play influence the roles played by others during your interactions, and their acceptance of your role-playing influences you.

. . . can be conscious or unconscious.

There will be times when you are highly aware of manipulating impressions to gain a favorable outcome and other times when your behaviors will be unconscious reactions you have learned over time.

. . . helps you follow social rules, laws, norms, and customs.

Without impression management, you couldn't behave properly in a given context, order couldn't be maintained, and you wouldn't be accepted.

. . . can vary in expressive control.

As defined by psychologist Mark Snyder, *self-monitoring* is the internal process that individuals engage in to pay close attention to social interactions so they can adapt to that particular situation.[18] Some people are high self-monitors and are very observant and flexible. Low self-monitors tend to listen to their own moods, feelings, attitudes, beliefs, and personality traits as the means to guide their interaction choices. Low self-monitors will seek out interactions with like-minded individuals or stay to themselves. They prefer situations where they can be themselves.

This self-monitoring scale developed by Snyder can help you begin to understand your preference for self-monitoring. You can access an online version at http://personality-testing.info/tests/SM.php.

Self-Test: Self-Monitoring Scale (Developed by Mark Snyder, 1974)[19]

Directions: The statements below concern your personal reactions to a number of different situations. No two statements are exactly alike, so consider each statement carefully before answering. If a statement is TRUE or MOSTLY TRUE as applied to you, circle the "T" next to the question. If a statement is FALSE or NOT USUALLY TRUE as applied to you, circle the "F" next to the question.

		T	F
1.	I find it hard to imitate the behavior of other people.	T	F
2.	My behavior is usually an expression of my true inner feelings, attitudes, and beliefs.	T	F
3.	At parties and social gatherings, I do not attempt to do or say things that others will like.	T	F
4.	I can only argue for ideas which I already believe.	T	F
5.	I can make impromptu speeches even on topics about which I have almost no information.	T	F
6.	I guess I put on a show to impress or entertain people.	T	F
7.	When I am uncertain how to act in a social situation, I look to the behavior of others for cues.	T	F
8.	I would probably make a good actor.	T	F
9.	I rarely seek the advice of my friends to choose movies, books, or music.	T	F
10.	I sometimes appear to others to be experiencing deeper emotions than I actually am.	T	F
11.	I laugh more when I watch a comedy with others than when alone.	T	F
12.	In groups of people, I am rarely the center of attention.	T	F
13.	In different situations and with different people, I often act like very different persons.	T	F
14.	I am not particularly good at making other people like me.	T	F
15.	Even if I am not enjoying myself, I often pretend to be having a good time.	T	F

16. I'm not always the person I appear to be. T F

17. I would not change my opinions (or the way I do things) in order to please someone else or win their favor. T F

18. I have considered being an entertainer. T F

19. In order to get along and be liked, I tend to be what people expect me to be rather than anything else. T F

20. I have never been good at games like charades or improvisational acting. T F

21. I have trouble changing my behavior to suit different people and different situations. T F

22. At a party, I let others keep the jokes and stories going. T F

23. I feel a bit awkward in company and do not show up quite as well as I should. T F

24. I can look anyone in the eye and tell a lie with a straight face (if for a right end). T F

25. I may deceive people by being friendly when I really dislike them. T F

Scoring Your Self-Monitoring Questionnaire
Self-monitoring is the ability and desire to regulate one's public expressiveness to fit the clues and/or requirements of the situation.

Scoring Key:
High self-monitors should respond with the following pattern:

F to questions 1, 2, 3, 4, 9, 12, 14, 17, 20, 21, 22, 23;

T to questions 5, 6, 7, 8, 10, 11, 13, 15, 16, 18, 19, 24, 25.

- To calculate your self-monitoring score, place a check mark next to the questions that match the "T" and "F" responses above.
- Count the total number of check marks that appear in the margin of your survey. That number is your self-monitoring score.
- A score between 0–12 would indicate that the respondent is a relatively low self-monitor; a score between 13–25 would indicate that the respondent is a relatively high self-monitor.

2.7 What Are Some Barriers to Perceiving Others Effectively?

As noted earlier in this chapter, how you perceive yourself, as well as the physical, emotional, environmental, intellectual, experiential, cultural, and mediated factors that influence all perceptions, will shape greatly your perceptions of others and your interactions with them. When you apply the perception process to others, you are engaging in what psychologist Solomon Asch defined in 1946 as impression formation.[20]

Impression formation (also known as person perception or social perception) refers to the tactics or approaches you use to form an impression of others. These tactics or approaches often become barriers for effective perception and lead to misperceptions. Because you may not be consciously aware of using a tactic or approach that becomes a barrier, it is important to practice and develop your perception skills.

Asch and many contemporary theorists have explored several barriers. Some of the most significant are negative bias, first and last impressions, stereotyping, attribution, self-fulfilling prophecy, and consistency.

Negative Bias

Although this may sound simplistic, we tend to favor negative impressions over positive ones. It is natural to recognize and attend to behaviors we perceive as negative, and we often allow positive behaviors to slide by unnoticed. Think about something you like and something you dislike. Then try to explain why you like it or dislike it. In most cases, you can be much more detailed about why you dislike something. This is true for impressions as well.

First and Last Impressions (Primacy versus Recency)

In one of his letters, St. Jérôme wrote, "Early impressions are hard to eradicate from the mind. When once wool has been dyed purple who can restore it to its previous whiteness?"[21]

The primacy effect suggests a bit of truth to St. Jérôme's statement when forming impressions of someone for the first time. Specifically, the **primacy effect** indicates that individuals are more likely to remember things that are at the beginning of a list or at the first encounter. For example, try to remember the first time you met your best friend or significant other—what you thought of him or her, where you were, what time of day it was, what you were doing, and so on. Odds are, the impressions you formed that day were strong and it took several more interactions to change them if need be. Next, try to remember meeting them a few encounters later. It is probable that you have no recollection of details for the later encounter.

Primacy effect suggests that first impressions are hard to reverse and that they set the stage for all other impressions. Some researchers argue that these first impressions are important to understand and appraise because they can screen what you perceive as you gain more information. This tendency to screen, notice, search for, interpret, and/or remember perceptions based on what you believe (your first impressions) is known as a **confirmation bias**. For example, if you find someone negative during a first encounter, you will likely attend to negative aspects of future encounters. Negative first impressions can be hard to undo, and positive ones can potentially obscure judgment. This type of impression formation can be a barrier to effective perception by continually supporting the existing first impression.

Conversely, the **recency effect** implies that the most recent (or last) impression of someone will be remembered the best. For example, if Danny struggles his first three years on the basketball team but becomes the star player in the season his team wins the championship, Danny could leave an extremely positive impression.

Recent events are easier to remember and seem to sway perceptions as much as first impressions. However, neither may be a great predictor of long-term behavior or effective perception.

Self-Check: First Impressions and Hidden Biases

Visit the site lovehasnolabels.com and watch the video. You can also take a quiz to see what hidden biases you may have. How did you perceive the people in the video? Did any of your first impressions turn out to be false?

Stereotyping

Most people tend to process information received about someone in one of two divergent ways. You tend to perceive the person either as a stereotype or as an individual. A **stereotype** is an oversimplified and generalized prejudgment, in this case applied to a person based on group belongingness or cultural patterns. We often need to use stereotypes on an initial level to respond quickly to the sheer number of stimuli we encounter or to make important fast decisions. For example, a masked individual walking up to a teller in a bank should quickly be stereotyped as a potential robber even when a snowstorm is raging outside.

However, when stereotypes are used as a means to dictate our interactions and reduce someone into a false reflection of who they are as an individual, stereotyping becomes a negative and unethical practice. Stereotyping in this manner leads to **prejudice**, or opinions formed about a person or cultural group based on little or no knowledge and illogical feelings. How we unfairly act or treat those we are prejudiced toward is **discrimination**. Most prejudices relate to race or ethnicity, language use, physical or mental abilities, social class, occupation, education level, age, religion, sexuality, or gender. Stereotyping by prejudgment can destructively distort your impressions and seriously undermine your interaction and ethics. You should avoid this type of stereotyping.

Attribution

As you learned in Objective 2.5, how you assign cause for your own behavior can skew your self-perception (self-serving bias) and it can influence your impressions of others as well. When we incorrectly assign cause to a person's behavior, we often commit overattribution or a fundamental attribution error, which is similar to a self-serving bias.

Overattribution

Overattribution occurs when you assign too much of a person's behavior to one or two of their characteristics—for example, "Marquette works out all the time because he is a guy" or "Megan studies harder because she is hearing-impaired." Marquette could have an underlying medical issue that requires he stay active. Megan might study harder because she wants to be a lawyer and getting into law school is very competitive. As with your own behaviors, their causes are more complex and can rarely be attributed to one characteristic.

Fundamental Attribution Error

Fundamental attribution error occurs when you overestimate a person's disposition or personality as the cause of his or her behavior and underestimate external factors such as situation.[22] Imagine that a waiter ignores you, seems distracted, and gives you bad service; you may attribute his behavior to not caring about his job or a poor attitude. However, his behavior could be the result of something completely different, such as a coworker's recent death. As with the self-serving bias, we tend to attribute others' negative behavior to personal traits and good behavior to external influences.

Self-Fulfilling Prophecy

As with your own perception of self, you can make a self-fulfilling prophecy with your perceptions of others. For example, suppose one of your coworkers previously worked for the person who is becoming your new boss. That coworker tells you that the boss is mean, unfriendly, and can't be trusted. When you start interacting with your new supervisor, your interactions with her are short, evasive, and cold. She reacts to your behavior toward her in much the same way. You have fulfilled the prophecy that she is not a nice supervisor.

The pygmalion effect and the golem effect are two forms of self-fulfilling prophecies. The *pygmalion effect* suggests that when you place greater expectations on others, the better they will perform.[23] The *golem effect* suggests that low expectations lead to decreased performance.[24]

Consistency

Consistency as a barrier to perception relates to psychologist Leon Festinger's **principle of consistency,** or our desire to keep things harmonious.[25] For example, Tori and Jane are in a relationship. Tori loves amusement parks and they both go often. Jane never complains about going and really enjoys herself. Tori perceives that Jane loves amusement parks too. However, Jane finds them okay but loves the times she is able to spend with Tori, given their busy lives. Tori is perceiving Jane's behavior to be consistent with hers. If Tori discovers that Jane may not be as excited about amusement parks as she is, Tori will experience conflicting feelings about taking Jane to the parks so much. Festinger calls Tori's discomfort from experiencing conflicting beliefs, ideas, values, or emotions **cognitive dissonance.** Even how we like or dislike someone can influence our perception of that person. If you like someone, you will perceive him or her as liking you. You want their feelings and perceptions to be consistent with yours.

And to change ourselves effectively, we first had to change our perceptions.[26]
Stephen R. Covey

2.8 How Can You Develop Better Perception Skills?

Given how much of what we perceive is unconscious and often a quick response, developing our perception skills is vital to effective communication and relationship development. Like other good habits, effective perception skills can slide right by without much notice.

You must be willing to invest time in uncovering misconceptions. So, here are some methods for developing your critical perception skills.

Engage in Perception Checking

Perception checking is the ability to critically evaluate your perceptions of others. Perception checking is important because your perceptions can be wrong, or the other person can be deceiving you.

Deception is the practice of deliberately making someone believe an untruth. Deception can be categorized as lies, exaggerations, half-truths, secrets, and diversionary responses.[27] Although rare but often well-publicized, some people may present a self that is a deception. Periodic critical re-evaluation of your perception of others can alert you to a deceptive self. This is particularly true for online perceptions where the lack of body-to-body communication may make it easier for someone to deceive.

So, how do you check your perceptions for error or deceptions? You can use two levels of investigation: indirect and direct.

Indirect Checking

You engage in *indirect* (or private) *perception checking* when you seek other information to verify or dispute the perception you are having. You may seek that information through more observation or by comparison to perceptions held by others.

For example, if Joe slams the door to his office as he quickly leaves, you might perceive that he is angry. Asking someone else in the office if there was something that caused Joe's behavior could help you confirm or disconfirm your feelings. Likewise, the time of day (Is it just before the hour or half hour?) or what Joe was carrying (a pen and pad) might suggest that he just realized he is going to be late for a meeting and his adrenaline kicked in. This act of private, or indirect, investigation can lead to a better understanding of how you should perceive Joe's behavior.

Direct Checking

Direct perception checking is the act of directly consulting the person you are perceiving. This is especially helpful in times of conflict. This level of investigation involves describing what you are sensing, offering more than one possible interpretation, and engaging in a conversation with the other person to understand if your feelings are correct. When doing this, you will create what is known as a perception-checking statement. For example, if you think your roommate is angry with you, you might say:

> I feel like you are ignoring me. Did I do something to hurt your feelings or make you angry? Is something bothering you?

Perception checking will help reduce the effects of deception, uncertainty, or ambiguity.

Chapter 6, Objective 6.4 offers more information on uncertainty reduction.

Be Willing to Change Your First Impressions

The *interaction appearance theory* (IAT) from communication scholars Kelly Albada, Mark Knapp, and Katheryn Theune explains how you finally change your original impressions (especially regarding physical attractiveness).[29] IAT suggests you will change your impressions of someone the more you interact with them. Be willing to withhold judgment based on first impressions until you have had time to interact more with that person. You might find that your first impression was wrong.

Beware of Selective Attention

Selective attention is the conscious or unconscious tendency to pay attention and expose yourself to a small scope of sensory information that satisfies you or supports something you believe—for example, hearing only what you want and ignoring the rest. Being conscious of this selective tendency will help you learn to widen your attention scope. The more information you attend to, the more likely your perceptions will be correct.

Seek Feedback from Others About Your Perception Skills

Others can help you evaluate your impressions. Ask if they agree with your impressions or what they see you doing that might influence the behavior of others. Such discussions can also help you see how you form impressions of others. This ongoing evaluation of your skills will help you develop a critical eye toward how you perceive and build your perception confidence.

Develop Identification

Develop your skills to be other-centered. Have you ever heard someone say, "You can't understand me until you have walked in my shoes"? This phrase reflects theorist and philosopher Kenneth Burke's notion of identification, as discussed in his book *A Rhetoric of Motives*. **Identification** (also called empathy) is the human need and willingness to understand as much as possible the feelings, thoughts, motives, interests, attitudes, values, behaviors, and lives of others.[30] Identification will help you cultivate your communicator competence by reducing uncertainty, increasing sensitivity, and highlighting details. Communication scholars Stephen Littlejohn and Karen Foss call this willingness to work toward understanding and communicating effectively with others **intercultural competence.** They identify three behaviors to emulate as an effective intercultural communicator, which are summarized in the table on the next page.[31]

Littlejohn and Foss's Intercultural Competence

The Components of Intercultural Competence	How Do You Emulate Each?	Example
Identity knowledge	Educate yourself about the other person's culture.	In your new friend's religion, eating certain foods or even using utensils that have touched those foods is inappropriate.
Mindfulness	Be conscientiously aware and pay attention to those distinctions.	Pay attention to your new friend's behavior when cooking or ordering foods, or educate yourself about these customs.
Negotiation skill	Respond to the differences through sensitivity, politeness, willing adjustment, and collaboration.	When going out with your friend, select restaurants that prepare each meal individually or avoid places that cook all meals on the same grill. Ask the waiter to explain dishes to you. Engage your friend in a discussion about where to eat and how to meet these needs.

Chapter 2 Review

Key Questions

2.1 What Is Perception?

Objective 2.1: **DEFINE PERCEPTION**

Perception is the ability to translate information into insight or awareness about something, usually people, places, events, or objects. Perception is learned, subjective, instinctive, cultural, and influential. You use perception to understand self and others.

See pages 38–39.

2.2 What Is the Process of Perception?

Objective 2.2: **DESCRIBE THE PROCESS OF PERCEPTION**

The process of perception consists of three phases: selecting, organizing, and interpreting. These phases can be conscious or unconscious. Selecting is the moment when some factor grabs your attention and forces you to focus on some stimuli and ignore others. Organizing is when you mentally arrange the information you gained from sensing something into more manageable patterns. Interpreting is when you attach meaning to what you have learned in the first two phases about a person, place, event, or object.

See pages 40–41.

2.3 What Factors Influence Perception?

Objective 2.3: **DESCRIBE THE FACTORS INFLUENCING PERCEPTION**

When you perceive yourself or others, numerous factors can influence your understanding. These factors can help or hinder your ability to form effective perceptions and therefore should be something you reflect on as you create and respond to your perceptions. They are:

- Physical factors
- Emotional factors
- Environmental factors
- Intellectual factors
- Experiential factors
- Cultural factors
- Mediated factors

See pages 42–45.

2.4 Who Are You?

Objective 2.4: **DISCUSS THE CONCEPTS OF SELF-AWARENESS, SELF-CONCEPT, AND SELF-ESTEEM**

Being self-aware involves recognizing who you are (self-concept) and determining how you measure up to your internal standards (self-esteem). Self-awareness is a heightened capacity for self-reflection and the ability to recognize who you are as a separate individual. Your self-concept is the knowledge you have of yourself. Your self-esteem or self-worth is the personal value (positive or negative) you hold of yourself.

See pages 46–47.

2.5 How Do You Create a Perception of Self?

Objective 2.5: **EXPLAIN THE WAYS YOU CAN CREATE A PERCEPTION OF SELF**

As you create a perception of self, understand:

- The perceptions and evaluations from your parents, siblings, friends, peers, and mentors continually shape your concept of who you are and help you form your perception of self (reflected appraisal).
- You are driven to evaluate your self by comparing it to others (social comparison).
- It is important to cultivate and protect who you are.

See pages 48–49.

2.6 How Do You Manage the "Self" You Present to Others?

Objective 2.6: **DISCUSS IMPRESSION MANAGEMENT METHODS**

Impression management is the process of controlling the impression you wish to make on others. You select which aspects of yourself to disclose, hide, or fake in your interactions. Impression management:

- Is conveyed verbally and nonverbally
- Requires you to manage multiple roles
- Is collaborative
- Can be conscious or unconscious
- Helps you follow social rules, laws, norms, and customs
- Can vary in expressive control

See pages 50–53.

2.7 What Are Some Barriers to Perceiving Others Effectively?

Objective 2.7: **DISCUSS KEY BARRIERS TO IMPRESSION FORMATION**

Impression formation refers to the tactics or approaches you use to form an impression of others. These tactics or approaches often become barriers, such as:

- Negative bias
- First and last impressions
- Stereotyping
- Attribution
- Self-fulfilling prophecy
- Consistency

See pages 54–57.

2.8 How Can You Develop Better Perception Skills?

Objective 2.8: **EXPLAIN METHODS FOR DEVELOPING PERCEPTION SKILLS**

- Engage in perception checking.
- Be willing to change your first impressions.
- Beware of selective attention.
- Seek feedback from others about your perception skills.
- Develop identification.

See pages 58–61.

Key Terms

Improve Your Communication

We all know that pictures posted on Facebook and other social sites send messages about who we are. You might even think twice about making posts that seem particularly negative. However, University of Pennsylvania researchers analyzed the word choice in all postings from 75,000 users and discovered the basic language choices you make can help others predict your personality.[32] At www.wwbp.org/personality_wc.html, you can see the "big five" personality traits (extraversion, agreeableness, conscientiousness, neuroticism, and openness) depicted in word clouds created from the language choices of the users. Take some time to analyze your use of social sites. Ask:

- What language choices do I make?
- How often do I tweet or post per day?
- What do I share, "like," or "favorite"?
- What do I say about school or work?
- How do I respond to others?
- Do I use a current photo of myself for my profile picture? If not, how does that prevent others from seeing who I am?
- What would all of this say to someone evaluating me for a job, getting into a school, or a long-term relationship?
- Am I really disclosing more than I want?

Researchers from the University of Cambridge, looking at only what 58,000 users "liked," were able to determine sexual orientation in men 88 percent or women 75 percent of the time or if a user was African American or Caucasian 95 percent of the time.[33]

Apply Your Knowledge

1. Over the next week, keep a diary of how you talk to yourself or engage in what some call self-talk. Try to note what you say to yourself that is negative. For example, do you say things such as: *I am not good enough. I will fail at this. I am afraid. Other people do not feel like this. What is wrong with me?* Once you have a list, try to turn the phrases into something more positive thoughts such as: *I can do this. I will reach for my best. Everyone has fears.* Learn to call yourself on negative self-talk. If you tend not to be negative, why do you think that is true?

2. Think of a person you formed a first impression of that over time proved incorrect. Now ask yourself:

- What information did you attend to that allowed you to form the first impression?
- What previous experiences help you interpret that information?
- What changed over time about that first impression?
- What errors in perception did you commit?
- What caused you to change your impressions?
- How long did it take?
- How can you prevent such errors in the future?

Other Resources

Here are some resources that offer additional information and support.

Self-Perception

Pachter, Barbara. *The Essentials of Business Etiquette: How to Greet, Eat, and Tweet Your Way to Success.* New York: McGraw, 2013. Print.

- www.ted.com/talks/amy_cuddy_your_body_language_shapes_who_you_are.html
- www.ted.com/talks/johanna_blakley_social_media_and_the_end_of_gender
- www.cmhc.utexas.edu/index.html
- www.mayoclinic.com/health/self-esteem/MH00129

Self-Perception and the Internet

Agger, Ben. *Oversharing: Presentations of Self in the Internet Age.* New York: Routledge, 2012. Print.

Cunningham, Carolyn. *Social Networking and Impression Management: Self-Presentation in the Digital Age.* Lanham: Lexington, 2013. Print.

Poletti, Anna and Julie Rak. *Identity Technologies: Constructing the Self Online.* Madison: U of Wisconsin P, 2014. Print.

Chapter 3
Verbal Communication

The limits of my language mean the limits of my world.[1]

Ludwig Wittgenstein

3.1 What Are the Characteristics of Language?

Verbal communication is the act of sending and receiving messages via language (words). These messages may be spoken, written, or signed (e.g., American Sign Language). **Language** is a systematic, rule-governed set of symbols (words) that have meaning for a particular group of people. According to Ethnologue.com, there are approximately 7,105 living languages.[2] You use language to make sense of things, to interact with others, to express your thoughts and emotions, to fulfill your needs, and to create and maintain your identity.

To understand how you use language, it is important to recognize the unique features of language.

Language Is Symbolic

As mythologist Joseph Campbell stated, "A symbol is an energy evoking, and directing, agent."[3] *Language* or, more precisely, a *word* is a symbol. A **symbol** stands for, represents, or suggests something. For example, think about the word *book. Livre* (French), *libro* (Italian), *bog* (Danish), *boek* (Dutch), and *buch* (German) are each a symbol (word) for *book* depending on the culture. Cultural members often use conventions and rules to determine which words symbolize the things, ideas, beliefs, actions, or material being represented.

Sometimes a word may have an association with or resemble what it represents. However, this connection between the word and the thing it stands for, represents, or suggests is still often subjective, personal, or idiosyncratic to the culture using it. The people of the culture connect the meaning with the thing. This brings us to the next language characteristic.

Language Is Meaningless Without People

Meanings are not in the words and sounds but in the significance people apply to those words or sounds. The relationship between a word and what it stands for is random, subjective, and coincidental. Therefore, words are **arbitrary**.

For example, nothing about the letters that make up the word *book*, or their arrangement, directly or logically relates to the thing you are reading from right now. If you happen to be reading from an electronic version of the book, the content may be the same, but we have a new series of sounds forming a new word (*ebook*). That relationship is understood only when you learn to associate the word (*book or ebook*) with pages bound between two covers or a digital version on a tablet or computer.

The classic movie *The Miracle Worker*, about the life of Helen Keller, features a scene in which Annie Sullivan teaches blind and deaf Helen the sign for water—a key breakthrough as Helen connects the word and the object together. At that moment, the word *water* became the symbol for that cold, wet substance Helen had felt for years; previously, she had no word or language to express it. The word now had meaning for Helen.

In their book, *The Meaning of Meaning*, Charles K. Ogden and Ivor A. Richards demonstrate how words (symbols) relate to the things they represent. Ogden and Richards created the "triangle of meaning" (also known as the semantic triangle), represented in the figure below.[4]

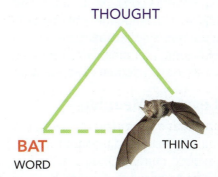

THOUGHT

BAT
WORD

THING

Notice that the bottom of the triangle is broken, and no direct relationship connects the word (*bat*) to the thing (the animal). Instead, the word must go through your thought process to connect to the living animal.

Language Meaning Is Complex

As noted in the previous section, the meaning of a word must go through your thought process for you to connect to the thing represented by the word. This detour into your thoughts makes giving meaning to words complex. To understand the complexity of language, you need to explore the notions that there are two levels of meaning for most words and that most words vary in degree of abstraction.

Two Levels of Meaning

The **denotative meaning** of a word is the commonly accepted meaning within a culture or co-culture. Often, it is the meaning found in the dictionary. For example, let's return to the word *bat* and look at its denotative meaning.

bat—a small animal like a mouse with wings that flies at night[5]

Sometimes a word can have more than one denotative meaning. Then, you must pay attention to the context surrounding the word. For example, the word *bat* could refer not to the animal but to a piece of sporting equipment.

bat—a long wooden stick used for hitting the ball in baseball[6]

Given this denotative meaning, hearing such statements as "He broke the bat" and "She threw the bat" is less alarming within the context of a baseball field.

The **connotative meaning** of a word is the emotional and personal reaction you might have to that word. Your reaction could be anywhere on a continuum from an emotional avalanche (a significant positive or negative response to a word) to an emotional famine (no real response at all).

For example, what if you are highly afraid of bats (the mammal)? Some people exhibit fear at just the thought of the word. Nothing in the word itself or its denotative definition should elicit that kind of response, but those individuals have had an experience with or a knowledge of bats that adds a negative connotative meaning for them.

Conversely, what if you are a zoologist and your specialty is the study of the Mexican free-tailed bat in California? Your response to hearing the word would more likely be excitement and interest. These differences in the emotional and personal reactions to a word add to your understanding and meaning of a word. The denotative and connotative meanings work in tandem to create your overall understanding and response to most words.

Degree of Abstraction

The abstraction level of a word relates to its degree of specificity. Semanticist Samuel I. Hayakawa, in *Language in Thought and Action*, discussed the levels of word abstraction and introduced the **ladder of abstraction**.[7]

As you can see from the figure on the right, the bottom of the ladder represents concrete words and the top represents abstract words. The varying steps in between represent differing levels of words that are neither really concrete nor extremely abstract. As you climb the ladder, the degree of abstraction and ambiguity is higher. Note how easy it is to visualize the wrong living thing, animal, or farm animal on the top three steps of the ladder. Toward the bottom, you get closer to the right living thing with "chicken" but reach the individual type of chicken with Zsa Zsa, the silkie bantam. It is easy to visualize her specificity.

If you use too much abstract language, your interactions can be confusing or misinterpreted. However, too much concrete language can weigh your interactions down in detail. The best way to deal with abstraction is to be aware of it as a feature of language and strive to use a mixture of both concrete and abstract words.

Living Thing
VERY ABSTRACT

Animal
MORE ABSTRACT

Farm Animal
ABSTRACT

Chicken
LESS CONCRETE

Zsa Zsa, the silkie bantam
CONCRETE

Language Is Governed by Rules

Rules are a set of explicit or understood regulations or codes governing how something is or should be done. We need rules to carry out daily communication and interaction. Otherwise, it would be impossible to interact or understand each other. Language rules help a native speaker communicate with other cultural members through standard language patterns. Often, you aren't even aware you are adhering to particular rules. The rule systems that you are most likely aware of are phonology, semantics, syntactics, and pragmatics.

Phonology refers to the accepted methods for combining sound or making sound patterns to create words. Not all cultures have the same sounds or accents, and not all co-cultures will adhere to the same combinations of sounds. For example, in Spanish, all letters have a unique sound; but in English, some letters have more than one associated sound. For instance, the letter "a" can be pronounced in different ways, such as in c**a**r, c**a**t, and c**a**ke.

Semantics refers to the process of understanding the meaning of words. This set of language rules helps you negotiate the complexity of language mentioned earlier in the chapter. Many words have literal meanings, figurative meanings, or meanings that change over time. For example, the phrase "please crack the window" typically means to open it slightly, not to break it. (This type of phrase is called an *idiom*. See Objective 3.5.)

Syntactics concerns the rules for determining word order, placement, and sequencing. For example, in English, the subject usually comes first, then the verb, followed by an object:

Nolan threw the ball.

For effect, legendary *Star Wars* character Yoda broke this language rule whenever he spoke, moving the subject and verb last. Instead of saying, "I like swamps," Yoda would say, "Swamps, I like."

Pragmatics deals with how you actually use language in everyday interactions, or how you say something to a person in a particular situation within a certain context.[8] This set of language rules is contextually and culturally specific. It takes into account such norms as how communicators take turns in conversation, how messages might be expressed, and what topics are taboo. For example, pragmatics guides you in knowing what is appropriate (or not) to say in front of your grandmother.

These rule systems were created around language use in traditional channels of oral and written communication. In mediated communication, such as online social networking and texting, these systems mix with language rules specific to mediated contexts. For example, you might use shortened forms of words in a text or tweet. Such rules are continually evolving, as cell phone and social media use keeps growing. In 2012, the Pew Research Center reported that 85 percent of U.S. adults own a cell phone and, of those owners, 80 percent send or receive texts.[9] As the figure below suggests, the high usage of Facebook and YouTube—on top of other social media like LinkedIn, Google Plus, and Twitter—adds even more opportunities for examining your language usage and how you present yourself.[10] The best approach in a mediated situation is to adhere to the same rules you would in other similar written communication situations. This is particularly true when you are communicating in a professional context, when you are only an acquaintance of the other person(s), and/or when your message will be widely accessible. See the Practicing Ethics box below for additional advice.

Social Media Use

% of adult Web users who ever use the following social networking sites, 2014

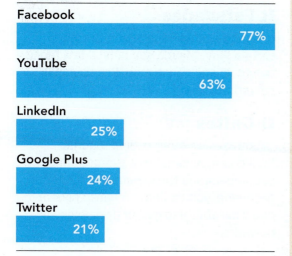

Facebook
77%

YouTube
63%

LinkedIn
25%

Google Plus
24%

Twitter
21%

Source: Pew Research Center

Practicing Ethics: Social Networking Language Rules

- Texting is more appropriate to use with friends and family. Professionally, restrict any texts to subjects like coordinating meetings or quick, informal notices: "The shipment has arrived!"

- Avoid using shortened words in formal contexts. Even informally, use them only if you know the rules well and you know the recipient(s) will understand you. Use full sentences, with correct spelling and grammar, to help with tone and clarity.

- Avoid using all caps or enlarged fonts to yell or shout.

- Don't use social media to break news about highly emotional events like a death, an accident, a serious illness, ending a relationship, or firing someone. These issues need body-to-body or other private interactions.

- Be considerate of when it might not be a good time to send an instant message.

- Sometimes the best message is no message or a delayed one: **do not text and drive**.

3.2 How Is Language Powerful?

Do you know the children's rhyme "Sticks and stones may break my bones, but words will never hurt me"? Parents often recite this to children when someone has called the child a hurtful name. Although the rhyme's intent is to teach a child to view words as powerless,

words are anything but powerless.

Here are some powers of language.

It Names

Language allows you to name experiences or things. For example, before Bill Wasik, senior editor for *Harper's Magazine*, staged the first "flash mob" in 2003, the term did not exist. You may now know that a flash mob is, as described by author Clay Shirky in *Here Comes Everybody*, "a group that engages in seemingly spontaneous but actually synchronized behavior" that is organized via email or texting, for example.[11]

It Persuades

Language can persuade you to act a certain way. Maybe you persuade a friend to join you in a flash mob. Persuasion is powerful.

It Unites

Language can bring people together for a common cause. For example, once you understood the meaning of the term *flash mob*, you could then participate in one. This ability to gather or mobilize is powerful.

"Hashtag" is the 2012 word of the year.[12]

American Dialect Society

It Divides

Unfortunately, language has the power to create and maintain inequality, to control, to hurt, and to disempower. This power can be conscious or unconscious, and history contains numerous examples. For instance, much of Adolf Hitler's power came from his persuasive speeches. Or think about the current use of the word *terrorist*. What images come to mind? Which of these statements might you consider true?

- Timothy McVeigh (Oklahoma City bombing) was a terrorist.
- Dzhokhar and Tamerlan Tsarnaev (Boston Marathon bombing) are terrorists.
- Muhammad Youssef Abdulazeez (Chattanooga shootings) is a terrorist.

Terrorism is commonly defined as politically motivated actual or threatened violence. A terrorist's nationality or religion has nothing to do with being labeled a terrorist, but since 9/11, many people tend to associate the label with certain national or religious ties. Today, some may not call McVeigh a terrorist because he was a U.S. citizen with a name that connoted citizenship and who "looked American," while these same people might brand Dzhokhar Tsarnaev and Abdulazeez as terrorists regardless of their being naturalized citizens. Yet all of their acts were seemingly politically motivated. Still others might see any attempt at mass destruction, such as the 2015 Charleston church or 2012 Colorado theater shootings, as terrorism.

It Empowers

Fortunately, language creates equality and frees, heals, and empowers—listen to the language used by activists such as Nelson Mandela, Robert Kennedy, Madonna, Wangari Maathai, Mary Robinson, Bono, and Malala Yousafzai—and that is powerful.

It Is Bound to Culture

As you learned in Chapter 1, *culture* is the system or learned patterns of beliefs, values, attitudes, norms, and behaviors shared by a large group of people and handed down from generation to generation. Language is a significant means for cultural members to perpetuate and document their culture. Likewise, much of this text demonstrates how one's culture influences communication choices and norms.

The Sapir-Whorf hypothesis, developed from the work of Edward Sapir and Benjamin Lee Whorf, emphasizes the idea that language affects the way we conceptualize our world.[13] There are two versions of the hypothesis. The first version is a "firmer" view known as **linguistic determinism**, which suggests that language limits and determines our knowledge, thoughts, and perceptions. The second and "softer" version, known as **linguistic relativity**, suggests that our language affects or shapes our thoughts, experiences, behaviors, or perceptions but is not as constraining as determinism.[14]

3.3 What Are Some Cultural Variations in Verbal Communication Styles?

Preventing communication breakdowns across cultures begins naturally with learning the language and cultural rituals of the specific culture or co-culture. However, to be interculturally competent, you need to understand and recognize how certain verbal styles or conversation styles can differ across cultures and co-cultures. What is a conversation style? Well, first imagine what might be important to a person when communicating a message.

Some cultures believe the nonverbal message is more important than the verbal or that written communication is more trustworthy than a verbal message. Still other cultures are very direct about their messages, while others take their time and are not straightforward. In some cultures, silence between communicators is uncomfortable; in others, it's viewed as a sign of respect. Therefore, it is important that you become sensitive to and recognize when someone is using a different conversation style.

A **conversation style** is how individuals exchange their thoughts, opinions, and feelings. The unique style can be personal, individualistic, and cultural. It can be ever-changing as the person grows as a communicator, develops a stronger relationship, or moves between contexts. A conversation style has verbal and nonverbal aspects that will help you interpret the message (Chapter 4 discusses nonverbal communication). The following sections discuss some of the most common variations in verbal communication styles between cultures and co-cultures.[15] Keep in mind, these are generalizations and individuals may respond differently.

Direct versus Indirect Style

A *direct style* is one where the verbal message straightforwardly reveals the intent, need, want, and desire. The direct style tends to be common in low-context and individualistic cultures. Countries like the United States, Australia, Great Britain, and Germany prefer this style—especially in business and formal situations. However, Great Britain and Germany are less direct than the United States. Phrases such as "get to the point," "give me the facts," and "don't waste our time" are common in direct styles. "Yes" and "no" are acceptable answers.[16]

An *indirect style* is a verbal message where the intent, need, want, and desire is less obvious or obscured. This style tends to be common in high-context and collectivist cultures. Saying "The dog is hungry" rather than "Would you feed the dog?" is an example of an indirect style. Africa, Taiwan, Korea, Japan, and China prefer this style.[17]

> ### TIP: Intercultural Conversations
> Language such as slang, clichés, idioms, and euphemisms can be unfamiliar and confusing across cultures. (See Objective 3.5.) Be cautious with their use to avoid misunderstandings. However, this language (especially slang) can be an important part of a co-culture's identity. Many co-cultures have languages all their own, which often helps them to navigate dominant culture oppression and to pass the culture on.

Elaborate versus Understated Style

An *elaborate style* stresses rich, expressive language. This type of communicator uses a lot of adjectives, sensory language, exaggerations, idiomatic expressions, similes, and metaphor. For example, note the difference of expressiveness in these two sentences:

> She finished the race.

> Weary and out of breath, she stumbled headfirst over the line.

Countries like Egypt, Iran, Saudi Arabia, and Lebanon use a generally elaborate style. However, we have great examples of this style of speech in the several famous inspirational speeches by Martin Luther King, Jr.[18]

> **Chapter 12** shows how to use expressive language techniques for public speaking.

An *understated style* stresses modest language, understatement, pauses, and silence. Cultures that tend to be high in uncertainty avoidance and high-context prefer this style.[19] The Amish and American Indian co-cultures prefer this style. For example, an Amish farmer who had a bumper-crop year in the fields would likely say, "We did all right," rather than expound on the details of personal success. Likewise, silence is often an acceptable response to conflict or when you can't say something positive.

Honorific versus Personal Style

An **honorific style** emphasizes a person's status in life (such as professional position, social status, age, and even gender). For example, turn-taking rights, word choice, and grammar can be different when communicating with someone of lower or higher status. The use of an appropriate title is often important. Countries that are collectivistic and high-context (such as Pakistan, Japan, Korea, China, and Taiwan) often use this style.

A **personal style** stresses equality and being personal. Individuals using this style tend to ignore titles and stress first-name usage, direct address, and equality. In recent years, the United States has moved even further to this style. For example, children today often speak to their parents or grandparents as equals.

Instrumental versus Affective Style

An **instrumental style** is the use of verbal language as a means to be goal-oriented. This style tends to be very factual and driven to complete a goal or fix a problem. It is often present in individualistic and low-context cultures. Directions given by a boss to an employee, a doctor to a patient, or a parent to a child are examples of this style.

An **affective style** tends to be more process-oriented. This style places the communicators in more of a transactional relationship. The communicators should pay attention to how each other is interpreting and reacting to the message. They should be concerned with how something is affecting the other and adjust. This style tends to be present in collectivistic and high-context cultures.

Silence Usage

We've already noted that silence is often a trait of an understated conversation style. However, silence can play a much more significant role in intercultural communication. It can show introspection, respect, thoughtfulness, or deference. In Finland, silence can be used to extend the length of a conversation, showing respect for the other person.[20] In Japanese culture, it is "generally associated with wisdom and power. A person who talks too much and self-discloses a great deal is considered less powerful than one who keeps personal opinions and knowledge private."[21] In Western countries, or individualistic cultures, it is often quickly (within seconds) viewed as painful and uncomfortable.

See Objective 4.3 for more on silence as nonverbal communication.

LISTEN HAS THE SAME LETTERS AS SILENT

Practicing Ethics: Being Culturally Mindful

Intercultural communication scholar Stella Ting-Toomey, in *Communicating Across Cultures*, offers these tips for being mindful about your verbal communication.[22]

- Try to understand and be sensitive to the cultural beliefs and values that support different conversation styles.
- Try to understand the different language rule systems of cultures you encounter.
- Develop "verbal empathy and patience." Speak more slowly and in simple sentences. Restate and paraphrase information. Ask questions; query for understanding. And ask for feedback.
- Use visuals to support your verbal message.
- Listen mindfully. Pay attention to verbal and nonverbal feedback. For example, when you ask someone from another culture if she understands, she may say yes even if she doesn't, to save face or to prevent you from looking bad. Watch for nonverbal signs that might counter the verbal messages.
- Use nonverbal cues to support your messages. Match your nonverbal communication to the message and use it to help your listener determine what might be important from the message.

3.4 How Does Gender Influence Verbal Communication Styles?

Many popular culture self-help books on gender would like us to believe that there are major differences between male and female behavior based on biological fact. Many TV sitcoms, such as *Friends*, *2 Broke Girls*, and *Mike and Molly*, base much of their comedic power on getting us to believe men and women are radically different. Therefore, it is no wonder we perceive radical differences between women and men when it comes to how they communicate and use language. However, if we truly explore the question above, we will discover that it *doesn't significantly* but it *does in very subtle ways.*

It Doesn't Significantly

In her article "Men Are from North Dakota, Women Are from South Dakota," communication scholar Kathryn Dindia notes that "sex differences exist but they are overwhelmed by similarities…. Differences between women and men are differences of degree, not kind." According to Dindia, "For many communicative, social psychological, and psychological variables, sex differences are small and approximately 85 percent of men and women overlap in their scores on these variables."[23]

Playing off of John Gray's book *Men Are from Mars, Women Are from Venus*, Dindia and communication scholar Nicolas Palomares, in "Explaining Gender-Based Language Use," argue that men and women who use the same overall language differ in their verbal communication so little that the metaphor of just being from neighboring states—or different blocks in the same neighborhood—is more accurate.[24] The idea of being from different planets suggests that men and women are radically different, to the point of having characteristics unique to one or the other. Palomares cites numerous scholars who assert that many contextual factors such as age, setting, status, or situation influence the language of men and women far more than gender.

Therefore, the view of women and men as radically different isn't correct and, as noted by communication scholar Julia T. Wood, fosters "dichotomous thinking and gender stereotypes" (only feminine and masculine).[25]

It Does in Subtle Ways

Different language tendencies can be recognized as being male or female—but only by trained observers and not average communicators (like most of us) with any accuracy, according to communication scholar Anthony Mulac. What Mulac noticed that makes these subtle tendencies important to our communication understanding is that the average observer does perceive the tendencies at some level—and the resulting perception influences how the observer views the person creating the message.[26]

The table below, based on Mulac, shows some of the female and male language features he studied. Communicators with the female features were perceived as having high social status and being literate, nice, and beautiful. Those with male features were perceived as strong and aggressive. These findings suggest societal norms play a role in teaching us to use language as well as in supporting the stereotypes of feminine and masculine. Being aware of what signals a particular perception for you is the first step to recognizing someone as an individual, not a stereotype.

Mulac's Female/Male Verbal Tendencies

Female Language Features	Male Language Features
Intensive adverbs: "really" or "awfully"	References to quantity: "It's 2.5 miles away."
References to emotions: "I was excited."	Judgmental adjectives: "That's a dumb idea."
Dependent clauses: "supposing that he likes her"	Elliptical sentences: "Nice boat."
Sentence-initial adverbials: "Actually, it's…"	Directives: "Bring that here."
Mean length of sentences is relatively long	Locatives: "We are at home."
Uncertainty verbs: "it seems to be"	"I" references: "I think we should go."
Oppositions: "The day was stressful, yet exciting."	
Negations: "Preparation will not make you not sound like a fool."	
Hedges: "We are sort of out of food."	
Questions: "Is that all right?"	

3.5 How Can You Use Language Effectively?

What are some movie lines that you like to quote or that stay with you long after the movie ends? Do you recall *Frozen* and who you'd melt for? Or *Captain America* and how you tell the good guys from the bad? Maybe you are a bit more classical and believe chocolates and life have a lot in common (*Forrest Gump*) or that we are not in Kansas anymore (*The Wizard of Oz*).

Movie quotations like these can be easily evoked in many people's minds because they are remarkable. They move us in ways other sentences don't. They are memorable, often becoming part of our culture beyond the movie or book where they were first created. They demonstrate effective language at work.

Crafting language may seem like something that is necessary only for formal or official purposes such as research papers, essay tests, speeches, job interviews, or work reports. But as you've seen, language matters when communicating across cultures and co-cultures, including gender. And using language effectively benefits you in all communication situations, from body-to-body relationships to informal mediated interactions. It helps you meet the practical, professional, public, and personal needs you learned about in Chapter 1.

An effective use of language includes being authentic, encouraging, appropriate, and clear. All of these characteristics are closely related, and the next few sections will help you understand how they can guide your language choices.

See Chapter 12, Objective 12.1, for more about correctness and using language effectively in a speech.

Be Authentic

In Chapter 2, you learned that deception is the unethical, deliberate practice of making someone else believe an untruth. Authentic, ethical communicators avoid choosing language that deliberately deceives others. They strive to use language effectively by making choices that are authentic, genuine, truthful, accurate, and original. To be authentic, you should:

- Do everything you can to speak the truth and use language that doesn't distort the truth. This doesn't mean you shouldn't keep something private when appropriate. Just don't hide or distort information to unethically deceive others.

- Use language that is clear, concise, and direct. For example, consider this intimate partner interaction:

  Joe: "What are you doing?"

  Pete: "Nothing."

  It is highly unlikely Pete is doing nothing, but his abstract language could be hiding a truth from Joe.

- Select language that emphasizes your true characteristics, beliefs, values, and attitudes. In other words, make language choices that suggest and support who you really are. So think carefully before lying about such things as your age, gender, status, race, religion, and political views.

In essence, choose language that helps you present a genuine self and message to others.

Be Encouraging

The use of encouraging language can foster connections, inclusion, and the participation of others in interactions. Discouraging language choices can inhibit, threaten, or outright prevent successful interactions. Here are some guidelines for encouraging interaction via language choices.

- Use language that creates a friendly and positive atmosphere. For example, if someone offers an idea that you don't agree with, you might say "that's a unique idea" rather than "that's stupid."

- Engage in small talk that makes you appear approachable and interested in the other person.

- Use "I" and "we" language rather than "you" language that seems to blame or criticize the other person. For example, say "I feel like you are mad at me" instead of "You are mad at me."

- Avoid **_trigger words_**, or verbal expressions that arouse emotions creating intense psychological noise in the other person. Trigger words are often sexist, homophobic, racist, or xenophobic. (See the next section for examples of inappropriate terms that can serve as trigger words.)

- Avoid falsely communicating a message that harms people or their reputations (known as defamation of character). For example, posting an untrue message that a particular person stole something or cheated on a test not only is deceptive, but also discourages positive interactions.

Be Appropriate

Remember that you co-create your message with others, whose denotative and connotative definitions of words may not be the same as yours. Also weigh the situation, the cultural environment, and your relationship with the person. Your success depends on selecting language that is constructive, not destructive.

- Avoid unnecessary **profanity**, or obscene, rude, or abusive language.

- Avoid singling out personal traits (e.g., age, disability, race, sex, sexual orientation) when they do not relate to the subject at hand. For example:

  AVOID:
  Joey, my gay friend, drove us to the party.

Your friend's sexual orientation has nothing to do with driving you to a party.

- Avoid the generic "he." It isn't generic. In a survey of college students, 87 percent of women surveyed assumed that the word referred only to men.[27] Use the plural form (they) or use both pronouns (*he or she*).

- Use the name for individuals or groups that they prefer, such as:

  African American or black; Asian or Asian American; American Indian or Native American; Hispanic, Latino, or Chicano; gay, lesbian, bisexual, or transgendered (avoid *homosexual*); a person with Down Syndrome; a person who uses a wheelchair

- Avoid language that is gender-loaded or promotes stereotypes. See the table below for suggestions.

Use Gender-Neutral Language

Avoid	Use Instead
man and wife	couple, partners, spouses
chairman or chairwoman, congressman	chair or chairperson, congressperson
housewife	homemaker, parent, or caregiver
pronoun *he* to represent both male and female or situations generally viewed as masculine (such as sports) pronoun *she* in situations generally viewed as female	the plural *they*, or replace with *one, you,* or *he or she* You can also reword to avoid using pronouns.
girl or boy (over the age of 18)	woman or young woman, man or young man
Miss and Mrs.	Ms. to refer to married and unmarried women
male nurse, lady lawyer or doctor, actress, stewardess, coed, fireman	nurse, lawyer, doctor, actor, steward or flight attendant, student, firefighter

Be Clear

Being clear begins with being correct. Although you can be somewhat less formal with your grammar in oral communication, you still want to adhere to correct grammar rules most of the time and when the context and situation demand it. Do not equate informal with incorrect. Your language should be free, as much as possible, of interpretation error and should adhere to certain standards. Using language incorrectly often leads to misunderstanding and low respect. When communicators use language incorrectly, they tend to use the wrong word, mispronounce words, use incorrect grammar, or use confusing language choices. For instance, you should avoid or use sparingly and appropriately *slang*, *clichés*, *fillers*, *idioms*, and *euphemisms*.

Be Clear by Avoiding or Carefully Using...

What Is It?	Examples
Slang: Typically informal language restricted to a particular context or group	cray cray, selfie, legit, bazinga
Clichés: Overused words or phrases that have lost their effect	needless to say, a matter of time, to tell the truth, without a doubt
Fillers: Sounds, words, or phrases that serve no purpose, do not help communicators understand each other, and may become distracting	ah, um, like, you know, actually, due to the fact that
Idioms: Phrases that have a meaning different from what the individual words mean and can be culturally specific	drop the ball, down to the wire, dancing in March, go out on top
Euphemisms: Mild or indirect words or expressions substituted for harsher, more blunt ones, to make the meaning more palatable	He passed away. Be careful with euphemisms that have double meanings or are socially unacceptable: He is no longer with us. He kicked the bucket.

Self-Check: Being Clear

Think of three examples of idioms or euphemisms you have used. Write them down and describe how you could explain their meanings to someone who has never heard them before.

Chapter 3 Review

Key Questions

3.1 What Are the Characteristics of Language?

Objective 3.1: **DESCRIBE THE CHARACTERISTICS OF LANGUAGE**

Verbal communication is the act of sending and receiving messages via language (words). Language is:

- Symbolic
- Meaningless without people
- Complex
- Governed by rules

See pages 68–73.

3.2 How Is Language Powerful?

Objective 3.2: **DISCUSS WHAT MAKES LANGUAGE POWERFUL?**

Language is powerful in that it helps us name things, places, ideas, and experiences; is persuasive; and brings us together or divides us. Language can create equality, freedom, and empowerment. Unfortunately, it can do the opposite as well. Language is also inextricably bound to culture.

See pages 74–75.

3.3 What Are Some Cultural Variations in Verbal Communication Styles?

Objective 3.3: **DISCUSS CULTURAL DIFFERENCES IN VERBAL STYLE**

A *conversation style* is how individuals exchange their thoughts, opinions, and feelings. The unique style can be personal, individualistic, and cultural. It can be ever-changing as the person grows as a communicator, develops a stronger relationship, or moves between contexts. A conversation style has verbal and nonverbal aspects that will help you interpret the message. Some cultural variations in verbal conversation styles are:

- Direct versus indirect style
- Elaborate versus understated style
- Honorific versus personal style
- Instrumental versus affective style
- Silence usage

See pages 76–79.

3.4 How Does Gender Influence Verbal Communication Styles?

Objective 3.4: DISCUSS GENDER DIFFERENCES IN VERBAL STYLE

- Gender *doesn't significantly* influence styles. Major communication research demonstrates that "sex differences exist but are overwhelmed by similarities."
- Gender *subtly* influences styles. There are sixteen subtle language male and female features used by many women and men. These features can influence how those that use them are perceived.

See pages 80–81.

3.5 How Can You Use Language Effectively?

Objective 3.5: EXPLAIN THE WAYS TO MAKE EFFECTIVE LANGUAGE CHOICES

- Be authentic. Make language choices that are authentic, genuine, truthful, accurate, and original.
- Be encouraging. Make sure you use language that encourages interaction with others.
- Be appropriate. Your language should suit you, your audience, and the context. Avoid profanity and remember to use culturally appropriate and unbiased language.
- Be clear. Make sure you use the correct words, pronounce words correctly, and use correct grammar. Be cautious of using slang, clichés, fillers, idioms, and euphemisms.

See pages 82–85.

Key Terms

verbal communication (68)
language (68)
symbol (68)
arbitrary (69)
denotative meaning (70)
connotative meaning (70)
ladder of abstraction (71)
phonology (72)
semantics (72)
syntactics (72)
pragmatics (72)
linguistic determinism (75)
linguistic relativity (75)
conversation style (76)
direct style (77)
indirect style (77)
elaborate style (77)
understated style (77)
honorific style (78)
personal style (78)
instrumental style (78)
affective style (78)
trigger words (83)
profanity (84)
slang (85)
clichés (85)
fillers (85)
idioms (85)
euphemisms (85)

Improve Your Communication

Improving your vocabulary will go a long way in making you a better communicator.

1. Read—and then read some more. Read anything you can get your hands on. Reading high literature or the classics will stretch your limits the most, but reading anything will help. Pay attention to the author's language choices. Don't just skip over words you don't know; look them up. Read the definitions several times and out loud.

2. Read the dictionary and thesaurus. Maybe this is not the coolest thing to do, but you will learn new words.

3. Make it a habit to learn three new words a day. Create printed or electronic flashcards for them. Include the definition and a sentence using the word. Periodically throughout the day, study the cards. Read them out loud and create new sentences using the words. Try to use them in your speech. As one of my undergraduate professors (Mrs. K) told me countless times, "Use it three times in a day and it is yours."

4. Write. Write poetry or stories, or in a journal, diary, or blog. Like an athlete, you have to practice and "just do it" to be better at it.

5. Follow *Word of the Day* on Twitter (@thewordoftheday) or get a word-of-the-day app.

6. Play word games. Group games include *Cranium, Apples to Apples, Charades, Reverse Charades, Trivial Pursuit, Scrabble, Quiddler, Word Crack,* or *Words with Friends.* By yourself, you can work word puzzles like the crossword puzzles in magazines or newspapers.

7. Learn a new language. Do this by taking a class, using online software or apps, or traveling to new countries. When you travel, make sure you force yourself to learn the language. Learning Latin will help you with your English. Many English words locate their roots in Latin. Ipsa scientia potestas est! ("Knowledge itself is power."—Wallace Bacon[28])

8. Speak it! When learning another language, don't just use it when it's necessary. Speak it with your friends.

Apply Your Knowledge

1. Make a list of words that have strong connotative meanings for you. Can you attribute your feelings about each word to a specific event, person, or place? Do the words help support stereotypes, powerlessness, or other negative cultural attributes? How can you work to erase those feelings or usages?

2. Which of the following terms are abstract or concrete? In general, what do you need to do to each of the abstract words to make them more concrete?

love	table
spoon	conservative
freedom	red
success	moral
hot	horse

3. Do you agree that women and men are more similar in their verbal usage than dissimilar? What are some popular misconceptions about how women and men verbally communicate differently?

4. How do texting and using social networking sites like Facebook and Twitter influence your language choices and skills?

Other Resources

Here are some language resources.

Vocabulary Building

Lewis, Norman. *Word Power Made Easy: The Complete Handbook for Building a Superior Vocabulary.* New York: Anchor, 2014. Print.

Cornog, Mary W. *Merriam-Webster's Vocabulary Builder.* Springfield: Merriam-Webster, 2010. Print.

- dictionary.reference.com/wordoftheday/
- wordinfo.info
- www.vocabulary.com
- www.wordplays.com
- www.dumblittleman.com/?s=tips+for+improving+your+grammar&submit.x=0&submit.y=0
- a4esl.org/q/h/grammar.html

Language Choices

Hayakawa, S. I. and Alan R. Hayakawa. *Language in Thought and Action.* 5th ed. San Diego: Harcourt, 1991. Print.

- www.marquette.edu/wac/neutral/NeutralInclusiveLanguage.shtml
- jerz.setonhill.edu/writing/grammar-and-syntax/gender-neutral-language/

Chapter 4
Nonverbal Communication

4.1 What Are the Traits of Nonverbal Communication?

The next time you are in a public place (e.g., the cafeteria, library, or mall) where you can watch others from afar, pay attention to how they communicate without using oral or written language. How do they sit? What do they do with their faces and bodies during their interactions? How are they dressed and how do they adorn their bodies? Do they use any items or touch? How do they use the space? What you are observing are their *nonverbal* interactions.

Here are some traits important to know in order to understand the role of nonverbal communication.

Nonlinguistic

Nonverbal communication is the intentional or unintentional transmission of a message or a portion of a message without the use of words that are spoken, written, or signed. In other words, *nonverbal cues*, or all nonlinguistical objects, observables, or behaviors, have meaning during an encounter. These cues are present in most of your interactions, even some of your mediated communication. You learn your nonverbal skills (as both a user and an interpreter of nonverbal cues) through interaction with others.

Like verbal communication, nonverbal communication has tremendous value in helping communicators encode and decode messages or share meaning. Some scholars would argue that as much as 60 to 93 percent of the message is carried by nonverbal cues.[1] Although these percentages might seem high, the point is that we use nonverbal communication to help us interpret messages far more than we realize, making it central to improving our overall communication skills.

Arbitrary, Ambiguous, and Abstract

Nonverbal communication, unlike language, has no documented code system to help us assign meaning. Adding to the ambiguity, nonverbal communication—and in this case, like language—has denotative and connotative meanings. For instance, think of some gestures that trigger emotions for you. Do you hate when someone other than an intimate partner touches your shoulder or hugs you, or are you a person who tends to hug a lot? Are there gestures that make you angry but don't seem to bother others? The meaning is not in the nonverbal behavior but in the agreed-upon assignment of meaning and your personal reaction. There is room for interpretation and misinterpretation.

Multichanneled

Nonverbal messages may be sent via the body, touch, the face, appearance, vocal cues, smell and taste, time, and the environment. To add to this already complex interaction, nonverbal cues can be sent simultaneously through multiple channels. Each of these channels may interact with each other and the verbal message, to make interpretation an elaborate collaboration requiring observation and concentration.

See Objective 4.3 for more about the channels for nonverbal communication.

Innate and Learned

How you develop nonverbal communication skills is different from how you develop your verbal ones. First, research suggests that a few nonverbal facial expressions (sadness, anger, disgust, fear, surprise, and happiness) seem to be culturally universal and appear to be inborn or innate as basic nonverbal instinct. However, the nuances of these basic nonverbal cues are informally learned. You must learn your nonverbal skills through observation and reinforcement with others. Seldom will people have formal training in nonverbal communication as they do with verbal language.

Contextual

In Chapter 1, you learned that all communication is contextual. This fact is worth stressing again. How you choose to nonverbally communicate, what you are communicating, and how it is interpreted are closely related to the contexts of when, where, and to whom.

In many ways, the subtleties in nonverbal variations across different contexts are amplified more than subtleties in your verbal options. For example, looking down as someone tells a sad story signals sadness and uneasiness. Looking down when in the presence of someone you fear signals anxiety and submissiveness. You might say to your intimate partner with a smile and a wink, "I miss you," in a public place; but the same verbal message in the same context with an intimate kiss and lingering hug is likely *too* intimate. In this latter example, you use rules to properly regulate or modify your nonverbal behavior. These ***display rules*** tell you what you can or can't, should or shouldn't, or must or must not do in certain contexts.[2] Display rules are dictated by the social situation and the culture, which leads to the next nonverbal trait.

Culturally Bound

Beyond helping you regulate what is acceptable, your shared cultural beliefs, customs, practices, and social behaviors influence your nonverbal communication—and how it is interpreted—just as they do your verbal message. For example, gender roles in Saudi Arabia evolved from Islamic law and tribal customs, often creating strict gender segregation. For a woman, touch, certain types of eye contact, and even most types of interaction are often forbidden unless she is chaperoned by a male family member. As another example, many collectivist societies prefer vocal deliveries that are lower in volume and draw less attention to the individual, whereas individualist societies tend to be louder and more flamboyant. Nonverbal behavior also aids meaning in culturally rich rituals, such as greetings.

Relational

Nonverbal communication helps you create and maintain your identity with others as well as define the type of relationship you want with another. For example, you may enlist certain types of nonverbal behavior when you want to create a positive image. You will likely dress in a flattering way, smile, use appropriate gestures and touch, signal an invitation to join you in conversation, maintain appropriate eye contact and posture, and use space appropriate to your relations with those you are engaging.

When working to define or build a relationship with someone, much of that relationship will reside in the nonverbal realm. You demonstrate how personal or impersonal you want to be primarily through nonverbal cues, which will change as your relationship develops. For example, the nonverbal behavior you display to your boss or coworkers on the first day at a new job will grow and change as you continue to develop the relationships. You may find yourself being slightly more personal with a close coworker and more impersonal with a boss that tends to be formal and distant.

Continuous

You can't really stop communicating nonverbally as you can with verbal language, which is considered discontinuous, intermittent, or based on disconnected units.[3] If you are verbally conversing with your friend and you stop, the verbal message stops. On the other hand, nonverbal is continuous, uninterrupted, or unending as long as you remain in an interaction with the other person. Some would even argue that if you leave the room or the interaction, you are still nonverbally communicating a reason for the exit and a change in the current relationship with that person.

Emotionally Expressive

Humans struggle to define, explain, and express their emotions. Your nonverbal messages often carry much if not all of your emotional state. Likewise, we often use our nonverbal cues to relay negative or difficult messages. For example, if you do something viewed as extremely wrong or hurtful to someone, that person might withdraw and leave the room rather than express pain or anger in words. The importance of nonverbal communication to express our emotions is the reason we use extra punctuation (????? or !!!!!), capitalization (I am so MAD at you!!!), or emoticons and emoji (like those to the right) in text-heavy mediated interactions. The strong need to express our emotions is one of the main reasons we regularly change our social media profile and cover pictures as well as digitally manipulate pictures to signal our moods. As humans, we have a primary need to convey our emotions nonverbally.

Emoticons and Emoji

Angry	**X-(** or **=/**	
Confused	**O.o** or **:–/**	
Crying	**:_(** or **:'(** or **T.T**	
Frown or sad	**:–(** or **:(** or **=(**	
Happy	**=)** or **:–)** or **:)**	
Heart or love	**<3**	
Kiss	**:–)*** or **:–*** or **:***	
Screaming	**:–@**	
Surprised	**=O** or **:–o** or **:o**	
Very happy	**=D** or **:–D**	
Winking	**;–)** or **;)**	
Yawn	**|–O**	

Powerful

In Chapter 3, you learned that language is powerful because it can name, persuade, unite, divide, empower, and create or maintain culture. Nonverbal communication is no different. Your nonverbal behavior allows you to express feelings and experiences indescribable in any other way. You can use it to influence others; people who have good nonverbal skills are often powerful communicators and effective at persuasion. You can unite with others by creating and maintaining relationships with your nonverbal communication, or you can destroy and divide relationships by withholding intimate nonverbal behavior or using disconfirming behavior. A hug can console, signal importance, and uplift. Your eyes or the volume of your voice can convey love, peace, pain, fear, or hatred. A gesture of the hand can draw someone close, push someone away, reveal deep love, or be offensive. That is powerful.

The believability we give nonverbal cues is powerful. Most people will believe your nonverbal communication over your verbal if there is a discrepancy. This believability evolves from our focus on some nonverbal behaviors as being spontaneous or unconscious, making them seem less controlled, calculated, or manipulated and therefore less deceptive. If our nonverbal messages are more spontaneous and unconscious, we can't deceive those we are interacting with as easily as we can when we craft our messages. Paul Ekman and Wallace Friesen note that when someone is deceiving, nonverbal *leakage and deception cues* can reveal deception or the true feelings of the messenger.[4]

See the Tip box below for some nonverbal behaviors that may indicate deception.

TIP: Detecting Deception

Researchers believe that you have about a 50 to 55 percent chance of detecting a lie.[5] Individuals particularly good at self-monitoring or people who lie so much (pathological liars) that they are sort of immune to any unconscious cues are especially good at covering a lie. Although nonverbal cues employed when deceiving will vary among different users, situations, and even reasons for lying, some scholars suggest that a few behaviors might signal deception. So watch for: false-looking smiles; blinking or pupil dilation; higher vocal pitch; speech error, such as vocal disfluencies; false starts; long pauses or long response times to questions; and fewer body movement cues than in truth-tellers.[6]

4.2 What Are the Functions of Nonverbal Communication?

Notice all the hands raised and displaying gestures for peace in the photograph below, taken in the 1960s. These activists may also be singing a peace song, chanting, or simply listening to a speaker we can't see in the photo. In any case, they are displaying a specific gesture symbolizing a call for peace. These activists are illustrating one of the functions of nonverbal communication.

As noted in Chapter 1, when you engage in communication, you use two code systems to facilitate your interaction. You express yourself verbally and nonverbally and often do both simultaneously. In doing so, you access the benefits of the inseparable nature of these two code systems. Because of their link to each other, it is impossible to really study one without considering the other. Nonverbal cues can be congruent (matching or fitting) with your verbal message or they can be incongruent (contrasting or different). In being congruent or incongruent, your nonverbal messages act as *metacommunication* to your verbal messages, or as communication *about* how you want your verbal messages interpreted.

In 1964, Paul Ekman identified six functions of nonverbal communication and demonstrated how they relate to a verbal message or serve as metacommunication.[7] The functions are to complement, accentuate, contradict, regulate, repeat, or substitute. The table on the next page will help you understand how each works. Keep in mind that the communicator could be using nonverbal cues to fulfill more than one of these functions.

Ekman's Functions of Nonverbal Communication

Function	What Is It?	Examples
To complement	Nonverbal messages serve to clarify, reinforce, or add to the meaning of the verbal message.	Wearing professional clothes to a job interview Employing a confident posture during a speech
To accentuate	Nonverbal messages emphasize a part of a nonverbal message. Some consider accentuating a form of complementing but with an emphasis on exact placement.	Using pauses in a formal speech to signal the importance of your next statements Hugging someone as you apologize after being angry or harsh
To contradict	Nonverbal messages are inconsistent with the verbal message.	Forcing a smile or an expression of gratitude when you receive something unwanted Being late for an event that you really do care about
To regulate	Nonverbal messages coordinate or facilitate verbal interaction.	Leaning into your conversation partner or nodding your head to signal you are ready to speak
To repeat	Nonverbal messages repeat or reiterate the verbal message.	Holding up two fingers as you say, "I would like two scoops, please"
To substitute	Nonverbal messages replace or stand in for verbal messages.	Glaring to tell someone to stop talking instead of making a verbal request

4.3 What Channels Do You Use to Convey Nonverbal Messages?

Fie, fie upon her!
There's language in her eye, her
  cheek, her lip,
Nay, her foot speaks; her wanton
  spirits look out
At every joint and motive of her
  body.

Ulysses, in Shakespeare's *Troilus and Cressida* IV.5. 54–57

In this dialogue from Shakespeare's play *Troilus and Cressida*, the character Ulysses comments on his interpretation of Cressida's nonverbal cues. Note how Ulysses suggests Cressida uses her eyes, cheek, lips, feet, and even joints in beguiling ways. Ulysses seems to suggest that every inch of Cressida's body calls out to entice all of the senses of those listening. Indeed, Ulysses understands that nonverbal communication can engage all of our senses through numerous channels. Those channels include your use of body movement, touch, facial expression, physical appearance, vocal cues, smell and taste, time, and environment.

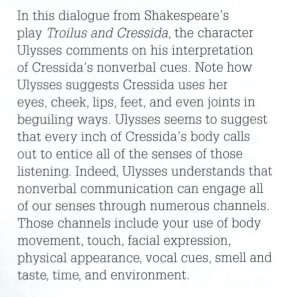

Variety of mere nothings gives more pleasure than the uniformity of something.[8]

Jean Paul Richter

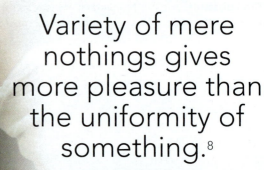

Body

How you use your body nonverbally can be categorized as posture or body gestures. Anthropologist Ray Birdwhistell labeled the study of the body in motion as **kinesics**.[9] Much of what we do with our bodies is culturally bound. However, our individual body types and abilities influence how we move, gesture, and hold our bodies. Let's look at how our posture and body gestures influence our communication.

Posture

Your **posture** is positioning of the body or how you carry your body, which can influence the perception others have of you and can offer clues to your emotional state.[10] Your posture can even influence how you feel by effecting such aspects as confidence.[11] Open and closed postures are two primary ways we use our posture to communicate. An *open posture* keeps the core of the body opened and exposed. You use this type of posture to suggest openness, readiness, friendliness, and acceptance. A *closed posture* protects the body core, usually by hunching forward while crossing the arms and legs. This stance indicates fear, hostility, apprehension, coldness, and unfriendliness.

Posture that reduces the amount of space between communicators and improves the ability to see each other (especially the eyes) suggests closeness, a willingness to engage, or a positive and open attitude. Likewise, parallel postures between two people signals equality and acceptance.

In this photograph of President Barack Obama and Russia's President Vladimir Putin, you can see both men displaying a *relaxed posture* by leaning back with asymmetrical leg position and relaxed hands. Generally, the higher someone believes his or her status to be, the more relaxed the posture.

Body Gestures

A *gesture* (also known as gesticulation) is the movement of a part of the body (such as the head, hand, and/or arm) to communicate. Most gestures are made with the hands or arms; you might use only one hand or a combination of both hands and both arms. Some gestures can be made with a nod of the head (pointing toward something with your head) or the body (a shrug or bow). Effective gestures should:

- Be appropriate to the communicators, situation, culture, and occasion.

- Vary, so that they do not become rhythmic or distracting. Using the same gesture often can limit its effectiveness and understanding.

- Be purposeful when conscious, adding to the message.

- Be used when speaking with individuals who struggle with language barriers, such as those listening to a nonnative speaker, or when communicating with young children.

Some Culture-Specific Gestures

Gesture		What Does It Mean?
	Benediction gesture Made by raising the right hand with the little finger touching the palm, while remaining fingers are raised	Used by Christian clergy while performing a blessing with the sign of the cross
	Crossed fingers	Signals good luck or the nullification of a promise if done as the person states the promise. In China, it is the symbol for ten. In Russia, it is a rude gesture for rejecting something.
	Fist bump or dap greeting	A form of a handshake popular in Western cultures
	Namaste gesture Made by pressing the hands together, arms a bit stiff, and with a slight bow	A customary greeting among people of South and Southeast Asian countries when individuals meet; also a farewell when they part

In 1969, Paul Ekman and Wallace Friesen identified five types of gestures: **emblems, illustrators, affect display, regulators**, and **adaptors**.[12]

Types of Gestures

Type	What Is It?	Examples
Emblems	Gestures that are speech independent and culturally learned, with direct verbal translations. An emblem may not mean the same thing in another culture, so be careful.	Shrugging your shoulders to convey "I don't know," forming a circle with your thumb and index finger for "OK," winking, nodding yes, waving hello or goodbye
Illustrators	Gestures that are dependent and closely linked to what is said	Putting up your finger as you say, "my first point…."
Affect display	Gestures that communicate emotion	Wringing your hands or twisting your hair when you are nervous or covering your eyes when you are afraid
Regulators	Gestures that control conversation flow. They include cues such as hand gestures, head nods, vocal displays, and posture changes. They can help you yield to another, maintain the right to speak, request a turn, or deny a turn.[13]	Signaling you are ready to speak by leaning forward, slightly raising a hand, slightly opening your lips, and drawing in a breath; or leaning back and lowering your volume at the end of a sentence to signal giving the conversation to someone else
Adaptors	Gestures that satisfy a personal need and are often learned early in life	Scratching your head, pushing up your glasses, or adjusting a tie

Touch

Touch is the first sense to develop in the womb and is the sense most essential to life and normal development.[14] You use your sense of touch to protect yourself from harm, to learn, to experience pleasure, and to relate to others. Even our love affair with technology—with such product descriptors and terms as multi-touch, touch technology, touch pad, touch screen, iPod Touch—suggests that touch is important to us. As a channel for nonverbal communication, touch is no less important. Frankly, because of its intrusion into our personal space, its ability to "touch our hearts" or cause tremendous hurt, and its strong cultural regulation, touch is one of the most commanding nonverbal messages.

Haptics is the study of touch behavior. Two common ways to consider how we use touch are according to its relational function and according to its meaning.

Touch and Its Relational Function

Psychologist Richard Heslin developed a system for how North Americans regulate touch based on its function.[15] Heslin's system is directly related to the relational situation in which the communication occurs. It is important to remember that the function of a particular touch within a relational situation might not be purely one or the other. For example, a touch that starts out as social–polite might evolve into sexual arousal. Heslin's system has five touch categories.

Heslin's Five Touch Categories

LESS PERSONAL

Functional–Professional
- Businesslike, unemotional, or apathetic touch
- Often fulfills a task or a service
- Examples: Touch that occurs during a transaction or during a visit to a doctor, dentist, or barber/hairstylist

Social–Polite
- Polite ritual social touch
- Much like functional–professional but within a social setting
- Examples: A handshake or placing your hand on someone's back to guide them through a doorway

Friendship–Warmth
- Touch indicating a special bond or relationship
- Expresses a liking for the person receiving the touch
- Examples: Short hugs, arm loosely around shoulders or waist, pat or slap on the back, or quick kiss, usually on the cheek

Love–Intimacy
- Touch reserved for romantic partners or family members
- Expresses a close, intimate relationship or attachment
- Examples: Lingering hug, sustained kiss, touch of the cheek, tight shoulder or waist embrace

Sexual Arousal
- Touch at the highest level of contact for arousal
- Expresses physical sexual attraction or sexual intent
- Examples: Foreplay, deep kissing, sexual massaging

MORE PERSONAL

The Meaning of Touch

In 1985, communication scholars Stanley Jones and Elaine A. Yarbrough studied touch as it relates to meaning.[16] Jones and Yarbrough asked 17 male and 22 female students to record their touch behavior over a three-day period. From the students' records, Jones and Yarbrough analyzed more than 1,500 acts of touching, which revealed 18 different meanings that can be grouped into seven overarching types.

- **Touch as positive and negative affect:** Touch can communicate positive emotions (support, reassurance, appreciation, affection, or sexual attraction) or negative feelings (anger, dissatisfaction, or frustration).

- **Touch as play:** Here, the meaning of a touch serves to lighten or reduce the seriousness of an interaction. These touches might be related to affection (teasing or tickling) or aggression (playing as if you are strangling someone).

- **Touch as control or influence:** Here, the touch becomes part of a persuasive goal to get the person being touched to respond. Control touches tend to seek compliance (direct behavior), get attention (serve to focus), or announce a response (calling attention to your current feeling).

- **Touch as ritual:** As ritual, touches can help control conversations (touching an arm to signal a turn to talk), move individuals in and out of an interaction (hello and goodbye greetings), or serve a ceremonial function (touching someone when offering a blessing).

- **Touch as function:** These touches directly relate to the need to complete a particular task. This is the same as Heslin's functional–professional touch. Combing a child's hair, helping an elderly person out of a chair, and conducting an airport pat down all employ touch that relates to the task at hand.

- **Touch as hybrid:** These are touches that combine two or more of the types mentioned above. For example, shaking someone's hand while leaning into a pseudo hug suggests an affectionate greeting or departure.

- **Touch as accidental:** Some touches occur accidentally (a brush of the body) and are perceived as unintentional and meaningless.

Face

The face plays a key role in your nonverbal messages. Two areas provide many of the nonverbal cues: facial expression and eye behavior.

Facial Expression

Psychologists and communication scholars use the term **facial primacy** for the tendency to give more communicative weight to the face than any other channel.[17] This notion may be supported by the almost limitless facial expressions we can create, our inclination to turn to the face for major identity factors (age, gender, race, emotional and health status), and our use of the face as the primary channel for emotions.[18] **Facial expressions** are the use of facial muscles to convey internal thoughts or feelings. Many animals use facial expressions, but humans seem to be the masters of this form of communication. Although you have thousands of different expressions, scholars suggest that six seem to be universal.[19]

Universal Expression	How Do You Make It?
Happiness	Raise mouth corners into a smile
Fear	Raise brows, open eyes fully, and open mouth slightly
Surprise	Arch brows, open eyes wide to expose more white, and drop jaw open slightly
Disgust	Raise upper lip and wrinkle nose bridge (which raises cheeks)
Anger	Lower brows, press lips together firmly, and bulge eyes
Sadness	Lower mouth corners and raise inner portion of brows

Some researchers believe these six expressions are inborn because children with certain physical challenges from birth exhibited these expressions in the same way.[20]

As you discover how to use your facial expressions as a form of communication, you learn to manage your expressions through certain display techniques. The techniques described in the table below help you hide, foreground, and diminish your display of emotion.[21]

Facial Expression Display Techniques

Display Technique	What Is It?	Examples
Intensifying	Exaggerating for increased effect	Exaggerating your smile and widening your eyes to increase your level of surprise and happiness when a child brings you a dandelion
Deintensifying	Reducing or softening your emotional expression for effect	Showing mild surprise when internally you are extremely happy at the amount of your raise
Neutralizing	Concealing any expression for effect	Masking sadness or a need to cry in front of your children in times of sorrow
Masking	Replacing a true-feeling facial expression with one that downplays the emotion or is more acceptable	Smiling and raising your brow in support when telling someone he or she looks great when you disagree

Eye Behavior

Oculesics is the study of eye behavior and is actually a subcategory of kinesics. When studying eye behavior, consider the following.

- *Eye contact* is the act of looking at someone else and usually with direct eye contact. Although cultural norms differ, Western culture prefers *direct eye contact*, or briefly looking straight into the eyes of the other person. Looking down usually connotes fear, uneasiness, or submission. Eye contact signals relational interactions, trustworthiness, turn taking, and attention.

- *Eye movement* relates to the involuntary and voluntary movement of the eyes (e.g., glancing at the clock because you want class to be over).
- *Gaze* is involuntary and voluntary intense staring to communicate desire (e.g., staring down that cupcake you want). A prolonged stare usually means aggression, while an averted gaze is often used to avoid contact, show a lack of interest, or maintain privacy.
- *Pupil dilation* is the change in pupil size. Beyond the physical change in pupil size due to brightness or darkness, pupil size signals attraction or positive or negative desire.

Appearance

Appearance as a nonverbal channel largely relates to attractiveness. Your **attractiveness** has to do with your looks as well as your personality, as perceived by others. Your attire, grooming habits, hairstyle, skin color, body type, facial symmetry, and choice of bodily accessories will send messages of attractiveness or unattractiveness based on cultural standards.[22] Additionally, people who have energetic, friendly, helpful, good-humored, and outgoing personalities are perceived as being more attractive than those who do not.[23]

All of the attractiveness factors function as forms of nonverbal communication influencing the perceptions others have of you and how you feel about yourself. That influence can be manipulated by you (e.g., how you dress to get noticed at a party or interview) or it may be uncontrollable (e.g., how people respond to your size, skin and natural hair color, or facial features).

Research studies have shown that if you are attractive, you have an immense advantage. You are more likely to get good jobs, have high self-esteem, be promoted to managerial positions (especially if you are a handsome male), viewed as credible, and have social power.[24]

In 1974, communication scholars James McCroskey and Thomas McCain concluded that the more you are attracted to others, the more you will communicate with them; and the more you communicate with someone, the more that person has influence on you. McCroskey and McCain went on to conclude that there are three types of attractiveness: social, physical, and task.[25] In 2006, Linda McCroskey, James McCroskey, and Virginia Richmond reexamined the appropriateness of types and added two more: background and attitude.[26]

The following table will help you understand each type. The last three attractions (task, background, and attitude) may seem less related to nonverbal communication. However, certain aspects of them can be relayed via nonverbal behavior, making them important to keep in mind here.

Types of Attraction

Type	What Is It?	How Do You Know You Are Experiencing It?
Social	Social attraction relates to how willing you are to interpersonally interact with the person you are perceiving.	Do I think the person could be a friend of mine? Would I want to carry on a friendly conversation with her? Would she fit in with my other friends and family? Do I wish I could spend more time with her? Do I wish to be more like her?
Physical	Physical attraction encompasses a person's physical and visual aspects that often stand out at first glance.	Do I find this person handsome, pretty, or sexy? Do I respond positively to his body type (tall, thin, stocky, heavy, muscular)? Do I like his hair color/style, clothes, shoes, jewelry? Are the clothes and artifacts he is wearing flattering to his body type? Do I perceive him as being well groomed and clean?
Task	Task attraction stems from your willingness to work with someone on a task.	Can I work with this person? Can she get work done on time? Will she be on time for work? Does she goof off too much? Is she knowledgeable? Could I study with her? Can we be creative together and have fun with our work? Note that several of these questions relate to time, which we will discuss as a nonverbal cue later in this chapter.
Background	Background attraction resides in that space where your background overlaps with another's, highlighting similarity.	Are we from the same social and economic class? Do we have similar experiences? Are we from the same town, state, region, country? Were our childhoods similar?
Attitude	Attitude attraction suggests that you are attracted to others who have similar behaviors, beliefs, values, and goals as you do.	Does this person behave like I do? Does he share my beliefs, values, and goals? Do we think alike? Does he treat others as I would? Do we have a lot in common?

Vocal Cues

How do you change the aspects of your vocal delivery when you say "goodbye" to a close friend, a lover, a child, or a pet? The word is the same, but the change in relationship compels you to change certain vocal cues. When you speak, you fluctuate or adjust some of these cues to create **vocal variety**.

The basic vocal cues we tend to change and modify are rate, pitch, volume, pronunciation, articulation, dialect, and silence and are known as *paralanguage*.

Rate

Your vocal **rate** is the speed at which you speak. The average rate a person can speak is between 120 and 150 words per minute. In parts of the country, people may speak faster (e.g., New York City) or slower (e.g., some southern states). You can manipulate your rate to add excitement, exhilaration, or urgency. You might speak slower when sad, sick, or unsure or when discussing complex or important ideas.

Vocal *pauses* are another way you can slow down your rate. Pauses can allow a listener to linger on a thought in order to apply meaning or gauge significance. Also, pauses can be used as a tool for enhancing or emphasizing a point. Do not be afraid to use pauses to help avoid using vocal fillers. Vocal fillers (also known as disfluencies) are extraneous sounds and words like *ah, um, like,* or *you know.* Vocal fillers distract the listener and hinder the interpretation of your message.

Removing vocal fillers is a process. The first step is to make a conscious effort to recognize that you are using fillers. Then, you must work to recognize when and why you use them. The next step is to preempt the usage, which takes time, dedication, and patience.

- Although not always possible in your daily interactions, thinking about what you are going to say and practicing your message will help prevent vocal fillers. We tend to use fillers when struggling to find our next words.

- Have someone signal you each time you use a filler. This might be intimidating at first, but it will help you eliminate them.

- When preparing for a formal speech, record your speech and listen for fillers. Hearing how fillers distract from your message can inspire you to use them less.

Pitch

Pitch is how high and low your voice is in frequency and is determined by how fast or slow your vocal cords vibrate. The greater the number of vibrations per second your cords move, the higher the pitch. One factor affecting pitch is how relaxed or stressed your body is. When you are excited, tense, or frightened, the muscles around your voice box (larynx) tighten, raising the pitch of your voice. This explains, for example, the difference between a calm statement, "The tree is falling," and a warning, "The tree is falling!"

Pitch is something you can work on if your voice is extremely high or low; and, as with many elements in your speech, variety in pitch is important. Varying your pitch (*inflection*) will help you demonstrate enthusiasm, excitement, concern, and dedication to interactions during a particular situation.

A constant pitch, known as *monotone*, is distracting and boring. Equally distracting and potentially problematic is the recent phenomenon for young women to talk at their lowest register, creating a low creaky vibration known as *vocal fry*. Britney Spears, Lady Gaga, and Kim Kardashian have made it popular. Using vocal fry over a long period can damage your vocal cords. It might be cool with friends, but research suggests that a person using it is perceived as less desirable, less hirable, less trustworthy, less competent, and less educated.[27]

Volume

Like your stereo volume, your vocal volume is how loud or soft your voice is. Your first concern with volume is to be loud enough to be heard within the environment in which you find yourself interacting with others. Second, you need to think about the emotions you are trying to convey or that are appropriate given the situation. Speaking too softly may send the message that you are afraid, unsure, or timid. Speaking too loudly can be viewed as harsh, mean, overbearing, or aggressive. Plus, being constantly loud can make people stop listening to you and can damage your vocal cords. Most often, the situation calls for you to slide your volume up and down as you communicate.

Pay attention to the cues your communication partners send you about your volume. They may lean forward if you are too quiet and turn their heads slightly to hear you better. If you are too loud, they may lean back, lower their chins slightly, and frown.

If you are from a culture where speaking softly is more acceptable, you might have trouble recognizing when you are too quiet. When giving a formal speech, practice with someone who will tell you to keep raising your voice until you reach a good volume, and then rehearse at that level several times. In interpersonal situations, if others are leaning closer to hear you, frequently ask you to repeat your message, or often ignore you, adjust your volume up a bit.

Pronunciation

Correct **pronunciation** is the standard or commonly accepted way to make a word sound. For example, do you know someone who incorrectly says the word *picture* like the word *pitcher*? The word *picture* should be pronounced "pik-chure," and *pitcher* should be pronounced "pit-chure." Poor pronunciation can, at the very least, slow down your communication partner's listening skills as he or she tries to figure out what you intend or, in the worst case, cause complete misunderstanding.

Recognizing when you mispronounce a word can be difficult, as you may not know you are doing it. Ask your friends and family to pay attention and tell you when you mispronounce a word. If you are unsure of how to pronounce a new word, look it up or ask someone who should know. Many online dictionaries allow you to play sound recordings of correct pronunciations. Not knowing how to correctly pronounce words can also significantly lower your credibility. Be diligent and find out the correct way to pronounce the words you plan to use.

Articulation

Articulation is how completely and clearly you utter a word—for example, saying "morning" instead of "mornin." Closely linked, and often used synonymously with *articulation*, is **enunciation**, or the distinctiveness and clarity of linked whole words—for example, saying, "Did you eat yet?" instead of "Jeat yet?" Speaking fast, mumbling, running words together, and dropping vowels or consonants (as in "drinkin") are all considered poor articulation or enunciation—commonly referred to as "lazy speech." Listeners may view these habits as inappropriate (especially in public forums).

Mumbling is a common problem. If you have this habit, make a conscious effort to eliminate it. If giving a speech in a formal setting, warming up your mouth can help. Before entering the speech location, open your mouth wide several times, stretching your jaw muscles (be careful if you have medical issues with your jaw), then hum as you rapidly vibrate your lips together. Like an athlete stretches legs or arms, you need to warm up your mouth's muscles. Interpersonally, mumbling can suggest that you are apathetic or uncaring. It can prevent someone with decreased hearing from receiving your message. Especially for those with complete hearing loss who rely on reading lips, your mumbling may make it extra difficult for them to understand you.

> **TIP: Pronunciation**
>
> If you know you have trouble pronouncing a word and cannot break the habit, use an alternative word if possible. This is especially important for formal communication situations such as speeches.

Dialect

All cultures and co-cultures have unique elements in their speech, known as dialects. A **dialect** is how a particular group of people pronounces and uses language. Dialects can be regional (e.g., the South) or ethnic (e.g., Jewish English). Dialects are important for establishing and maintaining cultural identity, so you do not automatically need to avoid using dialect. However, if your dialect is significantly different from that of your communication partners, it can distract them and decrease your message's effectiveness.

When a dialect interferes with communication, it is usually because grammar and vocabulary cause the misunderstanding. For example, in the Boston area, you might hear a water fountain called a bubbler. When communicating with others from outside your region or culture, use the more standard vocabulary. Doing so will help you prevent misunderstanding and distraction, while maintaining your individual identity.

Silence

Silence is the absence of words and any of these previous vocal cues. Silence isn't just the space between our linguistic messages, it is a tool that helps us often to communicate anger, shyness, anxiety, sadness, embarrassment, or that we have nothing to say. Silence can even create a monastic space for religious contemplation and prayer.[28] You may use silence as a form of intimacy to get closer to the one you love or as a means to reprimand (the "silent treatment"). One cross-cultural study exploring marital conflict discovered five uses for silence: avoidance of conflict, control of conflict, protection of self, protection of other, and maintenance of harmony.[29] If you reconsider the cultural differences discussed in Chapter 1, you can see how culture influences silence. For example, if a culture tends toward the high-power, collectivist, and/or high-context cultures, people in that culture will likely use silence more often and for longer time periods. For cultures like this, silence can demonstrate respect, agreement or disagreement with the larger group and harmony or consensus.[30]

Silence can be comfortable or unpleasant. It can be controlling and hurtful or empowering and respectful. We can feel so uncomfortable about not being in the majority that our voice is silenced.[31] In turn, we can use the right to be silent to protest, as the LGBTQ community does with the "Day of Silence." So, remember to pay attention even to the silent spaces.

Smell and Taste

Although it may seem strange to consider smell and taste nonverbal communication, these senses can be. Your sense of smell in particular gives you lots of information about your surroundings and even those you interact with. Smell and taste are known as chemical senses. Both help you experience flavors and identify substances but are separate senses.[32]

Smell

You smell something when a substance in the air passes through your nose and stimulates the olfactory nerve.[33] The study of smell as a nonverbal message is known as **olfactics**. What smells good to some may smell bad to others, and smells can be culturally influenced. Humans tend to use smell communication for the purpose of safety (smelling food for freshness, checking for gas or smoke odor, or smelling breath for alcohol consumption); recognition/memory (the aroma of baking bread reminds you of your grandmother, or the smell of barbeque makes you think of spring/summer); and interpersonal attraction (using lotions, perfumes, soaps, or candles, or even noticing a person's particular body smell).[34]

Taste

Taste, or gustation, occurs when your taste buds respond to something in your mouth.[35] Much of what we sense as taste is related to smell. Taste can be classified by sweet, sour, salty, bitter, and savory or fusion of taste/touch sensations (pungent, cool, astringent, fatty, spirituous, metallic). Much like your sense of smell, your ability to taste can offer up a message about safety (spoiled or spicy food), help you identify a substance, or invoke a memory.

The essays in the book *Food and Culture*, collected by anthropologists Carol Counihan and Penny Van Esterik, highlight the social, symbolic, and political-economic role of food and therefore taste in our global world. There are foods that are acceptable or prohibited, foods that perpetuate stereotypes, foods that help express belongingness or status, foods that are ritual, and foods that help us story our lives and relationships. Food often becomes a means of communicating who we are, where we belong, and what is important to us.[36]

Time

When we talk about time, we often mean past, present, or future. However, consider these phrases: "You are on island time now." "Don't waste my time!" "I don't have time for that!" "It is just a matter of time." These phrases reference how time is used, how it should be structured, how it should be perceived and reacted to, and how it should be interpreted. Studying how we use, structure, perceive, react to, and interpret time is known as **chronemics**.[37] Your use of time is greatly influenced by your culture and co-cultures. According to anthropologist Edward T. Hall, "Time is a core system of cultural, social, and personal life."[38] Hall argues that most cultures are either monochronic (M-time, or one thing at a time) or polychronic (P-time, or several things at once) time users.

Self-Check: Biological Time

Personal biological time orientation impacts your mood and physical energy, which can influence your communicative effectiveness.

1. Do you prefer to wake early and feel most energetic and ready to seize the day just after you wake up? Do you prefer to work day shifts? Do you go to bed early? If so, you are a morning person or a "lark."

2. Do you work better during the evening or prefer the night shift? Do you go to bed late? If so, you are a night person or an "owl."

3. Your preferences may fall between these two extremes as well (known as intermediates).

Monochronic people tend to:

- Do one thing at a time (*mono*)
- Emphasize promptness, schedules, and deadlines
- Concentrate on one thing and commit to it
- Prefer to stick to the plan
- Follow rules and respect private property

Polychronic people tend to:

- Do multiple things at once (*poly*)
- Not worry as much about schedules and deadlines
- Stress involvement of people and human relationships
- Prioritize time based on human relationships
- Place their jobs below kindness to others
- Be flexible with plans
- Lend and borrow personal property
- Build lifelong relationships and be very family oriented[39]

Clearly, when people from different time orientations interact, there can be serious perception issues and misinterpretations. Likewise, people who adhere to one or the other can limit their interaction skills and observations.

Even your biological time orientation can influence your mood, perception skills, communicative effectiveness, and attractiveness. See the Self-Check box to determine when you are at your peak.

Environment

Your environment is your physical surroundings from contact with your body outward and including objects and things (artifacts) that decorate that space. For example, the style of your house, décor, selections of objects like your car or computer, and even landscape choices send a message to you and others. According to communication scholar Mark Knapp, you perceive environments in terms of formality, warmth, privacy, familiarity, constraint, and distance.[40] Elements such as color, lighting, sound, arrangement, environmental smell, and space usage influence how you and others feel within a space. Even our use of personal space and territory figures into how we interact and is greatly affected by our personal preferences, our gender, the situation, and our relationship with those around us.[41] What we do with our environments reveals a lot about who we are and how we want to interact. Two major elements of your environment communication are personal space and territory.

Personal Space

Personal space is the space around your body that you perceive as yours. As Edward T. Hall noted in *The Hidden Dimensions*, you are often very protective of your personal space and are easily excitable when it is misused or invaded. ***Proxemics*** is the study of personal space as communication.

Hall identified four personal space zones used by most Western cultures, below.

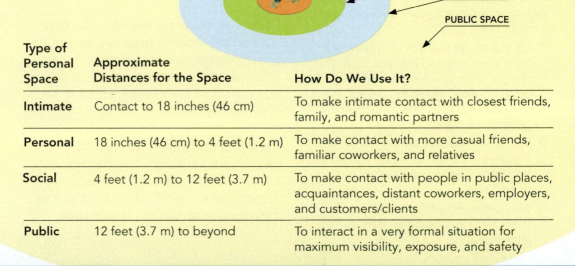

INTIMATE SPACE

PERSONAL SPACE

SOCIAL SPACE

PUBLIC SPACE

Type of Personal Space	Approximate Distances for the Space	How Do We Use It?
Intimate	Contact to 18 inches (46 cm)	To make intimate contact with closest friends, family, and romantic partners
Personal	18 inches (46 cm) to 4 feet (1.2 m)	To make contact with more casual friends, familiar coworkers, and relatives
Social	4 feet (1.2 m) to 12 feet (3.7 m)	To make contact with people in public places, acquaintances, distant coworkers, employers, and customers/clients
Public	12 feet (3.7 m) to beyond	To interact in a very formal situation for maximum visibility, exposure, and safety

Territory

Territoriality refers to behavior we display toward the space and objects that we permanently or temporarily claim as our own—ownership that we will often defend.[42] In other words, territory deals with one's own space or things and is closely linked to how we use space. How have you set or marked territories in your residence hall room, apartment, or house—or your space if you have been in the military, where personal territory is often difficult to maintain? How would you feel if someone hacked your Facebook or Twitter account? We send signals as to what is our territory and often feel violated when someone invades or misuses it. Social psychologist Irwin Altman distinguishes three territory types discussed in the table below.[43]

Altman's Territory Types		
Territory	**Distinguishing Features**	**Examples**
Primary	Space or objects claimed for your primary or sole use	Your desk at home, purse, wallet, cell phone, tablet, computer, eating utensils, home, apartment, room, backyard, car, social network sites, or body
Secondary	Space and objects not central to your life or necessarily owned by you but associated with you	Your desk in a particular classroom, the TV in a common area, the kitchen if you cook often, your neighborhood, a specific library table, or your spot on the couch
Public	Space and objects available for temporary possession but open to anyone	Park bench, seat on the subway/bus/train, restaurant, green space, beach, pool, theatre, mall, or study room

Every culture has different and certain expectations about how to use space as well as territory and what constitutes a violation. However, the longer we know someone, the more comfortable we might be with violation. The more intimate a relationship we have with someone, the more likely he or she can invade our personal space or a specific territory.

Space speaks.[44]
Edward T. Hall

4.4 What Are Some Cultural Variations in Nonverbal Communication?

Now that you have seen what constitutes nonverbal communication and how we use it, let's look at what can influence it. The next time you are able to watch individuals from different cultures or co-cultures interact, notice how important nonverbal behavior becomes. It can be the only and best method for intercultural communicators to understand each other—especially if they don't share a verbal language. However, nonverbal cues can be misunderstood and even destructive when they vary across cultures and are misinterpreted.

Throughout this chapter, you have learned a few variations in nonverbal behavior across cultures. For example, you know that there are a few mostly universal facial expressions, that food choices or taste can communicate different cultural messages, and that space is often used and negotiated in culturally specific ways. The table on the next page serves as a quick tip sheet for a few more variations to be mindful of as you interact. Be aware that it is impossible to note all the variations. So keep your eyes and ears open for more as you encounter the wonders of other cultures.

Select Cultural Differences in Nonverbal Style[45]

Body	Postures related to bowing are important in Japan (bows may be informal, formal, or very formal, and usually the inferior person bows deeper, longer, and more frequently).
Touch	U.S. and UK citizens and, even more so, the Japanese tend toward rarely touching in social settings.
	Latin Americans, Middle Easterners, Southern Europeans, and many African cultures touch much more and might even seem more intimate with touch (two men holding hands to signal friendship).
	Touching someone on the head (it is sacred) can be offensive to Asians.
	In the Middle East, touch or the transfer of objects with the left hand (it is seen as unclean) is inappropriate.
Face	Gazing is more common during conversations for Arabs, Latin Americans, and Southern Europeans.
	Winking can be viewed as rude in China or as a romantic or sexual gesture in Latin America.
	Direct, sustained eye contact with those in authority (Latin America, Asia, Middle East, Native American culture) or the opposite sex (for Muslims) can be disrespectful, bold, and forward.
	Russians, Japanese, and Koreans display a high level of facial control.
	Asians tend to smile more to conceal sadness, anger, embarrassment, or other awkward situations.
Vocal cues	Lower volume is generally more acceptable for Asians and Western Europeans.
	U.S. citizens are uncomfortable with silence but others see it as a sign of respect, contemplation, and introspection.
Time	Latin America, France, the Arab part of the Middle East, and sub-Saharan Africa are highly polychronic (may conduct meetings in open spaces and appointments can be changed) and the United States, Canada, and Northern Europe are highly monochronic (compartmentalize, concentrate, and stay on time).
Environment	High-power cultures tend to give more space to those in authority.
	People from crowded places (New York City, Hong Kong) will cope better with personal space violations.
	Private territory (the home) is sacred to Germans and an invitation to anyone other than a close family member is special.

4.5 How Does Gender Influence Nonverbal Messages?

Given the fact that much of our nonverbal communication is created with the body or its relationship to things, and given the fact that men's and women's bodies are so physically and socially different, it is no wonder each sex uses nonverbal communication uniquely.

As with the verbal message, women's and men's nonverbal communication is very similar when they are socialized by the same culture. However, each culture accentuates the differences between the sexes by supporting specific nonverbal behavior. For example, women in the United States tend to shave their legs and underarms; wear makeup to emphasize eyes and mouths, jewelry common to mainly women, and clothes that highlight the breasts; and walk with their legs close together and their arms close to their bodies. Men in the United States often work to show off their strength by building muscle mass in the biceps and abs, may grow facial hair to mark their masculinity, rarely cry or display that type of emotion, are expected to play rough, and walk "like a man" (legs wider apart and arms away from trunk).

As communication scholars Virginia Peck Richmond, James C. McCroskey, and Mark L. Hickson suggest, these differences between men and women appear to be caused by modeling (learning behavior by watching others and imitating) and by reinforcement or conditioning (if behavior is reinforced, it will increase). They believe genetics is less likely to play a role in the differences.[46]

Gender Nonverbal Behavior Differences[47]

Women's Nonverbal Behavior	Men's Nonverbal Behavior
Are judged more often and negatively for unattractiveness	Are judged negatively for unattractiveness but less so than women
Throaty vocalics seen as ugly or boring, breathiness as sexy or shallow	Throaty vocal quality viewed as older or mature, breathiness as young and artistic
Tend to talk more softly (especially in the United States)	Tend to use nonverbal cues such as greater vocal volume and inflection to demonstrate control or power
Tilt head and twist at the hips	Hold head upright and have erect posture
More facially expressive and will smile more but will be interrupted more when smiling	Internalize their emotions and mask more
Take up less territory and bodily space (notice how women cross their legs)	More likely to have a special space or room that is off-limits and will physically take up more space (notice how men sit and cross their legs)
Their space will more likely be invaded and they are expected to yield it	React more negatively to crowding
Use more head and hand gestures but they are smaller	Make sweeping gestures
Touch others more and are more likely to cross-gender touch	If heterosexual, tend to rarely touch other men and are more likely to view a touch by a woman as sexual
More accurate in sending and receiving nonverbal messages	Tend to move more during interaction
Make more eye contact	Tend to use more vocal fillers and pauses
Tend to sit closer to other women	

Practicing Ethics: Gender and Touch

Touch can be interpreted differently based on location. Touching a woman's head, back, hands, or face can be viewed as intimate or friendly—and, in certain situations, as sexual harassment. Men are less likely to view this type of touch as too intimate.[48] Cross-culturally, any type of touch might be taboo (especially men touching men or women initiating touch with men). Observe, inquire, and think before you touch.

4.6 How Can You Improve Your Nonverbal Communication?

Because so much of nonverbal communication can be culturally bound, gender specific, and unconsciously decoded or encoded, it is important for you to foster effective nonverbal behavior as an interpreter and user of it.

Develop Your Interpreting Skills (Decoding)

Here are some suggestions for improving your skills as an interpreter or consumer of nonverbal communication:

- Be other-centered. Try to see the behavior from the point of view of the person doing it.

- Remember that nonverbal messages can be very complex and blend together. Don't key in on only one aspect.

- Be mindful of culture and gender differences. Put yourself in situations that can help you learn about these differences. Don't communicate only with individuals similar to you.

- Remember to perception-check your observations and assessments of someone's nonverbal behavior. Reflect on the meaning you assign to his or her behavior and try to locate other information to confirm or disconfirm your interpretations.

  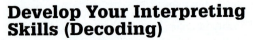 **See Chapter 2, Objective 2.8**, for more on perception checking.

- Check your interpretation of others' nonverbal behavior against their verbal message.

- Ask the communicator for clarification. Ask someone else in the situation what his or her feelings are about the nonverbal cues.

- Be aware of the situation. Realize that mediated communication can skew nonverbal messages or prevent them altogether

- Remind yourself of nonverbal cues that act like emotional triggers. Are your individual emotional reactions feeding your interpretation?

- Be willing to say your interpretations could be wrong or slightly off, or that you may simply be reading something into a behavior that was unintentionally created.

- Be aware of the expectancy violation theory. See the Practicing Ethics box.

Cultivate Your User Skills (Encoding)

- Carefully craft your nonverbal messages and try to be aware of what you do unconsciously in a particular situation. Self-monitor what you do nonverbally.

- Be other-centered. Imagine how others might interpret your messages.

- Be mindful of culture and gender differences. Educate yourself about how others might interpret and respond to your messages.

- Make your nonverbal behavior as consistent as possible with your verbal message.

- Use intimate nonverbal cues with caution (i.e., invading intimate or personal space or touching).

- Be aware of the situation. Realize that mediated communication can skew nonverbal messages or prevent them altogether. Others may not understand or could misinterpret your verbal message if they don't have your nonverbal cues.

- Ask for feedback about your nonverbal cues or others' interpretations of them. Accept input on how to be a better nonverbal communicator.

- Be willing to live with the results of your nonverbal message. Once it is sent and received, you can't delete it. Be polite.

- Be aware of the expectancy violation theory. See the Practicing Ethics box.

- Practice your nonverbal communication.

Practicing Ethics: Expectancy Violation Theory

Because many factors (such as culture, gender, and personal, idiosyncratic behavior) can influence what we say and do, we can violate what others expect our behavior to be. Judee Burgoon's *expectancy violation theory* explains how unusual behavior will increase uncertainty and be regarded as positive or negative by those receiving the message. Often, if you perceive a person positively, you will perceive their violation of your expectations as favorable and vice versa.[49] For example, if you hug a lot, your hugging behavior will more likely be expected and perceived as a positive by someone else who hugs a lot. If the other person is not a hugger, your behavior may seem unexpected and negative. However, if the non-hugger has a positive view of you, that person may view the hug more favorably. It is your ethical responsibility to be mindful of how your expectancy influences your interpretation of another person's behavior.

Chapter 4 Review

Key Questions

4.1 What Are the Traits of Nonverbal Communication?

Objective 4.1: **IDENTIFY THE TRAITS OF NONVERBAL COMMUNICATION**

Nonverbal communication is the intentional or unintentional transmission of a message or a portion of a message without the use of words that are spoken, written, or signed. Nonverbal messages are:

- Nonlinguistic
- Arbitrary, ambiguous, and abstract
- Multichanneled
- Innate and learned
- Contextual
- Culturally bound
- Relational
- Continuous
- Emotionally expressive
- Powerful

See pages 92–97.

4.2 What Are the Functions of Nonverbal Communication?

Objective 4.2: **DISCUSS HOW YOU USE NONVERBAL COMMUNICATION**

Nonverbal cues can be congruent (matching or fitting) with your verbal message or they can be incongruent (contrasting or different). In being congruent or incongruent, your nonverbal messages act as *metacommunication* to your verbal messages, or as communication *about* how you want your verbal messages interpreted. You use your nonverbal cues to complement, accentuate, contradict, regulate, repeat, and substitute.

See pages 98–99.

4.3 What Channels Do You Use to Convey Nonverbal Messages?

Objective 4.3: **EXPLAIN THE CHANNELS YOU USE TO TRANSMIT NONVERBAL MESSAGES**

Nonverbal communication can engage all of our senses through numerous channels. Those channels include:

- Your body, including posture
- How you use touch
- Your face
- Your appearance
- Your vocal cues and how you use silence
- Smell and taste
- Your use of time
- Your use of and relationship with your environment

See pages 100–117.

4.4 What Are Some Cultural Variations in Nonverbal Communication?

Objective 4.4: **SUMMARIZE SOME CULTURAL DIFFERENCES IN NONVERBAL STYLE**

Nonverbal communication can be the only and best method for intercultural communicators to understand each other—especially if they don't share a verbal language. However, nonverbal cues can be misunderstood and even destructive when they vary across cultures and are misinterpreted. It is important to stay mindful when interacting across cultures because it is impossible to note all variations. For example, U.S. citizens are uncomfortable with silence but other cultures view it as a form of respect, contemplation, and introspection.

See pages 118–119.

4.5 How Does Gender Influence Nonverbal Messages?

Objective 4.5: **ARTICULATE GENDER DIFFERENCES IN NONVERBAL STYLE**

As with the verbal message, women's and men's nonverbal communication is very similar when individuals are socialized by the same culture. However, each culture accentuates the differences between the sexes by supporting specific nonverbal behavior. For example, compared to men, women tend to:

• Be more facially expressive and smile more

• Take up less territory and personal space

• Allow their space to be invaded more

• Touch others more

• Make more eye contact

• Send and receive nonverbal messages more accurately

See pages 120–121.

4.6 How Can You Improve Your Nonverbal Communication?

Objective 4.6: **DEMONSTRATE METHODS FOR IMPROVING NONVERBAL SKILLS**

Because so much of nonverbal communication can be culturally bound, gender specific, and unconsciously decoded or encoded, it is important for you to foster effective nonverbal behavior as an interpreter (decoder) and as a user (encoder) of it.

See pages 122–123.

Key Terms

nonverbal communication (92)
nonverbal cues (92)
display rules (94)
leakage and deception cues (97)
metacommunication (98)
kinesics (101)
posture (101)
gesture (102)
emblems (103)
illustrators (103)
affect display (103)
regulators (103)
adaptors (103)
haptics (104)
facial primacy (106)
facial expressions (106)
oculesics (107)
attractiveness (108)
vocal variety (110)
rate (110)
pitch (111)
pronunciation (112)
articulation (112)
enunciation (112)
dialect (113)
olfactics (114)
chronemics (115)
personal space (116)
proxemics (116)
territoriality (117)
expectancy violation theory (123)

Improve Your Communication

Putting yourself in situations where you must rely on your nonverbal communication will help you develop your skills and understand your responses to nonverbal cues. Here are a few suggestions that might help you improve.

- Play games like *Cranium, Guesstures, Reverse Charades, Charades,* or *Catch Phrase.*
- Create your own games focusing on nonverbal cues.
  - Have someone put fragrant things in separate paper bags; without looking in the bags, smell each and note the memories invoked.
  - Have someone cut faces out of magazines and try to determine the emotional state of each face.
  - Write expressive words on note cards and act each out. Think about which could be expressed with only your face. (Word examples: confused, perturbed, proud, curious, jealous, thrilled, offended, discouraged, caring, or eager)
- Join an improv or acting group.
- Self-test your decoding nonverbal skills at the following online resource: http://nonverbal.ucsc.edu/

Apply Your Knowledge

1. Can you describe the emblems that go with the following phrases or words?

It's hot or cold
What time is it?
Blah blah
Peace
Victory
Hitchhiking
Requesting a truck driver to honk the
   horn
Check, please!

2. What nonverbal cues do you look for when trying to gauge if someone is lying or not? How are these similar to or different from those discussed in the chapter? Are you better at telling whether or not someone is lying when you know them well?

3. Consider how you generally dress, your hairstyle, and other items you wear on your body. What might these things say about you?

4. Do you believe that emoticons or emoji add to your online communication? Why or why not?

5. Discuss how food works to convey messages in your culture.

Other Resources

See the following sources for more on nonverbal communication.

Using Nonverbal Communication

Matsumoto, David, Mark G. Frank, and Hyi Sung Hwang, eds. *Nonverbal Communication: Science and Applications.* Los Angeles: SAGE, 2013. Print.

Vrij, Aldert, Katherine Edward, Kim P. Roberts, and Ray Bull. "Detecting Deceit Via Analysis of Verbal and Nonverbal Behavior." *Journal of Nonverbal Behavior* 24.4 (2000): 239–63. Print.

Williams-Forson, Psyche, and Carole Counihan, eds. *Taking Food Public: Redefining Foodways in a Changing World.* New York: Routledge, 2012. Print.

Cramer, Janet M., Carlnita P. Green, and Lynn M. Walters, eds. *Food as Communication: Communication as Food.* New York: Lang, 2011. Print.

- www.ted.com/talks/amy_cuddy_your_body_language_shapes_who_you_are
- www.diresta.com/vocal-fry-can-hurt-your-presentation-and-job-interview/
- www.fastcompany.com/3032208/hit-the-ground-running/4-speech-habits-that-are-undermining-your-job-chances
- www.helpguide.org/mental/eq6_nonverbal_communication.htm

Nonverbal Communication Across Cultures

- www.harley.com/writing/time-sense.html
- www.rheawessel.com/clips_istheretimetoslowdown.htm
- www.worldwidewords.org/turnsofphrase/tp-pol2.htm

Chapter 5
Listening

The most basic and powerful way to connect to another person is to listen. Just listen. Perhaps the most important thing we ever give each other is our attention.[1]

Rachel Naomi Remen

5.1 What Is Listening?

In her book, *The Zen of Listening*, speech/language pathologist Rebecca Z. Shafir writes, "Welcome to the Age of Distraction!"[2] Others call it an age of information overload, infobesity, or infoxication.[3] Whatever we name it, it is an age in which listening is important and effective listening skills are a must. Understanding what listening is and how it works is the first step in doing it well.

More Than Hearing

Hearing happens when sound waves strike the eardrum and spark a chain reaction that ends with the brain registering the sound. This is the physiological awareness of sound that most people are born with. People who are deaf or have severe hearing loss hear by watching via a language of gestural, facial, and body movements. According to the National Institute on Deafness and Other Communication Disorders:[4]

- Approximately 15 percent (37.5 million) of U.S. adult citizens report some degree of hearing loss.
- About 2 to 3 out of every 1,000 children are born with a detectable level of hearing loss in one or both ears.
- It is estimated that approximately 15 percent (26 million) of citizens between the ages of 20 and 69 have high frequency hearing loss due to exposure to loud sounds at work or in leisure activities.

Hearing is the first step in listening and is typically an automatic function. In contrast, you must choose to listen. **Listening** is the conscious learned act of paying attention, assigning meaning, and responding to a verbal and/or nonverbal message.[5]

A Major Portion of Your Communicative Life

For years, scholars have tried to measure the amount of time the average person spends listening. Most studies suggest that you spend 40 to 80 percent of your day listening.[6] This large range in the percentages seems to be connected, at least in part, to the situations being studied. For example, if the study measures listening time for students, the percentage goes up for school-related time but goes down in other situations. Likewise, many of these studies measure only body-to-body interaction or, at the most, include television and radio.

In 2009, communication scholars Laura Janusik and Andrew Wolvin conducted the first study to look at time in different communicative activities for 12,000 students in different situations (school, friends, work, and family), and they considered more mediated influences.[7] See the figure below. Given the creation or advancement of smartphones, video calling, instant messaging, and other interaction tools since the collection phase of this study, these percentages have likely changed even more. However, listening and speaking skills still dominate your communicative life.

Time in Communicative Activities

- Listening
- Speaking
- Internet
- Writing
- Reading
- TV
- Phone
- Listening to radio & music
- E-mail

5%, 6%, 7%, 8%, 8%, 9%, 13%, 20%, 24%

A Process

It is important to realize that listening is a process. A process, at its basic level, is the act of inputting something into a series of phases that results in a particular output. The listening process has five phases: receiving, attending, understanding, responding, and remembering.

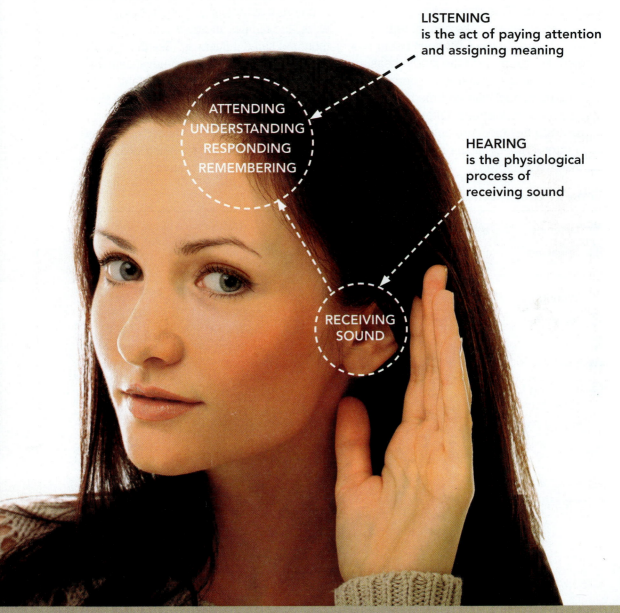

LISTENING
is the act of paying attention and assigning meaning

ATTENDING
UNDERSTANDING
RESPONDING
REMEMBERING

HEARING
is the physiological process of receiving sound

RECEIVING
SOUND

Receiving is the physiological process of hearing. The ears collect the sound (or, if hearing is impaired, the eyes collect visual stimuli), converting and transmitting it to the brain.

Attending is the phase where you make your brain pay attention to a given sound or equivalent stimulus. For example, stop and listen to the sounds around you now. You may be able to hear birds outside, music, people talking next door, or the soft whoosh of air coming from the air conditioner or heater. Now, imagine a friend speaking in the middle of this symphony of sound, and pay attention to his or her words. If you are able to do so, you will no longer pay attention to some of those other sounds. The sounds do not go away; you are still hearing but not attending to them. If your hearing is impeded for any reason, you will attend only to the message you can see. In either case, you have chosen to concentrate on your friend's message and exclude others.

Understanding occurs when you apply literal and emotional meaning to what you are attending to—and is where communication really begins. If someone yells "Stop!" with urgency, you might understand that message to mean you are in danger if you continue on. If that same person yells "Stop!" with anger, you might stop what you are doing because it is annoying that person.

Responding is the phase where you give feedback or a reply to the messages you have processed. Some communication scholars say the listening process ends with understanding because the communication was either successful or not. However, the communication process is transactional, and most listeners offer verbal or nonverbal feedback, silence, or some combination of these as their response. This part allows you to fulfill your responsibility as a communicative partner.

Remembering, or retaining what you hear, is the final stage. Most of the messages you receive go into your short-term memory. You remember them just long enough to make sense of the interactions or to fulfill a need, such as remembering a room number long enough to locate it. Other messages are deemed important enough to move into your long-term memory, where you store the information for a longer period of time. For example, your teacher might use memory games or assignments for the first few classes in a semester to help everyone remember names of those in the class. These games or assignments often require you to hear, focus, associate, or repeat names until they are remembered.

TIP: Listening With All Your Senses

No matter your physiological level of hearing, attend to both the verbal and nonverbal elements of a message. Listen with all your senses. Remember, too, that mediated interactions may not include message detail. Try to be open to and aware of alternative interpretations.

5.2 Why Is Listening an Important Skill?

Former CEO of Amgen (a biotech giant) Kevin Sharer once said, "Listening is the threshold skill; if you don't have it, you will fail, but having it doesn't mean you will necessarily succeed.... Most people underappreciate the complexity of listening, the skill needed, and the value of doing it well."[8] Good listening skills will influence your knowledge, enjoyment, relationships, and professionalism and help fulfill your role as a communicator.

Your Knowledge Increases

You may have found yourself in a math or chemistry class where you struggle to understand the information and your anxiety causes you to tune out the teacher. Or you might be distracted at work as your manager explains a new procedure. Like other students or employees, you must make a conscious effort to learn and engage in discussion. This is where your listening skills come into play as an information-gathering tool. Listening allows you to take in, process, and use information. Listening helps you develop your expertise or skill with a subject. It allows you to collect information to make your daily life easier and more enjoyable. It can improve your grades, make you more productive, or improve your self-confidence.

Listening also tells us about ourselves. For example, make a list of what really makes you sit up and listen. What topics can hold your attention for hours? What topics or people do you find easy to listen to? What types of music do you enjoy? The answers to these questions will feature what you value, agree with, or find interesting. Taking an inventory of what you listen to will begin to draw a picture of your self-identity.

You Fulfill Your Communicative Responsibility

As you learned in Chapter 1, a major reason scholars view the communication process as transactional is because each partner actively participates and is not a passive vessel. Listening and responding help complete the transaction between the partners. Communicators who believe that the person initiating the message is entirely responsible for the effectiveness of the message are falling prey to **passivity syndrome**. For example, have you ever said a person was boring and therefore you refused to listen? If so, you have incorrectly placed all responsibility on the other person. For effective communication to occur, all involved in the interaction must work at completing and understanding the message.

Also, try to always support the freedom of expression with active listening. For example, if a government is illegally or unethically muting individual or co-cultural voices, and we are in a position to listen, it is our ethical duty to do so. As journalist Walter Lippmann wrote, "While the right to talk may be the beginning of freedom, the necessity of listening is what makes the right important."[9] In other words, what is said is only as valid as the listener's willingness to listen and ability to comprehend and evaluate what is said. We should actively listen to and analyze messages and situations, not ignore them or be passive listeners.

You Build Better Relationships

Listening allows us to build and maintain healthy relationships with our families, significant others, friends, teachers, and coworkers. Just as listening can teach you about yourself, listening to others will help you know what is important to them. Their words will give you clues to their identity. Through understanding how our identities interlock, you build relationships and strengthen them. Once you choose to maintain a relationship, listening allows you to deal with conflict or help the other person cope with or resolve a crisis in his or her life. Much like what you learned about language choices in Chapter 3, being a good listener will encourage others to interact with you.

Listening shows others that you value and care about them and what is important to them. Effectively listening is the best gift you can give them.[10] It is a means of being with them, and greater interaction brings greater intimacy and bonding. Introduced in 2001, **affection exchange theory** suggests that our use of affectionate behavior (hugging, kissing, holding hands, and, yes, even listening) contributes to our survival and promotes bonding with those we consider potential intimate partners.[11] Good communication is vital in every stage of relationship development. The failure to communicate and listen in an interpersonal relationship will result in a languishing relationship at best and, more likely, an unhappy or negative relationship.

You Improve Professionally

"Can I help you?" "What kind of car are you looking for?" "Can you describe your pain for me?" "What are your company needs?" These are all examples of questions you might ask as a professional. Each of these questions requires good listening skills in return. A quick search on the Internet of things to consider in an employee evaluation highlights several main factors. The most common are job performance, attitude, cooperation, listening ability, commitment, ability to interact, and desire to learn. Notice most deal with some aspect either directly or indirectly related to listening. Clearly, many people believe listening is a key to success and tied to effective leadership.[12]

In 1990, the Secretary of Labor created a commission (Secretary's Commission on Achieving Necessary Skills, or SCANS) to determine the skills that people need to succeed in the workforce. The commission completed its work in 1992 but recommendations are still valid today. The commission lists reading, writing, math, speaking, and listening as the basic skills needed for successful employment. As the commission report noted, "…very few of us will work totally by ourselves. More and more, work involves listening carefully to clients and co-workers and clearly articulating one's own point of view. Today's worker has to listen and speak well enough to explain schedules and procedures, communicate with customers, work in teams, understand customer concerns, describe complex systems and procedures, probe for hidden meanings, teach others, and solve problems."[13] However, SCANS estimated that less than half of all young adults have the minimum reading and writing skills, lower math skills, and very little training with listening and speaking skills. Effective listening may prevent you from missing a professional opportunity, it may save you time and money, and it may advance your career.

You Experience Enjoyment

Listening for enjoyment is an intentional act. In other words, you seek out listening opportunities that allow you to have fun, relax, or engage certain emotional responses you appreciate or need. For example, listening to your favorite TV show or music, the birds singing in the woods, the sounds of a video game, or a poetry reading could be part of a pleasurable experience. Engaging in pleasurable relaxed events (e.g., listening to music with a slow tempo of 50–60 beats per minute) can even be healthy by lowering your blood pressure and heart rate.[14] Here, listening becomes pleasurable with benefits.

Practicing Ethics: Unplugging

Electronic device distractions are plentiful and enticing these days. Choose to be an ethical attentive listener, and be "unplugged" when communicating outside of a mediated context.

Self-Test: Assess Your Listening Skills

In her book, *Rule #1: Stop Talking! A Guide to Listening*, author and corporate trainer Linda Eve Diamond suggests that a good warm-up exercise for improving your listening skills is to assess them using self-reflection. Diamond offers the following self-test to send you on your way to understanding your listening abilities.[15] Record a yes or no to the following questions.

		YES	NO
1.	I like to multitask and think about other things when people are talking.	❑	❑
2.	If people aren't going to take my advice, they shouldn't waste my time telling me their problems.	❑	❑
3.	I'm usually bored when the conversation doesn't center around my interests.	❑	❑
4.	When someone is slow to get a point across, I interrupt to get things moving.	❑	❑
5.	When people speak to me, they most often have to compete with a number of distractions.	❑	❑
6.	I tend to be involved in a lot of misunderstandings.	❑	❑
7.	A person's appearance, grammar, or style of speaking affects how much attention I give them.	❑	❑
8.	I have trouble keeping a confidence (a secret).	❑	❑
9.	I usually feel that making my case is more important than someone else's feelings.	❑	❑
10.	When I don't understand something, I will often fake it and smile instead of asking questions.	❑	❑
11.	I am good at looking like I am listening when I am not.	❑	❑
12.	I tend to talk when I should listen.	❑	❑
13.	I trust my intuition and it serves me well.	❑	❑
14.	I can usually tell when people aren't being honest.	❑	❑
15.	I am good at soothing conflict.	❑	❑

A "no" to questions 1–12 and a "yes" to 13–15 would be a perfect score. Note any "yes" answers for 1–12 and "no" answers for 13–15 that you have. These are areas you might want to work on as you improve your listening skills.

5.3 What Are the Types of Listening?

When you engage in the process of listening, you do so to achieve a goal. The four listening goals are to appreciate, empathize, comprehend, and be critical. You will always have one of these goals as your overarching reason for listening. However, listeners often use a combination to achieve the main goal. (For example, you may be listening for information but at the same time evaluating it critically for believability.) Each of these goals corresponds to a type of listening.

Appreciative Listening

Appreciative listening happens when you listen for recreation or enjoyment. Examples of appreciative listening are:

- Listening to a comedy show
- Listening to your favorite band
- Listening to birds singing
- Listening to the cooing of your baby or the voice of a lover
- Listening to a speech that has the goal to entertain

Empathic Listening

Empathic listening occurs when your purpose is to give emotional support to another person. Examples here could be:

- A religious leader listening to a congregation member
- A counselor listening to a patient
- A friend listening to another friend in need

Emphatic listening emphasizes carefully attending to whom you are communicating with; supporting by listening more than responding; and empathizing, or feeling as the other person feels. Also, this type of listening is grounded in identification with the other person. In Chapter 2, you learned that this is an important skill for developing your perception of others. Identification is at the core of being other-centered in your communication.[16]

Informative Listening

Informative listening occurs when you want to gain insight or comprehension. This approach to listening emphasizes concentrating on language, ideas, and details as well as remembering the knowledge. In classes, you use informative listening when you pay attention to your professors. Other places where you might engage in informative listening could be:

- When a friend gives you directions to his new apartment
- When you are in the developmental stages of a relationship
- At the hardware store as a sales associate tells you how to install tile
- When a doctor gives you medical instructions

In all of these examples, you listen for clarification of the language, you concentrate on the necessary details, and you engage in some sort of activity to help you remember (e.g., taking notes).

Practicing Ethics: Being a Critical Listener and Thinker

Critical listening and critical thinking are such important parts of communication that you should almost always engage in a certain level of each. For example, you may be listening to gather information, but you should never assume information is correct simply because the person says so. This is true even in your personal relationships. Ask:

- Could any of this information be incorrect or incomplete?
- Is this person trustworthy and unbiased in this context?
- Could there be alternatives?

Critical Listening

Critical listening takes place when you listen carefully to a message in order to judge it as acceptable or not. This is the type of listening behavior you use when listening to:

- A presidential debate
- A salesperson trying to sell you a new sound system
- A friend when you are trying to decide if she is telling you the truth

Critical listening is the root of critical thinking. Theorists Brooke Moore and Richard Parker define **critical thinking** as "the careful, deliberate determination of whether one should accept, reject, or suspend judgment about a claim [or information] and the degree of confidence with which one accepts or rejects it."[17] Astronomer Carl Sagan called this your "baloney-detection kit." Sagan's suggestion was to "equip yourself with a baloney-detection kit … and be able to tell what is baloney and what is not."[18]

You currently live in a time when informative and persuasive acts bombard you from all sides. They come at you from social media, radio, television, the Internet, T-shirts, billboards, and even cereal boxes. You must be able and willing to ask such questions as: Why? Where did that information come from? How old is it? Who benefits from it? Who will get hurt? See the Practicing Ethics box on this page for more on being a critical listener and thinker.

5.4 What Can Prevent Effective Listening?

Most people would define noise as unpleasant sounds that might be loud, startling, irritating, or unwelcoming. In the process of communicating, *noise* refers to any barriers that prevent you from listening effectively to a communication partner. They can be pleasant or unpleasant things. They can even be unethical.

For example, you might find the deep, melodious voices of actors James Earl Jones and Morgan Freeman so pleasing that you focus more on the beauty of their voices than on their messages. Or you might feel that the harsh, nasal voices of actors Fran Drescher (as her character in *The Nanny*) and Gilbert Gottfried (comedian and the original voice of the AFLAC duck) are so annoying that you stop listening to the words spoken. Either of these vocal qualities could become a barrier and therefore noise, preventing you from attending to what is important about the message.

Noise is not always connected to the person creating the message; it can be something like a clock ticking, someone tapping a pencil, a text alert or Facebook notification, distracting thoughts, poor listening habits, being bored or generally lazy, or hunger. Understanding what can become noise is the first step to preventing it from distracting you. Two general categories of noise influence communication: internal and external. Closely related to these categories are nonproductive listening habits and your "go-to" listening style.

Internal Noise

Internal noise is any barrier to effective listening that originates within the body or mind of the listener. Internal noise can be either a physiological or a psychological barrier.

- *Physiological barriers* are bodily conditions that prevent or constrain your ability to process information.

- *Psychological barriers* are emotional conditions or a mental state that prevents you from focusing on and absorbing a message. For example, your communication anxiety may prevent you from listening to the speech given just before yours, or your fear of a boss could prevent you from listening to his or her comments. A fight with your best friend or worries over how to make a car payment may preoccupy you. Perspective differences (seeing the message from different points of view) between a teenager and a parent can prevent listening when they do not share the same attitudes, values, beliefs, or expectations. Even the respect or credibility you perceive in the other communicator can create a psychological barrier.

External Noise

External noise is any barrier to effective listening that originates outside of the communication partners' bodies and minds. External noise can be either an environmental or a linguistic barrier.

- *Environmental barriers* occur when something within the room or area where the interaction takes place interrupts your ability to concentrate.

- *Linguistic barriers* happen when the verbal and/or nonverbal messages are unfamiliar to or misunderstood by the listener. Even the speed of someone's message can influence your ability to listen. The average person can speak at about 125–175 words per minute, but you can listen at about a rate of 450 words per minute.[19]

INTERNAL NOISE		EXTERNAL NOISE	
Physiological Barriers	**Psychological Barriers**	**Environmental Barriers**	**Linguistic Barriers**
Headache	Boredom	Environmental sounds	Jargon
Lack of sleep	Fear	Smells	Awkward sentence structure
Pain	Don't-care attitude	Disruptions	Difficult vocabulary
Illness	Preoccupation	Bad ventilation	Unfamiliar or distracting nonverbal communication
Hearing or visual impairments	Anger	Room temperature	
Hunger	Anxiety	Uncomfortable seats	
	Frustration	Lighting	Poor organization
	Prejudice	Electronic devices	
	Perspective differences		

Nonproductive Listening Practices

How you respond to internal and external noise can manifest itself in nonproductive listening practices. The following table outlines the most common ones. Familiarizing yourself with each will help you recognize when you enter into such behavior and will help you regulate nonproductive habits.

Nonproductive Listening Habit	What Is It?
Pseudolistening	Pretending to listen. You might pretend to listen when you are not interested, dislike something, are sick, feel you might be rejected or hurt the other's feelings, or think someone will like you better.
Superficial listening	Paying attention to superficial things rather than the complex message. This type of listening can happen when you find people attractive and pay more attention to their looks or how they are talking. Conversely, you can listen superficially when you dislike someone as well.
Selective listening	Tuning into only a part of the message or listening to only what you want to hear. You will most likely do this type of listening when you are looking for positive or negative content related to you.
Defensive listening	Taking comments as critical or hostile attacks. This has more to do with how you interpret messages, and you tend to view all the messages as critical or hostile toward you no matter what they are or contain.
Literal listening	Paying attention to and interpreting only the denotative verbal message. For example, say someone sarcastically says she loves your humor and you keep doing it because you missed the sarcasm cue.
Dominating (or monopolizing) listening	Listening for moments where you can turn the focus back on yourself. This type happens often with empathic listening—for example, if you respond to a friend's grief over losing a job by turning the talk back to your past employment woes.
Ambushing	Careful listening for the purpose of attacking the other. For example, you listen only for errors or content that can be used against someone.
Multitasking	Although not a listening behavior, this behavior of attending to several things at once can negatively influence your skills. Although this behavior can be a positive for getting things accomplished, it is almost always a poor way to interact with others.

Your "Go-To" Listening Style

In 1995, researchers Kittie W. Watson, Larry L. Baker, and James B. Weaver III devised a 16-item profile (Learning Styles Profile, or LSP) designed to determine your common ("go-to") style of listening.[20] More recently, researchers Graham Bodie, Debra Worthington, and Christopher Gearhart revised the LSP into a 57-item profile (LSP-R).[21] Both sets of researchers noted four distinct styles and that most people tend toward one, but we can adapt to use them all in a particular situation. As you look at the two sets of styles in the tables below, note where they align or don't (e.g., action and content seem to align with critical). Think about how you generally listen. Do you tend to rely heavily on one style, no matter the situation? Which styles do you struggle with the most and might need to work on? Remember that you should be willing to adapt to any of them given the situation. Adhering to only one or using one that might not fit the situation can be a barrier to effective listening.

Listening Styles Profile

People-oriented	I listen to understand the emotional state of others. I am attuned to detecting nuances of conversations and am nonjudgmental.
Action-oriented	I am concerned more with precision or concise, error-free communication rather than emotions.
Content-oriented	I am concerned with systematic processing, details, and a need for cognitive stimulations.
Time-oriented	I have a limited amount of time to listen or there may be a limit to how long I am willing to listen. I am likely to interrupt.

Listening Styles Profile—Revisited

Relational	I listen to understand the feelings of others and to build/maintain relationships.
Critical	I often detect errors in other communicators' logic or message and notice contradictions by paying attention to details.
Analytical	I suspend judgment until I have all the facts and consider alternatives.
Task	I like to stay focused on topic and task. I am impatient with rambling or not quickly getting to the point.

5.5 How Can You Listen Effectively?

Effective listening is the responsibility of everyone committed to an interaction. It begins with the messenger, requires the follow-through of the listener, and ends only when the conversation does. Both the messenger and listener must commit to knowing their communication partners and controlling the environment.

Be aware of barriers your partner might have toward you, the message, or the situation. Take time to learn what you can about the culture or gender of those you engage. In a world where you can watch television, use a computer, send text messages and email, or talk on a phone almost anywhere, listening doesn't seem to have a chance. Identify what might be a distraction and eliminate it.

Employ Messenger Strategies

- **Create effective verbal and nonverbal messages**. Get your partner's attention. Use appropriate language and be aware of words that might trigger an unnecessary response. Organize your thoughts, even in informal situations. Make sure your nonverbal and verbal messages are congruous, and consider cultural difference when crafting them.

- **Be confident**. Speaker credibility might seem obvious and necessary when giving a formal speech, but it is equally important in your daily interactions. If you, as the messenger, seem timid, unsure, or untrusting, this will likely influence your communication partner. A partner may have trouble listening if her or his sympathy for a low-confidence messenger is too great. If she or he

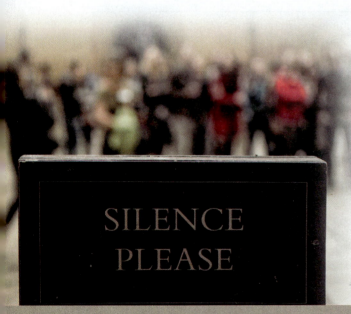

SILENCE PLEASE

doesn't believe the content of the message or is afraid for some reason, listening well can be difficult.

- **Listen to your partner and ask questions.** As you speak, be attentive and mindful of your partner's verbal and nonverbal responses. Ask questions to measure his or her understanding and reaction to your message.

Employ Listener Strategies

- **Commit to being a better listener.** Research suggests that, at best, we recall 25 percent of what we hear; therefore, we can say that most of us aren't good listeners.[22] Listening takes time and energy that you must commit to giving. Prepare yourself and the space around you to help you focus.

- **Quiet your mind.** Try to set aside time and space for your interactions. Gather your thoughts and focus on the present and not the past or future. If appropriate, be honest with your partner about your stress or focus level if you can't control it.

- **Dedicate your full attention when necessary**. Although multitasking is acceptable sometimes, it should not be the norm. Know when it is not appropriate. If you often find yourself responding to others with "I'm listening," you are not listening effectively—and that is the message you are sending. Lean in and make appropriate eye contact. It is hard to daydream or fake listening if you are close to your partner and maintaining eye contact. Eliminate technological/media distractions.

- **Listen appropriately for the situation.** Engage in the best type (appreciative, empathic, informative, or critical) or the best style (see Objective 5.4) for each situation. Be willing to adapt.

- **Listen for main points.** Don't get bogged down in trying to remember everything. Take notes if necessary.

- **Build your verbal and nonverbal vocabulary.** Listening is difficult if you don't know the vocabulary or cues.

- **Offer feedback and ask questions**. Remember this is a transaction and you both are creating meaning. Active listening supports shared understanding.

- **Be an ethical and critical thinker.** Don't listen just for your benefit. Avoid nonproductive listening practices (see Objective 5.4), especially defensive and dominating listening or ambushing. See the Tip box below.

TIP: Critical Listening

Critical listening takes time and practice. These tactics will help you:

- Listen carefully and ask questions.
- Avoid *counterfeit questions*, which mask a message as a question. "Are you finally off the computer?"
- Explore alternatives.
- Maintain a childlike curiosity—everything is interesting and possible.
- Suspend judgment until detail is given.
- Define criteria for making judgments.
- Be open-minded and willing to adjust.

Chapter 5 Review

Key Questions

5.1 What Is Listening?

Objective 5.1: **DISCUSS THE CHARACTERISTICS OF LISTENING**

- **It is more than hearing.** Hearing is physiological and only the first step of listening. Listening is the conscious learned act of paying attention, assigning meaning, and responding to a verbal and/or nonverbal message. Hearing is typically an automatic function. In contrast, you must *choose to* listen.

- **It is a major portion of your communicative life.** Research suggests that, as a student, you spend approximately 24 percent of your day listening.

- **It is a process.** The process of listening includes receiving, attending, understanding, responding, and remembering.

See pages 130–133.

5.2 Why Is Listening an Important Skill?

Objective 5.2: **IDENTIFY THE WAYS EFFECTIVE LISTENING IMPROVES YOUR LIFE**

When you employ good listening skills, you will:

- Increase your knowledge
- Fulfill your communicative responsibility
- Build better relationships
- Improve professionally
- Experience enjoyment

See pages 134–137.

5.3 What Are the Types of Listening?

Objective 5.3: **EXPLAIN THE WAYS YOU LISTEN**

When you engage in the process of listening, you do so to achieve a goal. The four types of listening related to your goals are:

- Appreciative listening
- Empathic listening
- Informative listening
- Critical listening

See pages 138–139.

5.4 What Can Prevent Effective Listening?

Objective 5.4: DISCUSS THE BARRIERS TO EFFECTIVE LISTENING

Noise refers to any barrier that prevents you from listening effectively to a communication partner. There are two general categories of noise influencing communication: internal and external. Closely related to these categories are nonproductive listening practices and your "go-to" listening style, which can become barriers to effective listening.

See pages 140–143.

5.5 How Can You Listen Effectively?

Objective 5.5: ARTICULATE STRATEGIES FOR IMPROVING LISTENING SKILLS

Effective listening is the responsibility of everyone committed to an interaction. It begins with the messenger, requires the follow-through of the listener, and ends only when the conversation does. You should employ messenger and listener strategies to be a more effective listener. Also be generally aware of potential barriers, and learn what you can about the culture or gender of those you engage.

See pages 144–145.

Key Terms

hearing (130)
listening (130)
receiving (133)
attending (133)
understanding (133)
responding (133)
remembering (133)
passivity syndrome (135)
affection exchange theory (135)
appreciative listening (138)
empathic listening (138)
informative listening (139)
critical listening (139)
critical thinking (139)
internal noise (141)
physiological barriers (141)
psychological barriers (141)
external noise (141)
environmental barriers (141)
linguistic barriers (141)
pseudolistening (142)
superficial listening (142)
selective listening (142)
defensive listening (142)
literal listening (142)
dominating (or monopolizing) listening (142)
ambushing (142)
multitasking (142)
counterfeit questions (145)

Improve Your Communication

Note Taking

Part of being a good student listener is taking good notes. Here are some tips.

- If possible, familiarize yourself with the topic before the lecture. Try to read the materials being discussed that day.

- Develop a note-taking shorthand, using symbols or abbreviations such as: i.e. (that is, in other words), & (and), # (number), @ (at), ! (important), ** (remember).

- Prepare yourself and your space for note taking. Put distracting things away and get out what you need to take notes. Try to make yourself comfortable. Sit in a location that will help you see everything and stay alert. The front row is often best.

- Listen for and record main points and pertinent subpoints.

- Use indentations and other similar outlining strategies to distinguish points. Notes that are neat and clear are the most beneficial.

- Use margins for questions or comments you may have.

- After class and as soon as possible, go over your notes, fill in, and summarize.

Focusing

With all the new technology at our fingertips, the sheer volume of information we have access to, our increased multitasking abilities, and almost constant interruptions, effective listening takes even more work. Be ready to focus—ditch the technology when listening.

Apply Your Knowledge

1. Make a list of your strengths and weaknesses as a listener in an interpersonal relationship you are in and when you are a student in class. Do you tend to have the same strengths and weaknesses in both situations? If so, how might you work to eliminate or lessen the influence of your weaknesses? In what situation(s) do you think you are a good listener or a poor listener?

2. Recall a moment when you felt like another person was not listening to you. Can you remember how you knew he or she was not listening? Can you think of issues in your communication that might lessen her or his ability to listen to you? What could both of you do to prevent this from happening again?

3. Explain this quotation by writer, editor, and teacher Brenda Ueland:

   Listening is a magnetic and strange thing, a creative force. You can see that when you think how the friends that really listen to us are the ones we move toward, and we want to sit in their radius as though it did us good like ultraviolet rays. This is the reason: When we are listened to, it creates us, makes us unfold and expand.[23]

Other Resources

Here are some listening resources:

Assessment Tools

- listenersunite.com/resources/Listening-Assessments---L.e.-Diamond.pdf
- psychologytoday.tests.psychtests.com/take_test.php?idRegTest=3206
- testyourself.psychtests.com/testid/3132

Listening Improvement

- www.listen.org
- listenersunite.com/blog/files/f072ee1e4d1e72a7ce20be9f2c4b5f84-144.html
- www.nytimes.com/2012/11/11/opinion/sund
- managementstudyguide.com/effective-listening-skills.htm
- www.experiential-learning-games.com/listeninggames.html
- www.listening-skills.net/index.htm
- www.blog.ted.com/8-talks-on-the-importance-of-listening-and-how-to-do-a-much-better-job-of-it/
- www.speedupcareer.com/articles/workplace-listening.html

Nichols, Michael P. *The Lost Art of Listening: How Learning to Listen Can Improve Your Relationships*. 2nd ed. New York: Guilford, 2009. Print.

Sayeekumar, Manimozhi. "Develop Effective Listening Skill." *Language in India* 13.5 (2013): 704–07. *Communication & Mass Media Complete*. Web.

"Effective Listening Skills." *Women in Business* 46.2 (1994): 28. Web.

"Listening Is Critical for Effective Communication." *Health Care Registration: The Newsletter for Health Care Registration Professionals* 23.9 (2014): 4–6. *Business Source Complete*. Web.

Chapter 6
Interpersonal Relationships

6.1 What Is an Interpersonal Relationship?

As a person going about your daily life and interacting with others, you have numerous interpersonal relationships, of varying types and closeness. For example, if you have a roommate, you will often develop a stronger bond with that person than with other college classmates. You learned in Chapter 1 that interpersonal communication is one of the ways you connect with others (see the figure below). This bonding process requires you to use your foundations of understanding and perceiving as well as your verbal, nonverbal, and listening skills.

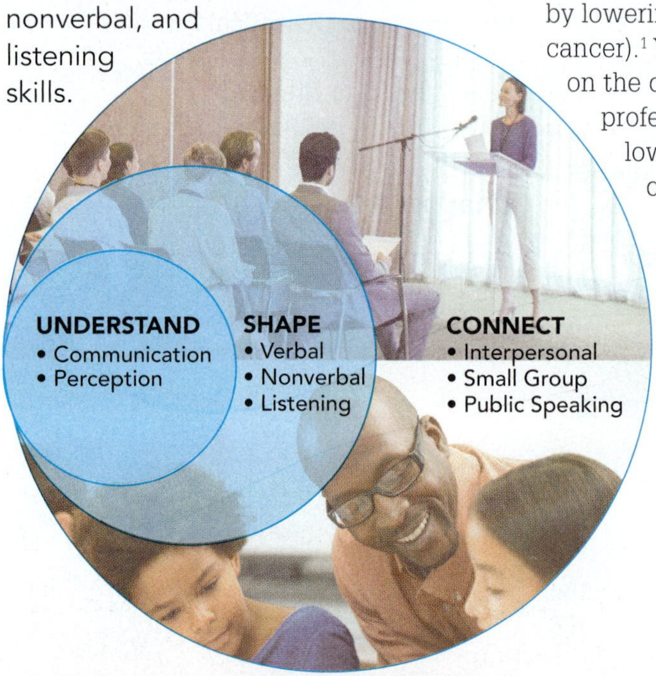

Interpersonal communication is the verbal and nonverbal interaction between individuals, usually two, who are in some sort of significant relationship developing over time. A *relationship* is the state of connectedness, with a heightened emotional involvement and commitment, that we have with another person or persons.

Research has demonstrated that healthy relationships improve your mental well-being (e.g., often lessening depression) and your physical health (e.g., improving your immune system and increasing longevity by lowering risks such as heart attacks and cancer).[1] Your relationships fall somewhere on the continuum between personal and professional, or high contact versus low contact. The personal and high contact sides of these continuums often relate to a heightened level of *intimacy*, or state of closeness evolving from physical, emotional, intellectual, and behavioral contact with one who is significant in your life.[2]

UNDERSTAND
- Communication
- Perception

SHAPE
- Verbal
- Nonverbal
- Listening

CONNECT
- Interpersonal
- Small Group
- Public Speaking

Before distinguishing the types of interpersonal relationships, it is helpful to understand the different modes of intimacy. All relationships have some level of intimacy.

Modes of Intimacy

Physical contact	A mother and baby bonding through cuddling; friends hugging; kissing and lingering touch of lovers
Emotional contact	Self-disclosure of personal feelings to friends, partners, or family
Intellectual contact	Developing a connectedness through sharing of knowledge
Behavioral contact	Spending more time with someone, in either body-to-body or mediated situations; displaying specific behaviors with that person

The most common categories of relationships today are family, romantic, friend, work, and online relationships. Keep in mind, these categories may not be mutually exclusive.[3] Your sister may be your best friend, your lover may be considered part of your family, or you may be developing a romantic relationship or friendship online.

Family Relationships

Family communication scholars Kathleen Galvin, Carna Bylund, and Benard Brommel define "family" as a "network of people who share their lives over a long period of time bound by ties of marriage, blood, commitment, legal or otherwise, who consider themselves as family and who share a significant history and anticipated future…."[4] This might include your biological or adopted mothers, fathers, siblings, grandparents, aunts, uncles, nieces, nephews, cousins, step-relatives, and anyone you would call a family member. As noted in Chapter 2, your close family influences your perception of self, and numerous studies suggest your early family experiences influence your willingness to form certain relationships and ability to maintain them.[5`]

The meeting of two personalities is like the contact of two chemical substances: if there is any reaction, both are transformed.[6]

C.G. Jung

Romantic Relationships

Sometimes closely related to your notion of family, a romantic relationship is one you have with a person that is extremely close, often marked by significant levels of intimacy, commitment, and passion (not only sex). For example, your junior high crush, your high school steady, and your lifelong significant other are all romantic partners. Psychologist Robert Sternberg developed the "triangular theory of love to help us visualize the elements of a romantic relationships."[7]

Intimacy
(closeness, connections, bondedness)

Love

Commitment
(loyalty, honesty, maintaining the love)

Passion
(romance, physical attraction, sex)

Sternberg suggested that the three elements are necessary for attaining a higher level of love. However, a more recent study suggests intimacy and commitment are more important for secure attachment and relationship satisfaction. "Passion may play a larger role in short-term relationships."[8]

One unique characteristic of a romantic relationship in most cultures is *monogamy*, or the practice of having only one sexual partner during a period of time. *Polygamy* occurs when a person has more than one spouse. It is called *polygyny* for men and *polyandry* for women. In countries where polygamy is practiced (e.g., parts of Africa, the Middle East, and Asia), it is usually only legal for men, and there is significant growing disapproval of the practice even in these countries.[9] Polygamy is illegal in all 50 of the United States. Many scholars, politicians, and activists emphasize the potential for polygamy to create abusive situations for women and unequal power between men and women.

In still other cultures (e.g., Amish, India, Islam, and ultra-Orthodox Jews of Israel), the initiation of a romantic relationship can be arranged by family members, relatives, or elders, and the couple agree to mark the pairing with marriage (known as arranged marriages).

Self-Check: What Is Love?

Consider Sternberg's elements as you reflect on your past romantic relationships—or on what you would like in a romantic relationship. Does that reflection give you insight into why a relationship is lasting, why others failed, what you want in a relationship, or how to begin a relationship? What was or is important to your romantic partner?

Friend Relationships

Your friend relationships constitute close, intimate relationships outside of the family or romance. Meaningful friendships are intentional on your part, often created with peers, and take time to develop. They grow out of such qualities as trust, honesty, respect, love, compassion, enjoyment, and support.

What do you mean when you refer to someone as a friend or, more importantly, as a best friend? We often call several people "friend" but only one or a few "best friend." As you will learn in this chapter, intimate, close, best-friend relationships are those that are reciprocal, deep, maintained over time, and with someone you share with often.

At certain points in your life, your friends can take on a more central role than family. For example, research suggests that on average adolescents spend 50 percent of their time with peers compared to only 20 percent with family.[10] Adolescent peers seem to have a particularly powerful influence on each other and rely on each other to fulfill needs.[11] Forming and maintaining friendships seems to help young people to learn appropriate social skills (i.e., how to treat people).[12]

The next time you are around other family members or friends, ask them who their friends were or are. Ask them to contemplate why their friends changed over the years, and what constitutes a "good friend."

Work Relationships

Interpersonal relationships at work influence you and the workplace. These types of relationships are most often peer co-worker relationships but may be superior-subordinate, mentor-protégé, or employee-client. Workplace relationships can positively influence productivity, provide other employment opportunities and professional growth, increase creativity and commitment, improve morale, reduce stress and job dissatisfaction, and lower employee turnover, to name just a few benefits.[13] However, workplace relationships that use power negatively or develop into complicated or prohibited romantic relationships can be detrimental to the individuals and the organization.

Online Relationships

Although not an exclusive type of relationship as the previous four can be, online relationships are becoming so common that they warrant individual consideration. You might maintain your family, romantic, friend, or work relationships online or you might have online-only relationships. Social and workplace networking sites (e.g., Facebook, Google+, Snapchat, Twitter, or LinkedIn), blogs, instant messaging, email, and video calling allow you to create and maintain relationships that otherwise might not develop or might end as people physically move in and out of your life. Interpersonal communication where the communicators are linked by technology is known as *mediated interpersonal communication.*

6.2 What Encourages Interpersonal Relationships?

What are some significant relationships you have cultivated over the years? Can you remember why you formed them and decided to maintain them? What roles did each relationship play in your life? What did you get out of each relationship? These questions are focusing on why you took the time to develop specific relationships.

Creating and maintaining healthy interpersonal relationships takes time and work. Indeed, these relationships are the most difficult to cultivate, but they give us the most in return. They are necessary from birth until death. As social work researcher Brené Brown notes:

> A deep sense of love and belonging is an irreducible need of all people. We are biologically, cognitively, physically, and spiritually wired to love, to be loved, and to belong. When those needs are not met, we don't function as we were meant to. We break. We fall apart. We numb. We ache. We hurt others. We get sick.[14]

Belongingness, reward, and attraction are all fundamentals that encourage interpersonal relationship bonding.

Belongingness

Later in this book, when you learn about audience analysis (Chapter 10), you will discover Maslow's hierarchy of needs, which demonstrates how people have specific needs or motivations that influence them to act in certain ways. Maslow classifies five needs, but one is especially important for this discussion—our *social needs*, or our strong motivation to feel that we belong, are loved, and can be close to others and have their support. In 1995, psychologists Roy Baumeister and Mark Leary formulated the **belongingness theory**, which states that humans have a strong fundamental motivation (not a want) for closeness and social belongingness.[15] Baumeister and Leary argue that the human desire to belong is innate and, therefore, universal; influences a broad range of behaviors; and leads to bad outcomes when prevented (e.g., poor health, mental stress or disorders, and poor reproduction levels).

Most humans will do just about anything to develop new and more rewarding relationships and to repair or dissolve ones that are defective. People resist losing or breaking attachments even when there isn't a pragmatic reason to maintain the bonds and will work to maintain them even when it is difficult. Interestingly, this could be the reason many of us spend hours scrolling through our Facebook accounts, reading tweets, viewing snaps, or sending instant messages.

Reward

The premise of the **social exchange theory** is that you when you put time and effort into something, you generally want something of equal or better quality in return (the cost-rewards).[16] Clearly, from this definition, you can see that social exchange is grounded in self-interest; people tend to maximize the reward and minimize the cost. For example, is it worth developing a workplace relationship with someone very different, to position yourself for a potential promotion or a lucrative contract? Cost-reward ratios change over time, and certain costs may be acceptable under certain situations. What might be a cost or reward to one person may not be to another.[17] Another important aspect is that it is an exchange—highlighting that you must be willing to give rewards if you want to receive them.[18]

Equality is important to this cost-reward element of relationships. The **equity theory** suggests that relational partners must both feel that the rewards and costs are balanced. If you have to give more and get less from the relationship, you feel *underbenefited*. If you receive more than you give, you are *overbenefited*.[19] In mediated interactions, your relational partner might assign a different level of reward to the interactions than you do. For example, your mother may find it more rewarding to hear your voice during a phone call, while you may prefer exchanging text messages.

Attraction

The **attraction theory** suggests that you form relationships on the basis of **interpersonal attraction**, or that you are drawn to another person for particular reasons.[20] As you learned in Chapter 4 (Objective 4.3), there are five main reasons for interpersonal attraction: *social attraction*, based on personal liking of another's personality; *physical attraction*, based on physical features and dress; *task attraction*, based on the ease of working with someone and his or her abilities; *background attraction*, based on similarities in your experiences; and *attitude attraction*, based on shared beliefs, values, and goals.[21] Elements that will help feed these orientations of attraction are proximity, similarity, complementarity, and attractiveness.

Proximity

Proximity (also known as *propinquity*) means *nearness* and interpersonally relates to increased exposure you have with others. The **propinquity effect** suggests that people tend to have interpersonal relationships with those they have more exposure to.[22] For example, your best friend as a child likely lived in your neighborhood or attended the same school you did. You likely dated someone who lived in your hometown, worked with you, or attended the same school. However, the use of technology has widened our understanding or proximity. It is easier to feel close to someone when using instant messaging and/or video calling.

Similarity

Similarity has to do with likeness, resemblance, and identification with others. This element of attraction suggests that you will be drawn to others who share your experiences, interests, and background.[23] In Chapters 2 and 5, you learned about Burke's notion of identification, or empathy with another. This works both ways. If you feel like you understand as much as possible about others' feelings, thoughts, motives, likes, attitudes, values, behaviors, and lives, you will be more attracted to developing relationships with them. Similarity can have a negative side as well. If you are too similar to someone, your behaviors might clash. This seems to happen in mother/daughter and father/son relationships. When considering similarity, you shouldn't be as rigid as looking for an exact clone. There will be things that are dissimilar and helpful to the relationship.[24] For example, one of you might be mechanically inclined and the other not, a difference that can help the nonmechanical person when it comes time to fix something. It can also offer an opportunity for the mechanically inclined individual to feel needed and an important part of the relationship. This is known as complementarity, the next element.

Complementarity

Complementarity is the state or quality of being complementary, or balanced opposites. This may seem to counter the notion of similarity. However, complementarity can be an effective encourager of bonding when the differences are seen as positive and a benefit to those in the relationship. For example, when I married my partner, he was overly organized and a bit obsessive about being tidy. On the other hand, I am a little disorganized and messy. After 24 years of living together, he is more accepting of untidiness and I am better at putting things in their rightful places. We each have benefited from living with the other.

This type of complementarity also works if both communicators view a difference as something they can accept, live with, grow with. It can have a bonding effect when two people connect over their dissimilarities. For example, my partner loves football and I love tennis. We each have learned to appreciate and even enjoy the other's favorite sport. This strengthens our love for each other.

Attractiveness

Attractiveness (as noted in Objective 4.3) has to do with your personal appearance and your personality. This element is important for the initiating stage of relationship development. You will be drawn to those who have appealing appearances and good personalities. You will resist connecting with those you do not find attractive and those who you think have horrible personalities. Likewise, according to Elaine Hatfield and Susan Sprecher, "people would prefer to date very attractive others, but, because rejection is costly, they end up choosing someone of about their same level of attraction."[25] There is evidence that matching on physical attractiveness occurs across numerous same-sex or opposite-sex relationships. For example, male friends, opposite-sex friends, couples who are dating, and committed couples were found to match with people approximately equal in attractiveness. However, evidence of female friends matching was less reliable.[26]

TIP: Attraction Isn't Everything

Keep in mind that always looking for certain attraction elements (such as appearance) can overshadow other awesome reasons for getting into or keeping a relationship. Think about what you are attracted to and what positive attractions you might be missing. For example, that hometown friend or romantic partner might be an easy relationship because of how similar she/he is or was to you, but a friend or partner with different core values and experiences might have a lot to offer as well. Likewise, your attraction might keep you from seeing major differences in the other person's view of relationship expectations/rewards. These types of attractions are often not healthy, mentally and physically, for you.

6.3 How Do Relationships Develop?

When you enter into a new relationship, you tend to go through a process of growing close to the other person. You take steps to start the relationship, you do things to test it out, and you act in ways to strengthen it. When relationships wane or don't work out, you go through a process of separation. These are predictable patterns to how your relationships develop.

In 1978, interpersonal communication scholar Mark Knapp proposed a dual system model of relationship growth (coming together) and deterioration (coming apart).[27] Knapp depicts the model as a two-way staircase, similar to the one here. The "coming together" encompasses the initiating, experimenting, intensifying, integrating, and bonding stages. The "coming apart" includes differentiating, circumscribing, stagnating, avoiding, and terminating stages. The figure helps you understand each stage.

Relational Maintenance

COMING TOGETHER

Bonding
Here, you often enter into a public ritual such as announcing commitments or engagements, getting married or holding commitment ceremonies, having children, creating business partnerships, and even, as friends, getting the same tattoo or sharing a living space.

Integrating
Where you become even more familiar with each other and might finish each other's sentences, have a special language, and so on. Romantic partners often initiate sexual contact and deep disclosure. Outsiders view you as a couple or friends, too. You tend to use "we" and "our."

Intensifying
If there is enough common ground and interest, you seek more intimacy, start to share more private information, and wait for the other to reciprocate. Spending more time together, touching more, and gift giving are just a few behaviors.

Experimenting
The stage where you explore, look for common ground, and learn about each other

Initiating
The initial contact where you form quick impressions (right or wrong) about the other person

The up arrow on the "coming together" side shows how the relationship escalates. The down arrow on the "coming apart" side demonstrates how a relationship can deteriorate. Although not all relationships will go completely through all the stages or the specific order suggested by the model, many will. Even the first two stages of deterioration are often experienced in healthy, long-term relationships as you grow close. Additionally, this model was developed from observing heterosexual romantic relationships but seems to apply to all types of relationships, including same-sex, friend, and workplace relationships. Can you identify moments in your life that signal some of these stages? Can you see how they work in your romantic, friendship, family, and work relationships?

> ### TIP: Don't Rush
> Next time you are in a relationship, try not to rush it. Move deliberately through each stage and use your knowledge to forge a stronger bond or establish whether or not the relationship is healthy.

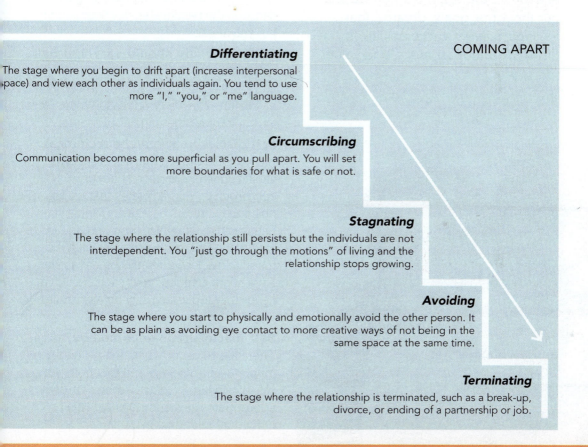

COMING APART

Differentiating
The stage where you begin to drift apart (increase interpersonal space) and view each other as individuals again. You tend to use more "I," "you," or "me" language.

Circumscribing
Communication becomes more superficial as you pull apart. You will set more boundaries for what is safe or not.

Stagnating
The stage where the relationship still persists but the individuals are not interdependent. You "just go through the motions" of living and the relationship stops growing.

Avoiding
The stage where you start to physically and emotionally avoid the other person. It can be as plain as avoiding eye contact to more creative ways of not being in the same space at the same time.

Terminating
The stage where the relationship is terminated, such as a break-up, divorce, or ending of a partnership or job.

6.4 How Does Self-Disclosure Influence Relationship Development?

Self-disclosure is the communicative process of revealing yourself to another person. It is the portal through which we build relationships. It allows us to move from being superficial strangers to best friends or intimate relational partners. It is when we share our thoughts, goals, dreams, fears, feelings, failures, successes, likes, dislikes, attitudes, beliefs, and values.

There are five main principles of self-disclosure:

- **Self-disclosure should be intentional.** Self-disclosure is the conscious revealing of what you want others to know about you.

- **Self-disclosure should be gradual.** Giving too much information too quickly can stop the relationship development or put you at risk.

- **Self-disclosure should vary.** Different situations and different relationships call for different types and depths of disclosure. Have a good reason to disclose and tailor your message appropriately.

- **Self-disclosure should be reciprocal.** Most people believe that self-disclosure should adhere to the social **norm of reciprocity**, which dictates that we are obligated to return a behavior with a similar behavior. For example, if you tell a friend your worst fear, you tend to expect that friend to disclose a significant fear as well. For a relationship to grow, each individual needs to self-disclose in generally similar ways.

- **Self-disclosure is governed by rules.** There are rules for when, where, and how much to self-disclose and to whom. All self-disclosure is governed by culturally appropriate rules and rules specific to individual relationships.

Increases Depth and Breadth of Intimacy

Psychlogists Irwin Altman and Dalmas Taylor formulated the social penetration theory to help explain how self-disclosure works. The **social penetration theory** states that over time, and as you develop your relationship with another person, you penetrate deeper into personal information and the identity of the other person.[28] This theory metaphorically works like peeling an onion. As you peel away the outer layer, you know basic and mostly observable things about the onion, and as you move to the center (or core) you know more individual detail. Self-disclosure allows people to do the same. In the public layers, information you offer or that is observable may include age, gender, ethnicity, employment, major, or hometown. In the personal layers, you convey more private information such as basic attitudes, beliefs, personal characteristics, and interests. In the intimate layers, you offer some limited insight into your significant values, beliefs, fears, and esteem as well as self-concept issues.

Social penetration is measured from depth to breadth. We can penetrate differently into each disclosure topic, such as those suggested in this figure (school, career, and love life). This is known as *depth of disclosure* and relates to the level you will allow the other person to penetrate to, or how personal your disclosure will get. *Breadth of disclosure* involves how many topics you will discuss with the other person. As your relationships grow, the depth and breadth of your disclosures and your intimacy will grow.

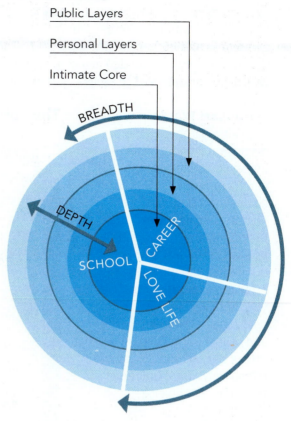

Public Layers
Personal Layers
Intimate Core
BREADTH
DEPTH
SCHOOL
CAREER
LOVE LIFE

Practicing Ethics: Respectful Disclosure

Because our lives and others' lives are so interwoven, be aware of how your disclosures might affect a third party. For example, if you tell a coworker that you are having a sexual relationship with someone, you have disclosed to your coworker very personal information about that other person—information he or she may not want public. Be cautious when your disclosure includes someone else.

Helps with Self-Awareness and Impression Management

An important part of being in any relationship is developing a heightened sense of self and managing the impressions others have of you (see Chapter 2 for more on self-awareness and impression management). The *Johari Window model* (also known as the disclosure/feedback model) is a helpful way to illustrate mutual understanding between relational partners and to assess how to improve your interpersonal relationships.

The *Johari Window model* is a self-awareness and disclosure model conceived by psychologists Joseph Luft and Harri Ingham ("Johari" comes from their first names—Joe and Harri) that is symbolically represented as a window with four panes, or quadrants.[29] Each pane represents information about you that falls in one of these categories: (1) known to you and others; (2) known to others but not you; (3) known to you only; or (4) unknown to you or anyone else.

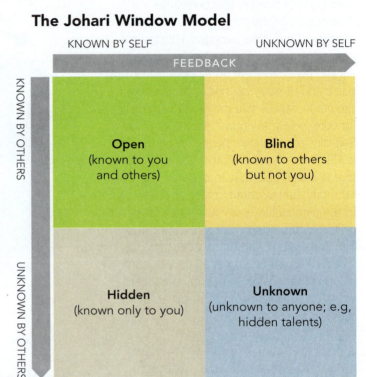

The Johari Window Model

KNOWN BY SELF   UNKNOWN BY SELF

FEEDBACK

KNOWN BY OTHERS

Open
(known to you and others)

Blind
(known to others but not you)

UNKNOWN BY OTHERS

Hidden
(known only to you)

Unknown
(unknown to anyone; e.g, hidden talents)

TIP: Foster Your Emotional IQ

Like improving your IQ, developing a healthy emotional intelligence quotient (EIQ) takes work. See the Improve your Communication section at the end of this chapter for advice on how to foster your EIQ.

The panes can change in size to reflect the evolving proportions of each pane as you disclose and develop your relationship. For example, as your relationship grows, the open pane should enlarge to demonstrate that your relational partner knows you better. It should be the largest quadrant. The blind pane will likely grow some as your partner sees new things in you that you don't. In healthy relationships, the knowledge represented in this pane helps you grow and develop through your relational partner's feedback. The hidden and unknown will grow smaller as you are exposed to each other more but will never completely disappear.

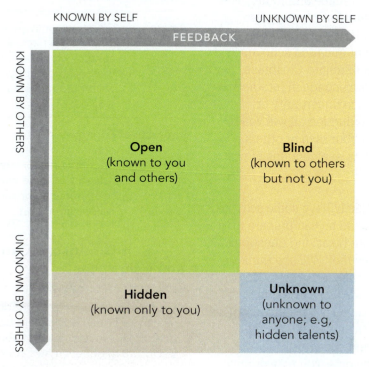

Closely related to the concepts behind the Johari window model is emotional intelligence.[30] Just as your IQ relates to overall knowledge abilities, your **emotional intelligence** relates to your abilities to recognize and manage your emotions and others' emotions within relationships. Answering such questions as these demonstrates how to expand and access your emotional intelligence.

- How do I view myself?
- How does my relational partner view me?
- How do I view my relational partner?
- How does my relational partner view herself or himself?

Exploring these questions leads to greater self-awareness and understanding between individuals as well as more robust and resilient relationships.

Reduces Uncertainty

As Knapp's relationship development model suggests, relationships begin with the assessing and discovering of each other through small talk or chitchat. You enter into this assessing/discovering phase to determine the worthiness of the relationship and to reduce ambiguity. The **uncertainty reduction theory** (also known as the *initial interaction theory*), developed by communication scholars Charles Berger and Richard Calabrese, asserts that you will engage in interaction as a means to reduce uncertainty or ambiguity.[31] This reduction allows you to predict or forecast your own or others' behavior or to create explanations of past behavior.[32]

For example, you likely have some self-talk going on in your head as you prepare for a first date. You might be asking questions such as *Will he like me? Will she think I am stupid? Will he like my dress? Will she like the restaurant?* All of these questions relate to the stress you are feeling about the ambiguity of the situation. As you engage in talk—and specifically self-disclosure—on the date, you may or may not be able to predict the answers to some of these questions. If the interaction occurs in a mediated situation, the potential for ambiguity can create even higher uncertainty. Berger argues that people tend to use *passive, active,* and *interactive* strategies to gain uncertainty reducing information. The following table explains these strategies.

Berger's Uncertainty Reducing Strategies

Passive	When you observe the environment and person to obtain information—for example, observing how your date seems to feel about the restaurant
Active	When you actively seek information through direct contact—for example, asking the best friend of your date what a good restaurant choice would be
Interactive	Engaging in actual conversation to gain information—for example, asking your date what restaurants he or she likes before going out

TIP: Self-Disclosure Can Be Risky Business

Self-disclosure comes with some risks.

- Your relational partner might decide to reject you or the relationship because of what he or she learns about you. Your disclosure might even hurt your partner.

- Your relational partner might find it difficult to reciprocate with similar disclosure and might become uncomfortable because he or she feels obligated. This may lead to avoidance or ending the relationship.

- What you tell others about yourself opens you up for harm if it is divulged to the wrong person or your partner uses it against you. Knowledge about your inner self can be powerful in the wrong hands.

Self-Check: Assess Your Levels of Self-Disclosure

On a sheet of paper, use two lines to divide the sheet into four sections. Label the first section with the name of a close family member; label the second with a close friend's name; the third with a coworker, boss, or acquaintance; and the fourth with "Post Online."

Close family member	Close friend
Coworker	Post online

Consider the following topics. Under each heading in your chart, write the topics you are likely to self-disclose or discuss to each person listed or post under each heading. When finished, draw a line under the last topic in each section. Next, write the statements that you are unlikely to self-disclose or discuss with each person or post.

Potential Self-Disclosure Topics

- My political views
- My views on abortion or the death penalty
- How much money I have in my bank account
- My biggest regret
- What I have done that might be illegal
- My feelings toward people who are different from me
- If I am in a relationship, my feelings about it
- My perfect romantic partner
- My sexual activity (current and past)
- How many sexual partners
- Naming my sexual partners
- My sexual fantasies
- My health
- My fears
- My drinking and drug usage

Now, consider the following questions:

- Who are you more likely to self-disclose with?
- Can you see a reason for why you self-disclose with that particular person? Does he or she disclose similarly with you?
- Do you tend to "tell all" to almost everyone? How might that influence your future relationships or put you at risk?
- How high is your level of self-disclosure online? Now that you have written down all these topics, are there some that you do or will consider taboo for posting about online? Can you live with the consequences of that information being available to just about anyone and into the future? What might some of those consequences be?

6.5 How Does Culture Shape Your Relationships?

Think about the last time you personally interacted with someone from another culture. Initially, you might have worried about your language choices or how to greet them. As your relationship continued, you began to worry about what topics you could discuss, if touching was appropriate, or why your friend rarely self-disclosed. This situation seems fraught with ambiguity and excitement all at the same time.

Clearly, the opening paragraph hints at how developing and maintaining any type of interpersonal relationship between individuals from different cultures can take more work. As you move from being just strangers or acquaintances to a more established relationship, the differences you encounter might increase and often become more crucial to relationship development. A person's ethnicity will likely be an influencing factor. However, co-cultures such as age, religion, and especially gender will shape how the relationship develops and what it becomes. Successful cross-cultural interpersonal communication requires diplomacy, an understanding of how culture prescribes relationship rules, and an understanding of how varying cultural dimensions influence behavior.

Requires Diplomacy

Later in this chapter, you will learn techniques for being a better all-around interpersonal communicator. Those techniques often help with intercultural relationships as well. Here are some guidelines for specifically negotiating cross-cultural relationships.

- Recognize that the ambiguity of the situation is unavoidable and will create a certain level of anxiety. Don't let your anxiety create ethnocentrism, intolerance, prejudice, or hatred.

- Try to set realistic expectations. Don't expect to agree on everything and accept the same behaviors.

- Attempt to educate yourself. Ask questions and seek out answers. Be willing to accept feedback and offer it.

- Don't make assumptions about how you are alike or differ.

- Treat your relational partner as an individual, not a stereotype.

- Remember that for many cultures and co-cultures, the situation can dictate or extensively change what is appropriate behavior or talk.

- Be willing to do things that affirm your and your partner's cultural identities.

- Respond to differences with sensitivity, politeness, willingness to adjust, and collaboration.

- Maintain a childlike curiosity. Be open-minded.

Prescribes Relationship Rules

All communication interaction is governed by rules. Rules are standards that help us act appropriately and effectively, telling us what "behavior is obligated, preferred, or prohibited in certain contexts."[33] There are rules that regulate each type of relationship (family, romance, friendships, workplace, and online; see Objective 6.7). Cross-cultural interaction adds another facet.

In 1980, communication scholar Susan Shimanoff identified the **rules theory**, which claims that interaction is most successful when the relational partners share the same rules.[34] One of the main reasons intercultural relationships appear challenging is that cultures tend to prescribe many of the rules regulating interaction—and when cultures rub up against each other, those rules can create uncertainty or even conflict. For example, a rule that is positive between friends in your culture (e.g., placing your arm around your friend's shoulders) might be negative in another. Rules in romantic and work relationships can especially vary from culture to culture. Mediated interactions, too, are subject to cultural rules. For instance, one culture might accept revealing lots of personal information or being negative about others in such forms as blogs, while another culture may find that extremely inappropriate.[35]

Influences Behavior Due to Varying Cultural Dimensions

The cultural dimensions discussed in Chapter 1 are often the reason for differing relationships rules. Geert Hofstede and Edward T. Hall defined seven cultural dimensions. These are high power versus low power, individualist versus collectivist, competitive versus nurturing, high-uncertainty avoidance versus low-uncertainty avoidance, long-term orientation versus short-term orientation, high context versus low context, and indulgence versus restraint.

See Objective 1.7 for a detailed discussion of each dimension.

Let's take Japan as an example. According to the website for The Hofstede Centre, Japan ranks somewhat high as a collectivist society; below average on uncertainty avoidance; high on restraint and power; and as one of the highest on the masculine, high-uncertainty avoidance, and long-term orientation dimensions.[36] On the other hand, the United States ranks fairly low on power and high on masculinity, favors the short term, prefers indulgence, and is one of the highest on the individualist dimension.[37] So, for instance, because of their difference in power distance, a student from Japan will likely treat a teacher with formal respect and prefer to speak when the teacher initiates conversation, while a U.S. student will prefer being treated as an equal to the teacher and is more willing to ask questions or debate.[38]

Intercultural communication researcher Min-Sun Kim notes that, for Japan, communication competency in these dimension rankings means being proficient at sending and receiving subtle, understated messages.[39] Likewise, Kim observes that meaningless or careless utterances are not respected or valued in Japan and that the Japanese embrace silence.[40] For the United States, competency is grounded in correctness and being highly communicative (verbally and nonverbally).[41] Silence is awkward, threatening, and unproductive for the U.S. culture, where the development of interpersonal relationships depends heavily on talk.[42]

William Gudykunst and Yuko Matsumoto, also intercultural communication scholars, argue that four of Hofstede's and Hall's cultural dimensions seem to be notably linked to interpersonal communication. The four significant dimensions are:

- individualist versus collectivist
- high-uncertainty avoidance versus low-uncertainty avoidance
- high power versus low power
- competitive versus nurturing

The following table offers selected relationship differences related to these four dimensions. Keep in mind that the individual you interact with might not adhere to these generalizations.

Select Cultural Differences in Intercultural Relationships[43]

Individualist versus collectivist	Individualists focus on self and personal happiness, will engage in competitive behavior, and cherish independence. They tend to self-disclose and exaggerate. Silence is discomforting.
	Collectivists emphasize group goals, needs, and views over their own; create strong bonds; have strong in-group relationships that influence their behavior; and tend to limit self-disclosure and be understated. They are even less likely to disclose in computer-mediated interactions. This may be due to collectivists distrusting online self-disclosure more than individualists do.[44] Collectivists are less likely to offer true feelings but will pay more attention to others' behavior. Silence can indicate truthfulness, embarrassment, or disapproval.
High-uncertainty avoidance versus low-uncertainty avoidance	High-uncertainty avoidance cultures tend to express emotions, worry about the future, view loyalty as a virtue, and be very ritualistic with strangers.
	Low-uncertainty avoidance cultures have lower stress levels, accept dissent better, and take risks.
High power versus low power	High-power cultures value obedience and conformity and will display a more authoritarian attitude. Power can be coercive. Wealth and status tend to be stressed.
	Low-power cultures tend to blur the lines between superiors and subordinates, will challenge and question, and believe that expert or legitimate power are more acceptable than coercive power. Happiness, knowledge, and love are stressed.
Competitive versus nurturing	Competitive cultures are highly motivated to succeed, especially at work, and it can interfere with personal things. May view same-sex relationships (friend or romantic) as a threat to traditional views and thus as problematic, which leads to self-disclosure, nonverbal expressiveness, attraction, and similarity issues.
	Nurturing cultures tend to focus more on relationships, feelings, quality of life, equality, and care for others. They tend to disclose more.

6.6 How Does Gender Impact Your Relationships?

"You are being too emotional, Liz!"

"Jeff, you never tell me how you feel about us!"

"Act like a man, don't cry!"

"I hate my boss! She is so aggressive, doesn't care about us, and only worries about deadlines."

"He is such a girl. He hates sports."

"Dude, pink is for girls!"

"Hey, girls can't drive."

Gender is a social construction or classification of what it means to be female or male in a specific culture at a particular time. The current Western cultural construct of **femininity** uses such qualifiers as nurturing, emotional, beautiful, gentle, sweet, timid, and submissive. The construct of **masculinity** uses unemotional, strong, brave, fearless, self-reliant, aggressive, successful, and determined. From birth, you begin the process of forming your **gender identity**, or your "view of self related to feminine or masculine traits, as well as one's vision of the roles or functions of people within a given culture."[45] Your gender identity and that of others begins to influence your behavior. This is especially true for opposite-sex romantic relationships, which are likely more grounded in the construct of femininity and masculinity—for example, the idea that men should ask women out or that women should date with the goal to marry. The following table shows some of the differences in these constructs. Keep in mind, though, that men and women are still more similar than dissimilar. For example, both men and women need to feel respected, to achieve and grow, to belong, to feel safe and secure, and to have a positive self-image.

Gender Differences and Relationships[46]

Men	Women
In Friendships	
Boys tend to disclose the same amount of information to friends of either sex. Men disclose more to women.	Girls tend to disclose less to boys than other girls. But young female adults disclose the same to both men and women. Overall, adult women disclose more than men.
Men tend to show less physical affection or offer fewer comments to male friends. They tend to use less verbal communication with male friends and talk about impersonal topics (e.g., sports). They tend to grow closer by doing things.	Women use verbal communication to create intimacy in all types of relationships. They tend to form more intimate female-female friendships than men do with other men.
Men disclosing to other male friends tend to use "joke speak" to frame serious talk or feelings in humor.	Women provide their female friends more emotional support than men do.
In Romantic Relationships	
During the early stages of relationship development, men typically initiate touch and sexual intimacy.	Women tend to discuss the nature of the relationship and engage in relationship maintenance activities more than men do.
Men tend to experience unrequited love and "love at first sight" more than women.	Women tend to experience more intense and volatile emotions.
Men express higher levels of sexual desire and have a more permissive attitude toward casual sex.	Women express slightly higher general sexual satisfaction. Both women and men are most satisfied when in an ongoing relationship.
In opposite-sex relationships, men are more assertive and will take the lead in sexual interaction.	Women tend to desire relationship support (maintaining and fostering) from their partners.
Gay men in a committed relationship are more likely than same-sex couples to have sex with another partner outside of the primary relationship. However, all men report more sexual partners than women do.	Lesbians are more likely than gay men to develop relationships with partners who were first their friends.
Men tend to view "friends with benefits" relationships as casual and emphasize the "benefits" aspect.	Women tend to view "friends with benefits" relationships as involved and emotional and emphasize the "friend" aspect.

6.7 How Can You Improve Your Relationships?

In *Harry Potter and the Order of the Phoenix*, J.K. Rowling wrote, "Indifference and neglect often do much more damage than outright dislike."[47] Indeed, this is often true of interpersonal relationships. If you do not find your relationships interesting or assign them significance or importance in your life, or if you simply ignore them, you will likely do as much harm as showing outright hatred or displeasure. Strong relationships are hard work but worth it.

Be Sensitive to Dialectical Tensions

Communication theorists Leslie Baxter and Barbara Montgomery suggest in their ***relational dialectics theory*** that relationships are not linear, are characterized by change, and are full of contradictions—or dialectics—that interact with each other in a "both/and" manner.[48] These dialectics, and they are numerous, pull at each other over time, creating tension in the relationship. They can be internal tensions between the partners or external tensions between the couple and larger community. Because we are talking about what you can do to improve your relationships, we will focus on the internal, or the tensions that occur within the privacy of the relationship. There are three primary internal relational dialectics:

- connection versus autonomy
- predictability versus novelty
- openness versus closedness

These tensions can occur in any type of relationship. The following table will help you understand each and offers some insight in to how to manage them. The overall management goal is to embrace the fact that both sides exist and to find a balance in navigating them.

Primary Internal Relational Dialectics

Dialectics	What Is It?	How Do You Manage It?
Connection versus autonomy	Relational strain created by the contradiction of needing to feel connected or interdependent versus autonomous and independent. For example, two young brothers want to share a bedroom but mark their own spaces within it.	Relational partners must realize that there must be boundaries for autonomy. Make rituals that mark connectedness (e.g., date night or family dinner night).
Predictability versus novelty	Relational strain created by the routine and the uniqueness of relationship. For example, John always fixes dinner on days Sam works late but decides to make a special romantic dinner for no particular reason.	Set up routines that mark the security and stability of the relationship (e.g., call when you are going to be late, kiss your partner goodbye in the morning). Use the element of surprise to bring a freshness to the relationship (e.g., cook something new together, take a last-minute getaway).
Openness versus closedness	Relational strain created by openly self-disclosing and being private. For example, Cooper doesn't think he should open Terry's purse to get money out of it even if she tells him it is okay, whereas Terry doesn't believe they should have things that are off-limits to the other.	Realize there must be somewhat equal disclosure between partners for relationship development. Don't disclose too much too soon. Embrace the fact that some secrets can be healthy as long as they won't harm the other. Constantly evaluate and be honest about your trust level of your partner.

Employ Maintenance Behaviors

Relational maintenance behaviors theory illustrates that we tend to use specific behaviors to effectively maintain relationships. Laura Stafford and Dan Canary observed five maintenance behaviors that can help you with your interpersonal relationships:

1. Positivity, or being friendly, cheerful, and supportive. For example, if Modhi is cheery, happy, lively, and kind, he will likely build his relationships.

2. Openness, or willingness to discuss the relationship. If Bhavin is willing to talk about himself and the relationship, he will likely build a stronger relationship.

3. Assurances, or offering messages that underscore your love, faithfulness, and commitment. When Joe reminds Sara that he loves her, wants to do things, and is committed, their relationship is more likely to grow.

4. Social networks, or bringing friends and family into the relationship. When Sherry takes Edin home to meet her friends and family, she is demonstrating the importance of the relationship to Edin.

5. Sharing tasks in the relationship and daily life. Doing simple everyday tasks such as fixing meals, taking out the trash, washing dishes, and mowing the lawn proves that you are willing to do the mundane things, too, for a healthy relationship.[49]

Remember Your Ethics

Sad to say, not everyone is ethical and that fact seems particularly harsh when dealing with the intimacy of interpersonal relationships. In Chapter 1, you learned the importance of being an ethical communicator—that you should be self-monitoring, truthful, knowledgeable, and caring. In interpersonal relationships, being unethical with any of these factors leads to deception, disconfirming messages, jealousy, and power issues.

Regulate Deception

Ironically, deception is extremely common aversive interpersonal behavior.[50] Online, people find it easier to deceive and will lie about identity, manipulate data or information, make false promises, or commit outright fraud. Types of deception related to relationships are *lies*, or the making up or twisting of information or outright cheating; *exaggerations*, or overstatements (*white lies* fall into this type); *playings*, or jokes (teasing, kidding, tricking); *concealment* (disguising, evading, omitting); *equivocation*, or being deliberately vague; or *understatement*, or softening the truth (*doublespeak* is a form of understatement).[51] As the saying goes, honesty is the best policy. Detecting deception is very difficult. Getting to know your relational partners by spending time with them is the best way to recognize potential deception leakages (language choices and nonverbal behaviors) that might signal deception by your partners.

Be Confirming

Individuals have a fundamental need to be validated by others.[52] We can foster this by using **confirming messages**, which are verbal and nonverbal messages that communicate empathy, worth, regard, respect for the other. The quality of these messages is more important than quantity. For example, you might say to someone, "I can't imagine how hard that was for you. Is there anything I can do to help?" **Disconfirming messages** are verbal and nonverbal messages that deny validation of the other person. For example: "Later, I don't have time for that now."

Check Your Jealousy

Called the "green-eyed monster" by Shakespeare, **jealousy** is the emotional resentment toward or suspicious fear of unfaithfulness of others, which feeds feelings of hurt, fear, anger, and mistrust. Jealousy in relationships often involves the presence of a third person. For example, Kian is jealous of how Steve flirts with Gretchen, or Youssef is jealous of how his boss treats his coworker Melvin. Unfounded or intense jealousy can be detrimental to a relationship. Evaluate your emotions critically, be emotionally intelligent, and discuss your feelings.

TIP: Networking

Growing professional relationships will build your career. When possible, meet new people in your workplace. A simple "hello" or current news discussion can be a start to something bigger.

Respect Power

In Chapter 7, you will learn how power comes in different forms and how it relates to conflict. For now, it is important to realize power is present in all interactions; power can have positive and negative influences; and it is important to work at balancing power between relational partners. **Power** is the ability to produce intended effects and the ability to influence the behavior of another person.[53]

For example, your parents had the power to determine who did which household chores or when you had to be home; your boss determines who gets a day off or a raise; and you may have the power over your roommate or friends to determine where you will go to eat or what movie you will watch. Abuse of power is unhealthy for any relationship. Work to make joint decisions in the relationship, minimize dominance, and use your power only when absolutely necessary. Do not use power to punish. On social media, where connectivity can sometimes give you power over others, do not harass, bully, or compromise those you have a relationship with. If you find yourself always in the subordinate position of the power equation, work to decrease your dependence on the other person and to increase your knowledge as well as connections to others outside of the relationship.

Play by the Rules When Appropriate

As noted earlier, relationships will develop and grow stronger if you play by a few expected rules. Here are some rules for each type of relationship you might encounter.

Workplace

The best way to discover workplace rules is to observe the culture and what is appropriate or not and to pay attention to formal organization documents (handbooks, memos, procedures, etc.). However, here are a few broad guidelines related to workplace relationships.

1. Respect others. Don't bully or harass others—especially do not sexually harrass or engage in workplace violence. Report such behavior.
2. Promote workplace harmony and help reduce conflict. Look for places to connect and agree.
3. Be competent and reliable.
4. Value the knowledge and strengths of others. Support the self-worth of others.
5. Be a productive team member.
6. Be honest and have integrity.
7. Be professional.
8. Be cautious about starting a workplace romance (it may influence your work or may be grounds for dismissal).
9. Above all, listen effectively.

Romantic

Communication studies scholar Leslie Baxter identified eight major romantic relationship rules.[54]

1. Acknowledge each other's individual identities and lives outside of the relationship (hobbies, activities, friendships, or work).
2. Express similar attitudes, beliefs, values, and interests (ultimately, you have to have more similarities than differences).
3. Enhance each other's self-worth and self-esteem (celebrate achievements and comfort during difficult times).
4. Be open, genuine, and authentic with each other (self-disclose and mean what you say).
5. Remain loyal and faithful.
6. Have substantial share time.
7. Put equal effort into the relationship.
8. Experience a mysterious and inexplicable "magic" in each other's presence (you must have and cultivate chemistry).

Family[55]

In your family relationships, you should:

1. Acknowledge each other as individuals.
2. Work to build family cohesion or emotional bonding.
3. Recognize family leadership, role relationships, and rules.
4. Focus on the family strengths.
5. Try to be consistent in your interactions.
6. Know what topics are inappropriate and with whom.
7. Cultivate family communication by self-disclosing, being specific, and listening effectively.
8. Be sensitive to family secrets.
9. Be kind and civil. That might seem a given but can often be forgotten in times of stress.

Friends

Studying across several cultures, anthropologists Michael Argyle and Monika Henderson identified 13 friendship rules that seem to be the strongest.[56] They are:

1. Give help when needed.
2. Respect privacy.
3. Keep confidences.
4. Trust and confide in each other.
5. Stand up for your friend.
6. Don't publically criticize.
7. Offer emotional support.
8. Strive to make your friend happy.
9. Be tolerant.
10. Don't be jealous or critical of your friend's other relationships.
11. Share good news.
12. Don't nag.
13. Repay debts, favors, and compliments.

Online

The digital ethics advice given in Chapter 1 will be helpful here as well. Netiquette advice specific to online interpersonal relationships includes:

1. Adhere to the same rules you would for a nonmediated relationship.
2. Set ground rules with the other person that will keep you safe and respected.
3. Recognize that some people are not comfortable in a mediated world. Don't use your power or comfort to be powerful over them.
4. Remember that some social sites are not private. Respect the privacy of your online partner.
5. Make your online interaction meaningful. Don't let the novelty of mediated interaction cut into body-to-body interaction.
6. Be civil and honest. Online stalking or cyberbullying is illegal and can be extremely detrimental.
7. Recognize that online relationships have cultural expectations and rules, too.
8. If you couldn't say it in person, don't say it online.
9. Listen.

Chapter 6 Review

Key Questions

6.1 What Is an Interpersonal Relationship?

Objective 6.1: DISCUSS WHAT CONSTITUTES INTERPERSONAL RELATIONSHIPS

Interpersonal communication is the verbal and nonverbal interaction between individuals, usually two, who are in some sort of significant relationship developing over time. A relationship is the state of connectedness, with a heightened emotional involvement and commitment, that we have with another person or persons. It is revealed in how we behave toward and feel about them. All relationships have some level of intimacy. The most common relationships are family, romantic, friends, work, and online.

See pages 152–155.

6.2 What Encourages Interpersonal Relationships?

Objective 6.2: IDENTIFY FACTORS THAT ENCOURAGE INTERPERSONAL RELATIONSHIPS

Belongingness, reward, and attraction are all fundamentals that encourage bonding in relationships. The *belongingness theory* states that humans have a strong fundamental motivation (not a want) for closeness and social belongingness. The *social exchange theory* suggests that when you put time and effort into something, you generally want something of equal or better quality in return (the cost-rewards). The *attraction theory* suggests that you form relationships on the basis of interpersonal attraction or that you are drawn to another person for particular reasons.

See pages 156–159.

6.3 How Do Relationships Develop?

Objective 6.3: EXPLAIN HOW RELATIONSHIPS GROW AND WANE

In 1978, interpersonal communication scholar Mark Knapp proposed a dual system model of relationship growth (coming together) and deterioration (coming apart). The coming together stages of Knapp's model are:

- Initiating—You form quick impressions through initial contact.
- Experimenting—You explore, look for common ground, and learn about each other.
- Intensifying—You seek more intimacy.
- Integrating—You reach a noticeable familiarity with each other that is evident by outsiders as well.
- Bonding—You seal the relationship with public rituals.

The coming apart stages are:

- Differentiating—You begin drifting apart.
- Circumscribing—Communication becomes superficial and you set more boundaries.
- Stagnating—You move toward independence and just go through the motions.
- Avoiding—You begin to physically and mentally avoid each other.
- Terminating—The relationship ends.

See pages 160–161.

6.4 How Does Self-Disclosure Influence Relationship Development?

Objective 6.4: **DISCUSS HOW SELF-DISCLOSURE WORKS WITHIN RELATIONSHIPS**

Self-disclosure is the communicative process of revealing yourself to another person. It is the portal through which we build relationships. Self-disclosure:

- Increases the depth and breadth of intimacy
- Helps with self-awareness and impression management
- Reduces uncertainty

See pages 162–167.

6.5 How Does Culture Shape Your Relationship?

Objective 6.5: **EXAMINE HOW CULTURE SHAPES RELATIONSHIPS**

Culture adds a dimension to relationships through:

- Requiring diplomacy. To negotiate cross-cultural interpersonal relationships, you need to recognize that ambiguity is unavoidable; set realistic expectations; educate yourself; don't make assumptions or stereotype; consider the situation; and affirm your partner's cultural identity. Be sensitive, polite, and open-minded.
- Prescribing relationship rules. All interaction is governed by rules and, according to the *rules theory*, interaction is most successful when the relational partners share the same rules. Cross-cultural relational partners must learn to negotiate these differences to be successful.

- Influencing an individual's behavior due to varying cultural dimensions, especially individualist versus collectivist; high-uncertainty avoidance versus low-uncertainty avoidance; high power versus low power; and competitive versus nurturing.

See pages 168–171.

6.6 How Does Gender Impact Your Relationship?

Objective 6.6: **EXPLORE HOW GENDER IMPACTS RELATIONSHIPS**

Because gender is a social and cultural construction of what it means to be female and male, as individuals develop a gender identity, that identity begins to influence behavior relationships—especially friendships and romantic relationships.

See pages 172–173.

6.7 How Can You Improve Your Relationships?

Objective 6.7: **ARTICULATE STRATEGIES FOR IMPROVING RELATIONSHIPS**

If you do not find your relationships interesting or assign them significance or importance in your life, or if you simply ignore them, you will likely do as much harm as showing outright hatred or displeasure. Valuable relationships are hard work but worth it. Try to:

- Be sensitive to dialectical tensions
- Employ maintenance behaviors
- Remember your ethics
- Play by the rules when appropriate

See pages 174–179.

Key Terms

interpersonal communication (152)
relationship (152)
intimacy (152)
belongingness theory (157)
social exchange theory (157)
equity theory (157)
attraction theory (158)
interpersonal attraction (158)
propinquity effect (158)
initiating (160)
experimenting (160)
intensifying (160)
integrating (160)
bonding (160)
differentiating (160)
circumscribing (160)
stagnating (160)
avoiding (160)
terminating (160)
self-disclosure (162)
norm of reciprocity (162)
social penetration theory (163)
Johari Window model (164)
emotional intelligence (165)
uncertainty reduction theory (166)
rules theory (169)
gender (172)
femininity (172)
masculinity (172)
gender identity (172)
relational dialectics theory (174)
relational maintenance behaviors
   theory (176)
confirming messages (177)
disconfirming messages (177)
jealousy (177)
power (177)

Improve Your Communication

Search the Internet for information on emotional intelligence (or the four branches of emotional intelligence) and study what it is. The University of New Hampshire's web page about emotional intelligence, by John D. Mayer and others, could be a good starting point. See www.unh.edu/emotional_intelligence/ and explore the links "What Is Emotional Intelligence?" and "Improving Emotional Knowledge and Social Effectiveness." Now, consider the following questions:

1. What are your emotional intelligence strengths and weaknesses?

2. How might you improve on your weaknesses and capitalize more on your strengths?

3. If you are in a close relationship (family, romantic, or friend), what do you think your relational partner's emotional intelligence strengths and weaknesses are?

4. Can you remember a time when either a weakness of yours or your partner's caused issues in the relationship? How could you have negotiated that issue better, given your knowledge now about emotional intelligence?

Apply Your Knowledge

1. Make a list of what would be too much to self-disclose on a first date, to your parents, during a job interview, to a coworker, in class, and on a social site. Ask a friend and someone older than you to do the same. Compare and evaluate what you thought was acceptable. Are there some items on your list that you should reconsider as appropriate?

2. When, where, and to whom might it be unsafe to self-disclose?

3. Reconsider the relationship maintenance behaviors in Objective 6.7. Make a list of behaviors you could work on within specific relationships that would grow and/or improve the relationship.

4. What confirming and disconfirming messages do you use (see Objective 6.7)? How could you increase confirming messages and decrease disconfirming messages?

5. Considering what you know know about listening (Chapter 5) and relationships (this chapter), explain this quotation by actor Henry Winkler:

   The ear is the center of all relationships. Listening is the beginning and the end.[57]

Other Resources

Here are some sources to help you improve your interpersonal skills and relationships:

Readings on Relationships

Chen, Guo-Ming. "The Impact of New Media on Intercultural Communication in Global Context." *China Media Research* 8.2 (2012): 1–10. Print.

Firestone, Robert W., and Joyce Catlett. *Ethics of Interpersonal Relationships.* London: Karnac Books, 2009.

Kowalski, Robin M., ed. *Behaving Badly: Aversive Behaviors in Interpersonal Relationships.* Washington: American Psychological Association, 2001. Print.

Rosh, Lisa, and Lynn Offermann. "Be Yourself, but Carefully." *Harvard Business Review* 91.10 (2013): 135–39. Print.

Interpersonal Communication Skills Test

- psychologytoday.tests.psychtests.com/ take_test.php?idRegTest=3199

Emotional Intelligence Information

Massari, Lauri. "Teaching Emotional Intelligence." *Leadership* 40.5 (2011): 8–12. Print.

- www.unh.edu/emotional_intelligence/

Interpersonal Relationships in the Workplace

- humanresources.about.com/od/ interpersonal-relationships/
- managementstudyguide.com/ interpersonal-relationship-at-workplace.htm

Chapter 7
Conflict

7.1 What Is Interpersonal Conflict?

"We always fight."

"We clashed over what was right."

"He hates me."

"She doesn't love me."

"We disagreed about everything."

"We are at war!"

When you use such language as seen in these examples, you are expressing potential responses to conflict.

According to communication scholars Joyce Hocker and William Wilmot, "***Conflict*** is an expressed struggle between at least two interdependent parties who perceive incompatible goals, scarce resources, and interference from others in achieving their goals."[1] Conflict happens in all relationships. It can be as simple as disagreeing on "What's for dinner?" or as complex as major clashes that end up with countries declaring war, companies collapsing, or relationships ending. However, keep in mind that conflict is not always evil or destructive (usually unresolved or repeated conflict)— and, therefore, it is not always something you should avoid. Conflict has a positive side, too.

Conflict has the potential to help you develop stronger, healthier relationships. As William Wilmot said, "What determines the course of a relationship, whether at work or at home, is in a large measure determined by how successful the participants move through conflict episodes."[2] For example, if you and a partner manage to effectively negotiate small conflicts (even as minor as where to eat), you will learn that you have the skills necessary for surviving larger, more stressful conflicts. At school or in the workplace, conflict can help teams think creatively, especially when making decisions and solving problems. Conflict can be constructive.

Not all conflicts can be resolved, but most can be navigated in a manner that is healthy and inspires relationship growth. Likewise, a feeling of euphoria, joy, ecstasy, or bliss often follows the successful navigation of conflict, which can increase your desire to be connected or close to the other person. You may want to relish in and celebrate the joy of overcoming the conflict. Conflict can help you grow as an individual by teaching you how to be a better thinker or debater and increasing your knowledge (i.e., you learn that there are other options). All of this is constructive conflict.

Economist Albert Hirschman and psychologists Caryl Rusbult and Isabella Zembrodt created a ***response typology*** to show one way to look at the constructive and destructive responses to conflict. They noted that we respond to conflict according to the dimensions of constructive/destructive and active/passive, with the potential responses of exit, neglect, voice, or loyalty.[3] When commitment is high, and we are happy and satisfied with a relationship, we are more likely to employ constructive responses.[4]

Active

Exit	**Voice**
Exit is active destructive behavior that ends in threatening to leave or leaving (e.g., walking or moving out, yelling and hitting, threatening to quit a job, or actually resigning or transferring).	Voice is active constructive behavior that tries to improve the conflict conditions (e.g., changing behavior, discussing feelings, trying to solve problems, asking others for advice with conflict).
Neglect	**Loyalty**
Neglect is passive destructive behavior that ignores active engagement of the issue and leads to deterioration of the relationship (e.g., letting things get out of control, often being late or absent altogether, doing just enough to get by).	Loyalty is passive constructive behavior demonstrated by optimistically waiting for conditions to improve (e.g., standing by a person or employer during turbulent times).

Destructive ——————————— Constructive

Passive

7.2 What Are Common Conflict Types?

Conflict related to how to pay family monthly bills may seem radically different from managers dealing with the cost of hiring new employees or the rising cost of materials. The personal issues you might feel with family money issues are different from the more removed business issues. However, how we classify conflict, and even somewhat how we respond to or manage it, is very similar across situations. This section will help you organize conflict into three specific types as noted by communication scholar Rebecca Burnett.[5]

Affective Conflict

Affective conflict (also known as relational or emotional conflict) involves interpersonal disagreement prejudices, antagonism, emotional tensions, trust or respect issues, attitudes, personality or power clashes, and other interpersonal struggles unrelated to a task or procedure. Questions like the following hint at affective conflicts: Do I like this person? Does he frustrate me? Do I see her as untrustworthy and/or undeserving? Do I ignore ideas proposed by certain people because of how I feel toward them? Am I unnecessarily harsh or critical of them, their actions, and/or their suggestions because of my feelings? Dealing with this type of conflict can be difficult. It is best handled when both parties recognize it and create straightforward methods or procedures for interacting.

Practicing Ethics: Pseudo Conflict

Have you ever argued with someone about something, only to realize you both were in agreement or saying the same thing? This is *pseudo conflict*, which occurs when people *think* there is a problem or disagreement, while in reality, there isn't. Be careful of jumping to conclusions. Ask the other person to explain his or her behavior, and be aware of how each of you is reacting. Be open.[6]

Substantive Conflict

Substantive conflict (also known as task or cognitive conflict) involves disagreement over issues related to the decision-making process. For example, parties may be considering or struggling with questions such as: What are the problems or issues? What are the solutions? What information or evidence is there? Relational partners and groups making effective use of this type of conflict use it to solve problems, induce creativity, form plans, and resolve misunderstandings or misinterpretations. There are four categories of disagreement that fall under substantive conflict.

- *Situational disagreement:* Do we have enough money to pay for a new car? How do we prevent low revenue in the next quarter?

- *Goal disagreement:* Should our family attend a weekly religious/worship service? Should our company become a "green company"?

- *Value disagreement:* Should our family value education? Should our company value civic responsibility?

- *Problem-solving disagreement:* Should our family eat out less to save for a new car? Should our company eliminate a line of products to increase quarterly earnings?

As you can see, effective substantive conflict is necessary for collaborative decision making or problem solving. If controlled, negotiated, and resolved, this is a very important and constructive type of conflict.

Procedural Conflict

Procedural conflict (also known as process conflict) is a disagreement over how to achieve a goal and resolution.[7] Procedural conflict can relate to aspects such as who should be involved in a decision, how to go about it, where you should meet, or what rules should be followed. Parents arguing over how to discipline children and business co-owners arguing over how to set a fair vacation policy are procedural conflict examples. Burnett notes that affective conflict can lead to procedural conflict. For example, if I don't trust you, why should I accept your ideas on how to proceed? Setting detailed goals and procedures early in your interactions will help prevent this type of conflict from having serious consequences.

These three types of conflict relate to the relational environment, or the context in which they occur. In addition, conflict is often categorized by the number of participants. This approach results in four categories:

- *Intrapersonal conflict* is conflict that takes place within the mind of an individual.

- *Interpersonal conflict* is conflict between two individuals.

- *Intragroup conflict* is conflict between small group members or team members (e.g., family, roommates, or work teams).

- *Intergroup conflict* happens between different groups and teams (e.g., two families or two companies disagreeing).

7.3 What Are Some Negative Conflict Behaviors?

In 1994, psychologist John Gottman observed four negative types of behaviors related to how married partners handle conflict. Drawing from a Biblical phrase, Gottman labeled the four behaviors as the *Four Horsemen of the Apocalypse*, signifying their negative potential to lead to divorce. According to Gottman, couples who divorce are more likely to have employed these behaviors, setting off a "cascade" of events. He believes that it isn't conflict that ends marriages but how partners handle conflict.[8]

Gottman discovered that the cascade depicted in the figure on this page was the most common. However, cascades can vary, and these negative conflict behaviors can occur in different types of close relationships (e.g., close friends, siblings, or coworkers). Recognizing these behaviors is the first step in preventing them or lessening their influence on a relationship.

Criticism

Criticism relates to negative communication that attacks or complains about the relational partner's personality or character rather than his/her behavior that bothers you. For example:

> You always get your way.
>
> You never listen to me.
>
> Why do you always have to make things an argument?
>
> You never think about anyone but yourself! You didn't answer your phone when you were out on the lake.

A productive critique of specific behavior can turn this into positive and healthy behavior. For example, instead of saying the last statement above, offer:

> I was worried when you didn't answer your cell phone. I thought we agreed you would carry it when you were out on the boat.

Criticism
Contempt
Defensiveness
Stonewalling
Relational break-up

Contempt

Contempt is negative communication that attacks or tears down the partner's self-worth with the intention of insulting or psychologically abusing her/him. This behavior is extremely harmful to the relationship and partners, especially if done repeatedly and publicly (such as putting down your significant other constantly in public). Other examples are:

Nonverbal contempt cues:
Rolling your eyes, sneering in disgust, using a mocking or sarcastic tone

Name calling:
You are a(n)... idiot, jerk, slob, [expletive]! or You are... stupid, fat, lazy, worthless!

Defensiveness

Defensiveness occurs when you start to see yourself as the victim and deny responsibility. This sort of behavior is fairly easy to fall into. The problem with it is that it allows you to deny responsibility or to avoid acknowledging your role in the conflict. Defensive examples are:

It's not my fault!

I didn't do that!

This is not fair!

Well, I acted like that because the last time we argued, you...!

Stonewalling

Stonewalling usually comes after the cascade of the other three and is the withdrawal from the interaction or, potentially, the relationship to avoid conflict. Simply put, it is refusing to interact. This can be confused with an attempt to defuse the situation; the difference is that when you stonewall, your goal is to completely stop engaging with the other person, and defusing should be a slowing down of emotional interaction. Examples of stonewalling would be:

Storming out and leaving

Being silent or "giving a cold shoulder"

Changing the subject

Speaking with simple words (monosyllabic) and sentences

Not making eye contact or moving away

If stonewalling persists, or relational partners rely on these four behaviors often, the relationship will suffer. Interestingly, Gottman found that men were significantly more likely to stonewall (85 percent) and women were more likely to engage in criticism. If women stonewalled, it was a significant predictor for divorce.[9]

> **TIP: Online Conflict**
> Be careful about taking your conflict behaviors to a mediated forum. Messages can be misread or taken out of context, emotions missed, and comments made that you wouldn't say body-to-body or face-to-face. Pause to cool down before writing or posting any reaction to a conflict.

7.4 How Can You Manage Conflict?

When you enter into a **conflict situation**, or a situation in which you and at least one other person appear to be at an impasse or in an incompatible state, you tend to use one or more explicit management styles. **Conflict management** is the process of managing and limiting the negative effects of conflict while capitalizing on its positive aspects. Managing conflict effectively in personal or professional settings will help you reduce stress, build your connection to others, develop leadership skills, build team spirit, and increase productivity.

For more than 35 years, the Thomas-Kilmann Conflict Mode Instrument (TKI) has been the leading measure of conflict behavior strategies. Drawing from the work of Robert Blake and Jane Mouton, management researchers Kenneth Thomas and Ralph Kilmann argued humans use two basic dimensions of behavior to respond to conflict: assertiveness and cooperativeness. Depending on where your conflict behavior falls between high or low aggressiveness on one axis and high or low cooperativeness on the other, there are five management styles or strategies.[10] See the figure on the next page. You may tend to rely on ones that have worked for you in the past or ones you feel more comfortable using. It is best to learn the pros and cons of each and when they would be the most effective responses.

By Collaborating

Collaboration is an assertive style that assumes a viable solution for all, or an "I win–You win" solution. It is grounded in analytic remarks/dialogue, show of support for others, and shared responsibility. Collaboration is often the most effective but takes time and energy. For example, you and your roommates might be experiencing money issues related to shared food expenses, Internet providers, or other utilities. This can cause major conflict among you, and collaboration might be a good way to respond: "Let's sit down and discuss our options."

ASSERTIVENESS

assertive

unassertive

COMPETING

COMPROMISING

COLLABORATING

AVOIDING

ACCOMMODATING

COOPERATIVENESS

uncooperative

cooperative

By Accommodating

Accommodation occurs when you cooperate at the highest level and let others have their way in relationship to the conflict. This level of cooperation can be at the expense of your own perspective, needs, goals, objectives, or desired outcome. The outcome tactic is "I lose–You win." Giving up/giving in, disengagement, denial of needs, and expression of harmony are all aspects of adopting this strategy. Examples include obeying rules that you might not agree with or letting a child win a game to lessen his or her stress over losing.

By Compromising

Compromise relies on discovering the most mutually acceptable solution. It is the most moderate in assertiveness and cooperation and supports an "I win a little–You win a little" solution. No one is completely satisfied, but all agree this is best. Compromise appeals to fairness, suggests a trade-off, and sometimes offers a quick solution. This strategy is usually a temporary fix (it settles the issue for now). This is often a better strategy than avoiding. For example, if a department has a problem with low productivity, individual members may compromise on changes to improve overall.

By Competing

Competition uses the outcome tactic of "I win–You lose" and occurs when you are very assertive about achieving your goal without the help of others or their perspectives. This style is often characterized by personal criticism, uncooperativeness, aggressiveness, domination, and denial of responsibility. It emphasizes your concerns over the concerns of others and relies heavily on your powers. An example would be standing up for your position or rights at the expense of another's.

By Avoiding

Avoidance occurs when you simply avoid the issue and don't pursue any resolution—an "I lose–You lose" tactic. Examples of avoiding behavior are denying conflict altogether, diplomatically sidestepping an issue (often culturally infused), changing the topic, employing passive behavior, and/or withdrawing verbally ("Let's not talk about it!"). Avoidance shouldn't be your preferred style. You might need to revisit the avoided conflict at a later date for the health of the relationship.

Managing Conflict Effectively

Style/Strategy	When Might You Use It?
Collaboration	When you want to discover, be creative, and learn; to commit to a decision; to problem-solve; to emphasize the importance of opposing positions; or to recognize the availability and value of diverse insights
Accommodation	When keeping the peace is important; to create goodwill and increase morale; to demonstrate levelheadedness, fairness, and loyalty; when the issue is more important to the other person
Compromise	When there is strain on the existing relationship; when a stalemate occurs; or when the parties are unable to negotiate effectively
Competition	When you know you are right and being so is extremely important; when quick, decisive action is necessary; when participants are being too thoughtful; when you are under attack; or when consensus fails
Avoidance	When the issue is just not worth the conflict; when the problem won't lead to more significant problems; or when the conflict is hostile

Keep in mind that everyone is capable of using all of these strategies in different situations.

Self-Test: Assess Your Conflict Management Style

Pinpointing exactly what conflict management style you will use in a given situation is a bit complex for a simple quiz. However, being cognizant of what behaviors you tend to rely on will help you understand your tendencies and can potentially help you change your behavior if needed.

As you read the following 15 statements, rate each with the following scale. Think about which ones seem the most reasonable or comfortable.

3 = Agree   2 = Somewhat Agree   1 = Disagree   0 = No opinion

___ 1. "We should all get along. That is what is important."

___ 2. "I just keep quiet when others disagree with me."

___ 3. "You have to win some and you have to lose some."

___ 4. "I need to make a decision about this issue but I want to hear what you think we should do."

___ 5. "I love a good argument."

___ 6. "You really can't do anything about most serious issues."

___ 7. "I like working with others on problems."

___ 8. "I often tell others how it is or what is right."

___ 9. "Let's meet halfway on this."

___ 10. "If this will make you happy, I will back off."

___ 11. "If you get that, I want this."

___ 12. "Let's consider everyone's feelings and concerns."

___ 13. "I prefer to avoid people who don't have the same opinions as I do."

___ 14. "I love the hunt for the right answer and the exhilaration of achievement."

___ 15. "I worry about what others need. I can back off of my point of view."

Now, place the ranking you gave each corresponding statement in the equation under the "Total" column. Add the equations to determine which style or styles you relate to the most.

Style	Corresponding Statements	Total
Accommodating	1, 10, 15	___ + ___ + ___ = ___
Avoiding	2, 6, 13	___ + ___ + ___ = ___
Collaborating	4, 7, 12	___ + ___ + ___ = ___
Competing	5, 8, 14	___ + ___ + ___ = ___
Compromising	3, 9, 11	___ + ___ + ___ = ___

7.5 How Can Culture Influence Conflict?

More than any other generation, you are likely to enter into an interpersonal relationship at home, school, or work with someone from another culture or co-culture. Social media, video calling, instant messaging, and smartphones allow us to venture into cross-cultural relationships with ease.

Our growing country also gives us more opportunity. According to the U.S. Census Bureau in 2012, the total U.S. population was 313,873,685. Of that population, 63% were white (non Hispanic/Latino), 16.9% Hispanic or Latino, 13.1% African American/Black, 5.1% Asian, 1.2% American Indian/Alaska Native, 0.2% Native Hawaiian/Pacific Islander, and 2.4% identified themselves as two or more races.[11] Because differing cultures, co-cultures, and daily experiences inform our values, attitudes, and beliefs, how we handle conflict—or even what we consider conflict—can vary.

Intercultural communication scholar Stella Ting-Toomey notes that our "cultural and primary individual orientation factors go hand-in-hand with situational features such as ethnocentrism and biased attributions, prejudice and racism . . . in shaping our interpretations of an intimate conflict situation."[12] **Biased attributions** refer to the errors we make when we evaluate others or their behaviors. If we make these attributions from our cultural and personal perspectives, we can misinterpret others' conflict behavior and/or view it as extremely negative.

Most research exploring the intersection of culture and conflict in relationships centers on the cultural dimensions of individualist/collectivist, low context/high context, and low power/high power distance. See the following table.

Below are some common findings of how the norms and rules of these cultural dimensions have the potential to influence conflict in the workplace. Keep in mind, these are generalizations; use them only as a starting point for understanding others.

Workplace Differences with the Potential to Intensify Conflict[13]

Individualist—Low Context—Low Power	Collectivist—High Context—High Power
More outcome-focused and content goal-oriented (conflict effectiveness)	More process-focused and relational goal-oriented (conflict appropriateness)
Often prefer moving quickly to a plan of action and reaching a concrete solution	May view moving too quickly to action or resolution—before building relationships and facework (saving our own or others' honor)—as threatening
May prefer moderate respect for those in power (parents, elders, boss) but will challenge and speak up (be persuasive, assertive of opinions)	Prefer respect and obedience (never or rarely question or contradict); offer collective opinions and ideas; very protective of in-group (a group with strong solidarity)
Prefer norms and rules grounded in fairness to resolve conflict	Prefer norms that focus on in-group and relational harmony to resolve conflict
Prefer direct (dominating) communication or saying exactly what you mean; may display more emotions (although not as true for the United States, especially in work groups)	Prefer indirect and face-saving communication or even silence; avoid confrontation and stress restraint in displaying emotions and opinions
Feel that listeners should be able to easily decode a message because it is well-constructed, persuasive, and clear	Feel that listeners should "read between the lines" and observe nonverbal nuances
Prefer resolving disputes through competing or collaborating	Prefer resolving disputes through compromising, integrating, or avoiding
Prefer short-term, individual rewards	Prefer long-term, group rewards
Tend to view the avoiding strategy as rarely effective because it is a "lose–lose" position from this cultural perspective	Tend to view the avoiding strategy as often effective because it is a "win–win" position from this cultural perspective

7.6 How Can Gender Influence Conflict?

"Leave me alone."

"Talk to me!"

"He never finishes a project."

"She's too aggressive."

You have likely heard such statements during conflicts in your private or work life, and each hints at differences in how men and women handle conflict. Although many women and men reject gender stereotypes, research notes some conflict behaviors and management styles that are generally male or female. Adding romance to the intersection of gender and conflict changes things further.

It Influences Behavior in General Conflicts

In workplace friendships and nonromantic partner relations, men and women exhibit some common general behaviors.[14]

- Men tend to distance themselves from or avoid conflict if possible. If they do avoid the conflict, they tend to not return at a later time to resolve it. When they don't work to avoid the conflict, or they initiate talk about a conflict issue, men tend to respond to conflict "consistent with their stereotype of being assertive and task-oriented. They tend toward the competing style."[15]

- Women tend to respond to conflict in "more conciliatory ways, consistent with their gender stereotype of being communal and relationship-oriented."[16] They tend toward the accommodating or compromising style. Women tend to store up feelings (such as sadness, anger, and disappointment) for longer periods of time. Women tend to want to talk about what they are experiencing during the heat of the moment and want men to do the same.

- Women tend to criticize more than men and men tend to stonewall.

- In the workplace, there tends to be little difference in how men and women respond to conflict.

It Influences Behavior in Romantic Conflicts

The intersection of gender and conflict between intimates has some of the most noteworthy differences between same sex and opposite sex partners.

For example, marital conflict researchers Richard Mackey and Bernard O'Brien found that, in opposite sex couples:

- Men may experience more anxiety than women when dealing with conflict in a face-to-face situation, which would suggest a preference for avoiding or quickly resolving it (compromising).
- However, African American couples in long-term relationships tend to prefer face-to-face styles of resolution.
- The competing style was often preferred by African American males.[17]

Observing gay, lesbian, and opposite sex couples discussing conflict issues, John Gottman and his colleagues noted:

- Same sex partners were generally better at handling conflict discussions. Creating and maintaining equality in the discussion and relationship seemed to be one reason for this.
- Women presenting conflict issues to men was the most common opposite sex pattern.
- Regardless of sexual orientation, women were more "sad" when confronted with a conflict issue than men were.

- Same sex couples began more positively in the way they presented conflict to a partner than opposite sex partners. Same sex couples were more positive in how they received the conflict. The same sex couples were able to maintain this positive state more steadily and for longer.
- There was less belligerence, domineering behavior, fear/tension, sadness, and whining in same sex relationships.
- Lesbians tended to be more emotionally expressive (positively or negatively) during conflict than gay men.[18]

An extreme behavior in romantic conflict is **intimate partner violence (IPV)**, or the actual or threatened physical, sexual, psychological, or emotional abuse by a current or former intimate partner.[19] In 2012, the Centers for Disease Control and Prevention reported that nearly 3 in 10 women and 1 in 10 men in the United States have experienced IPV.[20] Although there isn't a simple solution to IPV, learning better techniques for responding to conflict and being willing to confront IPV in varying ways will help limit such violence. Regardless, know that mental and physical abuse or violence is *not* a normal aspect of healthy relational conflict. If you find yourself in a threatening situation, reach out—help is available.

See page 207 for more help with responding to IPV.

7.7 How Can You Improve Your Conflict Negotiation Skills?

So far, you have learned what conflict and its types are, as well as about negative conflict behaviors, how individuals manage conflict, and the influences culture and gender have when people disagree. All of this is helpful knowledge, but it can be difficult to translate into exact behaviors, skills, and methods to negotiate conflict. Let's consider how to effectively negotiate conflict.

Embrace the Inevitability of Conflict

As noted throughout this chapter, conflict is a natural part of human interaction. You will be much more effective at negotiating conflict if you embrace the fact that it is going to happen and that it can often lead to positive outcomes. If you refuse to engage in conflict, it will not go away. And you will miss an opportunity to strengthen the relationship or to engage in effective problem-solving strategies. In the workplace, you will be appreciated and valued more if you can demonstrate your ability to navigate conflict rather than to ignore it. In your personal life, you will be respected, admired, loved, and accepted more if you can effectively work through conflict with those close to you. However, keep in mind that relational partners might need to "agree to disagree" on certain issues and, therefore, dodge those in future interactions.

Peace is not the absence of conflict, but the ability to cope with conflict by peaceful means.[21]

Ronald Reagan

Avoid Detrimental Behaviors

Here are some behaviors to avoid when negotiating conflict.

- Don't be closed-minded. There is usually more than one side to an issue or more than one way to solve a problem.

- Avoid defensive acts such as denying a problem exists, exercising your power over others to suppress their feelings, using sarcasm, or being overly critical.

- Avoid using trigger words (words you know will provoke a negative response), which you learned about in Chapter 3.

- Don't engage in what George Back and Peter Wyden called *gunnysacking* and *kitchen sinking*.[22] **Gunnysacking** is storing up a complaint and then, when the "sack of emotions" bulges, you bring it up, catching the other person by surprise. **Kitchen sinking** is rehashing old arguments or bringing up totally unrelated issues when you get into an argument.

- Avoid blaming and attacking.

- Avoid being so competitive that the other person always has to lose for you to win.

- Don't say things that make you appear to have the ability to read the other person's mind. "I know you don't care about me." "You think I am careless."

- If the conflict is via technology, do not engage in bullying or **flaming** (hostile and insulting Internet interaction).

- Don't give in to anger. Regulate it. Above all, don't be coercive, mentally abusive, or physically violent.

Utilize Constructive Behaviors

Constructive and confident behaviors can make all the difference when people disagree. Here are a few guidelines.

- Build relationships on trust and respect *before* conflict happens.

- Take responsibility for moving toward resolution rather than an impasse.

- Focus on the issue, not on hurting others.

- Recognize that there might be cultural, gender, and individual differences at play.

- Control your emotions—try to keep a positive attitude and stay calm.

- Use your emotional intelligence to recognize how you are feeling about the conflict, and pay attention to the emotions of others.

- Speak up, be assertive but not overly so, and articulate your feelings and position.

- Listen with your undivided attention.

- Search together for a mutually agreeable solution, if possible.

- Recognize and be willing to accept when it is time to call the relationship over, if the conflict is that destructive.

- Seek assistance from outside the relationship if it becomes abusive and violent.

- In a group situation, try to be impartial and promote team problem solving.

- When you successfully negotiate conflict, celebrate with your partner.

The next section offers a method for moving through conflict resolution step by step.

Commit to a Resolution Method

Coming to a successful conflict resolution takes dedication and fairness by everyone involved. There are numerous models and notions about the necessary steps to effectively negotiate conflict and for problem solving. Harvard Negotiation Project members and scholars Roger Fisher, William Ury, and Bruce Patton, in *Getting to Yes: Negotiating Agreement without Giving In*, argue for a method called "principled negotiation." This method supports fair and decent negotiations by separating the people from the problem, focusing on what is truly important to each person (interest), inventing options for mutual gain, and insisting on objective criteria for making a decision.[23] These may seem lofty goals, but they are attainable if you take the right steps and find tactics that work for you and your relational partner(s).

Chapter 9 discusses strategies for problem solving in small groups. For personal conflict moments, try the **MUSE model** described in the figure on the next page. Keep in mind that the word *muse* means to think, ponder, consider, deliberate, contemplate (often in silence), and meditate. In Greek mythology, the muses are the goddesses that inspire art and science. Both of these understandings of the word "muse" help create a fitting metaphor for conflict resolution. The best way to resolve conflict is for the relational partners to consider, deliberate, contemplate options, listen to each other, and find inspiration for agreement. The MUSE model has four steps: Meet, Understand, Solve, and Employ.

If the situation is highly complex, the conflict has escalated to an intense level, or there is a deadlock, those involved in the process may need help from a neutral person. Known as **mediation**, this method brings in a neutral party to help facilitate the resolution process, so those in conflict can come to an agreement. In extreme cases (e.g., labor disputes, custody cases, or divorce resolutions), resolution may only be achieved through **arbitration**, or when a third party imposes a decision that both sides must adhere to.

The MUSE Model of Conflict Resolution

MEET

- Be proactive, but calm, and initiate a meeting with those involved in the conflict. Leave outsiders out of this meeting unless they are taking on the role of a fair mediator.
- Select a meeting place that will be comfortable for everyone.
- Establish ground rules.

UNDERSTAND

- Understanding will only happen if you talk and listen. Give each person the opportunity to express his or her feelings, perspective, and potential solutions. Use "I" statements ("I feel like you don't trust me.") rather than "You" statements ("You don't trust me.").
- Be an active listener and don't judge.
- Try to identify with others' perspectives. Be mindful of them.
- Once everyone has spoken, discuss your understanding of the situation. Try to eliminate misunderstanding.

SOLVE

- Consider all the options that are available and/or acceptable. Brainstorm.
- Consider the impact and consequences of each solution. Is any acceptable to everyone?
- Strive for mutual agreement.
- Agree to a solution or agree to simply live with disagreeing.

EMPLOY

- Actively work to employ the solution, compromise, or negotiate an "agreeing to disagree."
- Remember to hold up your end of the bargain and to reevaluate/follow up on how everyone feels after a short period.
- Keep the dialogue open if necessary. Remember that decisions can be revised.

Chapter 7 Review

Key Questions

7.1 What Is Interpersonal Conflict?

Interpersonal conflict is an expressed struggle between at least two interdependent parties who perceive incompatible goals, scarce resources, and interference from others in achieving their goals. Conflict can be either constructive or destructive to the relationship.

See pages 186–187.

7.2 What Are Common Conflict Types?

Interpersonal conflict can be:

- *Affective conflict* (also known as relational or emotional conflict) involves interpersonal disagreement prejudices, antagonism, emotional tensions, trust or respect issues, attitudes, personality or power clashes, and other interpersonal struggle.

- *Substantive conflict* (also known as task or cognitive conflict) involves struggles erupting from disagreement over the partners' or group's goal or outcomes.

- *Procedural conflict* (also known as process conflict) is a disagreement over how to achieve a goal and resolution.

See pages 188–189.

7.3 What Are Some Negative Conflict Behaviors?

Psychologist John Gottman observed four cascading negative behaviors related to how partners handle conflict. They are:

- *Criticism*, or negative communication that attacks or complains about the relational partner's personality or character rather than his/her behavior that bothers you

- *Contempt*, or negative communication that attacks or tears down the partner's self-worth with the intention of insulting or psychologically abusing her/him

- *Defensiveness*, which occurs when you start to see yourself as the victim and deny responsibility

- *Stonewalling* is the withdrawal from the interaction or, potentially, the relationship to avoid conflict—refusing to interact

See pages 190–191.

7.4 How Can You Manage Conflict?

When you enter into a *conflict situation*, or a situation where you and at least one other person appear to be at an impasse or in incompatible state, you tend to use one or more explicit management strategies. Kenneth Thomas and Ralph Kilmann argued humans use two basic dimensions of behavior to respond to conflict: assertiveness and cooperativeness. Depending on where your conflict behavior falls between high or low aggressiveness and high or low cooperativeness, there are five management strategies: collaboration, accommodation, compromise, competition, and avoidance.

See pages 192–195.

7.5 How Can Culture Influence Conflict?

Objective 7.5: **EXAMINE HOW CULTURE INFLUENCES CONFLICT**

Our cultural and primary individual orientations can influence how we interpret and react in a conflict situation. We can make errors when we evaluate others or their behavior based on how we would react or expect others to react (biased attribution). How we react or expect others to react is often related to the cultural dimensions of individualist/collectivist, low context/high context, and low power/high power distance.

See pages 196–197.

7.6 How Can Gender Influence Conflict?

Objective 7.6: **EXPLORE HOW GENDER INFLUENCES CONFLICT**

Although many women and men reject gender stereotypes, research notes some conflict behaviors and management styles that are generally male or female. For example, men tend to avoid conflict and women tend to respond in a conciliatory way. Women tend to criticize more and men tend to stonewall. In the workplace, there seems to be little difference between how men and women respond to conflict. Adding romance to the intersection of

gender and conflict changes things further. Because men tend to avoid or resolve with compromise, intimate face-to-face conflict produces more anxiety for them. Same sex partners generally handle conflict discussion better. An extreme behavior in romantic conflict is *intimate partner violence (IPV)*, or the actual or threatened physical, sexual, psychological, or emotional abuse by a current or former intimate partner.

See pages 198–199.

7.7 How Can You Improve Your Conflict Negotiation Skills?

Objective 7.7: **ARTICULATE METHODS FOR IMPROVING CONFLICT NEGOTIATION**

To effectively negotiate conflict, you need to:

- Embrace the inevitability of conflict.

- Avoid detrimental behaviors (i.e., don't be closed-minded or defensive; avoid using trigger words, gunnysacking, kitchen sinking, blaming, or attacking; don't be overly competitive; and don't give in to your anger—regulate it).

- Utilize constructive behaviors (i.e., build trust and respect; focus on the issue, not the person; recognize individual, cultural, and gender differences; use your emotional intelligence; listen; and celebrate successful conflict negotiation).

- Commit to a resolution method such as the MUSE model (Meet, Understand, Solve, and Employ).

See pages 200–203.

Key Terms

Improve Your Communication

Gottman notes that some conflict issues are easier than others to resolve. He refers to these as *functional problems*, which can add up to create significant conflict or gridlock.[24] If you and your partner are open and willing to change, use the following prompt to help determine disagreements that might be fixable. Decide on one or two to work on, discuss how to do that, and try to implement change.

I would like my (roommate, coworker, spouse, friend, sibling, or other partner) to do the following:

_____

_____

_____

_____

_____

Apply Your Knowledge

1. From your family, romantic, work, and online relationships, think of constructive and destructive conflicts from the past. What made them either constructive or destructive? Can you see a better way to respond and/or resolve the conflicts? Were you willing to be flexible or not? Why?
2. Which conflict management styles do you tend to use? Is there a pattern to what you use? Do you tend to rely on just one or a few?
3. What emotions do you tend to exhibit in interpersonal conflict situations? Frustration? Anxiety? Anger? Confusion? Disappointment? Hurt? Others? Are there things you can do to minimize these emotions?

Other Resources

Here are some sources to help you navigate conflict.

Dealing with Workplace Conflict

Kim-Jo, T., V. Benet-Martínez, and D.J. Ozer. "Culture and Interpersonal Conflict Resolution Styles: Role of Acculturation." *Journal of Cross-Cultural Psychology* 41.2 (2010): 264–69. Print.

McAllum, Kirstie. "Workplace Conflict: Three Paths to Peace." *IESE Insight* 18 (2013): 48–55. Print.

Weiss, Joyce. "Conflict Resolution." *Sales & Service Excellence* 9.9 (2009): 8. Business Source Complete. Web. 5 Apr. 2015.

• www.forbes.com/sites/mikemyatt/2012/02/22/5-keys-to-dealing-with-workplace-conflict/

• hrweb.berkeley.edu/guides/managing-hr/interaction/conflict/resolving

• blogs.hbr.org/2014/06/manage-a-difficult-conversation-with-emotional-intelligence/

Violence Prevention

• www.cdc.gov/violenceprevention/

• www.womenshealth.gov/violence-against-women/types-of-violence/domestic-intimate-partner-violence.html

Intimate Partner Violence: Getting Help

If you find yourself in an abusive or violent situation, here are some ways to get help, along with key points to remember.[25]

• If you are in immediate danger, you can call 911. Go to a hospital if you are hurt.

• The attacks usually begin as emotional abuse and move to physical.

• Your partner may try to make it seem like it is your fault. Abuse is *not* your fault.

• Abusive partners need help from a professional. They may try to convince you that they will get better on their own.

• Create a code word to use with friends or family to let them know you are in danger.

• Reach out to people you trust. They can offer you emotional help.

• You can call the National Domestic Violence hotline at 800-799-SAFE (7233) or 800-787-3224 (TDD). Or, look up state or local help.

Chapter 8
Group Communication and Leadership

Coming together is a beginning; keeping together is progress; working together is success.[1]

Henry Ford

8.1 What Makes a Small Group?

Team sports, meal preparation with your family, and group assignments all require interacting as a small group. Engineers creating a product, medical personnel saving lives, and most others employed work in small groups. A **small group** is a group of three to approximately seven interdependent people united over time as a cohesive unit with a common goal. The understanding, shaping, and connecting associated with small group communication creates remarkable relationships. Let's look at the main characteristics of a small group.

Size

Clearly, the word *small* indicates that size is a factor. Small could be two, 20, or more, depending on what you are comparing it to. However, some parameters can help you define what constitutes a small group in communication. First, two people communicating with each other is called a *dyad*. According to Katherine Adams and Gloria Galanes in *Communicating in Groups*, dyads function differently from small groups because they immediately cease to exist if one person leaves the dyad, and they do not have multiple communication networks or leadership hierarchies. Therefore, a small group must include at least three people. The upper number is more complicated. Indeed, if you asked several communication scholars for a limit, most would say it falls somewhere between seven and 20, with the majority preferring seven to 12 communicators. Adams and Galanes say the group has to be small enough that individual members can "perceive each other and are aware of each other as individuals as they interact…. Most practically, small groups usually consist of 3 to 7 members."[2]

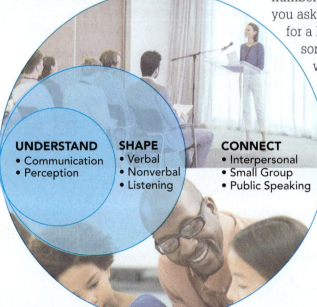

UNDERSTAND
- Communication
- Perception

SHAPE
- Verbal
- Nonverbal
- Listening

CONNECT
- Interpersonal
- Small Group
- Public Speaking

Interdependent Members

Seven strangers sitting in an airport lounge waiting for a flight do not make a small group, even if they are all interacting. To be a small group, those seven people need to be interdependent. **Interdependence** means each member is connected or interacting with the others in some significant way and that all members depend on each other for assistance, support, cooperation, success, and, ultimately, survival of the group. For interdependence to be present, the group needs sense of a collective identity, a belief in synergy, and cohesion.

A **collective identity** is a shared sense that each individual belongs to the group and is responsible for the group goal. Interestingly enough, a strong sense of self and self-worth is an important part of this. Being able to see the strengths and weaknesses you bring to the group, and those of others, allows the group to capitalize on the diversity of the members as it creates a new, stronger collective identity. This process of taking individual members and mixing their strengths together to form something stronger, better, and more effective is known as **synergy**.

Cohesion is the state of joining and working together as a unit, coupled with the wish to remain part of the unit. Student groups often fail at this condition. When you simply divide tasks and go work on your own parts without interaction, the group is not cohesive. Think of families that enjoy doing things together versus those that don't. It is from these types of families where the phrases "Families that eat together, stay together" or "Families that play together, stay together" gather their importance. Cohesiveness can be vital to the longevity of a group and is primarily fueled by social relationships within the group. How hard it is to become a member of the group, the amount of time the group spends together, and the intensity of emotion evolving from the group situation (or a perceived threat to the group) tend to create a stronger cohesive group.

Different groups will have a different mix and intensity of these elements. Some groups will even have a significantly high feeling of each element. For example, *teams*, such as sports, firefighting, or surgical teams, are all small groups that tend to be effective when there is a very strong sense of collective identity, high level of cooperation, wide diversity of skill, and intense commitment.[3]

Rules and Norms

Later in the chapter, you will see how rules and norms are a critical step in the development of a group. Both rules and norms help ensure group survival; they help the group to express their values and to perform their function or reach their goal.

In the Chapter 6 discussion about interpersonal relationships, you learned that all communication interaction is governed by rules. For small groups, rules are formal (usually written and official) procedures, directions, and policies set forth by someone in authority, such as a boss or a teacher. Say, for example, that all employees must wear safety helmets and goggles on the plant floor, or students must submit all assignments to Turnitin.com. Rules let people know what they should and should not do in specific situations.

Norms are informal (usually unwritten or implicit) guidelines for appropriate actions and behaviors. Most norms can be categorized as behavior norms or task norms. *Behavior norms* give guidance on what day-to-day interaction behavior is appropriate or not. For example, treating others with respect and maintaining confidentiality are behavior norms. *Task norms* (also known as work norms) regulate the performance and productivity of the group and its members. Task norms focus on how to make decisions and solve problems and what procedures are necessary (who will make room reservations, take notes, or write up a formal response; who should be notified if you will miss a meeting; what are the deadlines; what is acceptable productivity, etc.). The more explicit a group is about norms, the better the group can function.

TIP: Advantages of Small Groups

Because effective small groups take time to work, we often fail to see their value. Small groups are advantageous because they tend to:

- Access all the assets of a diverse membership
- Make better decisions—especially for complex issues
- Improve productivity
- Use critical thinking or objectivity, if the group functions properly
- Be creative
- Increase motivation, dedication, and commitment to outcome and organization
- Create a team spirit
- Create a sense of empathy and identification for others connected to the group
- Build individual self-esteem and confidence

A Common Goal Over Time

Another reason why those seven people sitting in an airport terminal are not a small group is that they are not fueled by a common goal for a period of time. In other words, they haven't spent a significant amount of time working toward a target, solution, objective, or goal. A small group needs a purpose for being convened. In any given small group situation, there are usually two types of goals: group and personal.

Group goals are the goals or charges given to the group as their purpose of existence. Why has this group of individuals been brought together? What should they accomplish? What is the group's reward or payoff? For example, a group goal could be to create a new ad campaign or develop a student civic-engagement project.

Personal goals are the purposes or reasons each member has for participating in the group and working toward its success. Why am I interested in being in this group? What do I want to achieve for myself? What is my reward or payoff? Personal goals can have a dark side when they lead to a negative **hidden agenda**, or an undisclosed motive or objective that adversely influences the group goal or others' personal goals. For example, a coworker may offer ideas that secretly aim to benefit only his or her department. On the other hand, a serious lack of personal goals—or mediocre personal goals—can lead to social loafing. **Social loafing** happens when people exert less effort as group members than they would working alone. If a member's personal goals are lower than those of some of the group, that member might loaf his or her way through the group work.

TIP: Disadvantages of Small Groups

As with most things that have a good side, groups also have potential disadvantages.

- The pace may frustrate members used to working quickly—it is time-consuming.
- *Groupthink*, or the willingness to conform to what the group thinks rather than engaging in critical decision making or thinking, can occur when members exert pressure on others to come to a premature or safe consensus. For example, if a group wants to pass a budget quickly, individuals may feel pressured not to question too many line-item costs. This often happens in extremely cohesive groups.[4]
- Unequal power issues within the group may lead to those in the low power position feeling marginalized or voiceless.
- Unproductive competition may arise between members or group-to-group.
- It can be easy for inequity in responsibility and accountability to occur.
- In an educational or work environment, a group's evaluation process can be complex.

Links to Personal, Public, or Professional Needs

Small groups help promote interpersonal relationships and accomplish a task. Because of these functions, groups can be clustered by need as personal, public, or professional.

- *Personal groups* include those groups that predominately provide members with affection, safety, solidarity, and socialization. Primary, social, and therapeutic groups fall into this cluster.

- *Public groups* primarily offer you the mechanism to support and help others or engage in public discourse. This cluster includes civic groups.

- *Professional groups* mainly offer members the ability to increase their knowledge and to complete a task in a professional setting. Learning and work groups are included in this cluster.

See the table below for more about the small group types.

Small Group Types

Needs	Types of Groups
Personal	**Primary groups** are your family and close friends that predominately offer you personal support, affection, safety, and solidarity. **Social groups** are formed with the primary goal of socializing by supporting personal interests and social opportunity (e.g., gourmet cooking clubs, car clubs, or amateur sports teams). **Therapeutic groups** are formed to assist and encourage members struggling with personal problems (e.g., grief recovery groups, addiction recovery groups, mental and physical illness support groups, weight loss groups, or assault crisis groups).
Public	**Civic groups** are principally charged with serving others (civic responsibility) through assisting with a worthy cause or discussing public issues (e.g., neighborhood restoration groups, charity organizations, or service-learning projects).
Professional	**Learning groups** are chiefly formed to help improve members' knowledge in some fashion (e.g., student project groups, study groups, and skill workshops). **Work groups** are more formal and are created to work on a specific task (e.g., workplace project groups, campus student government, or jury duty).

Work and civic groups usually have specific tasks they must accomplish. For example, a work group could be public relations specialists designing a new PR campaign. A civic group might be several volunteers working together to feed the elderly and homeless. See the table below for types of task-oriented work or civic groups.

Most often these types of small groups are conducted in person, or body-to-body. Mediated channels, such as the phone, video calling, Facebook, LinkedIn, or instant messaging, may assist with interactions at times. However, some groups reside largely in the virtual world.

Virtual small groups function much like other small groups, only they may never, or rarely, meet in person; they interact primarily through electronic media. Virtual work groups use traditional technology but will often use web or audio conferencing (e.g., WebEx or GoToMeeting). These types of groups take more time to cultivate and build trust, and they require better verbal and nonverbal listening skills of the members and the leader. It is absolutely necessary for the members to know what their formal roles and tasks are in order to be successful. Virtual work teams can often be global or intercultural, requiring greater sensitivity to issues such as how decisions are made.

See Chapter 9 for more on virtual groups.

Types of Work or Civic Groups

Task-Oriented Groups	What Do They Do?
Decision-making group	A group that draws conclusions and decides policies for action
Problem-solving group	A group united to solve a particular problem
Focus group	A group that addresses an issue and searches for the best solution
Brainstorming team	A group charged with generating ideas but not evaluating them
Project team	A group consisting of members with the necessary expertise to perform all the activities required to create and produce a product or service
Advisory group	A group of experts who offer skilled advice to an individual or group that needs to make a decision
Quality assurance group	A group that works to improve the quality of an organization's products or services

8.2 How Do Groups Develop?

Like interpersonal relationships, discussed in Chapter 6, small groups must go through a process of development. A number of systematic theoretical models have explained group formation.[5] Many of them tend to follow a similar path of development. One of the most commonly used and cited models is *Tuckman's group development model*. The original model had four stages: forming, storming, norming, and performing. Later, Tuckman, along with Mary Ann Jensen, added a fifth stage, of terminating/reforming.[6]

Forming

In the *forming* stage, the group creates its identity, seeks the leader's guidance and direction (if one exists at this point), learns about the group task, and begins to determine membership roles. Members gather information about each other and avoid conflict issues. This stage is much like a combination of the initiating and experimenting stages of Knapp's relationship development discussed in Chapter 6. It is important for members with group experience to begin to mold appropriate group behavior.

Storming

As the group becomes comfortable, it starts focusing on its goal; but this may become complex as power and relationship issues emerge and they enter the *storming* stage. This stage can be filled with arguments, posturing for leadership if needed, and anxiety over uncertainty of the group and task. This stage can feel uncomfortable but is necessary for the development of the group. Respect of the individual is important during this stage. The leader and members need to embrace the positive turbulence, which should lead to creativity and cohesion. The group leader must manage the group, set time limits, and give voice to all members, as well as remain calm and open.

This model is a linear process, but keep in mind that a group might move around within the process. For example, members might skip much of the forming stage if their group is reforming, or they might return to the storming or norming stage later in the process.

Terminating/Reforming

The *terminating/reforming stage* marks the end point for the entire group. The group is done with that task and either disbands or reforms with a new goal. This ending might be marked by a significant ritual. Examples include a formal rollout event of a new product created by the group or an informal gathering at a local restaurant or pub to mark the event.

Performing

Performing is the "real work" phase where the group conducts the work necessary to make a decision or solve a problem and implement the outcome. This should be a highly motivated, empowered, and energized stage, with reduced uncertainty if possible. Leadership communication is imperative and often very active during this stage.

Norming

Norming occurs after the conflict of the storming phase is expressed and addressed. The members identify their goal and begin to outline necessary tasks and assignments. Members take ownership of the group decision in this stage. Explicit rules should be formulated and the group should begin to establish and use implicit norm behavior to regulate the process.

TIP: Group Development

Identifying the stage a group is having the most trouble with will help you assist the group to move on and to be productive.

8.3 How Do Group Members Interact?

When you hear the word *network* today, you most likely imagine a computer network or the wired or wireless system that allows information to transmit from one computer to another. The Internet is a huge network that allows you to access information from almost anywhere. Small groups have similar networks that allow members to communicate or interact with each other.

There are two categories of small group networks. The first includes **informal networks**, which form out of friendship, common interest, work situations, or proximity and are not controlled by the larger organization. They often serve the self-interest of those willing to participate. Work or school grapevines and social networking sites are informal networks. Interestingly, grapevines can be viewed as more trustworthy at times.[7]

The second category of networks is made up of the **formal networks** that form specific interaction patterns when a group has a defined identity and goal. Power structures within the group and the organization housing the group can influence which patterns form. Likewise, the physical arrangement of a room or business, and whether the group is body-to-body, face-to-face, or some virtual configuration, will impact the patterns. One pattern is really not better than the other. Determining which is best evolves from evaluating the situation, the task, and the time constraints.

Formal networks can be *wheel, chain*, or *all-channel* networks.[8]

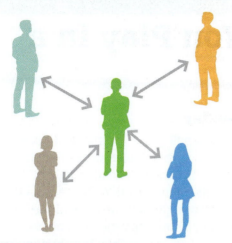

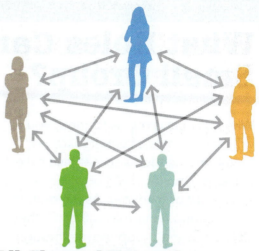

Wheel Networks

Wheel networks are communication arrangements that require a gatekeeper, such as a manager, who takes on the role as the collector and transmitter of information. The *gatekeeper* is someone in the group who has the power to control communication access between members and to regulate content and delivery of specific messages.

All-Channel Networks

All-channel networks are arrangements in which communication is open between and among all members; they can communicate actively with each other (e.g., a forensic team in a lab). This type of network is decentralized (no leader regulating communication flow), with low power distance. If the group is large, this type of network might travel over a mediated channel.

Chain Networks

Chain networks are communication arrangements where members interact with the persons above and below them in rank. For example, a company might have a chain where a vice president interacts with directors, directors interact with managers, managers interact with assistant managers, and assistant managers interact with technicians. This upward and downward flow follows the group's hierarchy and helps maintain power structures. This network can be unreliable, as it travels through different individual interpretations.

8.4 What Roles Can You Play in a Small Group?

When a small group is formed, you will play the role of either leader or member. A leader is sometimes called a chairperson (or chair) or will be a supervisor or manager. As a member of the group, your role will be further defined as the group moves through the development phases.

Leader

During small group communication, a leader is a person who guides the group toward its goal by influencing them through communication. Leaders need to analyze a group's membership to determine strengths and weaknesses. Leaders will also analyze the situation surrounding the group's task and the broader audience that its decisions will affect. She or he will develop a specific purpose that encapsulates the group's goal, which will focus group activities. In some groups, although rarely in a working group, you may not have a leader. This absence of leadership usually evolves and works best when each member has equal influence and status or in groups such as advisory or focus groups.

Practicing Ethics: Ethical Leadership

- Lead by example. Embody trustworthiness, integrity, civility, straightforwardness, and dependability.
- Be sensitive to feelings, perspectives, and emotions. Seek to empower.
- Educate yourself about cultural and gender differences (see Objectives 8.5 and 8.6).
- Create an environment where others can disagree with you. Listen!
- Be willing to adapt and change.
- Keep others informed when possible.

Types of Leader

As the table below suggests, there are three types of leaders: implied, designated, and emergent. They differ by how the leader is chosen.

Type of Leader	How Is This Leader Chosen?
Implied leader	When other group members defer to a member because of her or his rank, expertise, or other characteristics
Designated leader	By election or appointment when the group is formed
Emergent leader	When a member evolves as leader during the early stages of the group's formation

Recognizing the type of leader you are will help you determine how to relate to other group members.

For example, Lachelle is a project manager and part of a group where several members report directly to her; it is likely that the group will defer to Lachelle as leader because of her rank over several of them. Because of her power as project manager, Lachelle, as the implied leader of the small group, may need to work harder to get those subordinate to her to speak up with their own opinions and to not always agree with her solely because of her rank. This will lead to groupthink.

Leadership Approaches

According to research, the success of a group and its members' satisfaction is directly correlated to the effectiveness of the group's leader.[9] Leadership is the process of influencing, directing, guiding, and managing meaning that helps advance a group to its goal.[10] Therefore, your approach to how you lead is important. There are numerous theories about how leaders lead. Four common ones are:

- Trait approach
- Functional approach
- Behavioral styles approach
- Situational approach

Trait Approach One of the oldest approaches—especially popular in the 1920s—is the *leadership theory of personality traits*. This approach suggests that leaders are born with or could potentially develop certain traits that make them great leaders. They have ambition, high emotional maturity, integrity, self-confidence, intelligence, common sense, and a motivational personality, just to name a few.[11] Having these traits is no assurance you will be a great leader, but they can greatly assist you if you use them effectively and consider the intricacy of leading others.

Functional Approach The *functional approach* views the leader as a facilitator, or the one who manages and supports the procedural and maintenance communication of the group.

Procedural communication includes the routine interactions necessary for group functions, such as:

- Establishing the places, dates, and times the group will meet
- Setting and distributing the agenda
- Finding a room, setting up equipment, and taking care of personal needs (water, coffee, comfortable space, etc.)
- Preparing and distributing materials
- Taking notes or minutes or appointing someone else to do so
- Summarizing at the end of each meeting

Maintenance communication includes the necessary interactions during the group meetings to keep the group on task and to maintain effective interpersonal relationships. These interactions include:

- Helping the group with decision-making or problem-solving processes
- Helping research and collect information
- Pushing the group to consider all options
- Offering criticism
- Controlling conflict and bad behavior
- Determining if members are fulfilling their tasks
- Creating and maintaining a supportive environment

Behavioral Styles Approach *Leadership behavioral style* refers to the leading or influencing behavior a leader chooses to use. There are three behavioral styles:[12]

Authoritarian leaders (also called *autocratic*) assume and maintain control over the group. Such leaders control the discussion and interaction, limit members' advice and involvement in major decisions, and rarely offer feedback. This style is not a license to degrade, abuse, or threaten, and it requires a wise use of power. It can create low cohesion and apathetic behavior.

Democratic leaders (also called *participative*) involve group members in decision-making and/or creative processes. These leaders guide the discussion, mediate conflict, encourage participation, take a socioemotional orientation, and offer insight by delegating authority. Here, either the group makes the final decision or the leader maintains control over the final decision. Democratic leadership creates group satisfaction and commitment, and such leaders help in completing complicated tasks.

Laissez-faire leaders (also called *delegative* or *free rein*) give group members complete freedom with the process necessary to reach the goal. Here, the leader may stay removed from the decisions but is ultimately responsible for them. This style is often misused, leaving the group confused, misdirected, and frustrated. However, it can work with highly motivated and knowledgeable groups.

Situational Approach Developed by Paul Hersey and Ken Blanchard, the *situational leadership theory* (also known as the *contingency theory*) argues that a leader should read the situation and adapt accordingly. Hersey and Blanchard suggest that you cannot use the same approach in every situation and that you must be fluid. In essence, the appropriate leadership style is contingent on the leader considering time limitations, group diversity, the maturity of the group, the specifics and complexity of the task, group identity, individual personalities, and outside influences. With this approach, the leadership styles can be categorized as delegating, participating, selling, and telling.[13]

high

level of leader support

PARTICIPATING
A leader who works with the group to share in the decision-making process.

SELLING
A leader who sells his or her perspective by providing information and direction. This style has more interaction and is sometimes called coaching.

DELEGATING
A leader who passes most of the work and responsibility off to the group members. This leader tends to just monitor the group.

TELLING
A leader who tells the group members what to do and how to do it with little interaction. This style is sometimes called directing.

low ← level of leader direction → high

Note how similar these are to the behavioral styles. Delegating echoes laissez-faire style, participating reflects the democratic approach, and telling/selling seems to mirror authoritarian style.

See Objective 8.7 for more on successful leadership.

Member

Usually, you will assume the responsibility of group member. Although the situation will dictate the number of group members, many communication scholars suggest that the most effective groups have approximately seven members and a leader. With too few members, you might not have the necessary knowledge base; too many members will impede the decision-making process. In a classroom setting, groups of four or five seem to work well. As a member, you will bring your expertise to the group, be given special tasks to complete, and take on certain membership roles.

Positive member roles are clustered as either group task or group interaction roles. If you take on a **group task role**, your behavior will assist the group with completing tasks and the group goal. A **group interaction role** helps create and maintain a positive climate and interpersonal relationships. Not all group member roles are positive, however. A member (or members) of the group might play a **self-centered role** by focusing on his or her own needs. Based on the work of Sandra M. Ketrow, Kenneth D. Benne, and Paul Sheats, the table on the following page outlines the various roles members may play in a group.[14] Keep in mind that, as an active group member, you are likely to take on multiple roles and to share roles with others.

Rarely will you find yourself as a member of a group without having a good reason to be involved in that group. Take pride in being asked or elected to join a group, and try to overcome your apprehensions. The effectiveness of the group depends on participation from everyone. If you are very concerned about openly participating, gradually participate by offering to take notes or being the one who encourages others to speak. Offer supportive nonverbal cues and/or statements. Eventually, you will find yourself contributing.

Complex group interactions can lead to unethical behavior such as disrespect, unfair competition, intolerance, and even oppression. Be polite, respectful, and considerate to all.

Self-Check: Avoiding Negative Membership Roles

Answering yes to any of the following questions suggests you might be taking on a self-centered role. Evaluate your behavior and move toward one of the positive roles.

1. Do you return to old issues, try to block progress, or refuse to support majority decisions?

2. Do you interrupt inappropriately, refuse to listen, criticize, or threaten others?

3. Do you avoid conflict rather than attempt to resolve it?

4. Do you engage in behavior that is distracting to other group members?

5. Do you plead for issues that may be detrimental to others or for the wrong reasons?

Group Task Roles (Positive)	**Initiator** proposes and prods the group for new ideas, goals, or plans.
	Elaborator asks for clarification, expands on ideas or suggestions, and develops thoughts.
	Coordinator puts ideas together, organizes, and promotes cooperation.
	Summarizer pulls work and ideas together and makes connections to previous work.
	Recorder takes good notes on the proceedings, prepares minutes, or creates reports.
	Evaluator thinks critically and offers effective analysis of ideas.
	Information giver or seeker researches for relevant data, facts, and other materials.
	Opinion giver draws conclusions about group actions or discussion based on his or her beliefs, values, interpretations, and judgments.
	Clarifier asks for more details to make the group's discussion less ambiguous.
	Consensus taker asks how the group feels about issues, discussions, or actions.
	Agenda setter suggests a procedure or how to make a decision.
Group Interaction Roles (Positive)	**Encourager** reinforces group cohesiveness by openly appreciating contributions.
	Supporter tends to follow the lead of other members by supporting and agreeing with others' proposals or ideas.
	Harmonizer works to relieve tension by mediating, compromising, or offering new suggestions.
	Gatekeeper allows all members to have a say in the process.
	Observer focuses on observing and commenting on the process.
	Standard setter helps set and enforce standards, rules, and norms.
Self-Centered Roles (Negative)	**Blocker** blocks progress by constantly objecting, repeatedly bringing up old issues, and refusing to accept or support a group decision.
	Attacker prevents effective collaboration by harshly criticizing and threatening others.
	Avoider does not contribute, refuses to deal with conflict, hides emotions, and cannot take a stance.
	Dominator controls, interrupts, and refuses to listen to other options or opinions.
	Attention seeker is always boasting and calling attention to herself/himself.
	Joker engages in games and humor that distract group work.
	Special-interest pleader pleads for his or her own subgroup or special interest at the expense of group time and resources.

8.5 How Can Culture Influence Small Groups?

With lots of interaction potential, small group participation will likely place you in situations with others whose backgrounds and work styles or ethics differs from yours. Your ability to hold virtual group meetings ups the probability even more. These conceivable cultural and co-cultural differences can greatly influence the small group process, the decision-making process, outcomes, and the prospects of future small group activity.

Influences Group Formation and Leadership

More and more, small groups and teams are being formed for complex and unique reasons. As this chapter and Chapter 7 have demonstrated, group work is a dynamically charged, synergistic process that brings distinct people together in good and conflicting ways. That alone can be challenging. Add the need to create cohesion among culturally diverse members and it seems almost impossible.

For more on how culture influences conflict, **see Objective 7.5**.

Recognize where there are cultural similarities and differences, and play to both as strengths. Here are just a few notable cultural differences that might influence small group formation and leadership.

- High power cultures might view the informality of using someone's first name as inappropriate, but low power might see it as polite, creating equality, and openness.[15] This could cause added stress.

- Cultures with a short-term orientation and/or individualist tendency might find the forming stage a waste of time and want to move on too quickly, whereas high context, collectivist, and nurturing cultures might linger here.

- Members from individualistic, competitive cultures may find the storming stage less stressful than collectivist or nurturing cultures.

- High-uncertainty cultures may struggle through the forming and storming stages but be comfortable in the norming and performing stages, where things are more certain and tasks are outlined.

- High power cultures may prefer an implied leader (based on rank, title, expertise) or one designated by someone in power. Low power–independent–competitive cultures allow for emergent leadership. Collectivist cultures tend to respect authoritarian leaders. Individualist cultures tend to prefer democratic leaders.

- All-channel or wheel networks may not feel comfortable for high-power cultures. For example, "You can always come to me for help," or an open-door perspective, may not work with high-power group members. They may not feel comfortable taking the initiative to engage someone with higher status.

- Research has demonstrated that cooperative leadership (soliciting participation, acknowledging contribution, active listening, and few overlaps in speech) seems to work best when cultures similar to U.S. and East Asian cultures (predominately China, Japan, Korea) work together. However, this same study found that a directive style (giving directions to members, minimal listening to others, and lots of interruptions) is the most common in these mixed-culture groups.[16]

Affects Group Perspectives and Interactions

In Chapter 1, you learned that ethnocentrism is the assumption that your own cultural or co-cultural group is superior. Often ethnocentrism starts as an inability to be self-reflexive about your own culture or co-culture as well as how others might view it. How often do you ask yourself questions like: What behaviors or norms do I view as positive or negative? How do others view me or people from my culture? Might they view my behaviors or norms as inappropriate? What stereotypes might others have about my culture or co-culture? What behaviors and norms might create these stereotypes (right or wrong)?

As one example, intercultural communication scholar Min-Sun Kim notes that the U.S. culture places a premium on the amount and frequency of talk between communicators.[17] If you are from the United States, this perspective could force you, consciously or unconsciously, to view less talkative cultures as ineffective. Conversely, someone from the other culture could view you as pushy, aggressive, and inconsiderate of power distance. Their negative response to their view of your behavior could feed your ethnocentrism and prevent ineffective interactions. This is true for any interaction but can be more significant when groups come together to negotiate, make decisions, and solve problems.

8.6 How Can Gender Influence Small Groups?

Women comprised 56 percent of college students in 2013.[18] According to the U.S. Department of Labor, women were nearly half (47 percent) of the workforce in 2012.[19] As of October 2014, more than 40 percent of mothers are the sole or primary breadwinners of their households.[20]

Given these statistics, the groups in your life are likely to be relatively gender balanced, making gender an important element. Most of the research connected to gender and small group communication looks at the workplace. For example, health, psychology, and equity researchers Larissa Myaskovsky, Emily Unikel, and Mary Amanda Dew discovered that, for the most part, having more than one gender in small groups is a good thing for small group outcomes. Surveying recent research, they noted that mixed-gender groups tend to perform better than same-gender groups.[21] If you look at what our culture sees as masculine versus feminine, this may not be too surprising, especially if contrasting skills are important. Women tend to seek consensus, resolve conflict by compromising, reward with equality, be relationship focused, and be emotional. Men tend to be decisive, aggressive, task-oriented, and nonemotional; they are risk takers and resolve conflict through win/lose strategies. All of these traits are important to group dynamics and leadership.

However, Myaskovsky, Unikel, and Dew uncovered some disturbing facts as well. In their study, they found:

- Women in mixed-gender groups tend to speak less and be less assertive than men.
- Men in mixed-gender groups tend to speak more, are more dominant and task-oriented, and are less friendly than women.
- Women are less task-oriented in mixed-gender groups than same-gender groups.
- Men are more task-oriented in mixed-gender groups than same-gender groups.
- Women solos—cases where a woman is the only one in a given group—tend to experience greater visibility and scrutiny of their work and are often delegated to stereotypically feminine tasks.
- Men solos tend to be evaluated more positively.
- Solo women tend to be less talkative than women in the majority.
- Solo men tend to be more talkative than men in the majority.
- Women tend to be negatively affected by solo status; men tend to be positively affected by solo status.

Gender communication scholar Diana Ivy notes that, as leaders, women tend toward a collaborative, participatory, democratic management style and people-oriented leadership skills. Men tend toward the autocratic management style and business-oriented leadership skills.[22]

These facts may not tell us everything there is to know about how men and women work together or how gender influences small group success, but they do hint at how small group behavior tends to mirror the division between men and women in some potentially "sticky" ways. Diana Ivy defines the **sticky floor phenomenon** as "factors that keep women in low-level, support roles in the workplace and that prevent them from seeking or gaining promotion or career development." This phenomenon relates mostly to the experience of pink-collar workers (e.g., secretaries, nurses, teachers, child care workers, or waitresses). The **glass ceiling**, according to Ivy, is the "transparent barrier in the workplace that allows professional women to look higher and see possibilities for advancements, but prevents them from attaining higher positions."[23] Documenting research by other gender scholars, Ivy lists family commitments, attitudes, stereotypes, and organizational structure as some examples of the factors keeping women "stuck," or affecting women's advancement to higher position levels.

If you consider Myaskovsky, Unikel, Dew, and Ivy's findings about how women and men interact in groups and lead them, you can begin to see how attitudes, stereotypes, and organizational biases could prevent qualified women from advancing.

8.7 How Can You Improve Your Small Group Skills?

U.S. professional soccer player Mia Hamm once said, "I am a member of a team, and I rely on the team, I defer to it and sacrifice for it, because the team, not the individual, is the ultimate champion."[24] Hamm's now-famous statement demonstrates that the power and success of a team/small group rest in its members' willingness to be a part of the group's synergy. Here's some advice to help you practice what Hamm highlights.

Set Group Guidelines

Although you may not be in a position to control or implement all of these, you should support similar rules.

- Create and distribute an agenda. Include subject details, requirements, deadlines, and beginning and ending times.
- Start and end the meeting on time.
- Come to the meeting prepared.
- Determine the appropriate decision-making process or method for problem solving.

  See Chapter 9 for more on decision making and problem solving.

- Create an environment where differences of opinion are welcomed. Challenge ideas, not people. Bring in an outsider to challenge ideas, opinions, and solutions. Try to prevent in-group pressure to conform. These guidelines will help prevent groupthink.
- Keep communication open among all members if possible.
- When the group comes to a consensus, support the decision.
- Outline the consequences of missing deadlines, not attending meetings, and other behaviors detrimental to the task.
- Make sure everyone leaves the meeting with a clear sense of the next step.
- Document progress (e.g., minutes).

Employ the 5-C Principles

To be a productive and ethical member of a small group, you must act in a responsible way. Recognize and dedicate yourself to the 5-C principles below.

Commitment: Be willing to give the group your complete attention, and align your personal goals with the group's goal. Do not impair or destroy the group goal by manipulating others for a personal goal. Be transparent about your goal and how you view the group goal.

Confidential: Often, sensitive issues are discussed by groups, so be respectful of privacy and personal conversation. Only share group discussions outside of the small group when appropriate.

Coalesce: Allow the group members to come together and work *with*—rather than *against*—each other. Mentor and socialize new members when necessary. Be sensitive to culture/gender issues. Avoid interpersonal conflicts by being civil, courteous, dignified, and respectful. Encourage all to contribute. Create trust.

Contribute: Use your talent for the betterment of the group and complete your tasks. An effective group requires every member to be responsible. Share what you know for the group's good. If you remain silent, accept that as agreement.

Concentrate: Stay on task and focus on the group goal. Do not hijack the discussion. Practice active and critical listening. Be curious or seek to understand rather than persuade or coerce.

Diminish Unproductive Behaviors

Earlier, you learned about the roles small group members can play (see Objective 8.4). Positive roles help move the group toward the goal. But negative, self-centered roles—blocker, attacker, avoider, dominator, attention seeker, joker, and special-interest pleader—can derail the group. Here are some tips to help with these less productive behaviors:

- Set NOSTUESO as a ground rule. This is an acronym for "No One Speaks Twice Until Everybody Speaks Once." If you set this rule at the beginning, you have the ability to minimize blockers, dominators, attention seekers, and special-interest pleaders; it might even help with attackers and jokers. It will force avoiders to participate if they know they will be called on.

- Set aside time at the beginning or end, during a break, or outside of the formal meeting for social time. This might keep a joker from controlling too much time during the meeting. Plus, it can help relieve the stress of the group activity.

- Give avoiders concrete tasks. Build time into the deadline for keeping them on task. Make sure they are aware of related group norms and consequences.

Ultimately, the group leader might need to confront the member with unproductive behavior, for the greater good of the group. However, all members should actively work to maintain productive behavior.

Chapter 8 Review

Key Questions

8.1 What Makes a Small Group?

Objective 8.1: **DISCUSS WHAT CONSTITUTES A SMALL GROUP**

A *small group* is a group of three to approximately seven interdependent people united over time as a cohesive unit with a common goal. Rules and norms help ensure group survival, help the group express their values, and to perform their function or to reach their goal. Each group fulfills a particular function clustered by satisfying a personal, public, or professional need.

See pages 210–215.

8.2 How Do Groups Develop?

Objective 8.2: **EXPLAIN THE FIVE STAGES OF GROUP FORMATION**

One of the most commonly used and cited models is *Tuckman's group development model*. The original model had four stages: forming, storming, norming, and performing. Later, Tuckman, along with Mary Ann Jensen, added a fifth stage, of terminating/reforming.

- Forming is the stage in which members get to know each other and the group creates its identity, seeks direction, learns about its task, and begins to determine membership roles.

- Storming is the stage in which the group starts to focus on its goal and may become complex as power and relationship issues emerge.

- Norming occurs after the conflict of storming is expressed and addressed. The members begin to outline necessary tasks and assignments to achieve their goal.

- Performing is the stage where the group conducts the "real work" necessary to make a decision or solve a problem.

- Terminating/reforming is the stage where the group either disbands after completing their goal or reforms with a new goal.

See pages 216–217.

8.3 How Do Group Members Interact?

Objective 8.3: **EXPLAIN SMALL GROUP INTERACTION NETWORKS**

There are two categories of small group networks. The first includes *informal networks*, which form when members are free to interact in any direction with any number of others or skip over other members or leaders. Work or school grapevines and social networking sites are informal networks. The second category of networks is made up of the *formal networks* that form specific interaction patterns called *wheel*, *chain*, or *all-channel networks*.

See pages 218–219.

8.4 What Roles Can You Play in a Small Group?

Objective 8.4: SUMMARIZE THE DIFFERENT SMALL GROUP ROLES

During small group communication, a *leader* is a person who guides the group toward its goal by influencing the group through communication. Types of leaders are *implied, designated*, and *emergent* leaders. There are numerous theories about how leaders lead. Four common ones are the *trait, functional, behavioral styles*, and *situational* approaches.

Usually, you will assume the responsibility of group *member*. Although the situation will dictate the number of group members, many communication scholars suggest that the most effective groups have approximately seven members and a leader. Positive member roles are clustered as either group task or group interaction roles. Negative member roles can cluster around self-centered behavior.

See pages 220–225.

8.5 How Can Culture Influence Small Groups?

Objective 8.5: EXAMINE HOW CULTURE INFLUENCES SMALL GROUPS

Cultural differences can greatly influence the small group process, the decision-making process, outcomes, and the prospects of future small group activity. You will negotiate these differences if you note how cultural difference can influence group formation and leadership as well as being self-reflexive to your own cultural perspective.

See pages 226–227.

8.6 How Can Gender Influence Small Groups?

Objective 8.6: EXPLORE HOW GENDER INFLUENCES SMALL GROUPS

Mixed-gender groups tend to perform better than same-gender groups. If you look at what our culture sees as masculine versus feminine, this may not be too surprising, especially where contrasting skills are important. Women tend to seek consensus, resolve conflict by compromising, reward with equality, be relationship focused, and be emotional. Men tend to be decisive, aggressive, task-oriented, and nonemotional; they are risk takers and resolve conflict through win/lose strategies.

See pages 228–229.

8.7 How Can You Improve Your Small Group Skills?

Objective 8.7: ARTICULATE METHODS FOR IMPROVING SMALL GROUP SKILLS

To improve your small group skills, you should:

- Set group ground rules or guidelines.
- Employ the 5-C principles of small group membership.
- Diminish unproductive behaviors.

See pages 230–231.

Key Terms

small group (210)
interdependence (211)
collective identity (211)
synergy (211)
cohesion (211)
norms (212)
hidden agenda (213)
social loafing (213)
groupthink (213)
personal groups (214)
public groups (214)
professional groups (214)
virtual small groups (215)
Tuckman's group development model (216)
informal networks (218)
formal networks (218)
wheel networks (219)
gatekeeper (219)
chain networks (219)
all-channel networks (219)
implied leader (221)
designated leader (221)
emergent leader (221)
authoritarian leaders (222)
democratic leaders (222)
laissez-faire leaders (222)
group task role (224)
group interaction role (224)
self-centered role (224)
sticky floor phenomenon (229)
glass ceiling (229)

Improve Your Communication

Researchers Nancy L. Harper and Lawrence R. Askling conducted a case study of six student groups completing major class projects. Harper and Askling found specific characteristics, "differences that make a difference," in the success of a student group related to leadership, openness, and proportion of active participators. The following describes successful behaviors:[25]

- Leaders were more active (attended class and meetings more), were perceived as more communicative by the membership, communicated more and better about necessary tasks, considered social issues and personal feelings of the membership, and successfully confronted conflict.

- Successful groups viewed themselves as a team (highly cohesive), had open conflict discussion, could handle criticism, and made group decisions via group interaction.

- The more active participation from more members, the more successful the group. This study demonstrated that 60–100% of the membership had to be either high or moderate participators to be successful.

Keep these productive characteristics in mind as you engage in group activities in all your classes and into the future.

Apply Your Knowledge

1. From your past experience with small group activities, consider groups that worked well and those that didn't. Can you pinpoint why the successful group was effective? How could you improve those positive attributes even more? Can you pinpoint why the unsuccessful group wasn't effective? How could you prevent those issues in the future?

2. When you lead, what kind of approach do you tend to use? Can you see times in your personal, professional, or public life that the other approaches might work best?

3. When you are a member of a group, which roles are you more comfortable fulfilling? Are there others you could do as well? Do you fall prey to any of the self-centered roles? If so, how can you minimize their influence over the group or turn them into a positive?

Other Resources

Here are some sources to help you develop and improve your skills.

Small Group Understanding and Skills

- www.referenceforbusiness.com/management/Gr-Int/Group-Dynamics.html#ixzz3705DC4SO

- www.med.fsu.edu/uploads/files/FacultyDevelopment_EffectiveGroups.pdf

- csumb.edu/writing/being-good-group-member

Leadership Development

DePree, Max. *Leadership Is an Art*. New York: Dell, 1989. Print.

Johnson, Craig E. *Meeting Ethical Challenges of Leadership: Casting Light or Shadow*. Los Angeles: SAGE, 2012. Print.

Maxwell, John C. *The 5 Levels of Leadership: Proven Steps to Maximize Your Potential*. New York: Center Street, 2013. Print.

Sample, Steven B. *The Contrarian's Guide to Leadership*. San Francisco: Jossey-Bass, 2003. Print.

- www.entrepreneur.com/article/226265

- www.cnn.com/2011/LIVING/08/03/good.leader.traits.cb/index.html

- gilpizano.com/personal-development/leadership-personal-development/48-great-sites-leadership-tips-ideas/

- www.greatleadershipbydan.com/2009/09/10-free-leadership-video-sites.html

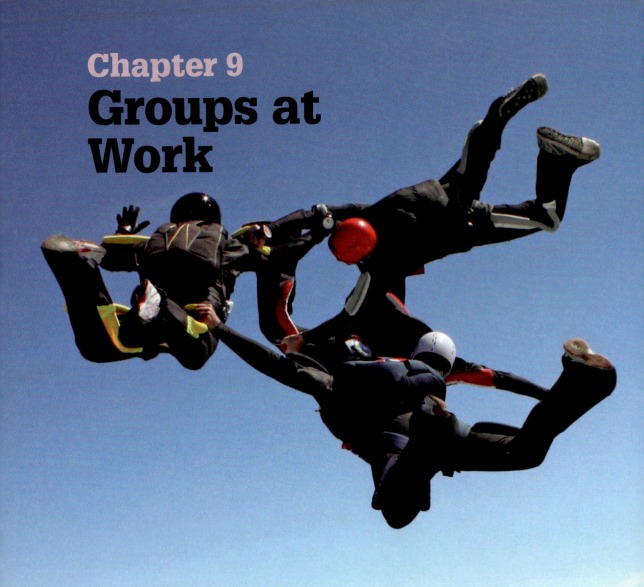

Chapter 9
Groups at Work

9.1 What Is the DECIDE Model for Decision Making and Problem Solving?

The work of small groups often takes the form of making a decision or solving a problem. *Decision making* refers to deciding what to do or distinguishing between alternatives (e.g., determining a type of computer to use company-wide). *Problem solving* is the process of finding solution(s) to an obstacle or concern (e.g., how to solve parking issues on campus).[1] You will find yourself in groups throughout your life, including college classes, doing this type of work.

Numerous decision-making and problem-solving processes are available, and many are variations of reflective thinking, first identified by philosopher John Dewey (1910).[2] This type of reflective thinking is often referred to as the *standard agenda method* today. Small group communication scholars Thomas Harris and John Sherblom outline one of these variations, called the **DECIDE model**, for decision making and problem solving.[3] Their unique approach makes it easy to remember the steps. The table on the next page explains each step. You can use this model as an agenda outline or to plan tasks for any group you are part of that needs to make a decision or solve a problem. The next time you are in a group with an assignment, think of the assignment as a process leading to a decision or solution. Then use the DECIDE model to help complete it.

Creativity and critical thinking are integral to decision making and problem solving. In the next section, you will learn methods for generating ideas, alternatives, or solutions. Once you have great options, your group will determine the final choice to be accepted or implemented. Objective 9.3 explains how formal or informal groups select a decision or solution.

The DECIDE Model

The Steps	What Needs to Be Established	Examples
Define the goal and problem	For whom is it a problem? What is the problem? Why, when, where, and how is it a problem?	The 5,000 jobs lost last year are a concern for the city, industry, housing market, and taxpayers, as they demonstrate a loss in growth and potential.
Examine issues preventing goal success	What is causing the problem and how severe is it? To reach your goal, what would be satisfactory, realistic, or achievable?	The closing of major industries and lost jobs in higher education and the medical field seem to be the sources of the problem. This job loss is 50 percent more than in 2014. Our goal is to reduce the number of jobs lost by 25 percent (still above 2014).
Consider alternatives	What are the standards for solving the problem? What are potential solutions?	Potential solutions are to rally for more state funding of higher education and medicine or to work at attracting new businesses.
Initiate a decision	Which solution is the best according to the group?	Because the state budget is being drastically cut, rallying for more state funds seems useless. Therefore, we should work to bring more new businesses to town.
Develop a plan	How will you implement the solution?	We will create tax cut incentives, build assistance programs, and step up public relations activities to attract growing industries.
Evaluate the results	Did the solution work? Was it too costly?	Although somewhat costly initially to the city and still high, the lost-job rate did drop 15 percent, which was better than for any other city in the state.

9.2 How Do Groups Generate Ideas, Alternatives, or Solutions?

Being creative nourishes the work of small groups. *Creativity* is the ability to "think outside the box" or to imagine new and original ideas, things, and solutions. Harris and Sherblom list a few thoughts that block creativity—*that is impossible, it's not exactly right, I might appear foolish, let's get serious, that's not logical,* and *that's not practical.*[4]

Brainstorming

Brainstorming is a process of creative thinking that jumps from one word or concept to another to generate a lot of ideas. Creativity theorist and father of brainstorming Alex Osborn defines brainstorming as the use of the brain to storm a creative problem in commando fashion.[5] This activity is often called "free association." Within the group setting, participants take turns calling out ideas to a moderator who lists them for all to see. During this imaginative stage, all ideas are accepted; "hitchhiking," or using others' ideas as a springboard for your thoughts, is encouraged; and ideas are not discussed.[6] Categorizing and evaluating the ideas occurs after this stage is concluded.

Brainstorming can be fun, create cohesion, and produce plentiful ideas. However, it can also have a few disadvantages. Brainstorming only works with a supportive and nonjudgmental group. One or two members can dominate the session, preventing the free flow of ideas. Plus, brainstorming can leave members who are in the minority, have less authority, are younger, are females in mixed-gender groups, or are males in same-gender groups feeling uncomfortable to freely participate. The next two techniques help diminish these disadvantages.

Nominal Group Technique

Nominal Group Technique (NGT) is a highly structured creative process for generating ideas, possibilities, or solutions and was created by management scholars Andre Delecq and Andrew Van de Ven.[7] The process follows these steps:

1. Define or state the question or problem to resolve.

2. Guided by a facilitator, the group takes a set time (10 minutes or so) to silently write down their ideas. This step can be computer-mediated as well.

3. Each member presents ideas in a round-robin session. The facilitator makes a master list of all the ideas.

4. The facilitator leads a discussion to consider the value of each item on the list.

This technique helps give voice to those who might not speak up during traditional brainstorming, allows for an anonymous vote, and prevents one or two members from dominating the conversation. It can benefit groups who think better in silence and larger groups where members may not know each other. Some disadvantages are that it can prevent creative cross-fertilization of ideas between individuals, may be too process oriented for some groups or topics, can be time consuming, and may not work well with extremely controversial issues.

Brainwriting

Brainwriting is a form of brainstorming that replaces the calling out of ideas with the private recording of an individual's ideas and adds cross-fertilization back into the process. Two common marketing brainwriting techniques are the *Pin Card* method and the *6-3-5* method.[8]

The Pin Card method asks 6 group members to write down 3 ideas or solutions in 5 minutes. Next, they pass their ideas to someone else. That member takes the other person's original ideas and has 5 minutes to do one of the following things: let the recorded ideas be an incentive for new ideas, which he or she adds to the sheet; make modifications to the original ideas created by the first member; or pass the card to the next person. The 6-3-5 method does the same thing, but each person can add only 3 new ideas to the sheet. At the end of the generation time period, ideas are collected, organized, and evaluated.

Brainwriting works well for groups of 6 or more.[9] It helps groups that have reserved members or conflict between members, and it prompts a lot of ideas quickly and without censorship. However, it can prevent development of ideas because of the speed—quantity over quality—and may prove difficult for members who are unable to write down ideas quickly.

9.3 How Do Groups Ultimately Select Decisions or Solutions?

Most highly organized groups have a constitution regulating how to conduct business and/or use a rule book, such as parliamentary procedure, to delineate rules, ethics, and customs designed to conduct meetings and official business. Even informal groups, such as family, friends, or social, therapeutic, civic, or learning groups, may use a form of parliamentary procedure to debate or reach group decisions. Most groups make decisions based on consensus, majority or minority rule, expert opinion, or authority rule.

Consensus

Consensus occurs when the entire group agrees or consents to a particular decision or solution. *Unanimous consensus* is the purest and occurs when all members agree (unanimity) that there is only one best decision or solution. Consensus based on consent can occur as well. This type of consensus happens when some members agree to a decision or solution even though it wasn't their first choice; they can live with it and support it. Consensus based on consent can be a healthy alternative if it isn't achieved through coercion, deception, impatience, or power pressure.

Reaching unanimous consensus can be difficult and is often limited to situations where the group decision has significant consequences (e.g., in a jury for criminal cases or when voting to reverse constitutional rules). Consensus can frequently provide the best, most creative results and strongest member commitment if you have the time to work through the process.

For consensus to happen, members must participate and behave ethically. They should critically listen, remain calm, view the process as collaboration, be open-minded as well as cooperative, and seek agreement.

Here are some favorable conditions for consensus:

- Small group size—three to seven is optimal
- A membership with the necessary knowledge, skill, and resources
- A high level of trust and respect within the membership
- A membership willing to dedicate the necessary time and energy
- A format where all members are given a voice and all ideas potential consideration
- A clear purpose and understanding of the issue
- Skillful leadership, facilitation, and preparation
- A group willing to prevent groupthink and to manage conflict via collaboration

| **See Objective 8.1** (page 210) for more on groupthink.

Practicing Ethics: Responsible Decisions

It is important for groups to make good, ethical decisions. Members should ask:

- Are we accomplishing the most important goal?
- Are there potential unintended or undesirable results? Is there a less harmful solution? If we were the ones influenced, would we still support it?
- What are the short- and long-term effects? What are the risks?
- Can we live with taking our decision public, or would we feel the need to hide behind the decision?

Majority Rule

Majority rule states that a group may make decisions or select solutions with a majority—one vote more than half of the group—or with a plurality. A plurality is sometimes necessary when there are more than two options and no one option receives 50 percent of the votes. In this case, a plurality wins, or the option with the most votes is selected.

Majority rule can cause tension within the group and therefore is best for insignificant decisions, when time is of the essence, when the group is large, when a stalemate is inevitable, or when it is required in the bylaws. The minority can end up feeling resentful, left out of the process, and not committed to the implementation.

If allowable by the group or organization, a *two-thirds vote*, requiring two-thirds of the membership to vote in favor, can be beneficial to limit majority rule disadvantages. For example, if you have a group of seven members, five must vote in favor for the decision or solution to be acceptable. If votes are sensitive, you can take this type of vote by private electronic or paper ballot.

Minority Rule

Although minority rule sounds like the opposite of majority rule, it really isn't. **Minority rule** is the decision process in which a small fraction of a larger group makes the decision for the larger organization. For example, the finance committee of an organization might decide on what insurance company to use, or a small student group may help make decisions about what is needed in a new student union. This type of voting can be efficient and effective if the smaller group is viewed by the larger organization as capable of making such decisions. However, it can create animosity if the larger group disagrees with the small group's decision or doesn't consider them fair, ethical, or experts on the issue.

Expert Opinion

Expert opinion decisions occur when one member has superior knowledge about the issues and that person is given the power to make the decision. For example, if a decision has legal ramifications, and one of the group members specializes in that type of law, the group could and probably should defer to that member's expertise. Like minority rule, this option can create animosity and the organization membership has to have faith in the individual's character and ability to make the decision.

Authority Rule

Authority rule decisions (also known as unilateral decisions) are made by a designated leader or person who has power over the situation. Extremely autocratic leaders use this form of decision making and it can be necessary when very quick decisions must be made. Some leaders might use a pseudo-democratic approach as well. For example, a group of students might be asked to put together a proposal on how to make campus safe, but the safety and security director or president makes the final decision on what to do. The membership may not be as dedicated to committing to and implementing the decision with this type of rule.

Although how to reach a final decision or solution is often preset or determined by someone else, the following table will help you determine the best route when you do have the option to select from these methods.

How to Decide on Deciding

Questions to Consider	Methods You Might Use
Are there organizational requirements or bylaws regulating how to make decisions?	If your organization has a governing handbook or constitution, that document can regulate what form you must use. For example, your handbook might say that you must use majority rule to change current procedures. It is best to always consult such documents early in the decision-making process. Do you need a quorum present to conduct a vote? A **quorum** is the minimum number of members (usually 50 percent plus 1) that must be present before business can take place at a meeting.
How much time do you have?	If you are pressed for time, consensus building may not be an option. Under extreme pressure, expert or authority rule might be best.
How creative or innovative should the group be?	Consensus and majority rule are going to involve more knowledgeable individuals and often rely on brainstorming, NGT, or brainwriting to be more creative and productive. Minority rule can as well if the group members are selected carefully.
Will the decision require expertise from multiple areas or significant research?	If the issue or problem is very complex, it is probably best not to use a single expert or authority figure to make the decision.
How important is community buy-in?	If it is important, consensus or majority rule is best.
Are there major conflicts that will impede the process?	If so, it is best to stay away from consensus. In extreme cases, a decision by *arbitration*, or having an external body or person make the decision for the group, might be the only option.
Is it a trivial or somewhat unimportant issue?	Forming a group for insignificant decisions or ones that can be made just as effectively by an individual is a waste of time and resources and will often frustrate the group members.

9.4 How Can Culture and Gender Influence Decision Making and Problem Solving?

Homogeneous groups are made up of like-minded members who are similar in culture and/or co-culture. *Heterogeneous groups* have memberships that are diverse in culture and/or co-culture. Small group and management researchers Poppy McLeod, Sharon Lobel, Taylor Cox, Jr., and Stacy Blake echo the prominent theme that companies need to manage diversity because of its inevitability in the global workplace. However, they also observed that it is a potential source of competitive advantage which they label as "value-in-diversity" or "valuing diversity."[10]

McLeod, Lobel, Cox, and Blake, as well as organizational and management researchers Nancy Adler and Allison Gundersen, argue that diverse groups possess the following benefits or value for an organization.[11] Heterogeneous groups that are managed effectively tend to:

- Be more productive
- Create better ideas and solutions to problems
- Engage in enhanced concentration
- Be less susceptible to groupthink
- See less turnover of staff and fewer sick days
- Access a better expert/knowledge base when diverse
- Understand diverse consumer behavior better for marketing purposes

Heterogeneous groups do have some potential downsides, especially when managed ineffectively. These groups risk experiencing outcomes opposite of those listed earlier. Negative outcomes may include:

- Greater losses due to faulty processes and employee turnover
- More challenges because team members find it more difficult to see, understand, and act on situations in similar ways
- Low cohesion and trust
- More difficulty coming to agreement or consensus[12]

The following Tip box offers some basic advice on how to manage diverse groups when you find yourself in such a leadership role. As a member of a group, you can use these tips to help the group and the leader positively negotiate diversity.

Let's take a closer look at some potential impacts of differences in cultural dimensions and gender.

Culture's Potential Impact

Just as it can when we are determining what to wear or eat, culture can make an impact on how we navigate making decisions or solving problems. In Chapter 8, you learned some ways that culture and co-cultures can influence the dynamics of small groups. Now let's look at how individuals from different ethnicities might react during each stage of DECIDE process. See the table on the next page. As you read through the descriptions, remember that it is easy to wrongly stereotype, or to make an oversimplified and generalized prejudgment about someone. Always view people as individuals.

TIP: Adler and Gundersen's Advice for Managing Diverse Groups[13]

1. Select members based on their relationship to the task. Members should be homogeneous in ability level and heterogeneous in attitude and culture/co-culture if possible.

2. Recognize and respect cultural differences. Educate yourself about the differences and be mindful and respectful. For example, the French believe that a manager should give precise answers to most work-related questions and the Dutch or Japanese will almost always make decisions or solve problems by consensus.[14]

3. Explicitly establish the group's goal or purpose. Remember that there might be some language barriers, so try to keep concepts straightforward. Engage in activities and question-and-answer sessions to determine if everyone understands. Some members may say they understand even when they don't.

4. Ensure equal participation. Use multiple techniques for gaining participation from all.

5. Minimize ethnocentrism and prejudice by creating mutual respect. Set ground rules if necessary. Plan how to respond to ethnocentric behavior or prejudice.

6. Give feedback. Diverse groups need encouragement to proceed through the decision-making process.

How Diverse Cultural Dimensions Could Impact DECIDE[15]

	High Power vs. Low Power	Individualist vs. Collectivist
Define the goal	**High power:** Need guidance and explicit direction from perceived authorities or experts. **Low power:** Prefer to be equal contributors. Defensive to authority.	**Individualist:** Ask: *What is the problem? How does it influence me?* **Collectivist:** Ask: *How is this a problem for my organization? What are communal goals and interests?* Might be reluctant to discuss problems ("losing face").
Examine the issue	**High power:** Consult those in authority or experts on the issue. Follow appropriate channels. **Low power:** Believe all need to offer input into what the issue is and how to resolve it.	**Individualist:** Ask: *How is this a problem for me? How can I solve this issue?* May aggressively explore the issue. **Collectivist:** Ask: *What is good or bad for the group? What can the group do?* Uncomfortable with confrontation, interruptions, and direct questions.
Consider alternatives	**High power:** Discourage challenging past procedures or management. **Low power:** Encourage questioning or challenging others.	**Individualist:** Ask: *What do I believe is best for me and my area?* **Collectivist:** Ask: *What is the will of the group?*
Initiate a decision	**High power:** Let senior managers make the decisions. **Low power:** Delegate responsibility or decide as a group.	**Individualist:** Let individuals decide. **Collectivist:** Prefer many people making the decisions, which takes time.
Develop a plan	**High power:** Let senior managers make the plan that is implemented by all. **Low power:** Prefer that plan design and implementation involve everyone.	**Individualist:** Assignments and responsibilities are given to individuals. **Collectivist:** No one person should make a plan alone unless he/she is an expert or authority. Assignments and responsibilities are collective.
Evaluates the results	**High power:** Don't question the decisions of leaders. Follow protocol and hierarchical structure. **Low power:** Evaluation and responsibility may not reside with leaders but with the whole group.	**Individualist:** I am responsible for my actions. **Collectivist:** Entire group is responsible for the results.

Long-Term vs. Short-Term Orientation	High-Uncertainty vs. Low-Uncertainty Avoidance
Long-term: Define with an orientation toward the past/tradition, present, and future. **Short-term:** Define with an orientation toward new, now, and future.	**High-uncertainty:** May view change as more uncertain than accepting the situation. **Low-uncertainty:** May embrace significant change.
Long-term: Ask: *What is achievable, realistic, or satisfactory even if it takes time?* **Short-term:** Ask: *What is quickly achievable to gain positive results?*	**High-uncertainty:** Ask: *How can we safely reach our goal or what is comfortably achievable?* **Low-uncertainty:** Ask: *How can we think differently about the goal?*
Long-term: Ask: *How does the plan fit with past/tradition and social, cultural, or organizational customs?* **Short-term:** Ask: *What does the plan cost (in money and time)?*	**High-uncertainty:** May prefer custom, ritual, and stability. **Low-uncertainty:** Embrace the unusual, new and innovative ideas.
Long-term: Take time with decisions. **Short-term:** Make decisions fast.	**High-uncertainty:** Tend to be safe and reject deviant ideas; seek truth and expertise. **Low-uncertainty:** Tend to take risks.
Long-term: Dedicated to past and long-term. Often see group members follow through in the long term. **Short-term:** Might develop a 5- or 10-year plan but focus on the present. Employees may come and go quickly.	**High-uncertainty:** Adhere to rules. Develop plans with greater predictability and certainty. **Low-uncertainty:** Explore new ideas and procedures.
Long-term: Value persistence, thriftiness, work ethic, structure, dedication to tradition, and status. **Short-term:** Make decisions fast, with immediate results, and with some emphasis on cost.	**High-uncertainty:** Ask: *Did the solution adhere to our traditions and values as well as solve the problem?* **Low-uncertainty:** Ask: *Was the risk worth it? Did it solve the problem?*

Gender's Potential Impact

In a 2001 lecture, then–appeals court judge Sonia Sotomayor said,

> Personal experiences affect the facts that judges choose to see. My hope is that I will take the good from my experiences and extrapolate them further into areas with which I am unfamiliar. I simply do not know exactly what that difference will be in my judging. But I accept there will be some based on my gender and my Latina heritage.[16]

In this quotation, Supreme Court Justice Sotomayor hints that gender (as well as culture) influences how individuals interpret information. You already know from Chapter 8 that diversity can affect group interactions and leadership. Here, we will see how it influences perspectives on decision making and problem solving. Sotomayor is not suggesting that she uses her gender and ethnicity to be knowingly biased, however. She is saying that they inform and focus what she sees and allow her to offer a unique perspective.

Political scientists Rebecca J. Hannagan and Christopher W. Larimer have posed the following question: "Does gender composition affect group decision outcomes?"[17]

Citing numerous studies, Hannagan and Larimer highlight the following differences in legislative situations:

- Women tend to exhibit a more democratic style of leadership and debate; men are more autocratic.
- Women tend to cue cooperation in groups and men tend to cue competition.
- In competitive decision-making settings, men discriminate against the out-group and women "boost" the in-group.
- Women tend to reach full consensus easier than men. Men often only reach a majority. Women's ability to read and decode nonverbal communication seems to be the reason for this, and they can determine the most amenable outcome more accurately.

The table on the next page offers some general gender differences that can influence how groups make decisions and solve problems. Keep in mind, gender is only one type of co-culture that might influence group outcomes. Be willing to learn about other cultures/co-cultures, pay attention to distinctions as they play out, and learn to negotiate differences.

How Gender May Impact Group Work

How men and women see problems	Men tend to view problems as only two-sided, or as an either-or situation. Women tend to seek out other options and ask more questions.[18]
Types of motivation	Women are more likely to report being motivated by altruistic concerns and to prefer a universalistic solution. Men are more likely to report being motivated by self-interest and to prefer a competitive solution.[19]
Levels of risk	Men are more likely to take risks or participate in risky behavior than women.[20] This could allow them to take chances with solutions that women may not. Likewise, women may research a risky solution more and make a potentially better risky decision.
Perceived expertise	Men are perceived as having more experience in most situations. This could be why they tend to evolve as leaders and be the ones a group will turn to for expertise.[21]
Ability to support	Women are somewhat more skilled at providing emotional support and responding to the distress of others.[22]
Alliances versus coalitions	In mixed-gender groups, women tend to form supportive alliances to gain support for their goals or perspectives. Men tend to form coalitions.[23]

Groups are a social microcosm of the wider society.[24]

Allen Brown and Tara Mistry

9.5 How Can You Effectively Communicate in Meetings?

Meetings are central to the work small groups do. They are a specific form of communicative interaction that can have different goals, such as sharing information, brainstorming ideas, making decisions, creating materials, or motivating the group. Some meetings are formal, conducted under strict rules, ethics, and customs. Usually formal meetings best fit civic organizations, clubs, and governments. Informal meetings are more common in the workplace but should adhere to rules, ethics, and appropriate customs.

As a Participant

Participants share the responsibility of using meeting time wisely and productively. As a participant, you should:

- Respond quickly when asked to participate in a meeting. You may be important to an agenda item, and the meeting may need to be rescheduled if you cannot attend.

- Read the agenda as soon as you get it, to see what you need to prepare. Anticipate how you might respond to questions about each item, and do your research.

- Be on time. This includes mediated meetings. Late arrivals are obvious and annoying. They will interrupt the flow of the meeting and could cause unnecessary repetition of information already discussed.

- Before the meeting begins, turn off your cell phone or unnecessary devices.

- During the meeting, actively listen and pay attention, focus on the agenda items, and keep your discussion to a minimum. Allow others to participate, and try not to interrupt. Be enthusiastic.

- Ask questions when appropriate, and write down your follow-up responsibilities.

- Be productive and do your part. A meeting is a group effort.

As a Leader

If you are leading the meeting, these guidelines will help you conduct an effective and productive meeting.

- Have a purpose and share it. Holding an unnecessary, undefined meeting wastes time and lowers morale.

- Create an agenda and send a copy to each attendee. Include the date, time, and location of the meeting. Depending on your group norms or what works for you as a leader, your agenda could simply list each item to be considered during the meeting, or it could be detailed. Detailed agendas often list how each item will be considered (for information, discussion, or action), who is presenting the item, and how much time will be spent on each item. In either case, you want your information to be specific enough that participants can prepare accordingly.

- If the meeting was called suddenly, quickly type an agenda to distribute at the beginning of the meeting or take a few minutes to outline orally what will be considered.

- If you will call on someone to speak, give the person enough notice before the meeting to prepare.

- Set beginning and ending times for the meeting, and share them with participants in advance. Make sure you can see a clock or watch during the meeting.

- Select a room large enough to accommodate known participants and a few extra, in case a participant invites a guest. Make sure all necessary equipment is present and working before the start of the meeting.

- Arrive early and chat with participants. By doing so, you personalize your relationship with the group and give them time to talk "off topic" about things that might otherwise come up later.

- Turn off your cell phone or unnecessary devices. Doing so in front of the participants hints that they should do the same. Close the door to minimize interruptions.

- Conduct introductions if new participants or guests are present.

- Keep control of the meeting. Do not let a participant take it over or monopolize the time. Limit the amount of time someone can speak, and try to engage all participants. Be energetic and focused.

- Save time at the end of the meeting to summarize, divide up responsibilities or tasks, ask for questions, and thank the participants.

- If needed, arrange a time and date for the next meeting.

> **TIP: Attentive Listening**
>
> Whether you are a group leader or member, *attentive listening* (paying careful attention and being observant) is key to effective group work. See Chapter 5 for more on listening.

In Virtual Settings

In 2012, according to Global Workplace Analytics, 2.6 percent of the U.S. employee workforce—or 3.3 million people—worked from home for a business, forcing them to work in the virtual world. This percentage is up 80 percent since 2005.[25] In 2011, Fortune 500 and larger companies surveyed by Brandman University noted that 40 percent of their employees work in some sort of virtual team.[26]

Given the global connectivity in the business world today, it is highly unlikely that you will complete your career without working in a virtual group. As you learned in Chapter 8, virtual small groups carry out their group activity predominately or completely via technology such as email, file-sharing websites, videoconferencing, electronic meeting systems, and telephone or computer conferencing. In Chapter 2, you learned that interactions that are not in real time (e.g., email) are *asynchronous engagements*, and *synchronous engagements* occur when groups interact in real time via mediation (e.g., telephone conferencing). ***Hybrid engagements*** occur when part of the interaction is in real time and a subset is not (e.g., part of a discussion is conducted face-to-face and part later via email). These engagements allow groups to function without being in the same place or even on the same time. For example, the author of this text is in Missouri, the editor is in Texas, the development editor is in Colorado, the design director is in London, England, and the main office for the publisher is in New York. The creation of the text occurred via telephone or computer conferencing and sharing of files via email or websites. Rarely did we meet body-to-body or face-to-face.

The self-check below will help you determine if you are using virtual meetings effectively, and the following page offers advice on effective behaviors for virtual participation.

Self-Check: Virtual Meetings

The "coolness" factor of using virtual meeting technology can sometimes cloud its effectiveness. As with any interaction, you should check the effectiveness of virtual meetings. Here are some evaluation questions.

1. Did the group effectively achieve its goal or outcomes? Did the group achieve the goal or outcomes within the set timeframe? If not, did the virtual meeting format cause the delay? Is there a way to fix that in the virtual world? Was this cost effective?

2. Did the technology work for this type of group? Did it add value? Was the best technology employed?

3. Was there enough leadership and coaching offline to help the process progress?

4. Did participants feel that the virtual group experience was effective and/or a good one? Do the participants look forward to other virtual groups?

Effective Behaviors in Virtual Settings

Develop an orientation phase to set the team into motion. This is often best done in person or via technology that allows face-to-face contact (videoconferencing, for example). Think about employing team-building exercises that build trust, help share personal values or experiences, or help develop information-sharing skills. (Search the Internet for "team-building games for virtual groups" if you can't have a body-to-body orientation.)

Remember that strong interpersonal skills are still important. Set up acceptable norms and rules. Build trust with each other. Incorporate emotions and personal thoughts into messages that can transmit as impersonal. Be aware of time or geographical differences that might influence interaction.

Select or appoint a leader who has strong technology and communication skills. The leader can help by setting boundaries, formal polices, and norms for the group. Create a good communication-sharing climate. Virtual leaders should communicate often with members. During meetings, leaders should keep participants focused and engaged.

Try to stay current on rapid technological advancements that can better facilitate the group's activities. Don't rely only on the easiest or most traditional methods for communicating. They may not always be the best.

Use the best technology or type of meeting (synchronous, asynchronous or hybrid) for the situation. For example, telephones or audio/video conferencing are the best when sharing complex information or when discussing the issue is vital. Email can be effective for sharing information if it needs to be documented or when written documents are best. Highly interactive technologies (e.g., videoconferencing or electronic meeting systems) are best for discussion, decision making, and creativity.

Plan and prepare for meetings. Long virtual meetings are hard to sustain (no more than 90 minutes is best). Create focused agendas, distribute necessary information before the meeting, and make sure the technology works. All participants need to prepare and participate.

Don't forget differences in cultures and co-cultures (such as gender). This can be easy to do when using text-based communication methods.

Remember to document virtual meetings. Written agendas and minutes are crucial to a dispersed group.

Remember to keep working between meetings. Not regularly connecting personally with other members or the leader can reduce your sense of responsibility to the project and the urgency to complete it. Keep a schedule and consult it regularly.

In Group Presentations

Groups often need to present their findings or results. For example, if you are given a group assignment to report back to the class on how social media influences interpersonal communication, you may be graded on how well you present your findings. Let's look at how to present as a group.

Determine the Format

The first step in presenting your finding is to determine the appropriate format. Usually, your assignment or the situation dictates or narrows your format options. See the table below for five group presentation formats.

Group Presentation Formats

Format	What Is It?
Group oral report	A speech reporting the findings, conclusions, and decisions of the group and given by someone from the group. A question-and-answer session may follow.
Forum	An interactive session between the audience and the small group. Here, the audience can offer their comments as well as ask questions. A forum may follow a symposium or prepared speech.
Symposium	A series of coordinated unique short reports by each group member, presented to an audience. A moderator introduces and connects each speech and summarizes after all are given. There may be a question-and-answer session.
Colloquium	A public discussion between the group members with divergent views in front of a public audience. A moderator usually facilitates and the audience may participate in a question-and-answer session.
Panel discussion	Usually led by a moderator or chairperson, this format is designed to give information about an issue, problem, or recommendation.

Create the Presentation

To create the content of your group presentation, you need to develop your ideas, research for potential content, and organize your thoughts. Other than having more than one person create the presentation, this process is just like that of a single person creating an informative or persuasive speech. Chapters 10–14 can help your group with the creative process for public speaking. Here's the basic procedure.

- Determine the goal and central idea of the presentation. This step requires analyzing your audience and the situation as well as narrowing your topic. Make sure each group member understands and supports the goal and focus of the presentation.

  See Chapter 10 for help with developing a central idea.

- Adhere to your presentation format.
- Assign individual tasks. If you agree to do something, do it.
- Create preparation and delivery outlines for each member. Think about electing someone to serve as moderator to help connect the individual parts. Moderators should also try to facilitate interaction between the presenters and the audience.

  See Chapter 11 for more on creating outlines.

- Use language appropriate to the audience and situation. Define any specialized terms.

  See Chapters 3 and 12 for more on language choices.

Give the Presentation

Most group presentations require all members of the group to participate. This can be more complex to work out and rehearse than an individual speech. Here are a few strategies:

- Create necessary presentation aids. If each member creates his or her own, try to coordinate them.
- Rehearse as a group several times, using the presentation aids, to uncover any trouble spots. Time your presentation to ensure you are within the limit. Panels and forums are usually extemporaneous or impromptu. Symposiums and oral reports may be delivered extemporaneously, from a manuscript, or from memory.
- Dress for the occasion.
- Use technology if appropriate and available.

  See Chapter 12 for help with delivery or presentation aids.

Listen and Evaluate

Adapting to your audience during the presentation is important to your success. Likewise, learn to evaluate your presentations so you can make the next one even better. Both of these tasks require effective listening skills. Your group should:

- Listen/watch for verbal and nonverbal feedback from your audience and respond.
- Be ready to take and answer questions.
- Evaluate the presentation for its effectiveness.

  See Chapters 5, 13, and 14 for guidance on listening and evaluating.

Chapter 9 Review

Key Questions

9.1 What Is the DECIDE Model for Decision Making and Problem Solving?

Objective 9.1: **EXPLAIN THE DECIDE MODEL**

Small group communication scholars Thomas Harris and John Sherblom outline the *DECIDE model* for decision making and problem solving. The steps in the process are:

- Define the goal or problem.
- Examine issues preventing goal success.
- Consider alternatives.
- Initiate a decision.
- Develop a plan.
- Evaluate the results.

See pages 238–239.

9.2 How Do Groups Generate Ideas, Alternatives, or Solutions?

Objective 9.2: **SUMMARIZE TECHNIQUES FOR GENERATING IDEAS, ALTERNATIVES, OR SOLUTIONS**

Creativity is the ability to "think outside the box" or to imagine new and original ideas, things, and solutions. Some techniques include:

- *Brainstorming* is a process of creative thinking that jumps from one word or concept to another to generate a lot of ideas.

- *Nominal Group Technique* (NGT) is a highly structured creative process for generating ideas, possibilities, or solutions.

- *Brainwriting* is a form of brainstorming that replaces the calling out of ideas with the private recording of an individual's ideas and adds cross-fertilization back into the process.

See pages 240–241.

9.3 How Do Groups Ultimately Select Decisions or Solutions?

Objective 9.3: **DISCUSS THE DIFFERENT METHODS FOR SELECTING DECISIONS OR SOLUTIONS**

- *Consensus* occurs when the entire group agrees or consents to a particular decision or solution.

- *Majority rule* states that a group may make decisions or select solutions with a majority vote or with a plurality.

- *Minority rule* is the decision process in which a small fraction of a larger group makes the decision for the larger organization.

- *Expert opinion* decisions occur when one member has superior knowledge about the issues and that person is given the power to make the decision.

- *Authority rule* decisions are made by a designated leader or person who has power over the situation.

See pages 242–245.

9.4 How Can Culture and Gender Influence Decision Making and Problem Solving?

Objective 9.4: **EXAMINE HOW CULTURE AND GENDER INFLUENCE DECISION MAKING AND PROBLEM SOLVING**

Homogeneous groups are made up of like-minded members who are similar in culture and/or co-culture. *Heterogeneous groups* have memberships that are diverse in culture and/or co-culture, and they tend to be more productive, create better ideas and solutions to problems, engage in enhanced concentration, be less susceptible to groupthink, see less turnover of staff and fewer sick days, access a better expert/knowledge base when diverse, and understand diverse consumer behavior better for marketing purposes. It is equally important for heterogeneous groups to realize how different cultural and gender dimensions can influence the decision-making and problem-solving processes.

See pages 246–251.

9.5 How Can You Effectively Communicate in Meetings?

Objective 9.5: **ARTICULATE METHODS FOR EFFECTIVELY COMMUNICATING IN A MEETING**

- As a participant, share responsibility for using meeting time wisely. Be prepared, focus on the agenda during the meeting, and ask appropriate questions.

- As a leader, follow guidelines for calling meetings, setting times and agendas, and keeping your meetings organized and focused.

- In virtual meetings, follow guidelines for effective behavior and technology use. Remember that interpersonal and intercultural skills are still important.

- In group presentations, the group must decide on the format (group oral report, forum, symposium, colloquium, or panel discussion), create the presentation, give the presentation, listen and watch for the audience's feedback, and evaluate the presentation.

See pages 252–257.

Key Terms

Improve Your Communication

As you learned from Chapter 8, group norms and guidelines are important to the group's success—so important that your instructor might require you to create a written group contract and have each member sign it. The University of Waterloo's Centre for Teaching Excellence offers some guidelines.[27] Make sure you delineate appropriate behaviors and the consequences if they are not followed.

1. Meeting times and dates will be agreed upon. Meetings will start five minutes after the agreed start time and end on time.

2. Everyone should attend the meetings. If you need to miss for an unavoidable event such as illness, you must notify the leader. You may miss only one meeting before it influences your grade by 10 percent each time. Being tardy or leaving early twice will be considered an absence.

3. All members will come to the meeting prepared.

4. All members should meet agreed-upon deadlines. Missing a deadline will influence your grade by 10 percent.

5. The group will actively seek a consensus of opinion based on the opinions of every member. Inappropriate behavior will not be tolerated.

6. The leader will create and distribute an agenda for each meeting.

7. One member will be selected each meeting to record minutes.

8. Any member can be voted out of the group at any time. Members breaking rules or not meeting deadlines will be confronted in writing (from leader) and

during a meeting. The instructor will receive a copy of the written document and will have final say on removing the student from the group.

Setting up norms like these, prior to having problems, will often prevent problems.

If your small group is charged with creating a document or presentation, here are some helpful hints for success:

- Set and meet deadlines.
- Plan the specifics of the format before anyone starts writing or composing.
- Share the duties. Consider everyone's talents when assigning duties.
- Remember to cite sources.
- Build leeway into the deadline—group work takes longer than individual work.
- Plan for revisions as a group or rehearse as a group.
- View the revision process and criticism as positive things (seek outside evaluation help from a colleague or writing center).
- Proofread and do a spelling/grammar check.

Apply Your Knowledge

1. Think about how you make personal decisions. Does this influence how you make professional decisions?

2. What do you view as appropriate behavior for small group membership? Be specific.

3. What aspects of your cultural or co-cultural background might influence the ways you make decisions or interact with others during the process?

Other Resources

Here are some resources to help you in your small group activities.

Group Work

Dittmer, Robert E., and Stephanie McFarland. *151 Quick Ideas for Delegating and Decision Making.* Franklin Lakes: Career Press, 2007. *eBook Academic Collection (EBSCOhost).* Web. 25 July 2014.

Mackin, Deborah. *The Team Building Tool Kit: Tips and Tactics for Effective Workplace Teams.* New York: AMACOM, 2007. *eBook Academic Collection (EBSCOhost).* Web. 25 July 2014.

Decision Making

- www.referenceforbusiness.com/ management/Gr-Int/Group-Decision-Making.html#ixzz3705QxRwa
- leadership.uoregon.edu/resources/ exercises_tips/organization/group_ decision_making
- www.uri.edu/research/lrc/scholl/ webnotes/Group_DM.htm
- www.cdc.gov/HealthyYouth/evaluation/ pdf/brief7.pdf
- www.hawaii.edu/mauispeech/pdf/ gpssteps.pdf

Chapter 10
Developing a Speech Topic

10.1 How Can You Be a Successful Public Speaker?

We often know when we hear or see successful public speakers, even if we can't always identify why we like them. While good public speaking habits seem to slide on by, unnoticed, the speakers can move us and change our lives. Beginning speakers often see perfection as the key to success—only to be disappointed. No one is perfect, but successful public speaking grows out of understanding, shaping, and connecting. The following qualities will help you achieve those goals.

Be Audience Centered

Speakers who are *audience centered* create and deliver their speeches while considering the unique characteristics of their audiences. Being audience centered will guide you in selecting appropriate topics and creating ways for your audience to connect with your speech.

- **Be knowledgeable.** Learn as much as possible about your audience, topic, and occasion.
- **Be creative.** Bring your topic to life for the audience by being creative. Think outside the box.
- **Be organized.** Successful speakers effectively organize their speeches to engage their audiences and focus attention on the speech topic.
  - **Use appropriate presentation techniques.** Most likely, you do not use the same language and speaking style with your friends that you do with an older relative. The same goes for speaking effectively in public. Think about your audience as well as the topic, situation, and intent of your speech when selecting your verbal and nonverbal behavior and your delivery style.

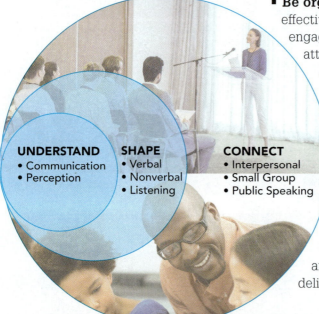

UNDERSTAND
- Communication
- Perception

SHAPE
- Verbal
- Nonverbal
- Listening

CONNECT
- Interpersonal
- Small Group
- Public Speaking

Be Ethical

A standard of ethics, as you know from Chapter 1, is absolutely necessary for maintaining your relationships in your personal and professional lives. Therefore, ethics should become a part of every decision you make as you create your speeches and judge the speeches of others. You should:

- Value diversity by being inclusive and respectful of all.
- Support and endorse freedom of expression for all.
- Be sensitive to the power of language.
- Cite sources to avoid plagiarism.

Plagiarism is an unethical and potentially harmful act that you commit when you intentionally or accidentally use all or a portion of the words, ideas, or illustrations created by someone else without giving proper credit. There are two common types of plagiarism. **Blatant plagiarism** can occur either when speakers take an entire speech or document and present it as their own or when a speaker takes parts of information from other sources and links the parts together, creating an entire speech out of someone else's words. *No-citation plagiarism* occurs when speakers fail to give source credit to a specific part of their speech that has been taken from another source. Be sure to cite all of your sources.

See Objective 11.4 for how to cite sources.

Be Confident

The uneasiness and fearfulness you might feel when preparing or giving a speech is **speech anxiety**. This is a form of communication apprehension, which you learned about in Chapter 1. The symptoms listed there often accompany speech anxiety as well. One of the first steps to controlling your anxiety is identifying the reason you are anxious. The most common causes of speech anxiety for beginning speakers are:

- Lack of public speaking experience
- Negative public speaking experience in the past
- Fear of looking "stupid" in front of peers
- Fear that the audience will laugh
- Fear of being the center of attention
- Fear of forgetting everything
- A belief that no one else feels like this
- Fear of speaking and using presentational equipment at the same time
- Fear of not being like the rest of the audience (especially true for returning students and nonnative students)
- Fear of failing the class based on speech performance

Often, just naming what we are afraid of will help us see how unfounded our fears might be. The techniques discussed at the end of this chapter can help minimize the influence of your anxiety (see the Improve Your Communication section). Preparing thoroughly for your speech will also help your confidence. However, a certain amount of intense reaction energizes you for the event.

10.2 What Is the Creative Process for Public Speaking?

Composing and presenting a speech may seem daunting if you view the process only as a whole, but you can break it down into workable parts. The chart on these two pages shows the four basic activities you will use to create a successful speech. Much of the information throughout this book will help you with the process, and Chapters 10–12 directly relate to each activity. In Chapters 13 and 14, you will use what you have learned about the creative process to generate informative and persuasive speeches. Although the process may look linear, you will frequently move back and forth between activities.

1 Developing

Chapter 10 (10.3 – 10.5)
GETTING TO KNOW YOUR AUDIENCE AND SITUATION
Know who you are speaking to as well as where, when, and why you are speaking.

Chapter 10 (10.6)
CREATING YOUR CENTRAL IDEA
Select a topic, define the purpose of your speech, and create and evaluate your central idea.

Chapter 11 (11.1 – 11.3)
LOCATING AND SELECTING SUPPORT MATERIALS
Learn how to effectively locate, evaluate, choose, and use a variety of support materials.

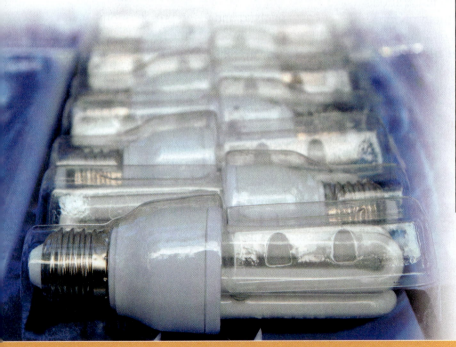

2 Creating

Chapter 11 (11.4, 11.7)
OUTLINING YOUR SPEECH
Start with a working outline, create a preparation outline, and include a citation page. Create a delivery outline to use during your speech.

Chapter 11 (11.5 – 11.6)
ORGANIZING THE SPEECH
Identify your main points and choose an organizational strategy. Craft your introduction and conclusion.

3 Presenting

Chapter 12 (12.1 – 12.4)
DELIVERING YOUR SPEECH
Use effective language. Strive to be natural, enthusiastic, confident, engaging, and appropriate in your delivery.
Practice!
❯See also Chapters 3 & 4

Chapter 12 (12.5 – 12.6)
USING PRESENTATION AIDS
Know when and how to use presentation aids to capture attention, enhance your credibility, and help your audience understand and remember your speech.

4 Listening & Evaluating

Chapter 5 (5.1 – 5.5)
LISTENING
Be an active, ethical, and effective listener who can overcome barriers to listening and who shares responsibility in the communication process. As a speaker, you should employ techniques to help others listen better as well.

Chapters 13, 14 (13.5, 14.8)
EVALUATING SPEECHES
Determine the effectiveness and appropriateness of a speech's topic, support materials, organization, and language, as well as a speaker's delivery and ethics.

10.3 What Do You Need to Know About Your Audience?

Audiences want you to recognize that they are unique groups of individuals, not one mass without personality, which means crafting your speech to be audience centered. This approach begins the moment you start selecting your topic and continues to the moment you finish delivering your speech. Speaking from an audience-centered standpoint begins with *audience analysis*—a systematic investigation of unique audience characteristics (attitudes, beliefs, values, and specific traits).

Attitudes

Attitudes are persistent psychological responses, predispositions, or inclinations to act one way or feel a particular way—usually positive or negative—toward something. For instance, you might like New York City better than Chicago or you may not trust anything found on the Internet. The longer someone holds an attitude, the more information he or she usually has to support it—and the harder it is to change. Your audience's attitudes can influence how they respond to you, your topic, the situation, and even smaller details such as your support material, delivery style, or presentation aids.

For example, if you are planning to give a persuasive speech on the positive attributes of tweeting and most in your audience hold a somewhat negative feeling about the overpopularity of electronic devices, the audience will be less likely to accept your position. Don't ignore their attitude or criticize it. Let the audience understand that you know their point of view, and try to move them in a positive direction from that vantage point.

Beliefs

Beliefs are those things a person accepts as plausible based on interpretation and judgment, such as believing in a religion or philosophy. For example, you may believe it is the responsibility of humans to take care of the planet, Internet bullying is harmful, or the United States has a responsibility to help other countries in times of disaster. Some beliefs may be easily accepted with only a little knowledge, whereas others take time to accept or may be very controversial. As with attitudes, beliefs affect how an audience perceives and responds to a speaker, a topic, support material, or other elements of a speech.

As another example, imagine that you are listening to a speech arguing that the world will end soon. Like most people, you wake everyday believing the world will continue and find it hard to believe that the end is near. Without verifiable data to support the prediction of a catastrophic event, the speaker has little hope of convincing you.

Values

Values relate to worth, or what a person sees as right or wrong, important or unimportant, desirable or undesirable, and they shape our attitudes and beliefs. Values are our principles, such as cherishing family over professional success. Other examples of values held by many in the United States are independence, progress, freedom of speech, life, good health, honesty, wealth, and education. When you are from or belong to a country, culture, co-culture, or religion, you may be expected to hold and share common values with the other members.

When speaking across cultures and co-cultures, you have to be extra sensitive to value differences to be an effective and ethical speaker. When giving a speech with the potential to challenge values, be extra careful with what you say. Be aware that different groups can be in your audience; don't assume everyone has had your experience or take an "our way is best" attitude. Remember that your message has consequences.

Beliefs, values, and attitudes make up the audience's **identity**. Knowing as much as possible about your audience's identity will help you make your speech more meaningful and you more confident.

> Your audience gives you everything you need....There is no director who can direct you like an audience.[1]
>
> Fanny Brice

Personal Traits

Personal traits (sometimes referred to as demographics) include age, gender, sexual orientation, household type, education, occupation, income, and disabilities. Each characteristic may help provide insight into what's important to your audience, how they will feel about given issues, and what they accept as true.

The key to using personal traits effectively is to make yourself aware of possible traits present in your audience but not to compartmentalize or stereotype the audience. *Stereotyping* is false or oversimplified generalizing applied to individuals based on group characteristics. Allow the traits to guide but not dictate your interactions.

Remember to:

- Be respectful of gender and sexual orientation. No matter whether your audience is predominantly male or female, gay or straight, being insensitive will hurt your reputation and perpetuates negative stereotypes.

- Recognize that you may have few "traditional" household members in your audience. According to the U.S. Census Bureau, only 2 percent of all U.S. households in 2010 were "traditional."[2]

- Remember that high levels of education do not always equate with intelligence. College graduates are not smart about everything, and some very intelligent people are self-taught. However, the more education your audience has, the more they are exposed to different topics and language.

- Be cautious about connecting income levels and occupations—not all lawyers are highly paid, for instance.

- Consider that you may have audience members with disabilities. They often have unique insights and may have certain communicative challenges.

Practicing Ethics: Stereotyping

- Avoid negative or damaging stereotypes.
- Understand that some traits can change due to significant events, trends, and opportunities during a particular time in history.
- Respect diversity, all the time!

The following table, based on *When Generations Collide* by Lynne Lancaster and David Stillman, describes some generational trends to help you understand how age might influence your audience.[3]

Generational Trends

Born before 1945
(Traditionalists)

Defining word: **loyal**
Marry once, "save for a rainy day," little formal education, conservative, respect authority and America, not easily persuaded

Born 1946–1964
(Baby Boomers)

Defining word: **optimistic**
More educated, committed to belonging, political, very competitive, spend rather than save, divorce and remarry, cynical of and challenge authority

Born 1965–1980
(Generation X)

Defining word: **skepticism**
Product of divorce, single parents, or blended homes; resourceful and independent; count on peers and friends more than on family; influenced by media; struggle with money

Born 1981–1999
(Millennials or Generation Y)

Defining word: **realistic**
Smart, confident, practical, tech savvy, concerned about personal safety, influenced by friends and media, appreciate diversity, can be very biased

Psychological Traits

The **psychological traits** of your audience pertain to their needs and motivations. In *Motivation and Personality*, psychologist Abraham Maslow outlined a classic theory demonstrating how people's needs motivate them to respond in certain ways. For example, if buying or doing something will help people satisfy a need, they are more likely to make that purchase or do that activity. Maslow fine-tuned his theory by identifying five levels of needs, which are *hierarchical*. In other words, you must fulfill some of the basic needs before the other needs become crucial. **Maslow's hierarchy of needs** is best represented as a pyramid, with basic needs at the bottom, giving support to the higher levels.[4]

Physiological needs are related to continued existence and include food, water, general comfort, and sex. These are the most basic and necessary for a person to live. A speech on "How to Eat Healthy on a Budget" highlights this level of need.

Safety needs relate to what we need to feel secure, such as a roof over our heads and security in our own homes. A speech demonstrating how to be ready in times of disaster evokes this type of need.

Social needs are those feelings we have about belonging. Most of us want to give and receive love, be close to others, and be supported. We have a strong need to feel a part of groups such as family, friends, or religion. Pep rallies and speeches given during new student orientations on college campuses strive to fulfill this need.

Self-esteem needs relate to our strong need for respect from others we view as important, much as you may have felt when you were a teenager and wanted your parents to trust you and be proud of you. Pride, prestige, self-respect, accomplishment, recognition, and the need for success are aspects of this need. Speeches given at graduations usually focus heavily on self-esteem needs.

Self-actualization needs relate to the need to feel achievement connected to personal identity, independence, happiness, and potential. An example of a self-actualization speech would be Grammy- and Academy Award–winning music icon, cancer survivor, and activist Melissa Etheridge giving a motivational speech to a group of breast cancer survivors. Her 2005 song "I Run for Life" characterizes this need.

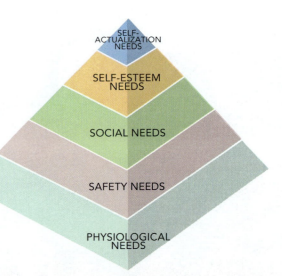

Social Traits

Your audience's **social traits** relate to how they are affected by or identify with other groups of people. Two types of groups can influence your audience—those by choice and those by birth.

Social Traits by Choice

The "by choice" group are people your audience members choose to connect with, such as political parties; hobby communities; athletic teams; and religious, professional, social, or civic organizations. Studying these group connections can give you obvious but significant insights into how your audience will relate to you and your topic. For example, avid hunters may react negatively to a speech arguing for new hunting regulations unless they see a benefit to hunters or the animal population.

Social Traits by Birth

The second group includes those relationships your audience members have with others by birth and by growing up within certain societies—specifically race, ethnicity, and culture.

Race is the biological differences of humankind, often noticeable in physical markers such as color and texture of hair, color of skin and eyes, shape of facial features, and bodily build and proportions.

Ethnicity stems from our national and religious affiliations.

In Chapter 1, you learned that *culture* is the system that teaches a set of objectives and rules that help us survive and gain societal acceptance within our community.

Race, ethnicity, and culture mold a person's identity and therefore will directly influence how he or she responds to issues.

For example, U.S. "minorities" tend to consider issues such as equal opportunity and immigration laws more carefully than people in the "majority." As another example, a *collectivist* culture like Taiwan stands for the group, so a collectivist audience may respond to an emphasis on community and duty. An *individualist* culture like the United States stands for self, and such audiences may respond to an emphasis on personal reward.

See diversity as an opportunity rather than an obstacle, with ethical appreciation in every stage of your speech process. Likewise, watch out for your own potential ethnocentrism. For example, don't view people who adhere to a sense of duty rather than personal gain (or vice versa) as inferior.

See Objective 10.5 for how to analyze your audience.

10.4 What Do You Need to Know About the Speaking Situation?

As noted in Chapter 1, the context for any communication includes the physical, relational, and psychological environments in which the communication takes place. Your audience analysis helps you to contemplate the relational and psychological. Your consideration of the speaking situation will help with exploring the physical.

Place

Imagine being a shorter-than-average person behind a large wooden lectern or giving a speech outdoors on a windy day—from loose manuscript pages. Both of these examples highlight how important it is to give attention to the environment where you will be speaking and to plan ahead. A simple, short platform for the first speaker prevents embarrassment. A manuscript printed on heavy paper and attached in a binder would help the second speaker.

You may be in a public speaking class and know that your classroom is where you will give the speech. But such familiarity is a luxury you rarely have, and even in the classroom, you need to prepare. Know what equipment you need and make sure it will be there. Make a backup plan if the equipment does not show up or is not working.

Audience Size

Find out how large the audience will be. Audience size could influence how formal (for larger audiences) or informal (for smaller ones) your style can be. For a large audience, you may need more equipment, such as a microphone or more powerful projection devices for presentation aids.

Time

Time has two factors. The first are general elements related to the time of day, day of the week, rotation of speakers, events before the speaking event, and length of speaking time. Each element has the potential to influence your speech positively or negatively. For instance, holding audience attention during an after-dinner speech can be challenging because the audience has just eaten and may be tired.

The second factor is time's influence on your relationship with the audience. For example, if this is the first time the group hears you speak, you will likely be careful to build your credibility. If they have heard you speak many times and have responded favorably, you might be a bit less formal. For example, try to recall how your professor or your boss related to you when you first met. How does she or he relate to you now? Is there a difference? Has your relationship evolved over time?

Occasion

Be aware of why your audience is gathered to hear your speech. How might the occasion influence their feelings about you and your topic? Are they a captive audience, required to be there, who do not feel like they can leave? Or are they a voluntary audience who made the choice to hear your speech?

Audiences required to attend an event, such as students at graduation or employees at a job-required meeting, can be apathetic, negative, or impatient. You might even experience some of these reactions in your classroom, as your audience has to be there regularly and must listen to many speeches. Captive audiences are not impossible to reach, but you must be more dynamic and interesting to gain their attention.

Mood is another factor. Is the situation celebratory? Somber? Businesslike? Your speech should reflect and respect the appropriate mood.

See Objective 10.5 for how to analyze your situation.

> **TIP: Building Your Confidence**
> Fear of the unknown is a major creator of speech anxiety. Analyzing your audience and the situation has the added benefit of helping you feel more comfortable in front of them. You can prepare for what can happen and prevent some stressors.

10.5 How Do You Analyze the Audience and Situation?

Adapting to your audience and situation begins immediately after you receive a public speaking assignment or engagement. The more you can predict about your audience and situation early in the speech-making process, the better you can prepare. If you don't know your audience, you could choose an inappropriate topic or select the wrong source materials.

Here are some helpful hints for how to gather information about your audience and situation:

- Based on both what you already know and what you need to know, brainstorm about the audience and situation.
- Ask friends, relatives, teachers, or peers what they know about the audience and your potential speech ideas. Sometimes fresh eyes can see connections and issues that we cannot.
- Do simple research on your audience, especially if they are part of a larger organization. Good sources are group websites, press releases, or news articles; opinion polls; census data, almanacs, or local government archives; and historical societies.
- Interview someone connected with the speaking event, a person familiar with the audience membership, or members of the audience.
- Create a survey or questionnaire to gather information from all or a large segment of the audience. (See Objective 11.1 for more on surveys.)

The following table offers questions to explore. Not all questions will apply to every speaking event, but you should do your best to know as much as possible about the audience and situation.

Analyzing Your Audience and Situation

Characteristics	Questions to Explore
Audience Identity	• What can I learn about my audience's attitudes, beliefs, or values?
Personal Traits	• What's the age range of my audience? What's the average age? • What's the gender ratio? • What do I know about their occupations? Education? Households? Disabilities? Average income or socioeconomic level? • What might the audience already know about my potential topics?
Psychological Traits	• What needs might my audience have? • Because of their needs, will my audience be positive, apathetic, or negative toward my potential speech topics? • How might I use their needs to show relevance to my topic or to persuade them?
Social Traits	• What organizations will sponsor the speaking event? • What organizations or other social affiliations might be represented at the event (such as hobbies or athletic teams)? • What professions, religions, cultures, ethnicities, and races might be represented?
Place	• Will I be giving the speech inside or outside? If outside, what are the plans if there is bad weather? • What are the stage arrangements? Is there a lectern if needed? • Will I have the equipment I need? What are my backup plans? • Can I practice with the equipment? • Can I control the heating, lighting, and sound if needed? • Whom do I contact for help with any logistics?
Audience Size	• How large will the audience be? In what arrangement? • Will I need to make any adjustments to be visible to or heard by the whole audience?
Time	• How much time will I have to speak? • What day of the week and time of day will I speak? • Where do I fall in the rotation of speakers? • Is there late-breaking news I should consider? • Is this the first time this audience will hear me speak?
Occasion	• Is this a special occasion? • What does the audience expect out of this event? Why are they here? What will be the mood of the day? • How will the audience respond to the topic? • Who's in charge of the event?

10.6 How Do You Create a Central Idea?

The key to any good speech is a first-rate topic and central idea. Unless your instructor limits you, your classroom topic could be almost anything that is suitable for you, your audience, and the class situation—which may seem overwhelming. However, outside of your class, most of your speaking opportunities will be professional or social. Your expertise or the speaking event may determine your topic choice. Following these steps will help you select an appropriate topic and create a focused central idea.

Identify Your General Purpose

Identifying the general purpose of your speech will help you narrow in on topic options. The **general purpose** is the unrestricted aim of your speech, which can fall into three different categories:

To inform. The giving of information is the aim of this general purpose. Speeches focusing on topics such as "How to Make a Gooseberry Pie," "The History of PEZ Candy," and "The Life and Career of David Letterman" are examples of speeches to inform.

To persuade. When your goal is *to reinforce, to change,* or *to influence* the attitudes, values, beliefs, or actions of your audience, you aim to persuade. Speeches arguing for tax reform in your state or rallying members of the Republican party to support a candidate are examples of speeches to persuade.

To accentuate a special occasion. *To entertain, to celebrate,* or *to commemorate* is the aim of a special occasion speech. A wedding toast, a graduation speech, or a speech given by a disaster survivor to other survivors each has the aim to accentuate a special occasion.

Your general purpose is the overriding goal of the whole speech, and you can only have one per speech.

Create a Topic Idea Bank

An **idea bank** is a list of general words and phrases that could be speech topics for you. Here's how to create an idea bank:

- Evaluate your speech assignment, the audience, and the speaking situation. Often this will help you limit your topic ideas.
- Write down your idea bank by hand. Using paper rather than a computer allows your mind to see connections and jump more quickly from idea to idea.
- Make a list of potential topics by brainstorming, searching for topic ideas, and exploring your general purpose.

Brainstorming

In Chapter 9, you learned about the creative process of brainstorming. You can use "free association," which is writing down everything you can think of that could be a topic and choosing one by a process of elimination. Or you can use "clustering," which is focusing a broad topic (e.g., cameras) that you then branch out from to discover more defined possible topics (e.g., famous photographers, digital cameras). The best way to start is to take a personal inventory of your interests, experiences, abilities, values, attitudes, or beliefs. Don't judge your potential topics during brainstorming, just write down anything that comes to your mind; it might lead to a great topic. You can eliminate what isn't appropriate later.

Searching for Topic Ideas

Another way to create an idea bank is by *searching*—browsing print publications, reference works, websites, or other media and materials for subject ideas. For example, you can look through acceptable newspapers or magazines you already have access to at home, online, or in a library, such as the Sunday paper in your area, *Time*, *National Geographic*, *The Week*, or *Smithsonian*. You can also watch a news broadcast, search an academic database at the library, or browse the Internet. A few places you might look include About.com, Ask.com, Librarians' Internet Index, or Yahoo! Directory. The idea bank shown below is one example created by searching the Librarians' Internet Index.

IDEA BANK

Ideas from Librarians' Internet Index

Bubbles – How to make tools & solution

Fortune-telling

Kites

Pioneer life

Digital vs. film cameras

Women photographers

Juggling

Political memorabilia (19th & 20th centuries)

Exploring Your General Purpose

Exploring your general purpose can also lead to speech topics. In situations where you are told what your general purpose must be, this method is a good place to start your topic selection process. You can create columns for the different types of speeches and topic categories that fit your purpose. The following table offers some categories you can use to generate ideas.

If Your General Purpose Is ...	Your Potential Topic Categories Are ...
To inform: To describe	Object, person, animal, place, or event
To explain	Concept or issue
To demonstrate	Process

If Your General Purpose Is ...	Your Potential Topic Categories Are ...
To persuade:	Attitudes, beliefs, values, behaviors/actions, or policies *(For topics under any of these categories, focus on reinforcing, changing, or creating new attitudes, beliefs, etc.)*

If Your General Purpose Is ...	Your Potential Topic Categories Are ...
To accentuate a special occasion:	Entertainment, celebration, commemoration *(These categories are not as straightforward and will depend on the goal of the speech. You must adapt to the occasion as well as the audience. Most special occasion speeches take place at events such as weddings, graduations, retirement parties, funerals, award ceremonies, fundraisers, campaign events, or conferences.)*

Below is one example of an idea bank created by exploring a general purpose.

IDEA BANK
To inform
To describe

Places
Island of Anguilla
Gettysburg
Mississippi Headwaters
San Diego Zoo

Animals/Insects
Canaries
Golden Retrievers
Butterflies
Bobcats in Missouri

Select Your Topic

Ask yourself a series of focus questions to help identify topics that will work well and eliminate topics that will not.

- Which topics in my idea bank will work for my general purpose?
- Which topics fit the speech assignment or request?
- Which topics are most familiar to me?
- Which topics am I most comfortable speaking about? (The self-check for self-disclosure in Chapter 6 can help.)
- Which topics have positive aspects for the audience, occasion, speaking event, or timing of the event? Which topics might cause a negative reaction from the audience or are not appropriate?
- Which topics are new or unique to this audience?
- Which topics are worth the audience's time and attention?

For example, suppose you are volunteering at the local historical society and you create an idea bank (see above right) because the society wants you to give an informative talk. You ask yourself the focus questions and cross out topics, such as "kites," that do not relate to the society's exhibits, because those topics may not interest visitors. You reason that visitors might like to hear a talk related to the recreated pioneer village on the property. Connecting this thought to your hobby of woodworking, you think that investigating how the pioneers built their homes will be a good topic. It passes the test created by the focus questions.

Idea Bank for Historical Society

~~Bubbles — How to make tools & solution~~

~~Fortune-telling~~

~~Kites~~

Pioneer life Pony Express

Building homes

~~Digital vs. film cameras~~

~~Women photographers~~

~~Juggling~~   ghost towns

~~Political memorabilia (19th & 20th century)~~

Do some preliminary research to see if you can locate current, quality materials on the topic. As you research, ask these questions:

- Are there enough materials to create a speech that fits into my allotted speech time?
- Is there a variety of quality materials for the topic?
- Will I be able to locate and review the materials in time to prepare effectively for my speech?

If you are having trouble finding support materials, you may want to return to your idea bank for a new topic.

Chapter 11 explains how to do research and evaluate support materials.

Practicing Ethics: Suitable Topics

Your topic should not be harmful to you or your audience, and it should not break any laws or rules.

Identify the Specific Purpose

Identifying your specific purpose is the first step in creating a focused central idea. The **specific purpose** of your speech is a single statement that combines your general purpose, your audience, and your objective. The **objective** of the specific purpose describes the outcome or behavior you want your audience to experience or adopt. Notice how the following specific purpose examples identify what the speakers want their audiences to take away from the speeches.

Examples of Specific Purposes

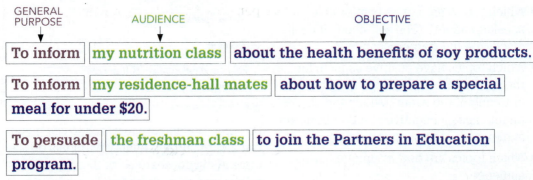

GENERAL PURPOSE · AUDIENCE · OBJECTIVE

To inform | my nutrition class | about the health benefits of soy products.

To inform | my residence-hall mates | about how to prepare a special meal for under $20.

To persuade | the freshman class | to join the Partners in Education program.

The above examples follow these guidelines for composing a specific purpose:

- Begin with an infinitive form ("To …") that reflects the general purpose, such as "To inform," "To persuade," or "To commemorate."

- Specify the audience. In the first example, the audience is "my nutrition class."

- State the objective. In the first example, the objective is to give the audience information "about the health benefits of soy products."

- Use clear, concise language. Avoid filler words or technical or long descriptions. For instance, the first example does not say, "the *awesome* health benefits of products *made with the fermented juice of a native Asian bean.*"

- Focus on only one speech topic. "The health benefits *and manufacturing* of soy products" would be two distinctly different speech topics.

Returning to your pioneer homes speech, you could construct a specific purpose this way:

GENERAL PURPOSE   AUDIENCE   OBJECTIVE

| To inform | Historical Society visitors | about how pioneers built homes. |

Your specific purpose should contain the key information and be concise, as the pioneer example shows. Once you have constructed a specific purpose, evaluate it using the self-check below. If you have a sound specific purpose, you are ready to identify and compose your central idea.

Self-Check: Evaluating a Specific Purpose

❑ Does my specific purpose contain my general purpose, my audience reference, and my objective for the speech?

❑ Is my specific purpose an infinitive statement (to inform, to convince, to motivate, to inspire)?

❑ Am I using clear, concise language?

❑ Does my specific purpose identify exactly what I want to discuss?

❑ Does my specific purpose focus on only one speech topic?

❑ Does my specific purpose relate to the audience? Does it work with the occasion and time? Is it appropriate for me?

❑ Will the scope of my specific purpose fit the time allowed for the speech?

Formulate the Central Idea

The ***central idea*** (also called a thesis statement, theme, or subject sentence) is a concise, single sentence summarizing and/or previewing what you will say in your speech. Any decision you make about your main points or support materials should connect back to the theme of this central idea. How the central idea differs from the specific purpose can seem confusing, but the difference lies in how each functions. First, the specific purpose identifies the objective of your speech. Then, the central idea summarizes and/or previews the ideas your speech will cover in order to achieve its objective. Here are a few examples demonstrating how the specific purpose relates to the central idea. The objective of each specific purpose is shown in blue.

If Your Specific Purpose Is …	Your Central Idea Could Be …
To inform my nutrition class about **the health benefits of soy products.**	Today's market offers several soy products that are beneficial to our health.
To inform my residence-hall mates **how to prepare a special meal for under $20.**	You can prepare a special home-cooked meal with a few basic utensils, an eye for a bargain at the supermarket, and your residence-hall kitchenette.
To persuade the freshman class to join **the Partners in Education program.**	As college students, we need to give back to the community by joining the Partners in Education Program, which pairs our college with a local elementary school.

Notice how the second central idea example—preparing a special meal—previews the speech's main points (utensils, supermarket bargains, and kitchenette). Some instructors may require you to preview your main points in this way as a standard part of your central idea.

What Does an Effective Central Idea Include?

Let's compose a central idea for the speech on pioneer home building. Start by looking at your specific purpose and identifying your objective.

SPECIFIC PURPOSE

To inform Historical Society visitors about how pioneers built homes.

OBJECTIVE

Your central idea will then summarize and/or preview what you will cover in your speech to achieve your objective. Here is one possible central idea:

CENTRAL IDEA

Pioneers moving westward built homes using available materials, basic hand tools, and general construction skills.

Notice how this example:

- Considers what your audience—the Historical Society visitors identified in your specific purpose—will need or want to know.

- Previews what your speech will include: in this case, the "available materials, basic hand tools, and general construction skills" pioneers used to build homes. This information comes from your preliminary knowledge and research.

- Focuses on only one speech topic: how pioneers built their homes.

- Uses simple, clear language that is not figurative or ambiguous. In the pioneer example, you could list the types of materials and tools, but if these types are no longer common, including them here could be confusing.

- Is a complete sentence, with a noun phrase and a verb phrase.

- Is a declarative statement, not a question.

These are all qualities your central idea should have in order to be effective.

The next section shows you how to evaluate a central idea for these qualities.

Evaluate Your Central Idea

To evaluate your central idea for effectiveness, study it from two perspectives. First, check the mechanics; that is, make sure your central idea is written correctly, with the proper parts, construction, and focus. Secondly, assess your central idea as it relates to your speech event and audience. Use the following guidelines and the self-check on the next page to help you evaluate it.

Mechanically Sound

To be mechanically sound, your central idea should meet all four of the following criteria:

- **Your central idea should be a complete sentence.** A complete sentence contains a noun phrase and a verb phrase and can stand alone.

INCORRECT:

Positive aspects of the low-impact Kickbike, a bicycle-scooter hybrid.

CORRECT:

The noun phrase

The Kickbike, a European bicycle-scooter hybrid, is a low-tech, low-impact, and high-intensity piece of exercise equipment.

The verb phrase

Although the incorrect example ends with a period, it is only a noun phrase; without a verb phrase, it is not a complete sentence. The correct version contains both noun and verb phrases and can stand alone.

- **Your central idea should be written as a statement, not a question.**

INCORRECT:

How safe is the radiation emitted by your cell phone?

CORRECT:

Cell phones emit tiny amounts of radiation, which scientists believe may be linked to certain types of brain cancer.

Asking a question—as in the incorrect example—can help you think about your speech, but your central idea needs to be a declarative sentence, as in the correct example.

> **TIP: Refining Your Central Idea**
> Your central idea might change slightly as you research and organize the speech. Be open to refining it as you move through the creative process.

- **Your central idea should use clear, simple, and direct language.** Use concrete words that are familiar to the audience. Avoid vague or filler language.

INCORRECT:

Some believe basically that the radiation silently emitted from cell phones can cause cancer.

CORRECT:

Cell phones emit tiny amounts of radiation, which scientists believe may be linked to certain types of brain cancer.

In the incorrect example, "some believe" is vague (who are the "some"?). "Basically" is a filler word that serves no purpose, and "silently" is unnecessary because all radiation is silent. The correct example drops the filler words and directly specifies "scientists believe" as well as what types of cancer may be caused by the radiation.

- **Your central idea should focus on only one speech topic.**

INCORRECT:

Kickbikes and elliptical trainers are low-impact, high-intensity pieces of exercise equipment.

Two nouns connected with a conjunction ("and") may indicate you have more than one speech topic.

CORRECT:

The Kickbike, a European bicycle-scooter hybrid, is a low-tech, low-impact, and high-intensity piece of exercise equipment.

CORRECT:

An elliptical trainer is a low-impact and high-intensity piece of exercise equipment.

In the incorrect example, "kickbikes" and "elliptical trainers" are two topics that could each get a speech-length treatment. Notice how the correct examples preview possible points ("low-tech," low-impact," etc.) while focusing on a single speech topic.

Appropriate for the Event and Audience

Your central idea should, at this stage, be appropriate and focused enough for the event. However, you need to continue to assess whether the topic is still narrow enough for the time allotted, interesting enough to grab your audience's attention, unique enough to not waste their time with something they already know, and accessible enough to not be too technical or confusing for them.

Self-Check: Evaluating a Central Idea

❏ Is the central idea written as one complete sentence?

❏ Is the central idea written as a statement (not a question)?

❏ Does the statement use clear, simple, and direct language?

❏ Does the central idea focus on only one speech topic?

❏ Can I cover this central idea in the time allotted for my speech?

❏ Is the central idea worth my audience's time and attention?

Chapter 10 Review

Key Questions

10.1 How Can You Be a Successful Public Speaker?

Objective 10.1: **IDENTIFY THE TRAITS OF A SUCCESSFUL PUBLIC SPEAKER**

- You strive to be audience centered.
- You are ethical.
- You are confident.

See pages 264–265.

10.2 What Is the Creative Process for Public Speaking?

Objective 10.2: **EXPLAIN THE CREATIVE PROCESS FOR PUBLIC SPEAKING**

The four basic activities you will use to create a successful speech are:

- **Developing** your speech material by analyzing your audience and situation; creating a solid central idea; and researching, locating, selecting, and testing effective support materials.
- **Creating** your speech by working through several types of outlines; identifying main points and choosing an organizational strategy; and crafting your introduction and conclusion
- **Presenting** your speech using effective language, delivery, and presentation aids
- **Listening and evaluating** as an active, ethical, and effective listener capable of successfully evaluating a speech; and helping your audience listen to you as a speaker

See pages 266–267.

10.3 What Do You Need to Know About Your Audience?

Objective 10.3: **SUMMARIZE WHAT YOU NEED TO KNOW ABOUT YOUR AUDIENCE**

As much as possible, you should know your audience's:

- Attitudes, beliefs, and values
- Personal traits such as age, gender, sexual orientation, household type, education, occupation, income, and disabilities
- Psychological traits related to audience needs and motivation
- Social traits by choice and by birth

See pages 268–273.

10.4 What Do You Need to Know About the Speaking Situation?

Objective 10.4: **SUMMARIZE WHAT YOU NEED TO KNOW ABOUT THE SITUATION**

The context includes the physical, relational, and psychological environments in which the communication takes place. Your audience analysis helps you to contemplate the relational and psychological. Your consideration of the speaking situation helps with exploring the physical. When exploring the situation, you should look at the place, audience size, time, and occasion.

See pages 274–275.

10.5 How Do You Analyze the Audience and Situation?

Objective 10.5: **EXPLAIN HOW TO ANALYZE THE AUDIENCE AND SITUATION**

The more you can predict about your audience early in the speech-making process, the better you can prepare. Consider what you already know, brainstorm, research, interview others, or create a survey to help you understand your audience and the situation. Explore how audience traits and situational factors might affect the way you construct your speech.

See pages 276–277.

10.6 How Do You Create a Central Idea?

Objective 10.6: **DESCRIBE HOW TO CREATE A CENTRAL IDEA**

Having a well-defined topic and central idea will help you create an effective speech. The following steps will help you create a focused central idea:

• Identify your general purpose.
• Create a topic idea bank.
• Select your topic.
• Identify the specific purpose.
• Formulate the central idea of the speech.
• Evaluate your central idea.

See pages 278–287.

Key Terms

Improve Your Communication

In this chapter, you learned how speech anxiety can influence your confidence level. Earlier in the book, you also learned a few general techniques for controlling any type of communication apprehension (Chapter 1). Remember that being somewhat concerned or anxious about giving a speech is normal and even important. It is your fears that will often push you to practice more, check your equipment, or help you increase your energy. However, there are always methods for minimizing the side effects of speech anxiety.

For example, dry mouth, tight throat, and shakiness seem to be the most common anxiety symptoms. Here are some additional suggestions for lessening their effects:

- **Dry mouth:** Using lip balm and taking small sips of water right before or during a speech might be helpful.
- **Tight throat:** Before the speech, hum softly, do vocal exercises, and breathe deeply.
- **Shakiness:** Exercise before the speech or minor movement during the speech can help. Try to gesture or move around during the speech, when appropriate, to relax those shaky muscles.

Apply Your Knowledge

1. Most likely, you will be asked to give at least one speech in this class. Is it important for you to analyze the audience for the speech? Why? What do you already know about the audience that might influence any speech you might give? What are their specific interests? If you have a topic in mind, can you begin to think about what should be covered for this specific audience? How much detail will they need? What could be potential audience expectations and reactions?

2. Examine the situation as well. What situational obstacles could affect your speech? For example, will the room be dark enough for slides if you use them? Is the room generally hot or cold, and is there anything you can do to help this? Is your class early in the morning, right after lunch, or late at night? How might this influence your speech choices?

3. Create topic idea banks for two speeches, one to inform and one to persuade.

Other Resources

If you are still struggling with pinpointing a topic or with researching your audience and situation, these resources might help you.

Topic Ideas

Janssen, Sarah, ed. *The World Almanac and Book of Facts 2016*. New York: World Almanac, 2015. Print.

Cohen, Richard E., James A. Barnes, Charlie Cook, Michael Barone, and John Bicknell. *The Almanac of American Politics 2016*. Bethesda: Columbia, 2015. Print.

Audience Research

- fedstats.sites.usa.gov
- gallup.com
- worldview.gallup.com
- pewresearch.org
- pewglobal.org
- ropercenter.uconn.edu
- infoplease.com
- norc.org

Chapter 11
Creating a Speech

11.1 Where Do You Locate Support Materials?

Research is the act of investigating, evaluating, and summarizing information. Good research skills help you find effective **support materials** (or evidence)—information that explains, elaborates, or validates your speech topic. Support materials come from different *sources* such as books, magazines, journals, websites, and interviews.

For example, Logan is preparing a speech on basketball and wants to use some startling statistics about one of the best professional basketball players of all time. However, he also wants to choose a player not everyone in his class knows. Logan asked a librarian for help. She recommended first searching the Internet for a list of great players and then looking for a specific player from that list. Within minutes, Logan had the opening to his speech:

> According to the NBA Encyclopedia Playoff Edition at NBA.com, as of June 2015, which NBA star is the only player to score 4,000 points in a season? Who set the NBA single-game record for most points (100) and the most rebounds (55)? Who was nicknamed the "Big Dipper"? If you answered Wilt Chamberlain, you are correct.

Because of the Internet and the quality of U.S. libraries, and the widening ability to interview experts or collect information from surveys, you (and Logan) have a vast amount of information at your fingertips. The next several pages will help you see the value of these resources and offer guidance on when and how to use them.

Commercial Websites

Commercial websites are created and maintained by for-profit businesses or organizations. These websites are typically promotional but can include newspapers, television networks, and video and image services (e.g., YouTube or Google Maps).

When to Use

- To locate information about a company
- To gather support materials from sites of respected news organizations
- To find current or popular-culture materials
- To find presentation aids (cite the sources)

Advantages

- Can offer information unavailable in print
- May be current (be sure to check dates)
- May be seen by your audience as reliable

Disadvantages

- Are often biased toward the interests of the site owner or paid advertisers, if any
- May require verifying information with other sources or may not be verifiable
- May not credit all sources of information

Tips on Locating

- Use a search engine (e.g., Google or Bing) to find a site or to search on your topic.

Sample Oral Citation

According to the story, "Water Efficient Maize for Africa," found on Monsanto.com on July 27, 2015, three-quarters of the most severe droughts in the last 10 years have occurred in Africa.

Nonprofit Organization Websites

Nonprofit organization websites are sites for local, national, and international not-for-profit groups dedicated to issues or causes such as UNICEF, MADD, the Special Olympics, or the Magic Johnson Foundation. Their URLs often end with ".org."

When to Use

- To locate detailed information about a particular issue or organization
- To locate emotional appeal examples

Advantages

- Can provide background and current information about a service or issue
- Are usually considered reliable sources
- Tend to use accessible language

Disadvantages

- Have set goals or agendas, which may bias how information is presented
- May not include author credentials
- May accept paid advertisements, which may signal the site's information is biased

Tips on Locating

- Search online using the name of the organization or the issue it supports.

Sample Oral Citation

According to centralmissouri honorflight.com on July 26, 2015, the Central Missouri program has "transported over 1,900 veterans to Washington" since 2009.

Blogs

A blog is a website or web page that contains regular postings by its author(s) and may allow visitors to comment. When created by authorities, they can offer unique, credible information; but keep in mind that most blogs will represent specific opinions or points of view. Types of blogs include personal, corporate (often for marketing), subject (e.g., politics), and media (e.g., videos).

When to Use
- To find new developments about your topic (to verify with other sources)
- To gauge if a topic is controversial or of current general interest

Advantages
- Can provide current information
- Can be helpful in gauging public opinion
- Can offer unique material

Disadvantages
- Are often biased toward the opinions of the blogger(s)
- May require verifying information with other sources
- May not be acceptable support in some classes. Ask your instructor.

Tips on Locating
- Use blog search engines (e.g., Google Blog Search, Blogarama, Technorati).

Sample Oral Citation
According to the White House blog on August 4, 2015, Air Force One totals 4,000 square feet of floor space on three levels.

Personal Websites

Personal websites are created by groups or individuals and focused on topics of personal interest. These sites, if created by a credible source, can offer personal or expert testimony. Much like blogs, personal websites can be created by anyone with the skills and equipment, and they may represent specific opinions.

When to Use
- To find material that humanizes your topic
- To find personal information about the site author(s)

Advantages
- Can be reliable support if author is a recognized expert on your topic
- Can offer unique material

Disadvantages
- Can be written by anyone, so be sure to research the author's credibility
- May require verifying information with other sources
- Are often promotional or biased toward the opinions of the author
- May not be acceptable support in some classes. Ask your instructor.

Tips on Locating
- Use a search engine (e.g., Google, Bing, Yahoo) to locate websites.

Sample Oral Citation
According to the official website of fiber artist Annette Kennedy on August 1, 2015, *Mountain Chapel* is an award-winning work from 2008.

Databases

Although search engines such as Google can help you find general information, they do not access everything. Most libraries subscribe to databases, or extensive collections of published works (such as magazine, newspaper, and journal articles) in electronic form, making material easy to search and locate. Databases contain descriptions and citation information, such as title of article and publication, author, and publication date, and they often include the full text of the articles. A database itself is not a source you will orally cite in your speech; it is a portal for finding a large amount of support materials from many different sources, all in one place.

Different databases may focus on various subject areas. For instance, ERIC (Education Resources Information Center) covers education research. Others specialize in arts, sciences, law, or business. Your reference librarian can tell you what databases are available at your library and what disciplines they cover. Your library's website will likely include a link to these databases.

Multiple-subject databases contain sources across a vast spectrum of disciplines and periodicals. Use these to research broadly and then to narrow your topic. Some common ones include:

- Academic Search Elite/EBSCOhost
- LexisNexis
- JSTOR
- Project MUSE

Specialized databases contain sources related to specific disciplines or topics. Use these to focus your research once you have your topic narrowed. Some common ones include:

- CQ Weekly (coverage of acts of Congress)
- ERIC (education)
- OVID (science and health care)
- Standard & Poor's NetAdvantage (business)

TIP: Using Databases

You search in databases much like you search in the library's catalog or with a search engine, with options for basic and advanced searching.

- Put limits on your search by defining attributes. You may be able to limit your search by discipline or subject, to full-text articles only, or to recent articles only. Always start with a full-text search. You may find all you need this way.
- Use broad key words rather than specific phrases or language for your initial search.
- If a database has more than one "search" box, use them. For example, you can search for "2015 drought," "California," and "Nevada."
- Check to see if the database has an online thesaurus to browse for subjects that match your speech topic. Once you have some results, look at the subject or descriptor field for related terms you can search on, and redo your search.
- Search more than one database.
- Ask your librarian for help if you have questions or find using a database intimidating.

Books

You might use any of several types of books for support materials. A book may be written by a single author, multiple authors, corporate authors, or government authors.

When to Use

- To find important detail and contextual information about your topic
- To locate facts, statistics, and examples

Advantages

- Often considered extremely reliable
- Usually contain a large amount of detailed information
- Often have bibliographies or source notes leading you to additional material
- Often contain quotable passages for emotional appeals

Disadvantages

- May not have current information (check the copyright date and verify information with current sources)
- Require more time to read and glean information, due to length

Tips on Locating

- Search Google Books.
- Search for your topic on sites such as Amazon or Library of Congress (www.loc .gov) to identify books to seek at the library.

Sample Oral Citation

In her 2011 book, *The Spunky Coconut Cookbook*, Kelly Brozyna offers several easy gluten-free recipes.

Newspapers

Newspapers are published daily, weekly, or biweekly and can be local, national, or international. They contain news, information, opinions, and advertisements.

When to Use

- To find current facts and statistics
- To locate extended examples
- To support current events or topics

Advantages

- Often viewed as current and reliable
- Feature condensed information
- Use accessible language

Disadvantages

- Rarely cite references
- May require finding other in-depth sources
- May be outdated quickly

Tips on Locating

- Search library databases.
- Public libraries often carry local and some national newspapers.
- Academic libraries often carry local, national, and international newspapers.
- Some newspapers are also online (online editions can be different from print).

Sample Oral Citation

A July 23, 2010, *Wall Street Journal* online article, "BP Managers Named in Disaster Probe" by Ben Casselman and Russell Gold, said testimony in a federal investigation indicated several reasons to anticipate a major incident.

Magazines

Magazines are published on a regular schedule (weekly, monthly, or quarterly) and contain a range of articles, often related to a theme or focus. Magazines are generally financed by advertisements as well as a purchase or subscription price.

When to Use

- To find facts, statistics, and examples
- To support current events or topics

Advantages

- Often viewed as current and reliable
- Feature condensed information
- Use accessible language

Disadvantages

- May not give background information
- May require finding other in-depth sources
- May be outdated quickly

Tips on Locating

- Search library databases.
- Libraries often have many magazines and may archive old issues.
- Some magazines have websites, but they may differ from print versions or contain only old issues.

Sample Oral Citation

This image, from Gregory Stone's September 2012 *National Geographic* article entitled "Mountains of the Sea," is an expanse of cabbage coral attached to the slope of a seamount.

Journals

Journals are academic and professional publications issued at regular intervals, such as quarterly. Journals are topic specific and exist in most major fields.

When to Use

- To find detailed facts and statistics
- To locate expert testimony
- When highly credible sources are needed
- With a highly educated audience

Advantages

- Have extremely high credibility
- Are written and peer reviewed by experts or specialists in the field
- Include extensive bibliographies where you may find further sources

Disadvantages

- Are written in a formal style that may need to be adapted for your audience
- Use language specific to the field that may be difficult to understand

Tips on Locating

- Search library databases.
- Academic libraries often carry selected scholarly/professional journals in print.

Sample Oral Citation

In her article "Geographies of Desire: Postsocial Urban Space and Historical Revision in the Films of Martin Scorsese"—published in the Spring/Summer 2010 issue of the *Journal of Film and Video*—Professor Sabine Haenni argues that . . .

Government Resources

Government resources are information sources created by local, state, and federal governmental agencies. They can include books, reports, bills, pamphlets, maps, websites, or other documents.

When to Use

- To locate statistics and facts
- To locate policy information
- To locate practical information

Advantages

- Are often viewed as highly credible
- Are often very current
- Often contain unique information
- Often have extensive bibliographies

Disadvantages

- May not include citation information
- May be difficult to locate a specific publication

Tips on Locating

- Search the Internet using the city or state name, or ask your librarian how to locate government holdings.
- Public libraries are often good sources.
- Go to www.usa.gov/Agencies/Federal/All_Agencies/index.shtml for a list of sites.
- The Government Printing Office website (www.gpoaccess.gov) offers information about federal government publications.

Sample Oral Citation

In 2010, the city's official website noted that more than 9,000 accidents occur yearly nationwide due to drivers' running lights.

Reference Works

A reference work is a compilation of information such as facts, data, and definitions arranged for easy access. Some examples are dictionaries, encyclopedias, thesauruses, or atlases.

When to Use

- To locate brief definitions or segments of information
- To locate statistics and facts
- To assist you in using language effectively
- To start your research and get a broad base of information to build on

Advantages

- Are great places to begin your research
- Are useful places to get brief statistics, facts, and quotations
- Are helpful in constructing your outline

Disadvantages

- May offer information that is too brief
- Can focus on obscure facts or definitions
- May be user-created sites, such as Wikipedia, which may not always be accurate and so are not viewed as credible

Tips on Locating

- Check the reference section of your library or ask a reference librarian.
- Check corresponding websites of printed reference works.

Sample Oral Citation

As defined in the *Longman Dictionary of American English*, dissonance is a lack of agreement between ideas, opinions, or facts.

Interviews

Explore groups, businesses, associations, or museums that might have helpful information related to your topic, and interview someone. Interviews are information-gathering sessions where you (the interviewer) ask either one person or a group (the interviewee/interviewees) a series of prepared questions.

Before the interview, set up a time and a location and decide how to record the session (i.e., note taking and/or audio or video recording, if you have permission). Write your questions after researching the interviewee and thinking about what information you might need. Use more open-ended than closed-ended questions. *Open-ended questions* encourage discussion or longer responses and may start with *who, what, where, when, why,* or *how. Closed-ended questions* prompt only "yes" or "no" answers.

During the interview, allow for *follow-up questions*, or new questions that occur to you. Be professional in appearance and conduct.

Sample Oral Citation

In a personal interview I conducted last month, local dentist Dr. Marvin Jones said he will donate free checkups.

Practicing Ethics: Interviewing

Be an ethical interviewer; obtain proper permissions and report information accurately.

Surveys

Surveys are similar to interviews in that their purpose is to collect information. However, they help you collect quantifiable information from a large group of individuals known as the **population**. The responses given to survey questions are not as wide open as in an interview, and the survey is usually self-administered—requiring careful construction of the questions.

As you create your questions, use clear and appropriate language, ask about only one issue in each question, and try to accommodate all possible answers. Closed-ended questions often work best.

You can find many survey tools available online for free. Search using phrases such as "free survey tools" or "free survey maker."

Once you have your survey written, you are ready to administer it. Most likely, you will only survey a sample, or portion, of the population you are researching. So, you should select individuals who represent subgroups across the entire population.

Sample Oral Citation

In my February survey of 85 out of the 120 new employees here at the plant, more than two-thirds indicated a high level of satisfaction with their jobs.

11.2 What Types of Support Materials Can You Use in Your Speech?

Using a variety of support materials not only supports your speech but also will improve your credibility and help keep your audience's interest. Whether you are informing the board of directors of your company about last year's revenue, trying to convince folks to vote for you in the next election, or informing your class about canine soldiers, you need materials such as facts, definitions, testimony, examples, and statistics to shape your speech. You can use quotations, paraphrasing, comparison, contrast, and analogy to further highlight your materials.

Facts

Facts are verifiable bits of information about people, events, places, dates, and times. Most audiences will accept a fact with minor support or a simple oral citation and not require extended logical proof. The fact must be typical and from a recent reliable source. For example:

> The Washington Monument was reopened to the public on May 12, 2014, after being damaged in a 2011 earthquake.

Definitions

Definitions are brief explanations designed to inform your audience about something unfamiliar. They can also be used as language or persuasive devices. How you define a word or phrase can persuade your audience to focus their attitudes or beliefs about that word or phrase in a certain way. For example:

> According to Judy Strauss and Raymond Frost, in their 2009 book *E-Marketing*, digital "piracy" is "installing computer software or other copyrighted intellectual property (such as music or movies) that the individual did not purchase."

Testimony

Testimony is firsthand knowledge or opinions, either your own or from others. It tends to be interpretive or judgmental. There are four types of testimony.

Personal testimony is from your own experience or point of view. You can use it in your introduction to build your credibility or as brief examples periodically in a speech. But you must support your knowledge with other sources; never use it as the main type of source.

Lay testimony occurs when an ordinary person other than the speaker bears witness to his or her own experiences and beliefs.

Prestige testimony draws its effectiveness from the status of the person testifying, which often stems from his or her popularity, fame, attractiveness, high-profile activities, or age, if older.

Expert testimony is from a person the audience recognizes as an expert. The expert must be in a field related to your topic—a teacher for an education topic, a scientist for a scientific topic, and so on. Identifying your source's expertise to your audience is crucial:

> During an August 23, 2012, online press briefing of the Centers for Disease Control and Prevention, the director of the Division of Vector-borne Infectious Diseases, Dr. Lyle Petersen, stated that "we're in the midst of one of the largest West Nile outbreaks ever . . . ."

Examples

Examples are specific instances or cases that embody or illustrate points in your speech. The content of the examples may embody or illustrate items, people, events, places, methods, actions, experiences, conditions, or other information. They act as samples, patterns, models, or standards that help your audience understand and accept your points. Effective examples bring life to your speech, making your topic vivid and concrete for your audience.

Hypothetical examples are based on the potential outcomes of imagined scenarios; they gain their power from future possibilities. An effective hypothetical example requires the speaker and the audience to have faith that the projected outcome could occur. For instance, in a speech on emergency preparedness, you might say:

> One hundred years ago, an earthquake erupted on the New Madrid Fault with a force so intense it changed the path of the Mississippi. If this occurred today, we could have major destruction and fatalities. Would you have enough supplies? Do you have a plan? Are you prepared?

You can use examples to:

- Start your introduction; often, an extended example works best.
- Clarify difficult ideas.
- Strengthen a point.
- Build emotional intensity.
- Give a personal touch to your speech.

Statistics

Statistics are numerical facts or data that are summarized, organized, and tabulated to present significant information about a given population (people, items, ideas, etc.). When you use statistics correctly, your audience will view them as factual and objective. Statistics should not scare or confuse you or your audience.

Types of Statistics

Descriptive statistics aim to describe or summarize characteristics of a population or a large quantity of data. For example:

> **Maya Moore, WNBA Minnesota Lynx player and 2014 MVP, has a career average of 18.3 points, 6.3 rebounds, 3.2 assists, 0.7 blocks, and 31.2 minutes of playing time per game as of July 27, 2015 (wnba.com).**

The average (or mean) of Moore's statistics over her career gives the audience an idea of her talent in a brief snapshot. As another example, if you survey your entire speech class and calculate the percentage results of the survey, you are generating descriptive statistics.

Inferential statistics aim to draw conclusions about a larger population by making estimates based on a smaller sample of that population. For example:

> **Americans gave Congress a 16 percent approval rating at the start of 2015 (Gallup.com).**

This example says that 16 percent of all Americans approve of the job Congress is doing. Yet the Gallup data, like most poll statistics in the news, are inferential. They come from only a portion of the population; if the poll is trustworthy, the portion is assumed to be representative of the whole.

Using Statistics

- Make sure your statistics are accurate. Check any calculations to confirm that they are correct.

- Verify important statistics with multiple sources for better validity.

- Do research to confirm that the collection, interpretation, and reporting methods for the statistics were ethical and valid and the sample is representative.

- If the statistics are based on a poll, any differences shown by the poll should be less than the poll's margin of error.

- Explain clearly to your audience what the numbers mean. Brief examples and visual aids often help make statistics understandable. See Chapter 12 for help with creating presentation aids.

- Use statistics in moderation. Too many can make your audience stop listening.

- Inform your audience of any biases the source of the statistics may have.

- Report the statistics in a manner that does not twist their meaning.

- Comparing statistics can help explain them. Be sure to compare like things.

Quotations and Paraphrasing

Quoting sources at key points can provide compelling additional support. Directly quoting from a source is generally more effective than paraphrasing. Quote precisely if the material is short and says something better than you can or is memorable. In your speech, signal a direct quotation orally by using a technique such as:

> Neil Shea writes in his March 2010 *National Geographic* article, "Dunga Nakuwa cups his face...."

Paraphrase when the section you wish to use is long, wordy, unclear, or awkward for you to say. *Paraphrasing* restates the content of the material in a simpler format and in your own words, using language appropriate for your audience. For example, here is a section of text from Aristotle's *Rhetoric:*

> The modes of persuasion are the only true constituents of the art: everything else is merely accessory.[1]

Here is how a speaker might paraphrase this:

> According to *Rhetoric*, Aristotle believed that logic was the only true method of persuasion and that everything else was merely ornamentation.

When you summarize, quote, or paraphrase the work of others, you must cite the source orally and in your outline.

Comparison, Contrast, or Analogy

You will use most support materials to clarify information, to hold your audience's attention, to help your audience retain information, and to prove a claim. The easiest and most common way to use support materials is to be straightforward. However, you might use them as an analogy, as a comparison, or in contrast. See below for examples of each.

> **Comparison:** Using support materials to point out similarities between two or more ideas, things, factors, or issues. For example:
>
> Diego Maradona and Pelé each made it to four FIFA World Cup finals.

> **Contrast:** Using support materials to point out differences between two or more ideas, things, factors, or issues. An example could be:
>
> Pelé won three FIFA World Cups in his career, whereas Diego Maradona won only one.

> **Analogy:** Using support materials to help explain by comparing and contrasting.
>
> **Literal analogy** compares and contrasts two like things.
>
> Although Maradona and Pelé came from different playing backgrounds, their similar career successes make them the greatest footballers of all time.
>
> **Figurative analogy** compares and contrasts two essentially different things.
>
> Diego Maradona is like a god to many Argentines.

11.3 What Should You Consider When Choosing Support Materials?

Picture the last time you searched for something on the Internet. After you typed in a key phrase, several hits came up. Some seemed more reliable and applicable than others. You might have even skipped over some because you didn't see them as appropriate or important. In doing so, you were choosing material you thought was best. This type of selection process is important to your speech material as well.

The power of your support material is only as good as how your audience views the material. Likewise, if you know you have interesting, current, reliable material, you can be proud of your speech and confident about giving it.

When you are choosing materials, two steps can help you make wise selections. First, evaluate information for accuracy, completeness, currency, trustworthiness, and suitability. Second, consider what variety of materials is appropriate. The Practicing Ethics box below and the table on the next page take you through these steps and offer advice for making effective decisions.

Practicing Ethics: Evidence

Deceptively manipulating support materials is extremely unethical behavior. Remember these ethical guidelines:

- Present hypothetical examples as such.
- Present prestige testimony honestly and not as expert testimony.
- Use statistics fairly and accurately.
- Research for alternate points of view.
- Use and quote materials in their correct context.
- Disclose any source agendas or biases.
- Give proper oral citations.

Choosing Support Materials

Evaluation Elements	How Do You Adhere to These Elements?
Accuracy is the correctness and truthfulness of your materials.	• Materials should be verifiable from the original source and supported by multiple sources. • Use your support materials within their original context. Don't twist information to fit an agenda that doesn't match the original intent.
Completeness relates to having enough materials to make your speech comprehensible and ethical.	• Two or three examples are not enough to prove your central idea or even show a trend. You may need to summarize several examples or incorporate wide-ranging statistics. • Persuasive speeches especially need complete information to be ethical and influential.
Currency demonstrates how recent or up-to-date your information is.	• If your topic is not changing rapidly, a general rule is to use information published or collected in the past five years. But changes can happen quickly, especially if your topic is unpredictable or related to current events.
Trustworthiness stems from how your audience views the credibility of your materials.	• Use trustworthy sources and let the audience know the author's or creator's credentials. • Select materials from unbiased sources. • Hold online sources to high standards of credibility. What is the site's purpose? Who sponsors or contributes to it? Has it been updated recently?
Suitability relates to how appropriate the materials are for the speech, audience, and occasion.	• Select materials that relate to your central idea. • Include information that shows your audience why the materials are relevant to them, to the topic, and to the occasion. Never use inappropriate material.
Source variety refers to the origin (primary or secondary) and target readership (scholarly or popular) of the materials.	• *Primary sources* are the original sources of the information; it is not quoted by a second party. *Secondary sources* cite, review, or build on other sources by quoting or paraphrasing primary sources. • *Scholarly sources* are written for specialists in their fields. *Popular sources* are for general readers. Choosing which to use depends on your topic, your audience, or class requirements.

11.4 What Are the Characteristics of an Effective Outline?

Organizing your support material begins and ends with creating an effective and appropriate outline. Successful speeches contain distinctive features and components that are carefully structured for particular functions and pleasing effects. Your outline is your speech's blueprint. Later in this chapter, you will learn more about the different types of outlines. For now, here are the basic characteristics of most outlines.

Includes Standard Parts of an Outline

An outline typically includes an introduction, body (with main points, subpoints, and links), conclusion, and source page.

- The *introduction* opens the speech, grabs the audience's attention, and focuses listeners on the topic.

- The *body* is the central portion of the speech. It contains:

  Main points, or the main ideas or claims you wish to cover or make. They directly relate to your central idea. Most speeches will have two or three main points, but some speeches (e.g., process or persuasive) may have around five.

  Subpoints, or the supporting material that relates back to the main point. You can have multiple layers of subpoints (e.g., your subpoints can have subpoints).

  Links (also called transitions), which serve to make logical connections between parts of your speech.

- The *conclusion* ends your speech and takes one last moment to reinforce your main ideas and "wow" your audience.

- Many instructors require a *source page*. You create it just as you do for a research paper, often using the style of the Modern Language Association (MLA) or the American Psychological Association (APA).

Adheres to Outlining Rules

Like most things that have a set structure, outlines follow rules that will help you create an effective one.

Record the Topic, Specific Purpose, and Central Idea

You should include the topic, specific purpose, and central idea at the top of the outline as a title framing the speech. This helps keep these elements at the forefront as you create the rest of the outline.

Use Full Sentences

Write each outline component in full sentences for a preparation outline (see Objective 11.7). This forces you to think in complete thoughts and will help you learn the speech as well as gauge its length.

Cover Only One Issue at a Time

Covering only one issue at a time in each outline component will help keep your speech simple enough for delivery and prevents you from writing the speech as a manuscript. The best method is to write only one sentence per component in the body of the speech.

INCORRECT

I. The City of Jackson needs to institute a plan to decrease the numbers of pigeons that infest it each year, breeding everywhere and roosting on buildings, because they spread diseases to humans and other animals and contaminate our waterways. The pigeons...

Avoid using words like **and**, **or**, **because**, or **but** to connect two independent issues in one sentence.

CORRECT

I. The City of Jackson needs to institute a plan to decrease the number of pigeons.
   A. Each year, thousands of pigeons flock to the city.
      1. They breed everywhere.
      2. They roost on many buildings.
   B. Pigeons spread disease.
      1. They carry germs that affect humans.
      2. They carry germs that affect animals.
      3. They can contaminate our waterways.

Use Correct Outline Format

The format of an outline should be very systematic, helping you to logically structure your speech and aiding you in your delivery. You should always use correct outline formatting in the body of the speech. The following guidelines will help you.

Distinguishing Main Points

Use Roman numerals to distinguish your main points.

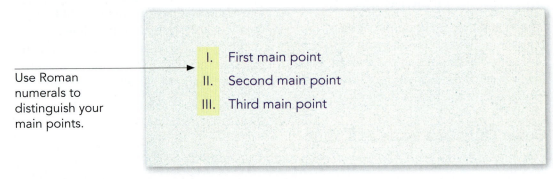

I. First main point
II. Second main point
III. Third main point

Pattern of Symbols

Use a consistent pattern of symbols (e.g., uppercase letters, numbers, and lowercase letters).

Related points (indicated here with colors) should use the same type of symbol.

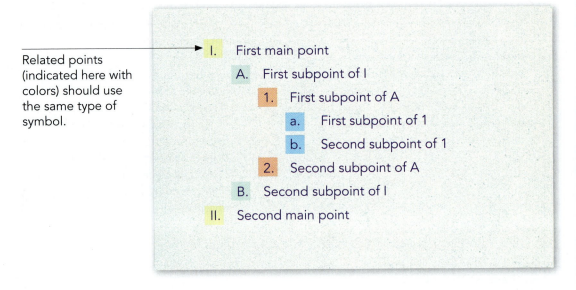

I. First main point
  A. First subpoint of I
    1. First subpoint of A
      a. First subpoint of 1
      b. Second subpoint of 1
    2. Second subpoint of A
  B. Second subpoint of I
II. Second main point

Subpoints

Each subpoint must have at least two subdivisions, if it has any. Think of it like cutting up an apple. If you cut up an apple, you have at least two pieces. You may end up with more pieces, but you cannot divide something without a result of at least two.

For example, subpoint A has two subdivisions, 1 and 2 (indicated here with colors).

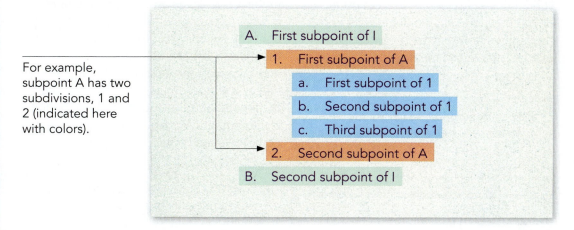

Alignment of Points in Your Outline

Your main points should line up closest to the left margin of the page, and each subsequent subdivision should be indented further to the right.

Each main point should align left (align the periods), and each level of subpoints should be indented further to the right.

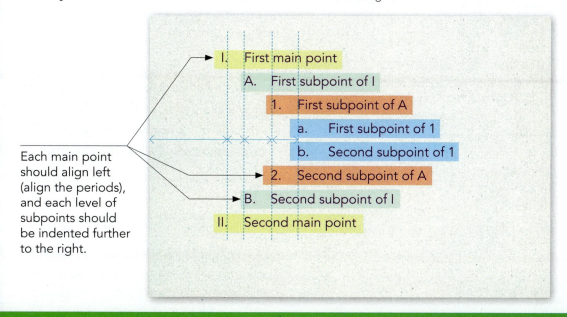

Use Balanced Main Points

Your main points should be equal in importance to each other. This is called a *standard of balance*. The main points will directly relate to the overall topic but should not overtly relate to each other. Each main point should coordinate with the others. For example, below are three relatively balanced main points:

Specific purpose: To inform my audience about the National Football League (NFL).

I. A brief history of the game of football explains the evolution of the NFL.

II. The NFL has come a long way since its beginnings.

III. Today, the NFL has a unique organizational setup.

Notice that each point is unique and relates back to the specific purpose.

Each of the above points is manageable in scope and should take roughly the same amount of time to present; the "brief history" in point 1 might be a bit shorter in duration.

Employ Subordination

The components of your outline following each main point should be properly subordinate to the point above them. In other words, any statement that comes under a point must not be equal to or of greater importance than the point directly above it. An easy test for this is to read the main point, mentally insert "because," and then read the subpoint. If doing so makes a logical connection between the main point and the subpoint, the subpoint is subordinate. For example, here is a main point followed by its first subpoint:

I. The City of Jackson needs to institute a plan to decrease the number of pigeons.
   A. Each year, thousands of pigeons flock to the city.

You can test the connection by mentally inserting "because":

Main point I

The City of Jackson needs to institute a plan to decrease the number of pigeons **because** each year, thousands of pigeons flock to the city.

Subpoint A

The test confirms that the main point and subpoint are logically connected and that the subpoint is subordinate.

Plan Out Formal Links

You should include links between major components of the speech. An effective speaker will lead the audience almost effortlessly from one point to another, and formal links will make this seem smooth, not jolting. There are four types of links.

Transitions are words or phrases signaling movement from one point to another as well as how the points relate to each other. Transitions include:

- Let's move on to . . .
- On the other hand . . .
- Also . . .
- In conclusion . . .

For example:

> Now we are ready to assemble the sound system.

Signposts are words or phrases that signal to the audience where they are with regard to related thoughts and/or what is important to remember. Some common signposts are:

- First . . . Second . . . Third . . .
- My first reason . . . My second reason . . .
- Above all, remember . . .

For example:

> The first step in planting a vegetable garden is to locate a well-drained, sunny location.

Internal previews are like mini-introductions and look like detailed signposts. These statements tell the audience what will be covered next in the speech. For example:

> Let's look at how the NFL consists of 32 teams, two conferences, and four divisions.

An internal preview is a great way to link your introduction and the body of your speech.

Internal reviews (also known as internal summaries) are like mini-conclusions. They summarize what you have just covered in the previous section of your speech. Here's an example:

> It is our responsibility to offer health care to every U.S. citizen, to improve access, and to lower care costs that currently drives the need for a universal system.

Often, you will combine internal previews and internal reviews with a transition, as in this example:

> Now that you have selected the right location for the strawberry patch, prepared the soil, and purchased the correct plants for your climate, it is time to plant the strawberries properly.

TIP: Effective Links

Creating your links ahead of time and placing them in the correct spots in your outline will help you remember to use them, and then you won't struggle for words during the delivery of the speech.

Use Proper Citations

Citing your sources on your outline and during your speech is an ethical responsibility and the only way to prevent plagiarism. If something is not original to you, the creator must be credited. Most instructors will ask you to follow a specific style manual (such as MLA or APA) for the outline citations and source page; the table below offers examples of two of the more challenging forms. For other examples, see source citations with sample outlines (pages 325, 387, and 429).

Sample MLA and APA Citations

Source	Citation
Web page– MLA (with government author)	United States. Dept. of Health and Human Services. Food and Drug Administration. "FDA Regulates the Safety of Packaged Ice." *U.S. Food and Drug Administration*. Dept. of Health and Human Services, 20 July 2015. Web. 27 July 2015.
Web page– APA (with government author)	U.S. Department of Health and Human Services, U.S. Food and Drug Administration. (2015, July 20). *FDA regulates the safety of packaged ice*. Retrieved from http://www.fdagov/Food/FoodborneIllnessContaminants/BuyStoreServeSafeFood/ucm197586.htm
Interview conducted by speaker–MLA	Jones, Timothy. Personal interview. 1 Nov. 2015. Jones, Timothy. Telephone interview. 1 Nov. 2015. Jones, Timothy. E-mail interview. 1 Nov. 2015.
Interview conducted by speaker*–APA	*APA normally does not recognize undocumented sources such as interviews. Because speakers often use interviews as source material, your instructor may ask you to include them as shown below. Jones, T. (2015, November 1). Personal interview. Jones, T. (2015, November 1). Telephone interview. Jones, T. (2015, November 1). E-mail interview.

Closely related to citing sources on your outline is citing them orally during the speech. There isn't an official style manual for oral citations. Follow your instructor's guidelines and/or the suggestions offered in the following table.

Contents of Oral Citations

Type of Source	What to Include
Website	Identify it as a website; give title of web page, site sponsor, and either the date of publication, last update, or when you accessed it; may include article title.
Magazine or journal	Identify it as an article; give name of magazine or journal, author and qualifications, and date of publication; may include article title.
Newspaper	Identify it as an article; give name of paper, author and qualifications, and date of issue; may include article title.
Book	Identify it as a book; give title, author and qualifications, and date of publication.
Government document	Provide title, name of agency or branch of government publishing it, and date of publication.
Brochure or pamphlet	Identify it as a brochure or pamphlet; give title, who published it, and date of publication.
Reference works	Provide title and date of publication.
Videotape, DVD, or CD	Provide title of tape or disk and date.
Television or radio	Provide title of the show, channel or network, and date of broadcast.
Interview conducted by you	Identify yourself as the interviewer; give name and identity of the person interviewed and date of interview.

When creating your oral citations, remember to use variety in how and where you place them, give them when you state the borrowed information (not all grouped at the beginning or end), and be enthusiastic when presenting your sources.

11.5 What Organizational Strategies Can You Use in Your Speech?

A strategy is a plan designed to achieve a goal—in this case, your specific purpose. Strategy is concerned with the relationship and arrangement of your main points. Most speakers choose from seven basic organizational strategies: topical, chronological, spatial, causal, comparative, problem–solution, and Monroe's motivated sequence. See page 330 for help with how to select the most effective strategy for your speech.

Topical

You will use the ***topical strategy*** (also called categorical) when there is a strong inherent or traditional division of subtopics within the main topic. If you give a speech about chocolate, for example, a natural topic division could be white, milk, and dark. For a topic such as taking a vacation to Orlando, you might divide the topic according to how people traditionally plan vacations—places to see, places to eat, and places to stay. Here's an example using the topical strategy to organize a speech on succeeding in school:

Specific purpose: To inform my audience about techniques to improve their schoolwork.
Central idea: To succeed in school, you need to organize your life, carefully manage your time, and focus mentally.
   I. Organization is the process of giving structure and order to your work.
  II. Time management is controlling or directing time into useful chunks.
 III. Mental focus is realizing what you have to do and concentrating hard on that single item.

Notice how each main point takes on a different subtopic—organization, time management, and mental focus. As individual subjects, these may seem unrelated, but in relation to the central idea, they are logically connected.

Chronological

You will use the ***chronological strategy*** when you need to move through steps in a process or develop a timeline. Depending on the topic and your general purpose, you might move forward or backward through the process or timeline for effect. This type of arrangement is especially helpful when stressing the history of an event, person, or thing or when demonstrating a process. For example:

Specific purpose: To inform my audience how to use a compost bin.
Central idea: Composting is an easy way to save space in our landfills while growing great vegetables or flowers.
  I. There are many types of composting bins, making it important to select the right one for your needs and budget.
  II. Where you position your composting bin can make composting either effortless or grueling.
  III. A few simple steps will help you maintain a sweet-smelling, productive compost pile.
  IV. Using the "black gold" from your pile will supply you with a bounty of produce or flowers.

Here, each main point walks the listener through the major steps of composting. The subpoints should do the same.

TIP: Demonstration Speeches
When you give a demonstration speech (a "how to do it" speech), you can use the chronological strategy to create a step-by-step organization.

Spatial

A ***spatial strategy*** recognizes space as a way to arrange the speech. This strategy is useful when you want to discuss your topic in relationship to proximity, a physical setting, or a natural environment. Examples might be speaking about your tour through the White House, room by room; telling the new freshman class about your campus, building by building. A speaker can even arrange an informative speech about the human tooth spatially—by beginning at the outermost part, the enamel, and working in to the soft center, or dental pulp. Here's another example:

Specific purpose: To inform my audience about the Grand Canyon.
Central idea: Carved by the Colorado River, more than 277 miles long, and more than a mile deep in places, the Grand Canyon National Park is like three parks in one when you visit the North Rim, the South Rim, and the Inner Canyon.
  I. The North Rim has a much higher elevation than the South, making it cooler, with better views of the Canyon.
  II. The South Rim is more accessible and has several historical sites.
  III. The Inner Canyon is the unpredictable lifeline of the park.

The spatial strategy is often a useful way to deal with a setting as large as the Grand Canyon. It helps you divide the space (North Rim, South Rim, and Inner Rim) into more manageable parts.

Causal

You will use the *causal strategy* when you want your audience to understand the cause and effect, or consequences, of something. With this strategy, you can either trace the path that leads up to a certain result or backtrack from the effect to the cause. Which way you go depends on what is most important to your specific purpose. For example, a speech explaining the causes leading up to the economic crisis beginning in 2009 would be a great candidate for this type of arrangement.

Specific purpose: To inform my audience about the causes of the 2009 economic crisis.
Central idea: The 2009 economic crisis in the United States can be explained by examining the chain reaction created by the declining housing market and global financial ramifications.
   I. An unsustainable real estate boom brought prices the average family could not afford.
   II. Bank losses created a major loss of capital.
   III. The average person feels the effects of a recession.

Depending on your topic, you may have one cause leading to a single effect, a single cause leading to several effects, or several causes leading to one effect.

Comparative

The *comparative strategy* uses the practice of compare and contrast. In an informative speech, you might use this strategy with new, abstract, technical, or difficult-to-comprehend topics. Here, you compare your topic to something the audience knows. This strategy only works when the two things you are comparing are comparable or analogous. For example:

Specific purpose: To inform new students about college life.
Central idea: Comparing what college might be like to your high school experience will help you anticipate the next four years.
   I. Your classroom experience will be unlike that of high school.
   II. Your social life will be different from what it was in high school.
   III. Your everyday responsibilities will be different.

Notice how this example uses the comparative strategy for informative purposes. This approach helps the audience understand and follow the speech by comparing the unknown (college life) with the familiar (high school experience). In a persuasive speech, this strategy can be used to convince an audience that one thing is better than another, by comparing the two. This is a common practice used by many salespersons and is often referred to as *comparative advantage*. Don't get carried away with the number of comparisons you make, which can be confusing. In a short presentation, five or fewer comparisons will suffice.

Problem–Solution

You will use the **problem–solution strategy** when you want to show your audience how to solve a problem, making it an arrangement suited for a persuasive speech. With this strategy, your speech will have two main sections, dedicated to the "problem" and the "solution." For example:

> **Specific purpose:** To convince my audience that artificial sweeteners are dangerous.
>
> **Central idea:** Artificial sweeteners are an easy alternative for the calorie conscious, but the toxic effects of their chemicals should prompt consumers to seek safer choices.
>
> I. **(problem):** Artificial sweeteners such as sucralose, aspartame, and saccharin cause major side effects that can be potentially dangerous.
>
> II. **(solution):** Gradually decreasing your intake of artificial sweeteners by drinking more water, unsweetened tea, or naturally flavored drinks is the solution for preventing future problems and improving your overall health.

Some persuasive speeches may need more than two main points, if the problem and/or solution is complex or if your audience might be unwilling to accept the problem and/or solution you propose.

Monroe's Motivated Sequence

Developed by Alan Monroe of Purdue University in the 1930s, **Monroe's motivated sequence** is really a more detailed problem–solution strategy.[2] Basing the speech on what motivates the audience, the speaker convinces the audience that the speaker has the solution to their needs. This strategy has five stages:

- Attention—Begin to direct your audience's attention toward your topic.
- Need—Demonstrate that your audience needs a change by suggesting that a problem exists and they need to solve it.
- Satisfaction—Propose a viable solution to the problem and support it as the best one with the appropriate evidence.
- Visualization—Help the audience visualize how great and beneficial the solution is.
- Action—Call them to action or tell them exactly what they must do to achieve the solution.

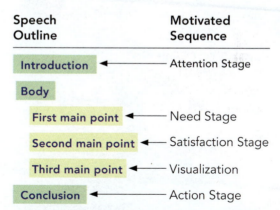

Speech Outline	Motivated Sequence
Introduction ←	Attention Stage
Body	
First main point ←	Need Stage
Second main point ←	Satisfaction Stage
Third main point ←	Visualization
Conclusion ←	Action Stage

11.6 How Do You Begin and End a Speech?

Think about the first and last few minutes of your favorite movie. Both sequences are often action-packed, thrilling, and spine-tingling. The introduction of your speech needs to be a bit like that to grab your audience's attention. Your conclusion needs to let them down easy, offer a response, and leave your audience breathless, speechless, or wanting to clap. You want to make them eager to listen and inspire them to remember your speech.

An introduction and a conclusion each have basic elements you should include. Here are two templates that suggest the most common arrangement for each. The next page will help you understand why this arrangement is effective.

INTRODUCTION

Attention-getter: ....
....

Credibility material: ....
....

Relevance to audience: ....
....

Preview of speech: ....
....

CONCLUSION

Summary statement: ....
....

Audience response statement: ....
....

WOW statement: ....
....

The Introduction

An effective introduction serves four functions. It should:

- Capture your audience's attention. An *attention-getter* is something you say, show, or do to get your audience to focus on you, your topic, and the goal of your speech. In most cases, it should be the first words spoken or the first images or actions shown. To grab your audience's attention with your words, you can use facts or statistics; quotations; stories, narratives, illustrations or anecdotes; humor; or questions.

- Build your credibility early. Employing an effective delivery style and noting a connection to the topic will help you establish initial credibility.

- Demonstrate audience relevance. An early statement about what your topic has to offer can demonstrate that the audience has something to gain from listening to you.

- Introduce the topic and preview the speech.

Your introduction should be no more than 15 percent of the total speech time, so you usually have under a minute to carry out these functions.

The Conclusion

An effective conclusion should serve four functions as well. It should:

- Signal the end of the speech. A vocal change, such as slowing down and beginning to lower your intensity; a physical change, such as moving from behind the lectern (often accompanied by a vocal change); and a language signal, such as "In conclusion…" are all ways to signal the end is near.

- Summarize or effectively and concisely restate your speech's main points.

- Elicit a response or tell the audience what you want them to do with the information you have just given them.

- Create an impact one last time. This is the "WOW" moment of the speech. As with your attention-getter, you might use statistics; quotations; stories, narratives, illustrations or anecdotes; humor; or questions. You might offer a challenge to the audience or refer back to the introduction.

Your conclusion should be no more than 5 percent of your speech time.

Everything that has a beginning comes to an end.[3]

Quintilian

11.7 What Are the Types of Outlines?

Speakers, especially beginning speakers, find it helpful to use outlining techniques at three main stages in the speech creation process. You can use a working outline during your research, a preparation outline as you craft the text of the speech, and a delivery outline when you present your speech.

Working Outlines

A *working outline* is a brief sketch of the body of your speech to keep you on track and give you direction while researching. It contains your topic, general purpose, specific purpose, and central idea—plus working main points. *Working main points* are early drafts of your main points. The working outline will be a combination of complete thoughts, words, and phrases. It is mostly for your eyes only. You should attempt to use correct outline form, but this is still a very free-flowing stage.

Preparation Outlines

Preparation outlines (also known as formal or full-sentence outlines) will be much longer and more detailed than working outlines. Designing a preparation outline allows you the opportunity to give the necessary time, effort, and thought to creating a successful speech. The entire outline will adhere to correct form and previously discussed characteristics. You should follow your instructor's requirements, but in most cases, it will be:

- Typed (double spaced)
- Formatted in a specific, consistent way
- Handed in prior to or on your speech day

Chapters 13 and 14 offer more examples of working and preparation outlines.

Here's a preparation outline by Brianna, a student, for a speech on pet adoption:

By labeling the parts of the introduction, Brianna is sure she has included all she needs to grab her audience's attention. When necessary, she includes proper in-text source citations. Her instructor requires MLA style.

Brianna Forester
October 15, 2012

COMM 110
Dr. Smith

Topic: Pet adoption
Specific purpose: To inform my COMM 110 class about the misconceptions of adopting a pet from a shelter.
Central idea: Viewing adopted pets as unhealthy, costly, and only as mixed breeds are three misconceptions about pet adoptions from a shelter.

INTRODUCTION
Attention-getter: It is estimated that about 62 percent of homes in the United States own a pet, according to "Pet Statistics" found October 10, 2012, on The American Society for the Prevention of Cruelty to Animals, or the ASPCA, website (ASPCA).
Relevance to audience: I surveyed this class, and 78 percent of you currently have a pet here at school or at home; 92 percent of you have had a pet at some time in your life. Some of you got your pets from family or friends for free. However, fewer than half of your adopted pets came from a shelter or rescue. The ASPCA states that "approximately 5 to 7 million companion animals enter animal shelters nationwide every year." Sixty percent of sheltered dogs and 70 percent of sheltered cats are euthanized each year (ASPCA).
Credibility material: As someone who has made the choice to adopt a pet from an animal shelter, I have reaped the benefits of pet adoption. I understand the importance of adopting from a shelter rather than purchasing a pet from a store or breeder. However, I understand that some people have concerns or serious misconceptions about pet adoption.

Brianna's main points mirror the order and construction of her preview.

Preview of speech: Today, I would like to discuss three misconceptions about pet adoptions from shelters. We will discuss the notions that adopted pets are unhealthy, that adoption costs as much as purchasing a pet from a store or breeder, and that you can't adopt purebreds.

(**Link**: Let's look at the first misconception.)

BODY
I. Pet adoption from shelters leads to unhealthy pets.
    A. The Humane Society of the United States —on its website, October 10, 2012—indicates that most shelters around the country provide full examinations as soon as an animal enters the facility.
        1. A board-certified shelter veterinarian conducts the examinations.
        2. The veterinarian treats any existing illness or injuries.
        3. The shelter staff evaluates the mental state of each animal for stability and best placement opportunities.
        4. The animals are wormed and given age-appropriate and animal-specific vaccinations (HSUS).
    B. As much as possible, the shelters maintain a healthy lifestyle for the animals while they are in the facilities.
        1. Our shelter here in town has volunteers to work as walkers, socializers, and foster parents or families, according the Central Missouri Humane Societies website on October, 10, 2012.
        2. The animals receive a healthy diet and a clean place to live.

(**Link**: Now that you understand adopted pets can be healthy and stable, let's look at misconception #2.)

Brianna distinguishes her main points with Roman numerals.

II. Pet adoption from shelters costs as much as purchasing a pet from a store or breeder.
   A. Adoption fees vary by geographic location and the type of agency you are adopting from.
      1. Larger cities can be more expensive.
      2. If you adopt purebreds from breed-specific rescues, they can be more expensive, according to CostHelper.com, accessed October 11, 2012.
      3. CostHelper.com suggests that adopting a dog from a shelter or breed rescue typically costs between $70 and $300.
   B. When considered in detail, shelter adoptions are usually cost effective.
      1. The Central Missouri Humane Society website quotes the following adoption fees.
         a. Puppies under 4 months are $120.
         b. Dogs (4 months and over) are $100.
         c. Cats and kittens are $100
         d. Adopting two cats at once is $150.
         e. Animals who have been in the shelter for a long time are $65.
         f. Animals over the age of 8 are $65.
         g. They have other fees for small animals like rabbits, and hamsters.
      2. Purchasing puppies from stores or breeders can average $300 to $5,000, according to CostHelpers.com.
         a. They suggest that pet-quality puppies can cost between $300-$1,500.
         b. Pet-quality puppies have an aesthetic flaw that would prevent them from being show animals but is not noticeable to the average person.
         c. CostHelpers.com states that show-quality puppies usually cost between $1,500-$5,000 but can go to $15,000 or more.
      3. You can even locate free pets in your local paper that are up for adoption.
      4. It is important to point out that those free animals are not totally free and that the ones purchased from breeders or stores have future costs many shelter animals don't.
         a. Most shelter adoption fees include the examination, fecal tests, worming, spaying/neutering, vaccines, and ID (tag or microchip).
         b. Spaying/neutering a dog can cost $150 to $300 and a microchip is usually $50, according to "Adopt a Pet" on Petfinder.com October 11, 2012.

She uses an appropriate pattern of symbols for related subpoints, such as the lowercase letters under subpoint 1.

All of Brianna's main points and subpoints are properly indented and aligned.

(**Link**: Now that you understand that adopting a pet from a shelter can be cost effective, let's look at our third and final misconception.)

Brianna includes all links in her outline.

III. Pet adoption from a shelter prevents you from owning a purebred.
   A. The Humane Society of the United States, on its website, estimates that 25 percent of dogs in shelters are purebred.

B. Purebred cats are less common, according to the Southeastern Wisconsin Purebred Cat Rescue website, October 11, 2012.
   1. Since 1999, the Wisconsin Purebred Cat Rescue has rescued thousands of neglected and abused purebred cats.
   2. In 2009, at the beginning of our economic crisis, their rescue was averaging 700 purebred cats a year.
C. In an October 10, 2012, article entitled "Shelters Seeing Increase in Purebred Dogs," written by Carole Carlson for the *Post-Tribune*, a *Chicago Sun-Times* publication, Carlson suggests that the current economic times are forcing many families to put their pets up for adoption.

CONCLUSION

Summary statement: Viewing adopted pets as unhealthy, costly to purchase for what you get, and not for those who want a purebred animal are all potential misconceptions about shelter adoptions. As with any major investment of time, money, and love, you have to educate yourself about the best options you have before making that purchase that will change your life.

Audience response statement: In my introduction, I noted that fewer than half of you have or have had a shelter pet. I hope that the information I have offered today will help you the next time you decide to bring a loving pet into your lives.

WOW statement: As George Orwell once stated, "All animals are equal but some animals are more equal than others" ("Pet and Animal Quotes").

As in the introduction, Brianna labels the parts of her conclusion, highlighting their functions.

Works Cited

"Adopt a Pet." *Petfinder.com*. Discovery Communications, 2012. Web. 11 Oct. 2012.

The American Society for the Prevention of Cruelty to Animals. "Pet Statistics." *ASPCA.org*. ASPCA, 2012. Web. 10 Oct. 2012.

Carlson, Carole. "Shelters Seeing Increase in Purebred Dogs." *Post-Tribune*. Chicago Sun-Times, 9 Oct. 2012. Web. 10 Oct. 2012.

Central Missouri Humane Society. *Central Missouri Humane Society*. CMHS, 2012. Web. 10 Oct. 2012.

"How Much Does Buying a Dog Cost?" *CostHelper.com*. CostHelper, 2012. Web. 11 Oct. 2012.

The Humane Society of the United States. *The Humane Society of the United States*. HSUS, 2012. Web. 10 Oct. 2012.

"Pet and Animal Quotes." *ThinkExist.com*. ThinkExist, n.d. Web. 11 Oct. 2012.

Purebred Cat Rescue. *Specialty Purebred Cat Rescue*. Purebred Cat Rescue, 2009. Web. 11 Oct. 2012.

For each source used in the speech, Brianna includes a proper citation on her source page. Again, she follows MLA guidelines.

Remember to double-space the source page and use a hanging indent for each entry.

Delivery Outlines

Delivery outlines will maintain the tight structure of the preparation outline but will eliminate much of the detail because you will know it by memory after writing the speech and doing some preliminary practicing. Create and use this outline as early as possible in the rehearsal stage of your speech. It is important that your "mind's eye" become familiar with the layout of this outline. If you find that you want to read directly from it most of the time, it has too much detail. A delivery outline will also have delivery and presentation hints highlighted at key points during your speech. You should set up your delivery outline format with what you find the most useful and comfortable, although some instructors may require that you use an outline containing only key words (eliminating all phrases). The following is only one example, showing note cards Brianna used. You should follow your instructor's requirements for delivery outlines.

CARD # 1

- 62% of U.S. homes own a pet (ASPCA) (slide)
- 78% of class own a pet now
- 92% have at some point owned a pet
- Fewer than half adopted a pet
- 5 to 7 million animals enter shelters yearly
- I adopted a pet
- Misconceptions--unhealthy, costly, no purebreds

(**Link**: The first misconception)

CARD # 2

I. Unhealthy pets
    A. HSUS indicates most shelters provide exams
        1. Board-certified vets
        2. Treatment of existing illnesses and injuries
        3. Evaluate for mental state and best placement
        4. Worming and vaccinations
    B. Maintain healthy lifestyle
        1. Walkers, socializers, foster programs (slide x3)
        2. Healthy diet and clean cages (slide)

                                        SLOW DOWN

(**Link**: Misconception #2)

CARD # 3

II. Cost of adoption ==(slide)==
    A. Varies by location and type of agency
        1. Larger cities more expensive
        2. Purebred rescue can be expensive (Costhelper.com)
        3. Shelter adoption $70 - $300
    B. Shelter adoptions usually cost effective
        1. CMHS fees ==(show slide with prices)==
        2. Store or breeders can charge $300 - $5000
        3. Can adopt free from paper or friends but....
        4. Perks included in adoption fees

(**Link**: Third and final misconception)

CARD # 4

III. No purebreds ==(slide)==
    A. 25% of dogs in shelters are pure (HSUS)
    B. Pure cats are rare ==(slide)==
        1. Wisconsin Purebred Cat Rescue
        2. 700 cats a year
    C. Caused by the economic downturn

CARD # 5

Conclusion
- Unhealthy pets, cost, and lack of purebreds are potential misconceptions
- I hope this information will help you in the future
- Orwell quote--"All animals are equal but some animals are more equal than others."

==(slide of me and Buster)==

Chapter 11 Review

Key Questions

11.1 Where Do You Locate Support Materials?

Research is the act of investigating, evaluating, and summarizing information. Good research skills help you find effective support materials (or evidence)—information that explains, elaborates, or validates your speech topic. Support materials come from different sources, including commercial websites, nonprofit organization websites, blogs, personal websites, databases, books, newspapers, magazines, journals, government resources, reference works, interviews, and surveys.

See pages 294–301.

11.2 What Types of Support Materials Can You Use in Your Speech?

You need facts, definitions, testimony, examples, and statistics to shape your speech and can use quotations, paraphrasing, comparison, contrast, and analogy to further highlight your materials. Using a variety of support materials not only supports your speech but also improves your credibility and holds your audience's interest.

See pages 302–305.

11.3 What Should You Consider When Choosing Support Materials?

The power of your support material is only as good as how your audience views the material. When choosing support material, it is important to first evaluate it for accuracy, completeness, currency, trustworthiness, and suitability. Second, consider what variety of materials is appropriate.

See pages 306–307.

11.4 What Are the Characteristics of an Effective Outline?

An effective outline should:

- Include the standard parts of an outline: introduction, body (main points, subpoints, and links), conclusion, and source citations and source page.
- Adhere to outlining rules: record the topic, specific purpose, and central idea; use full sentences; cover only one issue at a time; use correct outline format; use balanced main points; employ subordination; plan out formal links; and use proper citations.

See pages 308–315.

11.5 What Organizational Strategies Can You Use in Your Speech?

A strategy is a plan designed to achieve a goal—in this case, your specific purpose. Seven of the most common organizational strategies are:

- Topical: highlights strong or inherent divisions
- Chronological: moves through a process or time
- Spatial: recognizes space as a way to arrange
- Causal: emphasizes cause and effect or consequences
- Comparative: compares and contrasts your topic to something else
- Problem–solution: outlines a problem and offers a solution
- Monroe's motivated sequence: a detailed problem–solution strategy with five stages—attention, need, satisfaction, visualization, and action

See pages 316–319.

11.6 How Do You Begin and End a Speech?

You begin by creating an introduction that has an audience attention-getter, a statement about your credibility, an audience relevance statement, and a statement introducing your topic and, if necessary, your main points.

Your conclusion should let the audience down easy by offering a summary statement, an audience response statement, and a "WOW" statement.

See pages 320–321.

11.7 What Are the Types of Outlines?

Speakers, especially beginning speakers, find it helpful to use outlining techniques at three main stages in the speech creation process. The three different types are:

- Working outlines, or brief sketches to organize your thoughts as you progress through the early stages of creating a speech—especially as you do research
- Preparation outlines (also known as formal or full-sentence outlines), are much longer and more detailed than working outlines
- Delivery outlines, or the outlines you use during your speeches, which maintain the tight structure of preparation outlines but will eliminate much of the detail because you will know it by memory after writing and practicing the speech. A delivery outline will also have delivery and presentation hints highlighted at key points during your speech.

See pages 322–327.

Key Terms

support materials (294)
population (301)
testimony (303)
personal testimony (303)
lay testimony (303)
prestige testimony (303)
expert testimony (303)
examples (303)
hypothetical examples (303)
statistics (304)
comparison (305)
contrast (305)
analogy (305)
literal analogy (305)

figurative analogy (305)
main points (308)
subpoints (308)
links (308)
transitions (313)
signposts (313)
internal previews (313)
internal reviews (313)
topical strategy (316)
chronological strategy (317)
spatial strategy (317)
causal strategy (318)
comparative strategy (318)
problem–solution strategy (319)
Monroe's motivated sequence (319)

Improve Your Communication

Selecting the right organizational strategy for your speech topic may seem like a difficult task. Most speeches can use more than one strategy. The most important consideration is to select a strategy that works with your general purpose, topic, and audience needs. This table summarizes some helpful hints.

Strategy	When Might You Use It?
Chronological	Useful for speeches about a process or development over time or plan of action
Topical	Ideal when your topic has inherent subtopics
Spatial	Useful when you need to walk your audience through a space or setting
Causal	Effective for speeches focusing on causes or consequences of something already present or possible
Comparative	Great when topics are abstract, technical, or difficult; beneficial for showing advantages
Problem–solution	Useful when trying to change attitudes or calling for a particular solution
Monroe's motivated sequence	Excellent strategy for a call-to-action speech

For persuasive speeches, the causal, comparative, problem–solution, and Monroe's motivated sequence often create the strongest persuasive arguments.

Apply Your Knowledge

1. Think of three topics for a speech that you might give to your current class audience. Where might you go to find support materials, and what types might you use? Try to be as creative as possible; include ideas from beyond the Internet and the library. Also, include a variety. Can you use one of each of the types of support materials discussed In Objective 11.2?

2. Using the same three topics from question 1, what organizational strategies might you use? Is there more than one possibility for a topic or topics? If so, which would be the best and why?

   (Hint: If you struggle to answer the questions above, ask another classmate to work with you to answer them and vice versa. Brainstorming with a classmate can inspire your creativity.)

3. Go to the Purdue Online Writing Lab (OWL) at owl.english.purdue.edu. What suggestions are given there for preventing plagiarism?

Other Resources

See the following resources for help with creating citations, preventing plagiarism, and outlining.

APA

American Psychological Association. *Publication Manual of the American Psychological Association.* 6th ed. Washington: APA, 2011. Print.

- owl.english.purdue.edu/owl/resource/560/01/
- www.apastyle.org
- www.wctc.edu/current-students/library/apa-citing.pdf
- www.studygs.net/citation.htm

MLA

Modern Language Association of America. *MLA Handbook for Writers of Research Papers.* 7th ed. New York: MLA, 2009. Print.

- owl.english.purdue.edu/owl/resource/747/01/
- www.mla.org
- www.library.cornell.edu/resrch/citmanage/mla
- mlaformat.org

Plagiarism

- owl.english.purdue.edu/owl/resource/589/01/
- www.plagiarism.org
- www.plagiarism.org/plagiarism-101/prevention/
- libraries.ucsd.edu/services/instruction/preventing-plagiarism/

Outlining

- owl.english.purdue.edu/owl/resource/544/01/
- www.lib.jjay.cuny.edu/research/outlining.html

12.1 How Can You Use Language Effectively in a Speech?

And when the night grows dark, when injustice weighs heavy on our hearts, or our best laid plans seem beyond our reach—think of Madiba, and the words that brought him comfort within the four walls of a cell:

It matters not how strait the gate,
How charged with punishments the scroll,
I am the master of my fate:
I am the captain of my soul.

What a great soul it was. We will miss him deeply. May God bless the memory of Nelson Mandela. May God bless the people of South Africa.

These words, spoken by President Barack Obama at the December 10, 2013, memorial service for Nelson Mandela, demonstrate the power of language for fashioning a story and stirring our emotions. In this ending, we hear Obama deliver words that he has carefully chosen. The language is poetic, appropriate, honorific, moving, and etched in our memories. Most of us will not give a speech of this magnitude at such a momentous occasion, but all effective language use begins with being correct, specific, conversational, and distinct. The following discussion offers advice, examples, and tools to help you use language to its fullest potential.

We are what we repeatedly do; excellence, then, is not an act but a habit.[1]

William Durant,
summarizing Aristotle

Be Correct

In Chapter 3, you learned that using appropriate language is important and that being correct is directly related to being clear. Using language incorrectly often leads to misunderstandings for the audience and low credibility for the speaker. Incorrect language in a speech could be a wrong word; words or phrases that are less known, less acceptable, or unnecessary (slang, clichés, fillers, idioms, or euphemisms); mispronounced words; or incorrect grammar. The following self-check will help you identify four common grammar errors. Use this to check your wording as you draft and refine your speech.

Self-Check: Avoiding Four Common Oral Grammar Errors

❏ Do I place modifying words close to the words they are modifying (avoiding misplaced modifers)?

INCORRECT: The man caught a bass wearing a purple hat.

CORRECT: The man, wearing a purple hat, caught a bass.

❏ Do I use the correct form of a pronoun for its function in a sentence? (Use pronouns such as *I, she,* and *he* as subjects; use forms such as *me, her,* and *him* as objects.)

INCORRECT: Him and me are best friends. INCORRECT: Mom yelled at she and I.

CORRECT: He and I are best friends. CORRECT: Mom yelled at her and me.

❏ Do I use *gone* (the past participle form) instead of *went* with a linking verb like *has* or *have*?

INCORRECT: I should have went to the party.

CORRECT: I should have gone to the party.

❏ Do I use correct subject/verb agreement? (A singular noun in the present tense uses a singular verb; plural nouns use plural verbs.)

INCORRECT: One of these coats are mine.

CORRECT: One of these coats is mine.

See Chapter 3 for more on making appropriate, clear language choices and using correct pronunciation.

Be Specific

Getting your message across in a straightforward manner is necessary in most communicative situations. In an instant, your listeners must interpret your message and formulate a response or commit it to memory.

Expanding your vocabulary will help you be more specific. Here are some additional tips:

- Be concrete. As noted in Chapter 3, most words vary in degree of abstraction. Concrete words focus on a particular person, object, action, or behavior and help listeners create a complete and, hopefully, accurate image. For example:

ABSTRACT:

The person saved the dog.

CONCRETE:

Firefighter Mancuso saved the husky from the frozen pond.

- Eliminate unnecessary words. For example:

WORDY:

Assigning students assignments that are not related to the class is not something Professor Miller would do.

MORE CONCISE:

Professor Miller would not give unrelated assignments.

- Speak primarily in the active voice. In the active voice, the subject is doing the action stated in the verb. In the passive voice, the subject is the receiver of the action.

ACTIVE:

The player caught the fly ball.

PASSIVE:

The fly ball was caught by the player.

Occasionally, passive voice can be effective when you want to emphasize the receiver of the action more than the doer. But use it sparingly. This example from the Declaration of Independence uses passive voice for effect.

We hold these truths to be self-evident, that all men are created equal, that they are endowed by their Creator with certain unalienable Rights, that among these are Life, Liberty, and the pursuit of Happiness.

- Avoid acronyms and abbreviations. *Acronyms* are words formed from the initials or other parts of several words. For example:

LOL = laughing out loud

NRA = National Rifle Association

or National Recovery Administration

Abbreviations are words created from shortening a longer word. For example:

limo = limousine

See Chapter 3 for more on how to avoid ambiguous language choices.

Be Conversational

If you have ever read a transcript of an oral conversation, you know that the way people speak is radically different from the way they write. Likewise, if you have ever heard someone read a paper aloud, you know that this format is much harder to follow than a conversational delivery and requires greater concentration on the part of the listener.

In oral style, you use more everyday language, personal pronouns such as *we* or *you*, contractions, and shorter sentences that put the subjects and verbs closer together. Plus, you have an extensive repertoire of oral communication signals (gestures, intonation, inflection, volume, pitch, pauses, and movement) to help you convey the message and draw others into the message. It is more difficult to access the benefits of these signals if you are reading or your message is very complex in language and logic.

| **See Chapter 4** for more on how to use nonverbal signals.

Here are the major differences between oral and written styles.

Characteristics of Oral Style	Characteristics of Written Style
Informal language	Formal language
Animated language	Technical language
Simple sentence structure	Complex sentence structure
Personally tailored messages	Impersonal messages
Repetition and restatement	Detailed and complex thoughts

Self-Check: Using an Oral Style

❑ Am I using language known to my audience or words that have fewer syllables than I might use in a written style?

❑ Am I using short sentences?

❑ Am I employing a variety of communication signals—gestures, intonation, inflection, volume, pitch, pauses, and movement?

❑ Am I focusing on what needs to be said and not bogging my audience down in details and complexity?

❑ Am I using pronouns such as *I, you, we*, and *me* to make the message more personal and to form a relationship with the audience?

❑ Am I using repetition, restatement, and other such devices to help others remember my message?

Be Distinctive

Distinctive language is lively, vivid, attention grabbing, and memorable. You can boost the distinctiveness of your speech by using language that appeals to human senses, embellishing your words, or using speech devices.

Appeal to the Senses

Using language that appeals to one or more senses can bring an object to life, invoke passion, or entertain. Although not every sentence should use a sensory appeal, watch for some ordinary statements that you can turn into sensory images. Use the table below to help you.

Senses	Why Might I Appeal to This Particular Sense?	Examples
Sight (visual)	To make a visual comparison between things or to restore a visual image from memory	"The water on the floor glimmered in sunlight."
Sound (auditory)	To help the listener understand how something sounds or to evoke a sound memory	"As the wind blew, you could hear the cracking and splitting of the tree limbs."
Smell (olfactory)	To take a person back to a place, time, or feeling, as people often associate smell with memories	"My favorite memory is the cool leathery smell of the brand-new football my dad gave me when I was eight."
Taste (gustatory)	To associate the taste of something with something known or to restore taste memory	"It tastes like chicken." "The sweet rolls were chewy and buttery."
Touch (tactile)	To create the feel of something or to evoke a relationship/feeling between the person and the object touched	"Think about the last time you played a video game and how the controller warmed to your intensity and vibrated softly as you fought your battle."

Embellish Language

You can use techniques called **_tropes_** to embellish or enhance ordinary words. The following table explains the most common tropes.[2]

Trope	What Is It?	Examples
Simile	An explicit comparison between two things, using _like_ or _as_	busy as a bee, clear as a bell, cold as ice, common as dirt, crazy as a loon, cute as a button, eats like a bird
Metaphor	An implied comparison	"Every day is an uphill battle." "That outfit is a train wreck."
Personification	Giving human traits to an object, idea, or animal	"My computer hates me." "The camera loves you"
Oxymoron	Connecting two ordinarily contradictory words	act naturally, Hell's Angels, jumbo shrimp, found missing, unbiased opinion
Rhetorical questions	Asking a question, but not for the purpose of receiving an answer	"Do you consume a lot of diet soda daily? Do you think it is healthier than regular soda?"

Use Speech Devices

The techniques of manipulating word order—or **_schemes_**—can help you create distinctive language. The table below explains a few common speech devices.[3]

Scheme	What Is It?	Examples
Repetition	Replicating the same words, phrases, or sentence emphasis	"Harriett Tubman had one piece of advice... If you want a taste of freedom, **keep going**. Even in the darkest of moments, ordinary Americans have found the faith to **keep going**."—Hillary Rodham Clinton, 2008 DNC speech
Assonance	Repeating a similar vowel sound	". . . the **odious apparatus** of Nazi rule."—Winston Churchill
Alliteration	Repetition of initial consonants in two or more words in close proximity	"Already American vessels have been **searched, seized**, and **sunk**."—John F. Kennedy, _Profiles in Courage_
Parallelism	Repeating the same grammatical patterns	**"Tell me and I forget. Teach me and I may remember. Involve me and I will learn."**—Benjamin Franklin

12.2 What Are the Methods of Delivery?

A public speech is a presentation that merges the written speech with the oral presentation, and both are open to interpretation. Your message and delivery work together to create the whole experience. Effective delivery does not draw attention to itself. It is natural and engaging, and it demonstrates confidence. Chapter 4 gave you specific information about the physical and vocal aspects of delivery. This section will help you understand the methods.

Extemporaneous Speaking

Extemporaneous speaking is the most acceptable contemporary method of delivery. Here, you plan out, rehearse, and deliver the speech from an outline consisting of key words, phrases, and delivery notes.

When Should You Use It?

This type of delivery is more audience centered than others because it is speaking "with" your audience and not "at" them. When your goal is to give an audience-centered speech, this is the method to use. In fact, you should try to use this method most of the time. Most classroom speeches require extemporaneous delivery.

Delivery Techniques

With the extemporaneous style, you will expand on the brief notes you have in front of you as you speak. You have rehearsed the speech so that you are not scrambling for something to say, which allows you to adapt to the audience and to sound more natural. Preparing the speech effectively and rehearsing it enough to become very comfortable with the topic are essential to this type of delivery.

See also Objective 12.3, "How Do You Prepare for an Extemporaneous Speech?"

Manuscript Speaking

Manuscript speaking occurs when you read word for word from a copy of the speech.

When Should You Use It?

This form of delivery is used when you must present the speech exactly as planned, so that you do not omit important details or misstate critical information.

Delivery Techniques

Make as much eye contact as possible, keep your gestures high and not hidden by the lectern or prompter, and keep your voice dynamic. Rehearse until you are comfortable with your delivery and message. Mark delivery tips on the manuscript.

Memorized Speaking

Memorized speaking means you rehearse the speech so much that you commit the full text to memory.

When Should You Use It?

Some speakers employ memorized delivery when accuracy and the appearance of spontaneity are equally important. This method works well for brief speeches, such as toasts.

Delivery Techniques

The key to an effective memorized speech is to rehearse it a lot and make it sound fresh. Keep your excitement high, and use effective verbal and nonverbal delivery techniques.

Impromptu Speaking

Impromptu speaking is the only method of delivery that has very little, if any, preparation or rehearsal. If any outline is used, it is simply notes jotted down quickly.

When Should You Use It?

Even though this type of speech is the least prepared, often uses a very basic organizational strategy, lacks solid evidence, and uses simplistic language, impromptu speaking is the delivery we use the most in our everyday lives and careers. You use this type of delivery when answering a question in a public forum (such as the classroom), when you need to offer information or dispute an issue during a meeting, and when you are asked to address an audience at a moment's notice.

Delivery Techniques

The best technique is to always be prepared with appropriate knowledge and information. You will almost always be asked to respond about something you should or do know. These steps will help you put your thoughts together:

- Pay close attention during the event.
- If you have time, write down key words or ideas and arrange them in a logical order.
- Limit your remarks to two or three points.
- Anticipate what evidence you can offer to support your points.

12.3 How Do You Prepare for an Extemporaneous Speech?

There is no magical formula for how many times you need to rehearse your speech for each of the following steps. Rehearsing is an individual process that will be specific to you. Do not assume that if your friend can give a speech with only two rehearsals, so can you. Pay attention to what does or does not work for you, and adapt your rehearsals to your needs. Even an excellent speech has room for improvement.

Read Aloud the Preparation Outline

At this step in the rehearsal process, you want to read aloud the preparation outline several times. Pay attention to the order of your points, how much support material you are using, and the order of the support materials. Include your links to see if they smoothly transition between points and parts of the speech. Read aloud the introduction and conclusion to see if they are interesting and flow well. Read the preparation outline one more time at a reasonable pace and time yourself. Make changes where necessary to correct issues or to adhere to the time limit. At this point, you should be under the time limit because you have not added verbal and nonverbal techniques or presentation aids that will take up time during your speech. Once you feel like you have a solid speech, move on to the next step.

TIP: Preparation Outline

Finish your preparation outline at least two days before the speech event (or as required by your instructor) so that you have time to practice and to trim it down to an appropriate delivery outline. Remember to follow your instructor's guidelines.

Consider Your Support Materials

Beginning speakers can unwittingly fall into poor delivery habits when they use support materials, particularly extended examples, narratives, or statistics. However, good delivery can bring your support materials to life. Here are a few suggestions:

- Understand your materials—and deliver them in a way that shows you do. For example, know the meanings of any terms, quotations, graphs, or statistics you use in your speech.

- Practice saying aloud the entire support material segment, especially if the material is a long narrative or example. Become so familiar with the words that they seem like your own. Practice statistics to the point that you do not need to look at your notes to remember them.

- Employ dramatic effect. Speak with enthusiasm that is appropriate for your topic and the occasion. Use dramatic pauses, stress important words, and vary your pace. If you are bored by your material, your audience will be, too.

- Use repetition and/or restatement to help your audience understand and remember your support materials.

- Consider using presentation aids to reinforce what you are saying. Presentation aids are exceptionally helpful when presenting statistical information. Conversely, refrain from putting extended examples on a visual aid and simply reading them.

Prepare Your Delivery Outline

Now, you want to reduce your preparation outline to only key words, phrases, and important quotations, statistics, or details. Try not to include too much of the introduction or the conclusion. You will tend to read it if you do, and direct eye contact is crucial. Also be aware of any format requirements by your instructor. After you have what you think is the final delivery outline, add delivery cues where you might need them. Also note cues for presentation aids. If you are struggling to remember details when using the delivery outline, back up a step. Check your logic, and read the preparation outline aloud again.

See Chapter 11 for more help creating a delivery outline.

Prepare Your Presentation Aids

Next, prepare the presentation aids exactly as you will use them in the speech event. Do not cut corners here. You want to practice with the finished aids to discover any problems and to make them seem a natural part of your speech.

See Objectives 12.5 and 12.6 for more on creating and using presentation aids.

Practice Multiple Times

Now it is time to put your speech on its feet. Practice your speech exactly as you plan to give it. Here are some hints:

- At this stage, always practice from the delivery outline. If you are struggling, read over the preparation outline and then return to practicing with the delivery outline.

- Practice a few times in front of a mirror or record your speech. Practice exactly the way you plan to give the speech. Watch for distracting behavior. Are your posture and gestures appropriate? Audio or video recording a rehearsal will allow you to focus on vocal quality. Video will also help you pay attention to how effective you are with your body language, eye contact, pronunciation, articulation, vocal rate, and pauses.

- Time yourself several times while using your finished presentation aids and necessary equipment, if any. Get as close as possible to the time limit.

- Practice with a rehearsal audience of family members, friends, or classmates. Ask them to offer feedback.

- Evaluate what you have learned from the rehearsal audience and from watching and listening to yourself. Change the speech message or your delivery style when necessary. Rehearse again, incorporating these changes.

See Chapters 13 and 14 for help with evaluating your speech.

Do a Final "Dress Rehearsal"

The last step in the rehearsal process is to do what actors call a "dress rehearsal." With this rehearsal, you want to simulate as closely as possible the exact event when you will give the speech. So it is important to:

- Rehearse in the space (or a close alternative) where you will give the speech.

- Use the exact delivery outline you will use during the speech. Make sure you number the pages or cards to prevent a mix-up the day of the speech.

- Use the exact presentation aids and necessary equipment.

- Try to rehearse at the exact time, to address possible issues with noise, lighting, temperature, and so on.

- Rehearse standing or sitting as you will during the speech.

- Wear the clothing you plan to wear, to see if it is appropriate and makes you feel confident.

- Ask a friend or colleague to watch your dress rehearsal and offer comments.

- Rehearse until you are as comfortable as possible, but do not wear yourself out. You will need energy for your speech event.

Prepare for Questions

Not all speaking situations will have an opportunity for an audience question-and-answer (Q and A) session. But like some impromptu speeches, a Q and A session may happen spontaneously, so be prepared:

- Anticipate questions you might get, and plan answers. Think about questions you hope for—or dread.

- Practice your answers.

- If your topic is complex, prepare a "Facts Sheet" with details that you can consult during the Q and A session.

- Remain calm, confident, and professional with aggressive or difficult questioners.

- Be honest if you do not know the answer. "I don't know" is an acceptable answer if you have demonstrated your knowledge in other ways. Offer to look for an answer and get back to the audience member if the situation allows you to do so.

- Give your speech to a practice audience and have them ask you questions.

Prepare for the Day of the Speech

The Day before the Speech

- Avoid activities that will stress your voice, mind, and body. Get a good night's sleep (eight hours), eat right, keep hydrated, and limit your caffeine and alcohol consumption. Avoid taking drugs such as antihistamines and expectorants.

- Prepare what you will wear.

- Practice at least once.

The Day of the Speech

- Don't forget to eat. If your body doesn't have the fuel it needs, nervousness may intensify and your memory will decrease. If your speech is within an hour of a meal, avoid eating throat-irritating foods, such as milk and chocolate.

- Get to the speech event early so that you are not rushed.

- Check all necessary equipment and deal with any issues you discover.

- If you will be speaking for a long period of time, keep water handy.

- Try to be by yourself just before the speech and prepare yourself mentally. Do vocal or physical activities to warm up.

- Look over your notes one more time to make sure they are in the right order.

- Walk to the front of the room confidently.

TIP: Boost Your Confidence

- The more you practice with your delivery outline and presentation aids, the lower your apprehension will be.

- During the speech, avoid apologizing or calling attention to your shortcomings. Your audience may not notice any. Don't dwell on them, or you'll lose your concentration and audience focus.

12.4 How Do You Prepare for a Mediated Presentation?

Increasingly, you may be asked to deliver a mediated speech. To prepare for a mediated presentation, you should establish the type of presentation, address unique factors, and practice. The next few pages will help you follow through with this preparation.

Establish the Type of Presentation

Mediated presentations use technology as a channel outside of the speaker or audience to exchange a message. For example, if you video record your speech and your instructor or classmates watch the video at another time, you are giving a mediated presentation. Likewise, if your boss asks you to give a presentation during a web-based virtual meeting or you give an opinion segment on the radio, you are giving a mediated presentation. Depending on the situation and technology available, you might need to give a mediated presentation using only a video recording device, or online mediated tools such as podcasts, webinars, screencasts, slide narrations, or hangouts (interactive group video chats).

Much of what you have learned about public speaking will assist you. However, the fact that your audience may be in another place, viewing or listening to you at a different time and through a different channel, changes the dynamics of the process. In Chapters 2 and 9, you learned about *asynchronous engagements, synchronous engagements*, and *hybrid engagements*. Mediating tools can be classified by which of these engagements they support (see the on the next page).

The type of mediated presentation you give will depend on what is required or will be best for your speech situation. If you are asked to give a mediated presentation in speech class, it is most often a prerecorded video shared electronically. However, a speech delivered with audience interaction via online tools, such as GoToMeeting or WebEx, is becoming more common. In the professional world, live, recorded, and hybrid presentations (combination of live and recorded) are common. See the table below. To determine the type, ask:

- Will this be a single-speaker event, an interview, or a panel discussion? How will the interview members or panel and the audience interact?

- Do I need to record the speech and electronically share it?

- Will my entire audience view the speech from a prerecorded video?

- Will a portion of my audience be either present in the room or able to interact via an online or other mediating tool?

- What tools are readily available for me to use? What do I know how to use?

- Given my general purpose, speech topic, and available mediating tools, which tools are best to use?

- Is the audience's real-time interaction important?

Some online speech courses require you to locate a specified number of adult audience members to be present as you record or give the speech. In this case, you know a portion of your audience is interacting in real time and the rest is not.

Type of Mediated Presentation	Engagement Styles	Examples
Recorded	*Asynchronous engagements* occur when the speaker and audience interaction is not in real time.	Sharing prerecorded video or audio—on YouTube, for example—where the audience is not present when the presentation is recorded (e.g., narrated slide shows or product demonstrations)
Live	*Synchronous engagements* occur when the speaker and the audience interact in real time via mediation.	Video or web conferencing or teleconferencing (e.g., real-time WebEx or Skype meetings where the entire audience is mediated)
Hybrid	*Hybrid engagements* occur when part of your audience is interacting in real time and a subset of the audience is not.	A speech with both a present audience and a mediated audience (e.g., some situations in web conferencing, teleconferencing, or events such as Google+ Hangouts where part of the audience is mediated)

Address Unique Factors

Universal Considerations

When giving any mediated presentation, you should consider some universal factors.

- Familiarize yourself early on with the equipment and tools.

- Always be aware that the technology could be on and recording you.

- Use a neutral background or one that will not compete with you. Make sure you are well lit, with the light in front of you.

- Coordinate your clothing. Muted colors often work well. Stay away from patterns, stripes, and flashy ornamentation. Be wrinkle-free. Look professional.

- Use vocal variety, but avoid abrupt changes. Speak as though you are telling an exciting story.

- Keep your hair out of your eyes and don't wear tinted glasses.

- Use some movement, especially with your hands. Try to keep hands in the lower portion of the video image but not out of sight if you are gesturing. Relax your shoulders. Stand, if possible. Keep your feet flat and about six inches apart. If you sit, try to sit slightly forward and straight.

- Try to keep your message as short as possible.

- Use interactivity with your audience or presentation aids, if appropriate and possible, to keep the audience focused.

Recorded Presentation Factors

Recorded presentations require equipment to make the video and a website or Internet-based platform (such as Blackboard, Pearson's MediaShare, YouTube, Google Video, or Vimeo) for distributing the video to the audience. Here are some guidelines for recording.

- Web cameras or cell phones will not produce the best recording for a formal speech. Use a moderate-quality or better digital video camera.

- Avoid focusing in on your face. If possible, keep half to three-fourths of your body in view. If you use a lectern, make sure part of it is visible.

- Make eye contact with the camera.

- Plan how to display presentation aids for the camera so they are viewable and readable in the recording.

- If your assignment requires the audience to be visible in the video, find a way to include them so you are not blocked. Children and pets should not be part of the audience.

- Limit your movement so you stay in camera view. If possible, practice first.

- Check your finished recording, both before and after uploading, to be sure it works properly.

Live Mediated Presentation Factors

Many of the issues for recorded presentations apply here as well. You are still in front of the camera; however, you now have an audience that is interacting in real time from a distance. Some factors to address:

- Take into account time zones when setting up the presentation. Parts of your audience might be in other zones.

- Keep your audience size small (no more than 10).

- Remember, there are numerous distractions for your audience and therefore you need to stay enthusiastic. Incorporate presentation aids or interaction when possible. For example, use chat or polling features.

Hybrid Presentation Factors

As noted earlier, this type of presentation combines asynchronous and synchronous engagements into one event. Therefore, all the factors discussed so far are relevant. Also keep the following in mind:

- Remember to make eye contact with the camera as well as the audience present in the room. Ignoring the camera could signal to the mediated audience that you don't care or can't be trusted.

- If you interact with the present audience, try to incorporate interaction with your mediated audience.

Practice

If there is ever a time you need to be very familiar with your speech, it is during a mediated presentation. Knowing your speech well will free you to focus on using the technology to its best potential and to deal with problems. Remember to:

- Practice the entire speech with the actual equipment, including any presentation aids or interactive features, and in the space where you will give the presentation.

- Time your speech using all the equipment and make adjustments as needed.

- Anticipate what might go wrong and prepare a multilevel backup plan.

- On the day of the event, test and practice with the equipment one last time.

- Prevent interferences. Turn off cell phones, pagers, calendar updates, Google Chat, or other notifications. Post a "Do Not Disturb" sign on the door.

> ### TIP: Creating a Mediated Speech
>
> Because mediated presentations can feel impersonal or distant, and listeners will often be distracted, be sure to involve and connect with your audience by using:
>
> - Image-rich and evocative language
> - Personal examples
> - Shared experiences of your audience

12.5 What Are the Types of Presentation Aids?

Presentation aids are two- or three-dimensional visual items, video footage, audio recordings, and/or multimedia segments that support and enhance your speech. Presentation aids can improve audience interest, comprehension, and retention. For you as the speaker, they can improve your credibility, help you with sending your message cross-culturally, convey emotions, and help you maintain an extemporaneous delivery.

Actual Items

You can use people, animals, or objects when they are the actual items you are talking about or relate to the topic of your speech and help relay your message. For example, if you are planning to give a demonstration speech on cake decorating, you might decorate cupcakes with different designs for easier transport and display.

Advantages:

- Can get your audience's attention
- Can demonstrate, illustrate, exemplify, or emphasize your topic
- Can be simple to add to your speech when you do not need to create them
- Can help the audience visualize persuasive issues
- Can add humor

Disadvantages:

- Can be scary or dangerous to your audience or inappropriate for the occasion or location of the speech (such as live spiders or snakes, guns, anything with a flame, cats if people are allergic)
- Can be too small to see or too large to bring
- Can be distracting for the audience

Models

Models are three-dimensional representations. Models are usually scaled to size—often smaller than the real thing, such as a model car, but sometimes larger, such as a model of a molecule.

Advantages:

- Are great alternatives when you cannot bring the actual items
- Can get your audience's attention
- Can demonstrate, illustrate, exemplify, or emphasize your topic
- Can be simple to add to your speech when you do not need to create them
- Can help you visually compare and contrast

Disadvantages:

- Can be hard to locate and expensive
- Can be too small for everyone to see
- Can be unpredictable if they have working parts
- Can be distracting for the audience

Practicing Ethics: Be Safe

Do not use dangerous, illegal, or prohibited presentation aids. If an aid could be harmful to you or your audience, use a model or picture instead.

Photographs

Photographs are two-dimensional representations of places, concepts, people, animals, or objects. They can be original photographs, posters of photographic images, or other types of print display.

Advantages:

- Can be as effective as an object or model
- Can condense a lot of material onto one aid
- Can create a sense of authenticity
- Can be easy to use
- Can help you compare and contrast
- Can appeal to the audience's emotions
- Can help you explain an abstract concept

Disadvantages:

- Can be hard for the audience to see
- Can be less effective than an actual item or model
- Can be overused if they are stock photographs, making them less effective than photographs created for your speech

Drawings

Drawings are maps, sketches, diagrams, plans, or other nonphotographic representations of places, concepts, people, animals, or objects. They may show a whole or part of an area or dissect the parts or workings of something.

Advantages:

- Can be very helpful when objects or models are not practical or available
- Can visually demonstrate how something works, operates, or is constructed
- Can sometimes be located ready-made
- Can show details, processes, relationships, or arrangements
- Can be used to emphasize location, geography, or topography (especially maps)

Disadvantages:

- Can be hard to locate or create
- Can be hard for the entire audience to see
- Can have too much detail
- Can lower your credibility

Charts and Tables

Charts are visual summaries of complex or large quantities of information. Two common charts are flowcharts and organizational charts. *Flowcharts* (see example below) diagram step-by-step development through a procedure, relationship, or process. *Organizational charts* illustrate the structure or chain of command in an organization. *Tables* consist of numbers or words arranged in rows, columns, or lists.

Advantages:

- Can make the complex understandable
- Can summarize a lot of information
- Can show relationships and potential cause-and-effect issues
- Can help an audience think through hypothetical situations (especially charts)
- Can help the audience understand exact numbers or information quickly

Disadvantages:

- Can be less memorable than other visuals
- Can require a lot of time to explain
- Can be confusing if too detailed
- Can be hard for the entire audience to see

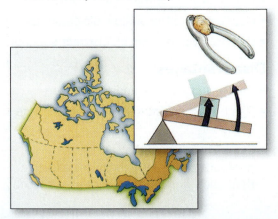

Graphs

Whereas charts and tables simply organize numbers and words, *graphs* are visual representations of numerical (statistical) information that demonstrate relationships or differences between two or more variables. There are four common types: line graphs, bar graphs, pictographs, and pie graphs.

Line Graphs

Line graphs contain numerical points plotted on a horizontal axis for one variable and on the vertical axis for another; you then connect the points to make a line. Be sure to clearly label horizontal and vertical axes so that your audience can see and understand them. See an example below.

Advantages:

- Can simplify complex statistical information
- Can be extremely easy to read if created effectively

Disadvantages:

- Can be less effective if you have more than three lines to plot
- Can require a projector

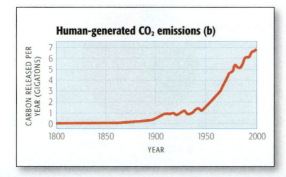

Bar Graphs

Bar graphs (also known as bar charts) are visuals consisting of vertical or horizontal bars that represent sets of data. Make sure your horizontal and vertical axes are clearly labeled.

Advantages:

- Can be easy for your audience to interpret if created effectively
- Can demonstrate change over time at a glance

Disadvantages:

- Can be less effective in black and white
- Can require a projector

TIP: Showing Time

When creating a line or bar graph for which time is a variable, always put time on the horizontal axis.

Pictographs

Pictographs (also known as pictograms) are bar graphs that use pictures instead of bars. Make sure to label the graph and assign a unit measure to the individual pictorial icons.

Advantages:

- Can make statistical information more interesting
- Can be easy for your audience to interpret if created effectively

Disadvantages:

- Can take time to locate appropriate pictures or icons to represent your data
- Can be unfamiliar to your audience
- Can be less effective in black and white
- Can require a projector

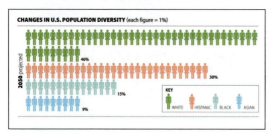

CHANGES IN U.S. POPULATION DIVERSITY (each figure = 1%)

Pie Graphs

Pie graphs (also known as circle graphs or pie charts) are circular graphs with sections representing a percentage of a given quantity. Use a pie graph when comparing segments of a whole. It is best to limit your segments to seven or fewer; you can combine the smallest ones if you have more than seven. Always make sure your pie adds up to exactly 100 percent. Labels should be brief and outside the segments if needed.

Advantages:

- Can help your audience quickly visualize the divisions of the whole item you are discussing
- Can effectively graph up to seven variables at once

Disadvantages:

- Can be difficult to clearly and visibly label the segments
- Should be in color

TIP: Finding Icons

These sites offer icons and graphics that might be helpful when creating a pictograph:

www.coolarchive.com

www.freegraphics.com

www.iconbazaar.com

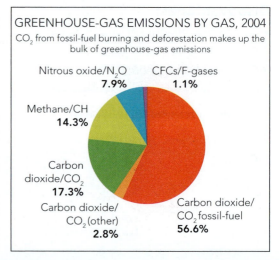

GREENHOUSE-GAS EMISSIONS BY GAS, 2004
CO_2 from fossil-fuel burning and deforestation makes up the bulk of greenhouse-gas emissions

Nitrous oxide/N_2O 7.9%
CFCs/F-gases 1.1%
Methane/CH 14.3%
Carbon dioxide/CO_2 17.3%
Carbon dioxide/CO_2 (other) 2.8%
Carbon dioxide/CO_2 fossil-fuel 56.6%

Media
Video and Audio

Audio and video clips can be effective presentation aids. **Video clips** are any footage you use from television, movies, or any other type of video. **Audio clips** are recordings of sound only.

Advantages:

- Can grab attention and make a speech memorable by appealing to your audience through sight, sound, and movement
- Can illustrate a point
- Can be linked to PowerPoint slides or a Prezi presentation
- Can increase your ethos when used properly

Disadvantages:

- Can require special production skills
- Can require special equipment
- Can require a lot of practice with the equipment to smoothly incorporate the video and audio into the speech
- Should only be used for short durations so that they do not become the speech or compete with the speaker
- Can increase the potential for errors, ineffective use, and equipment failure

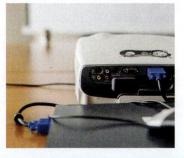

Multimedia

Multimedia refers to the combination of multiple presentation aids (still images, graphs, text, sound, and video) into one choreographed production. The most common multimedia aids incorporate computer-generated slides/presentations such as either PowerPoint or Prezi.

Advantages:

- Can be very creative and appeals to almost all senses
- Can be very professional
- Can increase your ethos

Disadvantages:

- Can be too flashy and distracting
- Can be costly and time-consuming
- Requires special equipment
- Can require special production skills
- Can be difficult to coordinate
- Should only be used for short durations so that the aids do not become the speech or compete with the speaker
- Can increase the potential for errors, ineffective use, and equipment failure

See the Improve Your Communication section at the end of this chapter for tips on using PowerPoint or Prezi.

12.6 How Can You Use a Presentation Aid Successfully?

To determine which presentation aids to use, establish a purpose for each aid; select the best types for you, your audience, and your topic; and explore options for displaying and producing the aids. For example, if you will be speaking to a large audience, a handwritten list of numbers on a flip chart will not do much to support your speech, whereas professionally created graphs presented in PowerPoint or Prezi can be helpful.

Determine What to Use

Establish the Purpose of the Aid

You should never use a presentation aid just because you can or to be glitzy. The important parts of any speech are you and the speech message. Your presentation aids should assist, support, and facilitate your message—not detract from or outshine it. So you first need to establish the purpose of each aid. You can do this by returning to your preparation outline and identifying where in the outline you need to use an aid to:

- Grab attention or maintain interest
- Promote understanding and clarity
- Appeal to your audience's emotions
- Help the audience remember key issues
- Aid in intercultural communication

TIP: Using Visuals Cross-Culturally

- Limit the number of words and, if possible, use the audience's language.
- Avoid words that might not translate well (technical words, jargon, slang, etc.).
- Avoid images that could be confusing or offensive.
- Be aware of cultural views of colors. For example, the color red symbolizes good luck in China, but in South Africa it is the color of mourning.

Select the Best Type of Aid

You should select the type of presentation aids to use by considering yourself, your topic, your audience, and the situation.

- When considering yourself as a factor, ask yourself questions such as these: What equipment am I comfortable with? What software do I need for the aids? Am I familiar enough with that software to be effective? Which aids would I feel comfortable using? Which types will raise my credibility? Which presentation aids do I have time to create and practice with?

- When considering your topic, start with your speech goal: Is it informative or persuasive? If informative, how can your aids help the audience visualize your message, challenge what the audience already knows, or simplify information? If persuasive, look at how your aids can support an idea, evoke emotions, demonstrate fulfilling a need, call the audience to action, or show audience relevance. How can each aid move through the speech to reach the conclusion?

- When considering your audience, ask yourself: What do they need to know about the topic, and which aids would be supportive? Will the information in the speech be difficult for the audience to understand? If so, which aids will best assist their understanding? Are there reasons why all or part of the audience would not be able to access a presentation aid? For example, are there factors that might prevent someone

from reading or seeing visuals or hearing video/audio clips?

- Where, why, and when you are speaking could significantly influence which type of presentation aids you use. For example, many visual aids will not work outside. Likewise, many special occasion speeches are given at events where certain presentation aids would seem strange. A PowerPoint presentation might seem inappropriate during a eulogy or a wedding toast. However, displaying an object or pictures that relate to the person being eulogized or raising your glass to signal the wedding toast would be acceptable.

Decide How to Display the Aid

Finally, you must choose how the aids will be presented for the audience. Various methods are available to most speakers. Your decision will be determined by what you are comfortable with, the size of the audience, the availability of equipment, what will work in the speech environment, cost, and effectiveness. Some common methods for displaying aids are chalkboards, whiteboards, posters, handouts, flip charts, and technology or media devices used with presentation software like PowerPoint or Prezi.

Craft an Effective Aid

In *Slide:ology: The Art and Science of Creating Great Presentations*, Nancy Duarte writes, "To succeed as a presenter, you must think like a designer."[4] Communication educators might add that you must think like an audience-centered communicator. Every decision you make about a presentation aid's design should aim to relay your message better and help the audience understand that message. To meet this goal, give yourself enough time to be creative and follow good design principles.

The time needed to be creative is difficult to predict. Duarte offers a time frame for creating an hour-long presentation with 30 slides.[5] If you adapt her recommendations to an eight-minute speech with four to six slides, your creation time might be similar to the following timeline:

- **1 to 2 hours** for researching and collecting ideas/information
- **1 hour** to evaluate audience needs and to outline your ideas
- **2+ hours** to create the presentation aids
- **30 minutes to 1 hour** to rehearse with aids

4.5 to 6+ hours total

This is merely an estimate. You are the only one who can predict how long it will take. If you don't know how to use the software or spend a lot of time on details, you will need more time.

Page 362 offers some advice on using presentation software.

Design principles relate to the arrangement and placement of various elements (color, text, line, images, space, etc.) for optimum effect. When you create two-dimensional presentation aids, plan out the arrangement and placement of visual elements on the page, poster, slide, or canvas. Likewise, when you think about the relationship of all of your aids within a given speech, you need to consider their overall arrangement and placement, to allow the aids to nourish your verbal message. See the table on the next page for five design principles to follow.

Practicing Ethics: Presentation Aid Sources

Remember to cite the sources for presentation aids that you did not create or the sources of information you put into an aid. For example, "This YouTube video, downloaded July 10, shows . . . " It is often wise to put a written reference to a source on a visual you didn't create or collect the content for. This will help you remember an oral citation as well. Place it at the bottom in a font large enough to read and include necessary citation information. Follow your instructor's suggestions for the exact style and placement.

Five Design Principles to Guide You

Unity	The principle of unity recognizes the need for the elements you use to relate to each other. If you use multiple aids, they should fit together as a unified whole to support your speech. Make sure your colors work well together (are complementary) and fit the tone of your speech. Images should relate to the text shown with them and your verbal message.
Pattern	The pattern principle recommends that you create a design format and use it consistently. Reusing patterns will help your audience quickly digest the material because the layout is familiar and not distracting. Keep your pattern simple and use consistent backgrounds, fonts, and symbols. Try to feature similar content for each main point.
Balance	Balance deals with equilibrium—a feeling of stability, symmetry, and calm. Balance in your aids will enhance your audience's feeling that your speech is balanced and organized. Choose easy-to-read fonts and font sizes—44 point for titles and 24 to 32 point for other text. Balance the elements with each other and with blank space.
Emphasis	Use aids that stress the important aspects of your verbal message. Use titles to emphasize and foreshadow your speech content. Bullets, color, images, text size, text structures (underline, bold, or italic), and music are ways to draw the eye or ear to what is important. Don't overuse them, however.
Rhythm	Rhythm has to do with a real or imagined sense of movement. The pacing of your presentation, animation/movement, and sound can create rhythm. Be careful that they do not distract from or compete with your speech message.

TIP: Use an Idea Bank

Use the same idea-bank process you used to narrow your speech topic to focus in on your presentation aid. At the beginning of the process, allow all options and open your mind to wild ideas. One of your wild ideas just might become the best idea. That's the beauty of the creative process.

Chapter 12 Review

Key Questions

12.1 How Can You Use Language Effectively in a Speech?

Objective 12.1: **EXPLAIN THE WAYS TO MAKE EFFECTIVE LANGUAGE CHOICES IN A SPEECH**

- Be correct. Make sure you are using the correct words, pronouncing words correctly, and using correct grammar.

- Be specific. Use active voice in your speech whenever possible. Use passive voice only to emphasize the receiver of an action when that is more important. Avoid acronyms, abbreviations, and other ambiguous language choices (many of which you learned about in Chapter 3).

- Be conversational. Compared to written style, conversational (or oral) style is less formal, more animated, simpler in sentence structure and language, tailored more toward the personal, and more repetitive.

- Be distinctive. Carefully select and craft your language for maximum effect.

See pages 334–339.

12.2 What Are the Methods of Delivery?

Objective 12.2: **IDENTIFY FOUR METHODS OF DELIVERY**

You may deliver a speech extemporaneously, from a manuscript, as a memorized text, or impromptu. Extemporaneous speaking is the most acceptable contemporary method of delivery. Here, you plan out, rehearse, and deliver the speech from an outline consisting of key words, phrases, and delivery notes.

See pages 340–341.

12.3 How Do You Prepare for an Extemporaneous Speech?

Objective 12.3: **DISCUSS THE PROCEDURE FOR PREPARING FOR AN EXTEMPORANEOUS SPEECH**

Rehearsing is an individual process that will be specific to you. Once you have prepared the speech preparation outline, you will:

- Read aloud from the preparation outline.
- Consider your support materials.
- Prepare your delivery outline.
- Prepare your presentation aids.
- Practice multiple times.
- Do a final "dress rehearsal."
- Prepare for questions.
- Prepare for the day of the speech.

See pages 342–345.

12.4 How Do You Prepare for a Mediated Presentation?

To prepare for a mediated presentation, you should establish the type of presentation, address unique factors, and practice.

- Establish the type of presentation. Types include recorded, live, and hybrid presentations. The mediating tools used for these types support asynchronous, synchronous, and hybrid engagements.

- Address unique factors of mediated presentations by familiarizing yourself with equipment, considering the presentation environment and audience, addressing vocal and nonverbal issues, keeping the message short, and using interactivity with your audience. If the presentation is recorded, consider the best equipment to use, avoid focusing only on your face, make eye contact with the camera, display presentation aids effectively, limit your movement, and check the final recording. With live mediated and hybrid presentations, consider all of these plus such issues as factoring in time zones, keeping audiences small, and interacting with the mediated audience as well as the audience present in the room with you.

- Practice and time yourself; use your equipment, outline, and aids.

See pages 346–349.

12.5 What Are the Types of Presentation Aids?

- Actual items, such as people, animals, or objects
- Models
- Photographs displayed on a document camera, posters of photographic images, or other types of print display
- Drawings, including maps, sketches, diagrams, plans, or other nonphotographic representations
- Charts and tables; two common types of charts are flowcharts and organizational charts
- Graphs, including line graphs, bar graphs, pictographs, and pie graphs
- Media, including video, audio, and multimedia

See pages 350–355.

12.6 How Can You Use a Presentation Aid Successfully?

- Determine what to use by establishing the aid's purpose, selecting the best type, and choosing the best way to display it.

- Craft an effective aid. Allow yourself enough time to be creative and to produce the aid. Adhere to design principles.

See pages 356–359.

Key Terms

Improve Your Communication

Software packages can help you create professional presentation aids incorporating text, images, charts, graphs, sound, and/or video. Two of the most common are PowerPoint and Prezi. No matter which software you use, be sure to:

- Have a backup plan in case the system fails.
- Rehearse using the finished presentation (in the speech event space if possible).
- Check the equipment the day of the speech.

Tips for presenting PowerPoint slides:

- Check the order of your slides against your delivery outline.
- Know how to display the slides in slide-show view.
- Learn slide-show commands. For example, when in slide-show mode, press the B key for blackout and the W key to return to the visual.
- Make sure you have saved all of the slides, sound clips, and video for transportation to the event.

Tips for presenting a Prezi presentation:

- Check that your path through the prezi relates to your speech outline.
- Know how to run the prezi. For example, pressing ESC exits full-screen mode; you can zoom in and out with a mouse wheel or the + or – tools on the right sidebar in presentation mode. The home icon takes you back to your global canvas. You can show the prezi in full screen by clicking on the button in the bottom right corner.
- Don't rush through the presentation.

Practicing Ethics: Presentation Aids and Copyright

You must observe copyright laws. Students and educators may use original work by another person for a class presentation, but they must follow these rules:

- You may use a very small amount (under a minute) of copyrighted film, video, or animation without permission.
- You may use less than 30 seconds of music or lyrics from one musical piece without permission.
- You can use an entire photograph or illustration, but only a small portion of images from a collection (less than 10 percent of the collection).
- You cannot post the presentation material back to the web without permission.
- You must display and mention the source, author/creator, title, and date of the material.
- You must display the copyright symbol (©) when necessary.
- Cite all sources of the material in your presentation aids and on your source page. These rules apply to materials legally downloaded from the Internet or obtained by other legal means. Illegally downloaded materials are never fair use. (See http://copyright.lib.utexas.edu for more information.)

Apply Your Knowledge

1. What are some ways you can make your language distinctive? Explain.

2. What are the differences between each of the four methods of delivery? Can you think of situations where you might use each of the four?

3. What are some ineffective ways to use presentation aids?

Other Resources

Presentation Software Help and Tutorials

- office.microsoft.com/en-us/powerpoint/
- prezi.zendesk.com/forums
- www.activehistory.co.uk/Miscellaneous/free_stuff/worksheets/Prezi.pdf

Creating Presentation Aid Content

Duarte, Nancy. *Slide:ology: The Art and Science of Creating Great Presentations*. Sebastopol: O'Reilly, 2008. Print.

Karia, Akash. *How to Design TED-Worthy Presentation Slides*. Akash Karia/CreateSpace, 2015. Print.

Chapter 13
Informative Speaking

13.1 What Is Informative Speaking?

You learned in Chapter 10 that all speeches have only one unrestricted aim (the general purpose): to inform, to persuade, or to accentuate a special occasion. At its essence, speaking to inform is the act of *giving*. The gift you give can range from a topic that seems indefinable, like the origin of life, to a practical topic like changing a tire. *Informative speaking* gives your audience completely new knowledge, skills, or understanding about your topic or increases their current knowledge, skills, or understanding.

Whether you are the CEO of a large corporation, a local automotive salesperson, or a parent involved in the community's educational system, informative speaking is the bread and butter of our daily communication. We are constantly asked to describe, explain, demonstrate, or report on almost every aspect of our lives. Informally, what you learn about public speaking can even help you teach a child how to tie her or his shoestrings, describe the ecosystem in your new car to a friend, and explain Taoism to a relative. The following Practicing Ethics box highlights the ethical benchmarks for an informative speech.

Practicing Ethics: Informative Speaking

The main benchmarks of great informative speaking are accuracy, unity, and inclusiveness. Ethically, these benchmarks translate into being:

- Truthful and reliable when selecting support materials
- Complete in your coverage of the topic, not simply relying on personal knowledge
- Organized enough to demonstrate how things "fit together" in the speech
- Evenhanded and unbiased when offering information
- Responsible in selecting an appropriate topic for you, your audience, and the situation

You can categorize most informative speeches as speeches to describe, explain, or instruct. Normally, the topic—or what your audience needs to know about the topic—determines the type.

- A **speech to describe** describes an object, a person, an animal, a place, or an event.
- A **speech to instruct** teaches or demonstrates a process.
- A **speech to explain** clarifies a concept or issue.
- In some speaking situations, you might be required to give an informative **speech to report**, which is an oral report or briefing. You will most often give this type of speech when you are part of a group or organization, including the workplace, and need to report on the progress of something.

The following table lists each type of informative speech, its corresponding topic labels, and examples of speech topics.

Type of Informative Speech	Topic Label	Sample Speech Topics
To describe	Object	To describe the features of a GoPro
		To describe the significance of the U.S. flag
	Person	To describe the events of Rosa Parks's life
		To describe the highlights of Aretha Franklin's music
	Animal	To describe the life cycle of the butterfly
	Place	To describe the Great Barrier Reef
		To describe the historical development of Gettysburg, Pennsylvania
	Event	To describe what happens at the Indianapolis 500 time trials
		To describe the significance of Veterans Day
To instruct	Process	To instruct about (demonstrate) creative ways to wrap a gift
To explain	Concept	To explain the basic principles of Islam
	Issue	To explain current issues related to illegal immigration
To report	Oral report or briefing	To report recent findings related to student parking needs on campus

13.2 What Is the Creative Process for Informative Speaking?

The previous chapters (especially Chapters 5, 10, 11, and 12) have prepared you for the basic speech process. This chapter will take you step by step through the process as it relates to informative speaking.

The first column of the table to the right briefly reviews the four basic activities of the creative process you learned in Chapter 10. Remember, the process is dynamic. Allow yourself to move creatively back and forth between each activity as you fashion an effective informative speech.

The last column of the table follows the example of how Liam, a college student in the Midwest, created his informative speech about trout. Spring break is around the corner, and Liam lives in northwestern Arkansas, where many of the rivers offer some of the nation's best trout-fishing opportunities. Although Liam's college is close to Arkansas, it is not in an area with many trout rivers. He surveyed his audience about their knowledge of fishing in general and discovered that most have some fishing knowledge and are very open to a fishing trip. Few of his classmates, however, knew there were different types of trout or how to fish for trout.

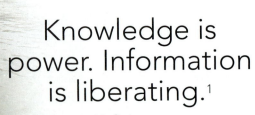

Knowledge is power. Information is liberating.[1]

Kofi Annan

The Creative Process		Informative Example
1 Developing	**13.3 How Do You Develop and Research an Informative Topic?** ▎**See page 370**	Liam created an idea bank, surveyed his audience, and created this central idea: **Many midwestern states offer an exciting opportunity to catch varieties of trout that differ in appearance, habitat, and population.** Liam searched fishing websites, found books on trout at the county library, and interviewed a local conservation officer.
2 Creating	**13.4 How Do You Outline and Organize an Informative Speech?** ▎**See page 376**	Liam constructed his main points around the four types of trout (a topical strategy). He ordered the main points by largest population to smallest, to mirror the Midwest population trends. I. **Rainbow trout are found in most states.** II. **Brown trout are found coast to coast, except for a few southern states.** III. **Cutthroat trout were originally native to only western North America.** IV. **Brook trout are native to the eastern United States and Canada.** In his introduction and conclusion, Liam used personal narrative to paint a picture of what it is like to trout fish.
3 Presenting	**13.5 How Do You Present or Evaluate an Informative Speech?** ▎**See page 388**	Liam created his delivery outline on note cards, using only enough key words to jog his memory. He also included delivery and presentation aid notes. Liam practiced several times before his speech date.
4 Listening & Evaluating		Liam's classmates and instructor offered constructive advice about his speech. He noted, for instance, that he should work on gesturing more for his next speech.

13.3 How Do You Develop and Research an Informative Topic?

As you prepare an informative speech, your analysis of the audience and situation should help you to determine:

- Your topic choice and the type of informative speech most appropriate for this audience
- What information you need to give this audience during this situation
- How to make your speech relevant to this audience
- How to select effective and interesting support material for this audience

Get to Know the Audience and Situation

If your topic is not appropriate to your audience and situation, you face an uphill struggle to engage your audience. Take time to learn about your audience and situation. Doing so will also help you determine what type of informative speech (to describe, explain, instruct, or report) to create. For example, if you are preparing to give an informational session on the iPhone 6 to a group of college students, and you know that most of them own a previous or similar model, your speech can focus on what makes this model unique. This audience will likely respond favorably to how the new phone will maintain their social and self-esteem needs. In contrast, an audience at a retirement center will more likely have a predisposed attitude toward a simpler model and how it might keep them safe.

Self-Check: The Informative Audience and Situation

❑ How will the attitudes, beliefs, values, and traits of my audience affect my choices?

❑ What do listeners know about my potential topics? What do they want or need to know?

❑ Why is the audience here, and what else do I know about the situation?

Create an Informative Idea Bank

Using the idea bank method from Chapter 10, make a list of potential topics that lean toward a specific purpose to inform—any topic you can explain, describe, or demonstrate. Your assignment may not allow you to do all three, but you can delete topics later if they do not work. Below is one example of an informative idea bank. Remember to accept anything as a potential topic at this point. Look around and let your mind free-associate. If you have trouble getting started, read through magazines or local papers, browse the Internet for ideas, or just look around your room or house. For example, what's the history of the Coke bottle shape? How was bubble gum invented? How can you make a pie out of the breakfast drink Tang?

Select and Narrow Your Informative Topic

You can now focus in on the broad topic that best fits you, your audience, and the situation. Use the process from Chapter 10 to narrow your idea bank. For an informative speech, especially explore these questions:

- Which topics might give completely new knowledge to your audience?
- Which topics would listeners like to know more about?

Suppose you created the idea bank below for class and are narrowing your selections. You focus on national parks, as many people like to travel, but "parks" is too broad. You've already begun narrowing the topic with free associations of Boundary Waters, Ansel Adams, and Yosemite. As your college is near the Boundary Waters and Ansel Adams is only peripherally related to parks, you choose Yosemite. This topic is still broad, but you can narrow it further later. For now, do some preliminary research to see if you can find quality information on the topic. If researching it seems difficult, you may want to revisit your idea bank for another topic or change the angle of this one.

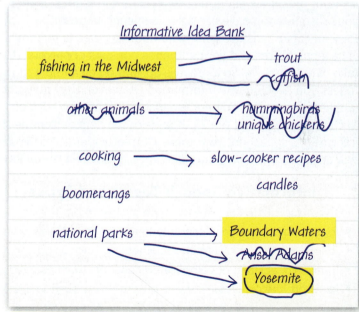

Identify Your Specific Purpose

A good specific purpose begins to shape your speech topic into a more manageable size. The specific purpose is a single statement merging together your general purpose, your audience, and your objective for the speech. For your Yosemite topic, you know your general purpose is to inform. Merging your general purpose with your audience and objective, your specific purpose would look like this:

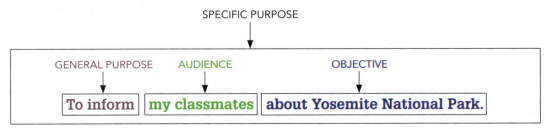

This specific purpose will help you keep your general purpose (to inform) and your audience (college students) connected to the objective of your speech (telling about Yosemite National Park).

Confirm the Best Type of Informative Speech

Earlier in this chapter, you learned that there are different types of informative speeches. Sometimes, simply labeling your topic as an object, person, animal, place, event, concept, issue, or process is enough to determine the type of speech you will create. For example, your Yosemite topic clearly fits as a speech to describe. If you do not yet have an angle for your topic, consider what your audience needs to know. For example, if your topic is baseball gloves and your audience consists of players, they probably know how to take care of a glove. So a process speech on cleaning a glove might not interest them unless you have unique information. However, they may not know how a glove is made (a different process topic) or the history of the glove (an object topic). Use the table in Objective 13.1 and the Tip box below to help determine the appropriate type of informative speech for your topic. Correctly identifying your type of informative speech will help you settle on a suitable organizational strategy later.

Identify Your Central Idea

Now you are ready to formulate your central idea (also called a thesis statement), or the concise one-sentence summary or preview of exactly what you want to say in your informative speech. This is the course you will take to achieve the objective of your specific purpose. Below are two possible examples of how the specific purpose of your Yosemite speech can become a central idea. The objective of the specific purpose is shown in blue type.

If Your Specific Purpose Is...
To inform my classmates about Yosemite National Park.

Your Central Idea Could Be...
Yosemite National Park is more than a park; it is an experience that can change people.

or

Yosemite National Park is more than a park; it is an experience that can change people through its adventures, its waterfalls, and the great Half Dome.

Either could be acceptable. Some speech instructors like the simpler form of the first, and others like the central idea to reflect your main points, as the second example does. Follow your instructor's guidelines. For some speeches, it might be difficult to establish the exact main ideas prior to doing research. You can always refine that part of the central idea as you begin to create your preparation outline. Use the Self-Check box to evaluate your central idea at every stage.

Self-Check: Evaluating an Informative Central Idea

❑ Does my central idea describe, instruct, explain, or report?

❑ Is my central idea written as a complete statement?

❑ Does the statement use clear and concise language?

❑ Does my central idea focus on one speech topic?

❑ Will this informative central idea offer my audience new information and be worth their time?

Create a Working Outline

At this stage, you should take a few minutes to map out a working outline to guide your research. As you collect support materials for your speech, add what you find to this working outline. This will help you see where you need more information or when you need to change something. Remember that your working main points might be questions you think need to be answered or simply phrases that relate to subtopics. As with your central idea, your main points will continue to evolve and become more defined as you create your speech. Identify what information your audience needs and explore how to incorporate that into three to five working points. Some things to remember:

- Try to limit your points as much as possible. You don't want to overload your audience's ability to understand and remember.

- Try to make your working points unique, such as new or novel information. This will help you gain and keep your audience's attention.

- Be flexible. The working points may change significantly as you discover new and innovative material better suited to teaching your audience about your topic. Although your working main points can be questions, in the preparation outline stage of creating your speech, you should always write your final main points as concise and complete declarative sentences.

TOPIC: Yosemite National Park

GENERAL PURPOSE: To inform

SPECIFIC PURPOSE: To inform my classmates about Yosemite National Park.

CENTRAL IDEA: Yosemite National Park is more than a park; it is an experience that can change people through its adventures, its waterfalls, and the great Half Dome.

I. What adventures are available at Yosemite?

II. What is important to know about the waterfalls?

III. What is important to know about Half Dome?

Remember, you may use questions for the main points in your working outline, but you should use declarative sentences in your preparation outline.

Conduct Your Research

The key to any good speech is a variety of acceptable support materials. Keep your eyes open for different possibilities, and do not rely on only one research tool (for example, only the Internet). Keep in mind your audience and its relationship with your topic to help you select appropriate materials. Most informative speeches will rely heavily on facts, definitions, testimony, and examples. Although you might use statistics, they should be used only to explain or describe, not to persuade.

When you are researching an informative speech, you want to find materials that will make your audience want to listen and learn. The best ways to do that are:

- Select materials that have a language level appropriate for your audience.
- Find materials that will interest your audience because they are relevant, unique, current, and easy to understand.
- If the topic is complex, make sure you use materials from multiple perspectives and means. Everyone learns differently.

Websites, books, newspapers, magazines, newsletters, journals, government resources, reference works, and firsthand personal knowledge are all effective sources of support materials for an informative speech. The Internet, libraries, interviews, and even surveys can offer a wealth of information. Government pamphlets and websites are often a good resource for speech topics that demonstrate or instruct.

If your topic directly relates to a local business, the staff there might be able to supply materials. For example, even if you do not live in the area of Yosemite National Park, most cities have travel agencies that will have information on Yosemite. If a national park is located near you, someone there might be able to help you locate information. You could also search newspapers near Yosemite or contact the park directly via phone or e-mail. Be creative when pinpointing possible locations for quality support materials.

See Chapter 11 for help with research.

TIP: Evaluating Your Support Material

To test your support materials, make sure they are:

- Accurate
- Complete
- Current
- Trustworthy
- Suitable

See Chapter 11 for specifics on evaluating support material.

13.4 How Do You Outline and Organize an Informative Speech?

Now that you have a focused topic, you need to organize your thoughts. For an informative speech, sound organization is critical if you want your audience to learn and remember. Outlining is the only way to tighten up your organization.

Start with Basic, Effective Outlining

Chapter 11 taught you the basics for how to outline a speech. Creating an informative speech outline requires an appropriate organizational strategy that unites the information you are presenting in a way that will help your audience understand and remember the content. Most speech instructors will ask you to complete a preparation outline at this point in the process. Remember, this outline is highly structured and at the minimum it should:

- Include necessary header information
- Contain an introduction, the body of the speech, and a conclusion
- Use complete sentences
- Cover only one issue at a time
- Use balanced main points
- Employ subordination
- Plan out formal links
- Use proper citations within the outline and include a source page (use the citation style that your instructor requires)

Use the format sample shown on the next page to create your informative preparation outline, or use the one suggested by your instructor.

Student name   Class
Date   Instructor name

Topic: Yosemite National Park
Specific purpose: To inform my classmates about Yosemite National
                          Park.
Central idea: Yosemite National Park is more than a park; it is
                          an experience that can change people through its
                          adventures, its waterfalls, and the great Half Dome.   ←

This example shows
how you would begin
to use the template to
create your Yosemite
speech.

INTRODUCTION
    Attention-getter
    Credibility material
    Relevance to audience
    Preview of speech

Begin filling in main
points as you have
them written. Use
only one sentence
per outline symbol,
whether it is a main
point or a subpoint.
You must have two or
more subpoints.

(Link from introduction to first main point)

BODY
    I. Yosemite's adventures are for all ages and cultures with
        varied interests.   ←
        A. Subpoint
        B. Subpoint
            1. Subpoint of B
            2. Subpoint of B
            3. Subpoint of B

(Link between first and second main points)

    II. Second main point
         A. Subpoint
         B. Subpoint
             1. Subpoint of B
             2. Subpoint of B
         C. Subpoint

Be sure to formally
write out your links.
In an informative
speech, the links help
your audience group
information for better
understanding and
retention.

(Link: If you continue your hike past the Vernal and Nevada Falls,
        you will reach what is possibly the most photographed place
        in the park—Half Dome.)   ←

    III. Third main point

          A. Subpoint
              1. Subpoint of A
                  a. Subpoint of 1
                  b. Subpoint of 1
              2. Subpoint of A
          B. Subpoint
          C. Subpoint

The introduction
and conclusion are
extremely important
to the effectiveness of
your speech. Spend
time on them. A
section later in this
chapter will help you.

(Link to conclusion)
CONCLUSION ←
    Summary statement
    Audience response statement
    WOW statement

                    Works Cited (or References)

Commit to a Strategy

Informative speeches can utilize a chronological, topical, spatial, comparative, problem–solution, or causal strategy. Knowing which types of informative speech these strategies fit with most comfortably should help you recognize which strategy you want. The best way to stay committed to a strategy is to choose one as you begin to construct your main points around what your audience needs to know. You may not finalize main points before selecting the strategy; and some strategies will not work for certain speech goals because you cannot create or support the main points necessary to use that strategy.

Strategy	What Types of Informative Speech Does It Fit?	When Might You Use It?	Sample Speech Topics
Chronological	To describe To instruct	When giving a speech related to time or history, or when you need to teach a sequence or process	• To describe the history of Savannah, Georgia • To instruct on the proper way to wax skis • To demonstrate how to make jerky
Topical	To describe To explain	With any informative speech that has natural, inherent subtopics	• To describe different types of butterflies in the West • To explain basic color theory
Spatial	To describe	To describe a place, event, or object based on its relationship to space	• To describe a film festival based on the different venues around town • To describe the human tooth from the inside out
Comparative	To describe To explain	To compare a complex topic to something your audience knows better	• To explain Islam by comparing it to Christianity
Problem–solution	To explain To report	When a solution has been implemented and you need to explain why	• To explain next year's tuition increase
Causal	To describe To explain	To describe or explain something based on how it is caused (or the reverse)	• To explain how secondhand smoke causes asthma

Construct Main Points

If you return to your working outline, you can see the basis of your main points in the questions you wrote. However, final main points cannot be questions, so these need some work.

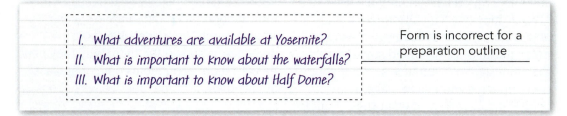

I. What adventures are available at Yosemite?

II. What is important to know about the waterfalls?

III. What is important to know about Half Dome?

Form is incorrect for a preparation outline

Main points need to be complete declarative sentences, written in a parallel structure, and balanced with each other. The working main points above could be rewritten as:

I. Yosemite's adventures are for all ages and cultures with varied interests.
II. Yosemite has several magnificent waterfalls, many of which are America's tallest.
III. Yosemite's most famous icon is Half Dome.

Organize Support Materials

Proper outlining requires you to demonstrate how your subpoints containing the support materials are subordinate to your main points and to any subpoints that precede them. For example, if you have your first main point of the Yosemite speech and have located appropriate support materials, you will be able to add the next level of the outline.

I. Yosemite's adventures are for all ages and cultures with varied interests.
   A. You can take it easy watching for wildlife like the black bear, bobcat, white-headed woodpecker, or mountain goat.
   B. Physical activities you could engage in include hiking, rock climbing, swimming, horseback riding, camping, and white-water rafting.
   C. Nightlife activities include stargazing at a vast, open sky or even having a cocktail at the Iron Door Saloon.

As you add the next level of support material detail, your outline will start to fill out even more.

How you organize the material under each point or subpoint depends on the strategy you are using. For example, the Yosemite speech can use a topical strategy at all levels of the outline, so it is really up to you to decide which point comes first.

Compose Your Introduction and Conclusion

Like a good movie, a speech should grab the audience's attention at the beginning and end by gradually leading up to a "WOW" moment. The introduction and conclusion of your speech can make or break its success. So spend some quality time crafting both, and use some of your best support materials to make them sing. Here's a review of what they should include.

Launch Your Speech

Don't forget the importance of *launching* into your speech. Your introduction should be one of the most exciting, moving, and interesting moments of your speech. An introduction for an informative speech should "pitch" your speech to your audience. It should tell them why they need to learn more about your topic or at least amuse them in some creative way about the topic.

End Your Speech

The conclusion of a speech is almost the reverse of the introduction, minus the need to demonstrate your credibility (your speech should do that). The informative speech conclusion should leave your audience hungry for more knowledge about your topic. Your ultimate goal is to inspire them so much that they go out on their own to find more information about the topic.

See the Tip box for guidance on how long your introduction and conclusion should be in relationship to the rest of your speech.

| **See Chapter 11** for more on introductions and conclusions.

> **TIP: Length**
> • Your introduction should be less than 15 percent of your total speech time.
> • Your conclusion should be less than 5 percent of your total speech time.

INTRODUCTION

This should be an exciting moment in your speech.

ATTENTION-GETTER: Several years ago, when I was about to embark on a serious life change and move half a world away from where I had lived since 18, I went to a place, a location, a mystical spot that had a healing and peaceful effect on me. I had to say "good-bye and thank you." Michele, my friend, and I had made it to the top of Half Dome in Yosemite National Park, and I felt like I was on top of the world! I was near heaven—almost close enough to reach out and touch it. I knew I would never forget this moment as a strange but oddly familiar feeling came over me. I had never felt so independent and free, nor had as much confidence in myself. I knew from then on that if I put my mind to it and had faith in myself, I could achieve anything.

State why you should give this speech.

CREDIBILITY MATERIAL: When I moved to Atwater, California, my grandmother told me that I must visit Yosemite. "It is awesome," she said. My teenage mind thought, "Yeah, right! As if nature could be all that exciting." In the end, I became a regular customer of this adventure, peacefulness, and beauty, making the 45-minute drive to Yosemite often.

Give them a reason to listen.

RELEVANCE TO AUDIENCE: Yosemite has a similar effect on almost all visitors. Conservationist and Sierra Club founder John Muir stated it well in *Our National Parks* when he said, "Climb the mountains and get their good tidings. Nature's peace will flow into you as sunshine flows into trees. The winds will blow their own freshness into you, and the storms their energy, while cares will drop off like autumn leaves."

Give them a road map to your speech.

PREVIEW OF SPEECH: Although my words and pictures could not do Yosemite justice, I hope to give you an idea of how wonderful it is by taking a glimpse at some general adventures the park has to offer, its waterfalls, and the awe-inspiring Half Dome.

CONCLUSION

What should your audience remember?

SUMMARY STATEMENT: Sadly, my speech has only given you a small piece of Yosemite, and it is ever changing with the seasons. In the winter, it is a vast wonderland of white beauty that is just indescribable. In the fall, the colors explode all around you. It is no wonder that John Muir spent so many years there and worked so hard to protect and defend it. And it is no wonder that Ansel Adams, the world-famous photographer, spent many years there photographing landscapes.

What do you want them to do with that information?

AUDIENCE RESPONSE STATEMENT: If you think national parks are only for family vacations and retirement visits, then you are seriously mistaken and will miss out on so much that you could experience and benefit from. Yosemite is a place to visit when you are young and healthy and can do all the physical adventures it has to offer.

Dazzle them one more time.

WOW STATEMENT: Yosemite healed my soul. It taught me what is important in life and that we can miss so much beauty. Until I did the research for this speech, I didn't realize that I was feeling the same motivations as John Muir and Ansel Adams a century before me. Don't you want to experience the same?

Preparation Outline for an Informative Speech

Your name   Class

Date   Instructor's name

Topic: Yosemite National Park

Specific purpose: To inform my classmates about Yosemite National Park.

Central idea: Yosemite National Park is more than a park; it is an experience that can change people through its adventures, its waterfalls, and the great Half Dome.

INTRODUCTION

Attention-getter: Several years ago, when I was about to embark on a serious life change and move half a world away from where I had lived since 18, I went to a place, a location, a mystical spot that had a healing and peaceful effect on me. I had to say "good-bye and thank you." Michele, my friend, and I had made it to the top of Half Dome in Yosemite National Park, and I felt like I was on top of the world! I was near heaven—almost close enough to reach out and touch it. I knew I would never forget this moment as a strange but oddly familiar feeling came over me. I had never felt so independent and free, nor had as much confidence in myself. I knew from then on that if I put my mind to it and had faith in myself, I could achieve anything.

Credibility material: When I moved to Atwater, California, my grandmother told me that I must visit Yosemite. "It is awesome," she said. My teenage mind thought, "Yeah, right! As if nature could be all that exciting." In the end, I became a regular customer of this adventure, peacefulness, and beauty, making the 45-minute drive to Yosemite often.

Relevance to audience: Yosemite has a similar effect on almost all visitors. Conservationist and Sierra Club founder John Muir stated it

This outline is only one example of a preparation outline. Be sure to follow your instructor's guidelines and remember to use a less detailed delivery outline when giving an extemporaneous speech.

Using descriptive language and emotional appeal can grab your listeners' interest.

well in *Our National Parks* when he said, "Climb the mountains and get their good tidings. Nature's peace will flow into you as sunshine flows into trees. The winds will blow their own freshness into you, and the storms their energy, while cares will drop off like autumn leaves."

Preview of speech: Although my words and pictures could not do Yosemite justice, I hope to give you an idea of how wonderful it is by taking a glimpse at some general adventures the park has to offer, its waterfalls, and the awe-inspiring Half Dome.

(**Link:** Let's begin with some general attractions at the park.)

BODY

I. Yosemite's adventures are for all ages and cultures with varied interests.

  A. You can take it easy watching for wildlife like the black bear, bobcat, white-headed woodpecker, or mountain goat.

    1. According to the National Park Service's web page for Yosemite, there are more than 400 species of vertebrates in Yosemite.

    2. The wide range of species is mostly due to the diverse habitats that have not been degraded by human activity.

    3. Paul Whitfield, in the 2011 book *The Rough Guide to Yosemite, Sequoia, and Kings Canyon* states that Yosemite embraces nearly 1,200 square miles and ranges from 2,000 feet in altitude to over 13,000 feet above sea level.

  B. Physical activities you could engage in include hiking, rock climbing, swimming, horseback riding, camping, and white-water rafting.

    1. White-water rafting takes place on the ferocious Merced River during the spring and early summer months, when snow from atop the mountains is melting into the river.

An engaging quotation can provide expert testimony and effective emotive language, to help build your ethos.

Including your oral citations on the outline will help you remember them during the speech and prevent you from committing plagiarism.

2. Although the waters are wild, there are rafting trips available for beginners and advanced levels.

C. Nightlife activities include stargazing at a vast, open sky or even having a cocktail at the Iron Door Saloon.

(**Link:** When you are exhausted, you can relax and take in the breathtaking beauty of the world-famous waterfalls.)

II. Yosemite's magnificent waterfalls are some of America's tallest according to the National Park Service website.
   A. May and June are the best months to visit most of the falls.
   B. There are hundreds of waterfalls in the park, but they begin to disappear in July as the last of the snow melts from atop the mountains.
   C. The most popular are Yosemite Falls, Bridalveil Fall, Vernal Fall, and Nevada Fall.
      1. The roaring and crashing of the water is so loud when you get close that you can't hear someone talking right next to you.
      2. It is overwhelming and makes you feel small.
      3. It made me realize that my problems were even smaller.
      4. As Paul Whitfield states in *The Rough Guide to Yosemite, Sequoia, and Kings Canyon*, Yosemite Falls is the highest in North America at 2,425 feet.
         a. Yosemite Falls is actually two falls—Upper Yosemite Fall and Lower Yosemite Fall.
         b. A steady breeze blows from the base of the lower fall due to the force of the air drawn down with the water and creates a steady spray.
         c. During a full moon in the spring and early summer, the spray creates "moonbows" at the base of the falls.

Interesting detailed facts and statistics support the main point about waterfalls. Details like this offer a great opportunity for appealing to the visual learners in the class. Remember to include graphs, charts, and pictures when possible.

5. The Bridalveil Fall is a mere 620 feet, notes Whitfield.
   a. The National Park Service's web page states that this is "often the first waterfall visitors see when entering the valley."
   b. In the spring, it is huge, but the rest of the year, it has its characteristic light, swaying flow that gives it its name.
   c. You can walk to the base up a steep trail.
6. Vernal Fall is 317 feet, according to Whitfield.
   a. The Yosemite Conservancy website observes that this fall is one of the valley's only year-round falls.
   b. This fall is not visible from the main valley, but you can see it from the Happy Isles Trail.
   c. The National Park Service notes that when the road is open, a wheelchair-accessible trail is available.
7. Nevada Fall is 594 feet, according to the National Park Service.
   a. This fall is active in September and October as well, with peak flow in late May.
   b. This fall is not visible from the main valley, but you can see it from the Happy Isles Trail.
   c. When the road is open, a wheelchair-accessible trail is available.

Include your links in the outline, and use them where you need to guide your audience to the next thought (usually between parts of the speech and the main points).

(**Link:** If you continue your hike past the Vernal and Nevada Falls, you will reach what is possibly the most photographed place in the park—Half Dome.)

III. Yosemite's most famous icon is Half Dome.
   A. The National Park Service states that Half Dome rises to 5,000 feet above the Yosemite Valley and 8,800 feet above sea level.

B. Getting to the top of Half Dome is a 17-mile hike that takes nine to 12 hours to complete, round trip.
  1. You must complete the trip in one day.
  2. You must obtain a Park Service permit to hike Half Dome.
C. The last 400 vertical feet is at an angle of 60 degrees that requires the use of steel cables and wooden two-by-fours to reach the summit.
D. If you have forgotten gloves, which we did, there are usually some stuffed under a rock at the base of the cables, left by fellow hikers and rangers.
E. Before climbing this last leg, be sure to heed the warning engraved on the steel sign that's embedded into the side of the granite mountain: "DO NOT ASCEND TO THE TOP OF HALF DOME IF THUNDERCLOUDS ARE VISIBLE ANYWHERE IN THE SKY. HALF DOME HAS BEEN STRUCK BY LIGHTNING IN EVERY MONTH OF THE YEAR."
  1. When we began to climb, the sky was a beautiful crystal-clear blue.
  2. After 15 minutes on top, in the midst of taking in the magnificence and feeling on top of the world, black clouds rolled in from out of nowhere.
  3. The 20 or so people on top of Half Dome were then all trying to get down at once and in a hurry, because both the peak and the steel cables attract lightning.
  4. We made it down fine by staying calm, but we were sad that we had to cut the summit visit so short after that long journey.

Personal testimony with a hint of emotional drama can build up to your conclusion.

Signal the conclusion with language and vocal delivery.

CONCLUSION

Summary statement: Sadly, my speech has only given you a small piece of Yosemite, and it is ever changing with the seasons. In the winter, it is a vast wonderland of white beauty that is just indescribable. In the fall, the colors explode all around you. It is no wonder that John Muir spent so many years there and worked so hard to protect and defend it. And it is no wonder that Ansel Adams, the world-famous photographer, spent many years there photographing landscapes.

Audience response statement: If you think national parks are only for family vacations and retirement visits, then you are seriously mistaken and will miss out on so much that you could experience and benefit from. Yosemite is a place to visit when you are young and healthy and can do all the physical adventures it has to offer.

WOW statement: Yosemite healed my soul. It taught me what is important in life and that we can miss so much beauty. Until I did the research for this speech, I didn't realize that I was feeling the same motivations as John Muir and Ansel Adams a century before me. Don't you want to experience the same?

> Evoke or give expert testimony whenever you can to build ethos.

References

Muir, J. (1901). *Our national parks.* New York, NY: Houghton Mifflin.

U.S. Department of the Interior, National Park Service. (2012, November 15). Yosemite National Park. Retrieved from http://www.nps.gov/yose/

Whitfield, P. (2011). *The rough guide to Yosemite, Sequoia, and Kings Canyon.* New York, NY: Rough Guides.

Yosemite Conservancy. (2012). *Day hikes in Yosemite.* Retrieved from http://www.yosemiteconservancy.org/experience-yosemite/day-hikes?page=1

> Include only sources cited in the speech and format them according to an acceptable style manual (APA style is shown).

13.5 How Do You Present or Evaluate an Informative Speech?

You have finally made it to where you can put your speech on its feet and learn to effectively evaluate speeches. As you move to the delivery stage, you need to pay special attention to the final language choices you make, how to effectively deliver the speech, and how to use the listening process as an evaluative tool.

Put Your Speech on Its Feet

Putting your speech on its feet requires paying special attention to your language and delivery. Chapters 3 and 12 highlight the importance and use of language. Your language should be accurate, appropriate, distinctive, and conversational. Especially for an informative speech, use simple, clear, and vivid language. Use previews and reviews to explain complex topics and aid the audience's memory.

Extemporaneous delivery is often central to the informative speech. For example, imagine demonstrating a process while reading a manuscript. As Chapter 12 notes, speaking extemporaneously allows you to be more natural, adaptable, and able to connect with your audience. Creating and practicing with a delivery outline is key. You should also:

- Use your voice and nonverbal communication to assist your audience's understanding. Use a vocal rate, volume, and posture that convey enthusiasm, but speak slowly enough for listeners to absorb information.

- Make eye contact often, especially when giving a speech to instruct.

- Use presentation aids to assist learning and retention.

- Include audience participation if appropriate and time allows.

Evaluate the Speech

Listening is crucial if the information in a speech is to be relayed effectively, and evaluating yourself and other speakers will help you improve your own techniques. If you are the speaker, explore how you can help your audience understand and retain information. If you are an audience member, listen critically. Evaluate the message for clarity, accuracy, and organization. Does the speech meet its informative goal? Assess the delivery. Keep a critical eye out for what works and what does not.

▌**See Chapter 5** if you need help with listening critically.

Use this checklist, or guidelines provided by your instructor, to evaluate informative speeches. This list can also help guide you as you create and practice a speech.

CHECKLIST FOR EVALUATING THE INFORMATIVE SPEECH

TOPIC
- ☐ Speech accomplished purpose to inform
- ☐ Topic appropriate to speaker, audience, and occasion
- ☐ Interesting topic

INTRODUCTION
- ☐ Gained attention and interest
- ☐ Established credibility
- ☐ Indicated relevance to audience
- ☐ Declared central idea
- ☐ Previewed speech

BODY
- ☐ Main points clear and obvious to the audience
- ☐ Points followed an appropriate organizational strategy
- ☐ Main points appropriately researched and supported
- ☐ Main points supported with appropriate presentation aids when necessary
- ☐ Oral citations included throughout speech
- ☐ Linked parts of speech

CONCLUSION
- ☐ Contained a summary statement
- ☐ Offered an audience response statement
- ☐ Effectively came to closure (WOW statement)

PRESENTATION
- ☐ Language was clear, concise, and appropriate
- ☐ Gestures/body movements were effective
- ☐ Consistent and effective eye contact
- ☐ Used vocal variety/emphasis/volume/rate
- ☐ Used appropriate delivery style
- ☐ Spoke with enthusiasm
- ☐ Spoke with conviction and sincerity
- ☐ Good use of delivery outline
- ☐ Presentation aids appropriate to speech topic (if applicable)
- ☐ Used presentation aids throughout entire speech (if applicable)
- ☐ Used professional presentation aids (if applicable)
- ☐ Speech met time requirements

Chapter 13 Review

Key Questions

13.1 What Is Informative Speaking?

> Objective 13.1: **DEFINE INFORMATIVE SPEAKING**

Informative speaking gives your audience completely new knowledge, skills, or understanding about your topic or increases their current knowledge, skills, or understanding. There are four types of informative speeches:

- *A speech to describe* usually describes an object, person, animal, place, or event.
- A *speech to instruct* teaches or demonstrates a process.
- A *speech to explain* clarifies a concept or issue.
- A *speech to report* is an oral report or briefing.

▌ See pages 366–367.

13.2 What Is the Creative Process for Informative Speaking?

> Objective 13.2: **EXPLAIN THE CREATIVE PROCESS FOR INFORMATIVE SPEAKING**

Informative speaking follows the general speech creative process—developing, creating, presenting, and listening/evaluating—but emphasizes awareness of what your audience knows and what you would like your audience to learn.

▌ See pages 368–369.

13.3 How Do You Develop and Research an Informative Topic?

> Objective 13.3: **EXPLAIN HOW TO DEVELOP AND RESEARCH AN INFORMATIVE TOPIC**

- Get to know the audience and situation.
- Create an informative idea bank.
- Select and narrow your informative topic.
- Identify your specific purpose.
- Confirm the best type of informative speech.
- Identify your central idea.
- Create a working outline.
- Conduct your research.

▌ See pages 370–375.

13.4 How Do You Outline and Organize an Informative Speech?

Objective 13.4: **DISCUSS HOW TO OUTLINE AND ORGANIZE AN INFORMATIVE SPEECH**

- Start with basic, effective outlining. Be sure your outline includes necessary header information, an introduction, the body of the speech, and a conclusion; uses complete sentences; contains source citations within the outline; and includes a source page.

- Commit to an appropriate informative strategy. Informative speeches can utilize a chronological, topical, spatial, comparative, problem–solution, or causal strategy.

- Construct your main points. Use elements such as parallelism and repetition to help your audience learn and remember.

- Organize your support materials. Anticipate what your audience needs to know or might have trouble understanding.

- Compose your introduction and conclusion. The introduction should include an attention-getter, credibility material, relevance to audience, and a preview. In an informative speech, it should "pitch" your speech to your audience. The conclusion should include summary, audience response, and "WOW" statements. It should inspire your audience to want to learn more.

See pages 376–387.

13.5 How Do You Present or Evaluate an Informative Speech?

Objective 13.5: **EXPLORE HOW TO PRESENT OR EVALUATE AN INFORMATIVE SPEECH**

- Put your speech on its feet. Language, delivery, and presentation aids (if any) should be crafted based on how they can help an audience learn and retain information.

- Evaluate the speech. Listen effectively. Evaluate the speech message for how clearly and accurately it informs. Evaluate the presentation for techniques that inspire an audience to listen.

See pages 388–389.

Improve Your Communication

How much support material do you really need?

It would be a rare situation when you would give an informative speech about something you are not familiar with. However, familiarity is not an excuse to ignore the value of quality support material. You should always seek out material to support what you know and to increase your knowledge. Additionally, using support material from credible sources will always improve your ethos. Your audience will view you as more of an expert and will see how others support the information you are offering. When giving more mundane speeches (such as "How to creatively wrap a gift"), you might need to be a bit more imaginative about sources and material. Locate creative quotations you can use in the introduction and conclusion. Interview experts at a local crafts store. Compare and contrast ideas in magazines or how-to books. Use instructions from other sources. There are always other sources, to support any topic.

How detailed should a process speech be?

To give an effective speech to instruct, you need to actually guide the audience through the process. The best way to do that is to do the process, or as much of it as possible, so that they can understand it. Think about cooking shows on television. They walk through the steps and illustrate the ones that would take too long to complete during the segment. We may not see them dry the beef jerky, but they illustrate how to do it. At the very least, each major part of the process should be supported with a presentation aid. Here are a few other suggestions:

- Try to collect tidbits of information to offer during longer moments of mixing, cutting, or building. For example, tell your audience about the origin of ramen noodles as you prepare the lettuce for a salad using the noodles. Cite the source of that information.

- Create a pamphlet or card containing the tools, steps, and other resources. Distribute the handout at the end of your speech.

- To save time, have ready before your speech event a premade example for each step, so you don't have to completely finish each during the speech before moving on to the next step.

Other Resources

Here are some sources to help you develop and improve your informative speeches.

Locating Support Material

To locate only websites, try these:

- The Open Directory Project dmoz.org
- Yahoo! Directory dir.search.yahoo.com

To locate relevant blog material, try these:

- IceRocket icerocket.com
- Technorati Technorati.com
- Regator regator.com

Beyond YouTube or Bing, Google, and Yahoo! videos, try these to locate multimedia material:

- Blinkx blinkx.com
- FindSounds FindSounds.com

Understanding Learning Styles

Sprenger, Marilee. *Differentiation Through Learning Styles and Memory.* 2nd ed. Thousand Oaks: SAGE, 2008. Print.

- www.learning-styles-online.com/overview/
- www.mindtools.com/mnemlsty.html

Avoiding Plagiarism

If you need more help with citing sources and understanding plagiarism, explore plagiarism.org.

Apply Your Knowledge

1. How do you confirm the best type of informative speech to give?

2. Make a list of potential speech topics for the chronological, topical, spatial, and comparative strategies. Select one topic with each strategy and write the potential main points for each.

3. Give examples of informative speeches using problem–solution and causal strategies. How would they differ from persuasive speeches using these strategies?

Chapter 14
Persuasive Speaking

At the end of reasons comes persuasion.[1]

Ludwig Wittgenstein

14.1 **What Is Persuasive Speaking?**

Persuasion is a deliberate attempt by the speaker to create, reinforce, or change the attitudes, beliefs, values, and/or behaviors of the listener. Persuasion can occur between two individuals or between a speaker and a larger audience. When you create a formal speech with the general purpose to persuade, you are engaging in *persuasive speaking*. Examining what a persuasive speech does will help you understand the complexities of persuasion.

Practicing Ethics: Coercion

Persuasion is not coercion! *Coercion* is forcing somebody, via threats or intimidation, to do something against his or her will. Persuasion gives the person the necessary knowledge to change or act differently via her or his own free will.

Focuses Listeners' Options

Persuasive speaking is like offering guidance to your listeners when they have several options to choose from and need your help to determine which is the best one. The job of the ethical persuasive speaker is to determine the best and safest option, support that decision logically, and offer information to the audience in a manner that allows them to make a wise decision.

Seeks a Response

In the persuasive speech, you have an audience response in mind. That audience response determines which of the three types of persuasive speeches you will give.

- When you want to create a new or change an existing attitude, belief, value, or behavior for your audience, you are creating a *speech to convince*.
- When you overcome apathy in your audience or reinforce an existing attitude, belief, value, or behavior, you are creating a *speech to stimulate*.
- When you ask your audience to take action, you are giving a *speech to actuate*.

Although you are seeking a response, you should not coerce your audience. See the Practicing Ethics box. Also, changing an attitude, belief, value, or behavior often takes time. One speech may simply open the door a bit.

Supports a Proposition of Fact, Value, or Policy

When you create a persuasive speech, you have an overarching argument (the body of the speech) that supports the assertion you are making in your central idea. The assertion you are making in your central idea is a proposition of fact, value, or policy. For example, if your central idea is

Foods marked organic are not necessarily healthier than conventional foods.

then the proposition you are supporting with this central idea is:

Organic foods are not healthier than conventional foods.

And once you have identified your proposition, you can determine if it is a proposition of fact, value, or policy.

- **Proposition of fact:** Seeks to prove something factual and answers "What is accurate or not?" For example:

  SUVs are safe.

  Lee Harvey Oswald was part of a conspiracy to assassinate President John F. Kennedy.

  Genetically altered vegetables are not healthy.

- **Proposition of value:** Seeks to make a value judgment and answers "What has worth or importance? What is good, wise, ethical, or beautiful?" For example:

  Funding after-school programs is a good use of tax dollars.

  Mandatory drug testing violates privacy rights.

  Plagiarism is unacceptable.

- **Proposition of policy**: Seeks to prove a need for a new or different policy and answers "What procedures, plans, or courses of action need to be terminated and/or implemented?" This type of proposition can ask the audience to immediately act (To persuade my audience to volunteer to clean the city) or to simply agree (To persuade my audience that the city should outlaw smoking in public buildings). Other propositions of policy include:

  All homeowners should be required to recycle.

  The City of Jonestown should not implement a tax on pet owners.

  The recreation center should be open 24 hours a day.

  The state needs stiffer laws related to child abuse crimes.

In your organic foods speech, your proposition looks at the *accuracy* of the assertion that organic foods are not necessarily healthier than conventional foods. Therefore, your central idea seeks to support a *proposition of fact*.

Knowing the type of proposition your central idea supports will help you select an organizational strategy for creating the body of the speech, which will be made up of smaller arguments. These arguments will ultimately sustain your central idea— for instance, that organic is not necessarily healthier than conventional.

14.2 What Is the Creative Process for Persuasive Speaking?

Influencing others through a persuasive speech is a remarkable task that requires you to be diligent and ethical in some ways that are different from those used in informative speaking. The previous chapters (especially Chapters 5, 10, 11, and 12) have prepared you for the basic speech process. The table to the right briefly reviews the four basic activities you use to create an effective persuasive speech. Remember, being creative is not a linear process, so move back and forth between each activity as you mold your speech.

In the example at the far right, Shimin, a student from Singapore, is studying in the United States. In an environmental class, she recently became aware of the staggering volume of plastic pollution in the United States. After her environmental class ended, Shimin joined the Clean Cities program in her college town. Now, she needs to give a speech about recycling to fellow students who live off campus.

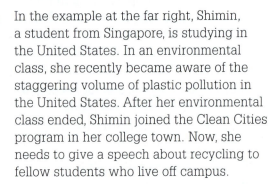

Shimin will give her speech at a Saturday workshop held once a month to bring off-campus students together to build community and to show them how to be better consumers and citizens. Shimin has been a part of the group for some time, so she knows many of her audience members, making her audience analysis relatively easy. She creates a working outline with four main points:

Main point #1: What is plastic?

Main point #2: How do we use it?

Main point #3: How is it influencing our environment?

Main point #4: What is the solution?

As she develops the speech, Shimin turns these points into complete statements and an expanded outline. This chapter will help you use some of the same techniques Shimin used in her speech.

The Creative Process		Persuasive Example

1 Developing

14.6 How Do You Develop and Research a Persuasive Topic?

| See page 410

Shimin creates this central idea:

> The amount of plastics thrown away daily is a serious problem, but a few simple steps on our part will lower plastic's impact on our future.

Using questions related to a proposition of policy to guide her, she conducts her research online and in the local public library. She also interviews a professor who specializes in waste management.

2 Creating

14.7 How Do You Outline and Organize a Persuasive Speech?

| See page 416

Shimin selects the problem–solution strategy for her speech and creates main points to fit that strategy.

Problem:

   I. Plastics are made from problematic raw materials.

  II. Plastics cause major environmental issues.

Solution:

  III. There are alternative forms of plastics and substitute materials.

  IV. There are alternative ways of using plastics.

She uses the environmental artwork of Chris Jordon to grab attention in the introduction and ends with startling statistics for her WOW statement.

3 Presenting

14.8 How Do You Present or Evaluate a Persuasive Speech?

| See page 430

Shimin adjusts her language to clarify her arguments and to be more interesting. She creates her delivery outline and her Prezi presentation aids. Shimin practices several times, including twice in the event space.

4 Listening & Evaluating

After the speech, Shimin asks the audience to fill out a short survey of their experience, and she asks close friends for comments about her speech.

14.3 What Are the Appeals You Can Use to Persuade?

Appeals (also called proofs) are the means by which you prove or establish the argument you are making. First discussed by Aristotle in the fourth century BCE, pathos, ethos, logos, and mythos are considered the traditional appeals by most scholars today.[2] Modern speakers can use other types of motivational appeals grounded less in the logical and more in the psychological.

Traditional Appeals

Appeal to Pathos

An appeal to *pathos* deals with the listener's emotions. In other words, you can use your audience's sympathy and imagination to affect their attitudes, values, beliefs, or behaviors. Eliciting your audience's emotions is a conjuring process and not a command. Emotive language and vivid description, especially by trusted experts who have firsthand knowledge, can be very moving. For example, President George W. Bush invoked pathos with these remarks during his address on September 11, 2001:

> Tonight, I ask for your prayers for all those who grieve, for the children whose worlds have been shattered, for all whose sense of safety and security has been threatened. And I pray they will be comforted by a Power greater than any of us, spoken through the ages in Psalm 23: *Even though I walk through the valley of the shadow of death, I fear no evil, for you are with me.*

Although it may seem unethical to play with your audience's emotions, philosophers and rhetoricians have long argued that logic may not be enough to get people to act.

Appeal to Ethos

Ethos is the credibility inspired by the speaker's character, or what Aristotle called *moral character*. You can have a strong argument and emotional appeal, but if the audience questions your character, you will have trouble persuading them. The key to using your credibility effectively is to realize that it resides in *how your audience views you*. Aristotle claimed that the speaker's credibility evolved from *competency* and *character*. In modern times, a third trait, *charisma*, has been recognized.

- *Competency* is the audience's perception of how knowledgeable you are about your topic. Mentioning your related experience or education, citing a variety of support materials from credible sources, and presenting a polished speech will help demonstrate your competency.

- *Character* is the audience's perception of your intentions and of the concern you have for the audience. Finding ways to connect with the audience, demonstrating that you have investigated alternatives and challenges to your positions, and emphasizing your concern for the audience (rather than just for yourself) will build your character.

- *Charisma* is the audience's perception of your personality. Do they see you as energetic, friendly, and vocally as well as physically pleasing? Be confident and assertive in a positive manner. Use language and gestures to demonstrate your dynamic personality and excitement about the topic.

Appeal to Mythos

The appeal to mythos is often fueled by emotion and not always viewed as a noteworthy appeal. **Mythos** relates to a sense of one's history in the larger culture and the need to be a member of that culture. For example, our sense of what it means to be a woman or a man evolves from a community-accepted understanding of what is valued in women and men. In the United States, patriotism, nationalism, faith, pride, and valor are strong traditions and values. A downside to mythos is that it can promote *ethnocentrism*, or the notion that one's culture or viewpoint is superior to that of others. (See Chapter 1.)

Appeal to Logos

The human ability to use logic can be a powerful persuasive tool. When you appeal to logic, or **logos**, in a speech, you appeal to the listener's ability to reason through statistics, facts, and expert testimony to reach a conclusion. Therefore, you engage in **reasoning**—the rational thinking humans do to reach conclusions or to justify beliefs or acts. You build arguments to influence your audience's beliefs, values, attitudes, and behaviors. Later sections of this chapter will explain arguments in more detail.

Practicing Ethics: Balanced Appeals

Ethical speakers balance their use of appeals. Don't rely too heavily on just one type.

Modern Appeals

Appeal to Need

This appeal recognizes that your audience members have needs they see as important and necessary to fulfill. Demonstrating, when possible, how your topic will help your audience fulfill a need can be an effective motivator.

In Chapter 10, you learned about Abraham Maslow's hierarchy-of-needs theory, which states that humans have a set of needs that must be met. The pyramid diagram below illustrates the five hierarchical levels of needs.[3] Appealing to your audience's needs makes for an effective persuasive speech. For example, persuading an audience to get a flu shot could appeal to good health, or the safety need.

This appeal relies on your knowing the audience's needs and paying attention to the hierarchy. For example, during a year following a light flu season, motivating listeners to get flu shots might be difficult.

Appeal to Harmony

In his book *A Theory of Cognitive Dissonance*, Leon Festinger introduced **cognitive dissonance theory**, which emphasizes the human need to be in a harmonious state (consonant state).[4] However, sometimes conflicting attitudes, values, beliefs, ideas, or behaviors cause an inharmonious feeling (dissonant state).

When listening to a persuasive speech, an audience may feel this sort of dissonance. Read the following proposition of value and note how it makes you feel:

> **Illegal downloading of music is stealing.**

You could agree, disagree, or feel apathetic (you don't care). If you don't think illegal downloading of music is stealing, the speaker must offer strong evidence to make you feel bad about your belief.

Creating an uncomfortable feeling in your audience can be unpredictable, especially if their beliefs in your topic are deeply seated. Just because you create dissonance does not mean your audience will accept your solution. They may discredit you or your sources, they may stop listening, or they may simply hear what they want to hear.

An appeal to harmony can also be used when your audience agrees with your proposition. In this case, your goal becomes to create a dissonance related to not acting on their beliefs.

Appeal to Gain

When you appeal to gain, you are recognizing that most people weigh or evaluate their actions based on what the actions might cost them. To help you understand how this appeal works, the **expectancy-outcome values theory** suggests that people will evaluate the cost, benefit, or value related to making a change in an attitude, value, belief, or behavior to decide if it is worthwhile or not.[5] People in such a situation will ask questions such as:

- Is this a good or bad idea?
- Will my family, friends, or colleagues approve or disapprove?
- If they disapprove, what are the ramifications?
- Will others think better of me if I do this?

People will try to determine what they will gain or lose by changing. During a persuasive speech, if you can demonstrate to your audience that what you are asking will be a gain and not a loss, you may be able to motivate them to agree.

For example, if you are trying to convince a group of college students to engage in community service or to sign up for an internship because potential employers like to see these activities on résumés, you are appealing to the students' need to gain something more important than the time it will take to participate in the service or internship.

Appeal to Commitment

Another appeal recognizes how audience members might interpret your message, depending on their commitment to critical thinking and involvement. The **elaboration likelihood model (ELM)** argues that people will process your message by one of two ways: **central processing** or **peripheral processing**.[6]

Processing Type	What Is It?
Central processing	Being motivated to listen and think critically
Peripheral processing	Not paying close attention to an argument; or superficially accepting an argument

The level of your commitment and involvement makes you process differently. As a speaker, you can use this knowledge to create a message relevant to the majority of your audience's interests. The challenge with using an appeal to commitment is that you need to know your audience and what they will process centrally. This heightens the significance of conducting effective audience analysis.

At a basic level, the ELM theory should signal a need to pay close attention to issues such as your appearance, your delivery, and the completeness of your message when giving any speech.

14.4 What Are the Parts of an Argument?

An *argument* is a reason or a series of reasons you give to support an assertion. You use arguments to support your persuasive speech proposition and central idea. In his book *The Uses of Argument*, British philosopher Stephen Toulmin notes that an argument has three main parts: a claim, evidence, and warrants.[7]

Claim

Earlier, you learned that a persuasive speech supports a proposition of fact, value, or policy and that your central idea summarizes or previews what you want to assert. Likewise, any smaller argument within your speech will have a claim that acts just as your central idea does for the whole speech. An argument's **claim** is the assertion and will be a claim of fact, value, or policy. A claim should be a single, concise sentence. For example:

> CLAIM OF FACT: People who wear seat belts tend to take better care of their health.
>
> CLAIM OF VALUE: Owning a gun is wrong.
>
> CLAIM OF POLICY: All public buildings should be smoke-free.

Evidence

Your support materials become **evidence**, or the information proving your claim. Let's say your speech is on the following:

> CLAIM OF POLICY: The city should change the current city ordinance to allow citizens to own a small flock of hens within the city limits.

To support your claim, you consult books for evidence such as the fact that naturally raised chickens and eggs have a better nutrient value than factory-farmed chickens.

Warrants

Just presenting evidence will not necessarily demonstrate that your claim is accurate. You also need **_warrants_**, or assumptions that act as links between the evidence and the claim. In this step, you help your audience draw a conclusion about your claim and the evidence provided.

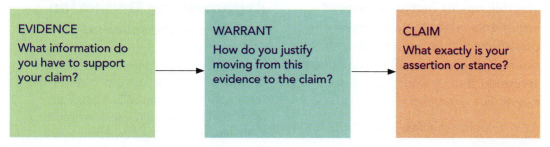

EVIDENCE
What information do you have to support your claim?

WARRANT
How do you justify moving from this evidence to the claim?

CLAIM
What exactly is your assertion or stance?

Staying with your topic about urban chickens, if you take two bits of information—one about the health benefits of chicken in general and one that naturally raised chickens tend to be more nutritious than chickens raised on factory farms—you could support your claim like this:

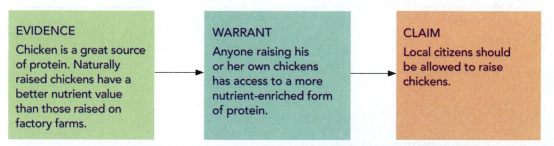

EVIDENCE
Chicken is a great source of protein. Naturally raised chickens have a better nutrient value than those raised on factory farms.

WARRANT
Anyone raising his or her own chickens has access to a more nutrient-enriched form of protein.

CLAIM
Local citizens should be allowed to raise chickens.

There are three types of warrants that can link the evidence to the claim:

- *Authoritative warrants* assume that the claim is accurate based on the credibility of the source of the support materials.

- *Motivational warrants* are based on the speaker's and audience's needs and values.

- *Substantive warrants* are based on the reliability of the support materials.

In the urban chickens example above, the warrant is motivational, based on the value of healthy eating—that naturally raised chickens are a desirable nutrient-rich source of protein.

> **TIP: Qualifying Your Claim**
> Rarely, if ever, can you prove that a claim is 100 percent correct. Claims can be qualified as "possible," "probable," or "beyond doubt."

14.5 What Are the Different Types of Arguments?

The differences between types of arguments relate to how they are constructed after you create your claim. Remember, a claim is a concise sentence stating what you want to prove. For example:

> All dolphins, whales, and porpoises are mammals.

Once you know what you want your audience to accept, you need to decide what type of argument you want to construct. There are five types of arguments.

Argument by Deduction

Argument by deduction (also known as reasoning by deduction) constructs a series of general statements, or *premises*, that together prove correct the claim/conclusion. When arguing by deduction, you can use one of two formats: a *syllogism* or an *enthymeme*. The **syllogism** is the classical form of deductive reasoning, with this structure:

MAJOR PREMISE
All mammals feed their young milk via mammary glands located on the female of the species.
— Includes a generally accepted statement

MINOR PREMISE
All female dolphins, whales, and porpoises feed their young milk produced by mammary glands on the female.
— Includes a specific observation

CONCLUSION
Therefore, all dolphins, whales, and porpoises are mammals.
— Includes a statement that ties the major and minor premises together

When you use deductive arguments in a speech, you will not usually be so methodical in how you phrase the argument. This same syllogism might be presented as:

According to scientists, there are several characteristics that define mammals, but the most significant is how they feed their young. All mammals have the ability to feed their young through mammary glands located on the body of the female of the species. — **MAJOR PREMISE**

Dolphins, whales, and porpoises all have this unique ability to allow their offspring to suckle. — **MINOR PREMISE**

We consider dolphins, whales, and porpoises to be marine mammals. — **CONCLUSION**

Sometimes, one of your premises will be obvious or common knowledge and you will not need to state it; this type of truncated syllogism is an *enthymeme*. In the example below, you would drop the obvious minor premise—that Jimmy Fallon is a human—and jump to the conclusion.

MAJOR PREMISE
All humans are mortal.

CONCLUSION
Therefore, Jimmy Fallon is mortal.

Deductive reasoning must present a sound argument. To be sound, the major and minor premises as well as the conclusion must be factual; if they are not, the result is a *faulty syllogism*. For example:

MAJOR PREMISE
All environmentalists are vegetarians.

MINOR PREMISE
Yeon is an environmentalist.

CONCLUSION
Therefore, Yeon is a vegetarian.

FAULTY SYLLOGISM

The major premise here is false because many environmentalists are not vegetarians. Yeon may be an environmentalist, but that does not necessarily mean Yeon is a vegetarian. Likewise, Yeon may be an environmentalist and a vegetarian, but being a vegetarian may have nothing to do with being an environmentalist. To make a sound deductive argument, you want to ask: "Can I prove the major and minor premises are true? Is the conclusion reasonable, given the two premises?"

Practicing Ethics: Ethical Arguments

Previously, you learned not to coerce your audience and, in Objective 14.8, you will discover how to prevent faulty arguments. However, it is important to always use persuasive argument for the good.

- Don't conceal your true intentions.
- Don't represent yourself as an expert unless you are.
- Don't distort, mislead, pretend certainty, or fail to support your arguments.
- Don't exaggerate to manipulate.

Argument by Induction

Whereas deduction deals with certainty, induction predicts probability. When you construct an *argument by induction* (also known as reasoning by induction), you will argue from specific cases to a general statement suggesting something is likely based on the specific cases. We often use this type of reasoning in our everyday lives.

For example, if you buy a box of assorted chocolates and you eat three or four pieces in the box only to discover they are stale, you do not keep eating and assume the next one will not be stale. Instead, you reason that if the first three or four pieces (the specific) are stale, the whole box (the general) is stale. Likewise, if you check out gas prices at 9 or 10 gas stations in your city and they are all $2.95, you reason that gas in your town will probably cost $2.95 everywhere.

The reliability of these claims resides in the quantity and quality of the specific cases. The same is true for a speech using argument by induction. The induction can be based on examples, statistics, facts, or testimony.

This diagram demonstrates how you might reason through specific cases to support the claim "ZZtravel.com has the best rates for a variety of travel needs."

SPECIFIC CASE #1
Student A purchased airline tickets and hotel reservations to Cancún from ZZtravel.com because the service was the cheapest.

↓

SPECIFIC CASE #2
Student B rented a car and made hotel reservations for a trip to Orlando from the same online service because it was the cheapest she could locate.

↓

SPECIFIC CASE #3
Student C purchased airline tickets to make a trip back home to Oregon from the same online service because it was the cheapest.

↓

SPECIFIC CASE #4
Student D purchased airline tickets and a Eurail pass for a trip to Germany from the same online service because it was the cheapest he found.

↓

CLAIM
ZZtravel.com has the best rates for a variety of travel needs and destinations.

TIP: Inductive Arguments
Inductive arguments are useful when you know your audience is against what you are about to claim.

Argument by Analogy

When you create an **argument by analogy** (also known as reasoning by analogy), you conclude that something will be accurate for one case if it is true for another similar case. In other words, if it is true for A, it is true for B because they are so similar. For example, many people who argue for a universal health-care plan in the United States do so by making a comparison to Canada. Their claim based on an argument of analogy might be something like this:

> **Because the United States and Canada are so similar and a universal plan works in Canada, then universal health care will work in the United States.**

As in this example, you will most often use an argument by analogy when giving a persuasive speech on a proposition of policy. As discussed in Chapter 11, there are two types of analogies: literal and figurative. An argument based on literal analogies (the comparison of two similar things) works better. Rarely will a figurative analogy (a metaphorical comparison of dissimilar things) prove a claim, and most of the time, a figurative analogy ends in faulty reasoning.

> **TIP: Faulty Arguments**
>
> When a speaker creates an argument, she or he can unintentionally or intentionally create a faulty argument or error in logic known as a fallacy. See Objective 14.8 for more on recognizing and avoiding fallacies.

Argument by Cause

Argument by cause (also known as reasoning by cause) attempts to demonstrate a relationship between two events or factors in which one of the events or factors causes the other. This form of reasoning may take an effect-to-cause or cause-to-effect form. Here are two claims suggesting this type of argument:

> **The increase in violence in our public schools is the effect of increased violence in the entertainment world.** — EFFECT-TO-CAUSE
>
> **Procrastinating on your assignments will cause you to get lower grades.** — CAUSE-TO-EFFECT

Argument by Authority

Argument by authority (also known as reasoning by authority) locates its power in the ethos of the testimony of others you might use to support your claim. When you use this type of argument, you collect testimony from individuals the audience will perceive as experts on the topic. Argument by authority works only if the audience perceives the experts as credible and unbiased. For example, if you wanted to support the claim that stoplight cameras decrease accidents and save lives, you might quote the chiefs of police in towns and cities successfully using these devices. For maximum effect, you should quote your sources directly, and you should always give their credentials.

14.6 How Do You Develop and Research a Persuasive Topic?

The process of developing your topic and researching it for a persuasive speech is very similar to that of informative speaking. However, knowing your target audience, understanding the complexity of what makes your topic debatable, researching multiple perspectives, and committing to a persuasive strategy mark the persuasion process in very different ways. Be mindful of what you are doing at every step.

Get to Know the Audience and Situation

You know from Chapter 10 that it is important to know your audience's attitudes, beliefs, and values as well as their psychological, personal, and social traits. Recall the definition of persuasive speaking: You are attempting to change, influence, or reinforce the attitudes, beliefs, values, and/or behaviors of an audience. Therefore, being audience centered is crucial. If you do not know where your audience stands on your topic or what their needs are, you cannot expect to persuade them. Understanding who is in your audience and what the situation is will help you appeal to the **target audience.** The target audience is the primary group of people you are aiming to persuade; it is the subset of the audience that you most want to engage.

Self-Check: The Persuasive Audience and Situation

❑ How will the attitudes, beliefs, values, and traits of my audience affect my choices?

❑ What topics might listeners be concerned with or find controversial? What might they know or think about those topics?

❑ Why is the audience here, and what else do I know about the situation?

Create a Persuasive Idea Bank

If you do not have an assigned or predetermined persuasive topic, your next step is to find one. For a persuasive speech, the topic should be controversial or debatable—in other words, there are two or more different opinions people may hold about the topic. Beginning speakers often have trouble getting started because they want to pinpoint the perfect "be all, end all" topic right away. Relax, investigate a wide variety of topics at first, and let your mind wander. Databases such as EBSCOhost, CQ (Congressional Quarterly) Weekly, and Opposing Viewpoints Resource Center, or periodicals such as the *New York Times*, your local newspaper, *Time*, and *The Week* are great places to locate current persuasive topics. As you browse, note topics that seem interesting. Let your brain free-associate other ideas. When creating a persuasive idea bank, use phrases noting a side to an issue ("everyone should"). This allows you to explore multiple points of view and related topics.

Select and Narrow Your Persuasive Topic

Now you are ready to narrow your ideas to a viewpoint or your stance on a debatable topic. The persuasive idea bank on this page shows one example. If you are still unsure of which general topic you want to use, return to analyzing the audience and situation. Ask yourself these questions:

- Are there topics that are just not persuasive enough?
- Will the audience be neutral, negative, or positive? Will they have an extreme reaction? Which topic will appeal to a solid target audience?
- Are there situational issues that will help you determine the best topic?

Before you commit to a topic, do some preliminary research. If locating current quality information on the topic is difficult, you may want to change the viewpoint or select another topic.

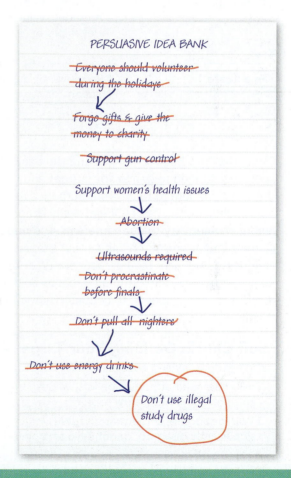

PERSUASIVE IDEA BANK

~~Everyone should volunteer during the holidays~~

~~Forgo gifts & give the money to charity~~

~~Support gun control~~

Support women's health issues

~~Abortion~~

~~Ultrasounds required~~

~~Don't procrastinate before finals~~

~~Don't pull all-nighters~~

~~Don't use energy drinks~~

Don't use illegal study drugs

Confirm the Best Type of Persuasive Speech

Before moving on to create your central idea, it is important to confirm the type of persuasive speech you should give. A persuasive speech will be a speech to convince, stimulate, or actuate. Knowing the type of persuasive speech will help you determine your organizational strategy and focus on the response you want your target audience to have.

Type of Persuasive Speech	Desired Audience Response	Examples
To convince	To convince my audience to change their attitudes, values, beliefs, or behaviors	A speech arguing that outsourcing harms the U.S. economy, presented to a group of CEOs
To stimulate	To stimulate the existing attitudes, values, beliefs, or behaviors of my audience	A speech arguing that animal theme parks are cruel, presented to an animal rights group
To actuate	To move my audience to action	A speech arguing to vote for medical marijuana use, presented at a rally supporting a medical marijuana initiative

Given that you need to understand the exact audience response you desire from the speech, you need to define your target audience in relationship to your new topic. Use the checklist here to refine your audience analysis. For example, Megan has decided to do a speech on the use of illegal study drugs. She knows that younger members of her audience might try to cut corners in studying by doing things that could be harmful. Her preliminary research shows that the use of prescription drugs as a study aid is significant. Megan's biggest concern is for the students who might not have enough knowledge about the harmful effects to hold an opinion one way or the other. She decides to give a speech to convince her younger classmates not to use illegal study drugs.

Self-Check: Defining Your Target Audience

❑ What does my audience know about my topic?

❑ What are their attitudes, beliefs, values, needs, and behaviors toward my topic?

❑ Will they agree, somewhat disagree, significantly disagree, or not have an opinion?

❑ Therefore, will I primarily be creating, reinforcing, or changing attitudes, values, beliefs, or behaviors?

❑ Do I want my audience to passively agree or to take action?

Identify Your Specific Purpose

To review, the specific purpose is a single statement connecting your general purpose, your audience (the target audience in this speech), and your objective. It needs to be clear and limited to only one topic. Let's see how Megan created her specific purpose. You already know that her topic relates to the illegal use of prescription medication as a study aid. She personally believes that this behavior, especially using ADHD drugs illegally, is extremely dangerous, and she wants to convince her audience to believe the same thing.

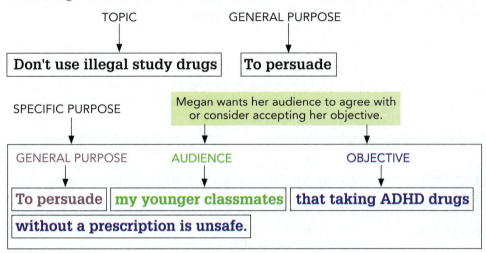

TOPIC

GENERAL PURPOSE

Don't use illegal study drugs

To persuade

SPECIFIC PURPOSE

Megan wants her audience to agree with or consider accepting her objective.

GENERAL PURPOSE

AUDIENCE

OBJECTIVE

To persuade **my younger classmates** **that taking ADHD drugs without a prescription is unsafe.**

This specific purpose will help Megan keep to her general purpose (to persuade) and focus the attention of her target audience (the 18–20-year-old students, because preliminary research demonstrated they are more likely to take illegal study drugs) on her objective (don't use ADHD drugs as illegal study drugs).

Identify Your Central Idea

Now you and Megan are ready to formulate your persuasive central ideas. As you know from Chapter 10, the central idea (or thesis statement) is one concise sentence summarizing or previewing exactly what you are going to claim. Megan's looked like this:

Megan's Specific Purpose:
To persuade my younger classmates **that taking ADHD drugs without a prescription is unsafe.**

Megan's Central Idea:
The use of ADHD drugs for nonprescription purposes is very dangerous.

At this point, it should be easy to see the overarching proposition that your speech—and Megan's speech—is trying to answer. Remember, all persuasive speeches support a proposition of fact, value, or policy. Megan's speech seeks to support a proposition of fact.

Overarching Proposition	Guiding Questions	Examples of Persuasive Claims
Proposition of fact	What is accurate or not? What will happen or not?	When consumed safely, coffee can be beneficial.
Proposition of value	What has worth or importance? What is good, wise, ethical, or beautiful?	Animal theme parks are cruel.
Proposition of policy	What procedures, plans, or courses of action need to be terminated or implemented? (This question can ask the audience to just agree or to act.)	The city should not implement a required recycling program.

Self-Check: Evaluating a Persuasive Central Idea

❏ Is the central idea persuasive in nature? Is it reinforcing or changing attitudes, beliefs, values, and/or behaviors?

❏ Does it support a proposition of fact, value, or policy?

❏ Is it a complete clear and concise statement?

❏ Can I cover this central idea in the time allotted?

❏ Is it unique?

❏ Is it worth persuading the target audience of this and worth their time?

Create a Working Outline

Before embarking on your major research, it is helpful to create a working outline to guide you. To review: Your working main points might be questions you think need to be answered, or they could simply be phrases that relate to subtopics. Later, when you get to your preparation outline stage, you want your main points to be concise and complete declarative sentences, not questions. Your central idea might hint at possible main points. Also, your target audience and your preliminary research should offer some insights and ideas. Here is Megan's working outline:

Working outline for "Don't Use Illegal Study Drugs"

TOPIC: The illegal use of ADHD drugs

GENERAL PURPOSE: To persuade

SPECIFIC PURPOSE: To persuade my younger classmates that taking ADHD drugs without a prescription is unsafe.

CENTRAL IDEA: The use of ADHD drugs for nonprescription purposes is very dangerous.

I. What are ADHD drugs?

II. What are the side effects of ADHD drugs?

III. Who is taking the drugs illegally?

IV. Why are they taking them?

V. What are some alternative solutions to study drugs?

Conduct Your Research

Depending on your topic, your central idea, and the arguments you are using to support your claim, different types of support materials will be more effective than others. You can use facts, definitions, testimony, examples, and statistics. For your arguments to be strong, effective, and ethical, your support materials must be accurate, current, complete, trustworthy, and suitable to the topic, audience, and occasion. Also, research as many angles as possible. Most debatable topics have more than two issues, solutions, or viewpoints. Complex topics require good detective work, and you will not find all the answers in one place. Here are a few tips:

- You can often locate current statistics on the web, and many professional organizations (expert testimony) are present there.

- Although some items you locate in the library can be found on the Internet as well, the library item can often be viewed in its original form for verification.

- There are numerous items in a library that you cannot locate on the Internet.

- Interviews can give you access to testimony that is often not available in print—especially expert testimony.

- Survey data can help you gauge the current reactions or beliefs of a group.

See Chapter 11 for help with research.

14.7 How Do You Outline and Organize a Persuasive Speech?

Constructing an effective preparation outline helps you create a persuasive speech that your audience can follow, that you can follow as you speak, and that can persuade others. Your audience needs to follow every detail of the argument you are presenting, so your organization must be appropriate to the topic and precise down to the smallest detail.

Start with Basic, Effective Outlining

Revisit Chapter 11 for a general review of outline creation if you still feel unsure. Remember that a successful preparation outline will:

- Include necessary header information.
- Contain an introduction, the body of the speech, and a conclusion.
- Use complete sentences.
- Cover only one issue at a time.
- Use balanced main points.
- Employ subordination.
- Plan out formal links.
- Use proper citations within the outline and include a source page (use the citation style your instructor requires).

As you create your persuasive outline, evaluating the strength of your argument will be easier the more detailed you are. Although important to any speech, strictly following these qualities for your persuasive speech will help you create a strong, effective argument that your audience can follow in the oral presentation. Your outline should adhere to either a format similar to the one on the next page or a format your instructor suggests.

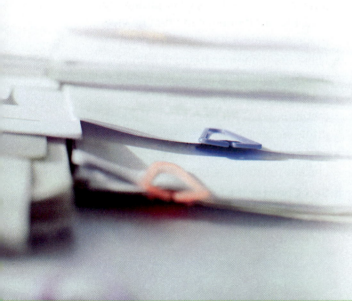

Student name   Class
Date   Instructor name

Topic: Illegal use of study drugs
Specific purpose: To persuade my younger classmates that taking
                    ADHD drugs without a prescription is unsafe.
Central idea: The use of ADHD drugs for nonprescriptive
                    purposes is dangerous, illegal, and not a good
                    study-aid solution.

INTRODUCTION
    Attention-getter
    Credibility material
    Relevance to audience
    Preview of speech

(Link from introduction to first main point)

BODY
    I.   Taking non-prescribed ADHD drugs is dangerous.
         A. Subpoint
         B. Subpoint
             1. Subpoint of B
             2. Subpoint of B
             3. Subpoint of B

(Link between first and second main points)

    II. Second main point
         A. Subpoint
         B. Subpoint
             1. Subpoint of B
             2. Subpoint of B
         C. Subpoint

(Link between second and third main points)

    III. Third main point
         A. Subpoint
             1. Subpoint of A
                a. Subpoint of 1
                b. Subpoint of 1
             2. Subpoint of A
         B. Subpoint
         C. Subpoint

(Link between third and fourth main points)

    IV. Fourth main point
         A. Subpoint
             1. Subpoint of A
                a. Subpoint of 1
                b. Subpoint of 1
             2. Subpoint of A
         B. Subpoint
         C. Subpoint

(Link to conclusion)

CONCLUSION
    Summary statement
    Audience response statement
    WOW statement
                        Works Cited

After conducting research and selecting a strategy, Megan reworked her central idea to include a preview of her (now three) main points. Note the differences from her original central idea on page 414.

Megan begins to fill in her main points, making sure they are full, declarative sentences and cover only one idea at a time. She will make sure to have only one sentence per outline symbol and fill in the support materials.

Megan doesn't know yet how many subpoints each of her main points will have. For now, she leaves a variety of subpoint placeholders in her outline.

Although this template shows four main points, Megan's speech will only have three, and you could have three to five. Short speeches are usually best, with three or four main points.

Commit to a Strategy

Select the best strategy for your type of persuasive speech and your overarching proposition, and strictly adhere to that strategy. It is easy to stray from the point or randomly string thoughts together, so be sure to write your main points so that they stick to the strategy. Periodically, you should return to Chapter 11—where the strategies are explained in detail, with examples—and make sure you are following your strategy.

What Factors Should You Consider When Selecting a Strategy?	Strategies
Speech to stimulate	
Audience viewpoint needs reinforcement	Monroe's motivated sequence, problem–solution, topical,* or chronological*
Speech to convince	
Audience is apathetic or uninformed and needs to create a viewpoint	Problem–solution, comparative, Monroe's motivated sequence, causal, topical,* or chronological*
Audience viewpoint needs to change because they disagree or are conflicted	Comparative, problem–solution, or causal
Speech to actuate	
Audience needs motivation to act	Most of the strategies work for this type, but Monroe's motivated sequence is often the best
Overarching proposition for your speech	
Proposition of fact	Causal, problem–solution, Monroe's motivated sequence, topical,* or chronological*
Proposition of value	Comparative, causal, comparative, or topical*
Proposition of policy	Problem–solution, comparative, causal, Monroe's motivated sequence, or topical*

*Remember, topical and chronological strategies are generally weaker persuasive strategies. They should only be used when nothing else works.

Megan selected and committed to the problem–solution strategy. She will spend most of her speech outlining the problems (the drugs are dangerous and illegal), and then she will offer alternative solutions to studying-related problems.

Construct Main Points

Depending on how you constructed your central idea or which strategy you selected, one or both of these components might suggest the main points you will need to cover in the speech. If your central idea has evolved since the working outline, study it again for three or four possible subtopics, or study the strategy you want to use and how it might influence your main points. Strategies such as Monroe's motivated sequence have certain steps that become main points and determine the focus of those main points. If your central idea or strategy does not help determine main points, make a list of what you want to convey in the speech, group items that relate to each other, and create main points from those groups. Select the three or four most important ideas. Remember that your main points need to be complete declarative sentences, written in a parallel structure, and balanced with each other, and they should cover only one idea per point.

After conducting research, Megan reconsidered her central idea and focused it more to preview her main points. Megan committed to three main points.

I. Taking nonprescribed ADHD drugs is dangerous.
II. Taking nonprescribed ADHD drugs is illegal.
III. Taking nonprescribed ADHD drugs is not the solution.

Organize Support Materials

Your arguments will become the subpoints supporting your main points. So it is time to decide which appeals to use, which types of arguments best fit your speech, and how to arrange the arguments. Make these decisions based on what you want to accomplish, your audience's relationship to the speech, and the needs of the organizational strategy. Once you have your arguments, you need to put them in a logical order. For example, Megan arranges the subpoints under her first main point using *induction*. She will offer facts about the physical problems caused by taking nonprescribed ADHD drugs and then end with her claim that it is dangerous.

Two additional models can help you decide how to arrange arguments:

- The *primacy model* suggests that you should put your strongest arguments first because you are more likely to persuade if you win over your audience early. This method is best if your audience opposes your viewpoint.

- The *recency model* is the reverse of primacy. Here, you begin with the weakest argument and end with the strongest. If your audience is unfamiliar with your topic, is apathetic, or already agrees with you, this method is best.

There is no set way to approach creating arguments, and the more you do it, the better you will get.

Compose Your Introduction and Conclusion

Even though the body of a persuasive speech takes a bit more time and thought to develop than that of other speeches, you must still create a strong introduction and conclusion. Make sure you allow yourself plenty of time by starting early on the persuasive speech.

Launch Your Speech

Keep your introduction stimulating, poignant, and fascinating. Megan uses a narrative, from a student who abused ADHD drugs, to grab her audience's attention and to appeal to pathos (the fear of what the drugs can do).

An introduction for a persuasive speech should focus your audience's attention on what you intend to claim about your topic. Megan cites statistics to logically demonstrate relevance to the audience. She then previews the proposition and main points of her speech.

Your audience will tend to wander off subject if you let them. So don't take too long to get to your point.

Your Speech's Finale

The persuasive speech's conclusion should leave your audience knowing your viewpoint and give them one more push to accept it or be influenced by it. Keep your specific purpose in mind as you construct the conclusion. In the example on the next page, notice how Megan specifies a response, summarizes, and "WOWs" her audience one last time.

See the Tip box for how long your introduction and conclusion should be.

See Chapter 11 for more on introductions and conclusions.

TIP: Length
- Your introduction should be less than 15 percent of your total speech time.
- Your conclusion should be less than 5 percent of your total speech time.

INTRODUCTION

This should be an exciting moment in your speech.

ATTENTION-GETTER: "My use of Adderall as a study aid, 20 mg every so often, quickly escalated into 100 mg+ daily doses within 6 months of meeting a student who'd sell me his entire script for $60 each month. Amphetamine tolerance builds very quickly, and soon I wasn't able to obtain the energy and focus for which I came to depend upon amphetamines. I finally got help for my addiction, but I had to take time off of school to heal the damage I'd done to my brain chemistry." –Female student, 20, Pittsburgh (Schwarz)

State why you should give this speech.

CREDIBILITY MATERIAL: Recently, in my psychology class, we conducted research related to college students' use of ADHD drugs (such as Adderall, Vyvanse, Concerta, Focalin, and Ritalin). I was shocked to learn how prevalent this usage is nationwide and even on our campus.

Give them a reason to listen.

RELEVANCE TO AUDIENCE: Citing a study conducted by researchers at the University of Kentucky, Aaron Cooper, in the September 2011 article "College Students Take ADHD Drugs for Better Grades," reports that these drugs are more abused than marijuana. Thirty percent of students at UK have reported use. A survey conducted at our three local campuses suggests we are no different. Odds are six of you are using some type of study drug this semester.

Give them a road map to your speech.

PREVIEW OF SPEECH: We can't ignore this problem any longer. Today, I would like to persuade you not to use ADHD medications as study drugs. The use of ADHD drugs for nonprescription purposes is dangerous, illegal, and not a good solution for your study needs.

CONCLUSION

AUDIENCE RESPONSE STATEMENT: Clearly, the decision to work a little harder to achieve one's goals and to be smart about it is far better than succumbing to the usage of nonprescribed drugs. I urge you all to opt for alternative solutions to cope with the stress of school and outside activities. These options are simple, safe, and legal. These options are what the successful students take—not a drug.

What do you want them to do with that information?

What should your audience remember?

SUMMARY STATEMENT: Using ADHD drugs as nonprescribed study drugs is dangerous, even life threatening. Using ADHD drugs as non-prescribed study drugs is illegal, with potential fines and prison time, and may influence what you can do with your future. It is a felony!

Dazzle them one more time.

WOW STATEMENT: Make smarter choices to be a better student by preparing each day. As an African proverb states, "For tomorrow belongs to the people who are prepared for it today" ("Future").

Preparation Outline for a Persuasive Speech

Megan Kramer   COMM 110
12 March 2013   Dr. Dailey

Topic: Illegal use of study drugs

Specific purpose: To persuade my younger classmates that taking ADHD drugs without a prescription is unsafe.

Central idea: The use of ADHD drugs for nonprescription purposes is dangerous, illegal, and not a good study-aid solution.

INTRODUCTION

Attention-getter: "My use of Adderall as a study aid, 20 mg every so often, quickly escalated into 100 mg+ daily doses within 6 months of meeting a student who'd sell me his entire script for $60 each month. Amphetamine tolerance builds very quickly, and soon I wasn't able to obtain the energy and focus for which I came to depend upon amphetamines. I finally got help for my addiction, but I had to take time off of school to heal the damage I'd done to my brain chemistry." –Female student, 20, Pittsburgh (Schwarz)

Megan uses a student's personal narrative to appeal to the audience's pathos.

Credibility material: Recently, in my psychology class, we conducted research related to college students' use of ADHD drugs (such as Adderall, Vyvanse, Concerta, Focalin, and Ritalin). I was shocked to learn how prevalent this usage is nationwide and even on our campus.

Relevance to audience: Citing a study conducted by researchers at the University of Kentucky, Aaron Cooper, in the September 2011 article "College Students Take ADHD Drugs for Better Grades," reports that these drugs are more abused than marijuana. Thirty percent of students at UK have reported use. A survey conducted at our three local campuses suggests we are no different. Odds are six of you are using some type of study drug this semester.

She starts with general national statistics and then narrows the scope to highlight the relevance to this particular audience.

Preview of speech: We can't ignore this problem any longer. Today, I would like to persuade you not to use ADHD medications as study drugs. The use of ADHD drugs for nonprescription purposes is dangerous, illegal, and not a good solution for your study needs.

(**Link:** First, let's explore the problem with taking these drugs without a prescription.)

BODY

I. Taking nonprescribed ADHD drugs is dangerous. ◄

> Megan uses a series of specific facts and other information to inductively support her claim at the end of this main point.

    A. This chart from the June 9, 2009, *New York Times* denotes that the common ADHD drugs used as illegal study drugs are either amphetamines or methylphenidates.

        1. Adderall and Vyvanse are amphetamines.

        2. Concerta, Focalin, and Ritalin are methylphenidates.

        3. Both classifications of drugs are powerful central nervous system stimulants.

    B. Their intended use is to treat attention deficit hyperactivity disorder (ADHD).

        1. According to the National Institute of Mental Health, ◄ ADHD is a common childhood disorder that can continue through adulthood.

> When possible, she uses material from highly credible sources.

        2. The specific cause is unknown.

        3. Symptoms of ADHD are difficulty staying focused and paying attention, difficulty controlling behavior, and hyperactivity.

    C. Each of these drugs has potentially harmful side effects noted by the manufacturers.

        1. After researching each drug on Drugs.com or LIVESTRONG.com, I discovered that each can have similar side effects (show list).

            a. Serious side effects across many of these drugs include seizures, fast or uneven heart rate, blurred vision, unusual behavior, twitching or tics, and extreme high blood pressure.

After discussing all ADHD drugs used as study drugs, Megan then focuses in on the drugs most commonly used as study drugs.

b. Less serious side effects can be insomnia; loss of appetite; headaches; stomach and intestinal issues; feeling restless, anxious, or jittery; and extreme dry mouth.

2. Adderall and Ritalin tend to be the most common study drugs, so let's look at their side effects specifically.

a. Adderall has major serious and less serious side effects.

i. Adderall's known serious side effects are fast or uneven heartbeats; pain or burning when urinating; talking more than usual; feelings of extreme happiness or sadness; tremors, hallucinations, unusual behavior, or motor tics; and dangerously high blood pressure (Drugs.com "Adderall").

ii. Adderall's less serious side effects are insomnia; stomach pain, nausea, or vomiting; loss of appetite; vision problems, dizziness, or mild headache; sweating; mild skin rash; numbness, tingling, or cold hands or feet; and weight loss (Drugs.com "Adderall").

b. Ritalin has major serious and less serious side effects as well.

i. Ritalin's known serious side effects are fast or uneven heartbeats; feeling like you might pass out; fever, sore throat, and headache, with a severe blistering, peeling, and red skin rash; aggression; restlessness; hallucinations, unusual behavior, or motor tics; and dangerously high blood pressure (Drugs.com "Ritalin").

ii. Ritalin's less serious side effects are stomach pain, nausea, or vomiting; loss of appetite; vision problems, dizziness, or mild headache; sweating; mild skin rash; numbness, tingling, or cold hands or feet; insomnia; and weight loss (Drugs.com "Ritalin").

Note how Megan uses proper outline symbols and only one sentence per outline point.

3. Without a doctor determining if you should take these drugs or monitoring your health as you do, you are taking your life into your own hands.

   a. Quoting the Substance Abuse & Mental Health Services Administration in her Feb. 10, 2013, article, Morris notes that "emergency room visits tied to use of an ADHD stimulant rose from 13,379 in 2005 to 31,244 just five years later."

   b. "The portion of those visits caused by non-prescribed use of the stimulants rose to half."

4. Our lackadaisical view on the nonprescribed use of these drugs begins early.

   a. Morris states that a survey conducted by the Partnership for a Drug-Free America discovered that "40 percent of teens think prescription drugs are 'much safer' to use than illegal drugs."

   b. "29 percent think prescription drugs are not addictive."

5. Because of these dangerous side effects, each drug requires a prescription.

6. The bottom line: Taking ADHD drugs without a prescription and supervision of a doctor is downright dangerous.

(**Link**: Now, let's consider the legal problems with taking these drugs without a prescription, as well as the practice of selling them.)

II.   Taking nonprescribed ADHD drugs is illegal.

   A. According to NOLO.com, March 2013, a site dedicated to helping consumers and small business with everyday legal questions, the legality of a drug is inherently tied to its use and who has the right to use it.

Here, Megan appeals to logic with current facts. Note that she uses quotation marks when directly quoting from the article.

Megan unequivocally states her first claim.

B. A prescription drug being used by someone without a prescription in the state of Missouri is considered the illegal possession of a controlled dangerous substance (CDS), as stated on CriminalDefenseLawyer.com, March 2013. ◄

When citing her source, Megan includes the date to demonstrate currency.

　　1. "It is a class C felony in our state to possess CDS without a valid medical prescription" (Steiner "Possession").

　　2. "Penalties for possession include a fine of up to $5000; and either up to a year in jail, or at the sentencing judge's discretion, at least two (and up to seven) years in prison" (Steiner "Possession").

C. Selling or distributing a CDS is a serious offense that can vary depending on the substance, amount, and if crossing state lines.

　　1. Illegal CDS sale or possession with intent to sell, in this case as a study drug, "is a class B felony."

　　2. In this case, a class B felony is "punishable with at least five (and up to 15) years in prison" (Steiner "Missouri Sale").

D. The course of your future can change; possessing or selling ADHD drugs as illegal study drugs is a felony, which, if you are convicted of, can keep you from pursuing your career choice.

(**Link**: Even though it may seem safe because "everyone does it," taking ADHD drugs is dangerous and not legal. Now that we have outlined the problem, let's look for better solutions.)

When creating this main point, Megan wrote it to signal the problem–solution organizational strategy and to alert the audience to where she is in the strategy.

III. All students experience pressure and stress, but taking nonprescribed ADHD drugs is not the solution.

A. When asked, students give numerous reasons for taking illegal study drugs.

　　1. Their parents have high expectations.

　　2. They commit to too much.

　　3. Getting into and staying in college is harder than ever.

4. They don't have the skills necessary to cope with stress.

5. Their peers pressure them to take the drugs, so they have more time to play. (Cooper, Morris, Schwarz, "Study Drugs")

B. The solution is better overall habits.

1. Dr. Crawford, the director of our student counseling service, offered this advice. ←

   Megan knew many of the students trust and admire the director of the campus counseling service. So, she interviewed her for the speech.

   a. Don't procrastinate and wait until the last minute to start that big project or study for a test.

   b. Don't take on more than you can manage.

   c. Be smart with your time.

      i. Do the homework first and use an outing with friends as a reward.

      ii. Use a calendar to help you manage your time and to break down large projects or study sessions into chunks.

      iii. Make exercise part of your routine.

      iv. Get enough sleep and make the time as routine as possible.

      v. Seek professional help from the counseling service to help you manage your time and deal with your anxieties.

2. StudentHacks.org, a site dedicated to productivity tips to help students study smarter, offers these suggestions.

   a. Eat frequent, small meals instead of large ones or starving yourself.

   b. Study when you're at your sharpest.

      i. Listen to your body clock, not to everyone else, about when you should study.

      ii. The morning is often the best time.

   c. Drink water often and caffeine only in moderation.

d. Prepare your study site for comfort and with only the things you need.

e. Take a short break every hour.

   i. Set a time—it is important to take the break before you realize you are tired.

   ii. Stretch during the break.

   iii. Study at the same time and place, which is dedicated to only studying.

(**Link:** Clearly, the decision to work a little harder to achieve one's goals and to be smart about it is far better than succumbing to the usage of nonprescribed drugs.)

CONCLUSION

Audience response statement: Clearly, the decision to work a little harder to achieve one's goals and to be smart about it is far better than succumbing to the usage of nonprescribed drugs. I urge you all to opt for alternative solutions to cope with the stress of school and outside activities. These options are simple, safe, and legal. These options are what the successful students take—not a drug.

Summary statement: Using ADHD drugs as nonprescribed study drugs is dangerous, even life threatening. Using ADHD drugs as nonprescribed study drugs is illegal, with potential fines and prison time, and may influence what you can do with your future. It is a felony!

WOW statement: Make smarter choices to be a better student by preparing each day. As an African proverb states, "For tomorrow belongs to the people who are prepared for it today" ("Future").

Megan uses repetition and parallelism stylistically here to highlight her language. She ends the summary with a pathos appeal to fear of what the drugs can do. This mirrors her introduction.

Works Cited

"Adderall." *Drugs.com: Drug Information Online.* Drugs.com, 2013. Web. 10 Mar. 2013.

"Concerta Side Effects." *LIVESTRONG.com.* LIVESTRONG Foundation, 9 Dec. 2009. Web. 10 Mar. 2013.

Cooper, Aaron. "College Students Take ADHD Drugs for Better Grades." *CNN.* Cable News Network, 11 Sept. 2011. Web. 6 Mar. 2013.

Crawford, Julie. Personal interview. 3 Mar. 2013.

"Drug Laws and Drug Crimes." *NOLO: Law for All.* NOLO, 2013. Web. 10 Mar. 2013.

"Focalin." *Drugs.com: Drug Information Online.* Drugs.com, 2013. Web. 10 Mar. 2013.

"Future" *ThinkExist.com.* ThinkExist, 2013. Web. 10 Mar. 2013.

"How to Study Effectively—8 Concentration Strategies." *StudentHacks.org.* StudentHacks.org, 2007. Web. 10 Mar. 2013.

Morris, Caitlin. "More College Students Abusing ADHD Drugs." *Troy Record.com.* Troy Record, 10 Feb. 2013. Web. 6 Mar. 2013.

National Institute of Mental Health (NIMH). *Attention Deficit Hyperactivity Disorder (ADHD).* NIH Publication No. 08-3572. Bethesda, MD: NIMH, 2008. Print.

"Ritalin." *Drugs.com: Drug Information Online.* Drugs.com, 2013. Web. 10 Mar. 2013.

Rose, Gianna. "Vyvanse Negative Side Effects." *LIVESTRONG.com.* LIVESTRONG Foundation, 31 Mar. 2011. Web. 10 Mar. 2013.

Schwarz, Alan. "In Their Own Words: 'Study Drugs.'" *New York Times.* New York Times, 9 June 2012. Web. 6 Mar. 2013.

Steiner, Monica. "Missouri Sale of a Controlled Substance Laws." *CriminalDefenseLawyer.com.* NOLO, 2013, Web. 10 Mar. 2013.

---. "Possession of a Controlled Substance in Missouri." *CriminalDefenseLawyer.com.* NOLO, 2013, Web. 10 Mar. 2013.

"'Study Drugs' Popular Among High School Students." *New York Times.* New York Times, 9 June 2012. Web, graphic. 6 Mar. 2013.

Megan's instructor requires MLA citation style. On her source page, Megan follows the proper MLA style for each citation and for the overall format of the page. She uses hanging indents, alphabetizes the entries, double-spaces, and makes sure each entry is correct.

Even though Megan's class assignment required a minimum of only three sources, she used many more to effectively persuade her audience.

14.8 How Do You Present or Evaluate a Persuasive Speech?

Now it's time to put your persuasive speech on its feet, by carefully choosing your language, polishing your delivery, and, if appropriate, preparing and practicing with presentation aids.

Put Your Speech on Its Feet

Effective language is a must if you intend to persuade. Emotive and stylistic language helps your audience follow your arguments, remember them, and be emotionally moved. Think about how your use of transitions such as *therefore* and *as a result of* might clearly signal the bridge between two steps in an argument, or how you can use language ethically to stir the emotions of your audience.

| **Chapters 3 and 12** cover language usage.

Practice your speech from the preparation outline the first few times, then use a delivery outline. Your delivery should be powerful, direct, and enthusiastic, to suggest a high level of confidence and trust. Rehearse your speech until you can get through it several times without major errors or glitches. Presentation aids are often necessary for a persuasive speech, to help your audience understand facts and figures or to follow the logic of an argument. Keep in mind that aids should support your speech and not be added on just because you can make them. Megan, in her study-drug speech, will use slides with tables, quotations, and photos.

| **See Chapter 12** for more on delivery and presentation aids for your speech.

Evaluate the Speech

Evaluate the Message

Evaluate the message for clarity, accuracy, and overall organization.

- Is the topic persuasive?
- Is the speech designed to speak to a particular target audience?
- Is the evidence effective and appropriate?
- Are the sources credible and current?
- Is the information presented believable? If not, did the speaker attempt to help the audience view it as believable?

A persuasive speech should never lose sight of its central idea, its proposition, its target audience, and what it is trying to change or reinforce in the audience. For example, Megan outlined the problem and argued for a preferred solution. On the Internet, Megan had located a *New York Times* article that included student interviews telling how ADHD drugs had influenced their lives, as well as persuasive legal material related to her state. The use of this support material allowed Megan to focus her message for her target audience (younger adult students in her state).

See the checklist on page 433 for a detailed evaluation format, or follow your instructor's guidelines.

Evaluate for Fallacies

One of the main ways a persuasive speech differs from other speeches is the reliance on effective arguments within the speech. When a speaker creates an argument, she or he can unintentionally or intentionally create a faulty argument or error in logic known as a ***fallacy***. Fallacies occur when you use evidence incorrectly or your interpretation of the evidence is incorrect. Whether you are the speaker or an audience member, you need to be able to recognize when an argument falls apart or does not make sense, making it a bad argument.

There are numerous fallacies, but the table on the following page explains some of the most common. For detailed discussions of these and additional fallacies, you can seek out books such as *Classical Rhetoric for the Modern Student* by Edward Corbett and Robert Connors and *An Introduction to Reasoning* by Stephen Toulmin, Richard Rieke, and Allan Janik.[8] You can also locate more types and descriptions online by searching the term "fallacies."

See the next page for a list of several common fallacies.

Practicing Ethics: Critical Thinking

As a member of a democratic society, you must be willing to ask the hard questions to ensure your safety and the safety of others: Is this true? Who stands to gain? Are these sources unbiased?

Fallacy	What Is It?	Example	How Can You Avoid It?
Non sequitur	Not connecting an argument's conclusion to the premises	If you do not buy this for me, you do not love me.	Be sure every step of your argument leads to the next and connects to the claim.
Hasty generalization	Drawing a general conclusion without sufficient support materials	Two of my friends bought that album and hated it. That band is horrible.	Use a significant number of current and quality cases to argue from the specific to the general.
Faulty use of authority	Using information or testimony from someone who is not a legitimate authority on the subject	My roommate agrees that the tuition increase is too high.	Make sure the person is a recognized expert related to the topic.
Post hoc ergo propter hoc	Assuming that because one event comes after another, the first event caused the second	Last month, the city council passed an ordinance banning smoking in public places. The ordinance caused two pubs to go bankrupt.	Verify with valid support materials that one event causes the other.
Ad hominem	Attacking the person instead of challenging the argument	Who are you to question my decision? You didn't finish school.	Focus your argument on the issues being discussed and not the people discussing them.
Appeal to tradition	Assuming something is best or correct because it is traditional	My grandfather bought a Ford, my father bought a Ford, so Ford must be best.	Base your claims on solid evidence and use tradition only to supplement that evidence.
Ad populum	Arguing a claim is accurate because many people believe it or do it	Most people in St. Louis voted for candidate A; the state of Missouri must be for candidate A.	Use popular opinion only to supplement other forms of evidence.
Slippery slope	Arguing that a small event sets off a chain reaction to disaster	If you drop out of school, you will take drugs, become a alcoholic, and end up in jail.	Always consider the middle ground as a potential end result, and do not be overly dramatic.

Evaluate the Presentation

Successful delivery techniques rarely draw attention to themselves, but they help the audience stay interested in the speech while the speaker (you or another) builds ethos. Persuading an audience is difficult and will not happen if the speaker does not effectively use voice, gestures, and enthusiasm, or use an appropriate delivery style or presentation aids. If Megan's enthusiasm is low, or she doesn't make good eye contact, or she is too lighthearted or insincere, she will not convince those audience members who don't view taking study drugs as a problem. She needs to use a delivery style that supports the urgency and seriousness of the topic.

CHECKLIST FOR EVALUATING THE PERSUASIVE SPEECH

TOPIC
- [ ] Speech accomplished purpose to persuade
- [ ] Topic appropriate to speaker, audience, and occasion
- [ ] Interesting topic

INTRODUCTION
- [ ] Gained attention and interest
- [ ] Established credibility
- [ ] Indicated relevance to audience
- [ ] Declared central idea
- [ ] Previewed speech

BODY
- [ ] Main points clear and obvious to the audience
- [ ] Points follow an appropriate organizational strategy
- [ ] Main points appropriately researched and supported
- [ ] Used effective proofs/arguments
- [ ] Main points supported with appropriate presentation aids when necessary
- [ ] Oral citations included throughout speech
- [ ] Linked parts of speech

CONCLUSION
- [ ] Contained a summary statement
- [ ] Offered an audience response statement
- [ ] Effectively comes to closure (WOW statement)

PRESENTATION
- [ ] Language was clear, concise, and appropriate
- [ ] Gestures/body movements were effective
- [ ] Consistent and effective eye contact
- [ ] Used vocal variety/emphasis/volume/rate
- [ ] Used appropriate delivery style
- [ ] Spoke with enthusiasm
- [ ] Spoke with conviction and sincerity
- [ ] Good use of delivery outline
- [ ] Presentation aids appropriate to speech topic (if applicable)
- [ ] Used presentation aids throughout entire speech (if applicable)
- [ ] Used professional presentation aids (if applicable)
- [ ] Speech met time requirements

Chapter 14 Review

Key Questions

14.1 What Is Persuasive Speaking?

Objective 14.1: **DEFINE PERSUASIVE SPEAKING**

Persuasion is a deliberate attempt to create, reinforce, or change someone's attitudes, beliefs, values, and/or behaviors. When you create a formal speech with the general purpose to persuade, you are engaging in persuasive speaking. Persuasive speaking should focus listeners' options, seek a response, and support a proposition of fact, value, or policy.

See pages 396–397.

14.2 What Is the Creative Process for Persuasive Speaking?

Objective 14.2: **EXPLAIN THE CREATIVE PROCESS FOR PERSUASIVE SPEAKING**

Persuasive speaking follows the general speech creative process—developing, creating, presenting, and listening/evaluating. Knowing where your audience stands on an issue, locating effective persuasive material, and putting together a strong argument are paramount when persuading.

See pages 398–399.

14.3 What Are the Appeals You Can Use to Persuade?

Objective 14.3: **EXPLAIN THE APPEALS YOU CAN USE TO PERSUADE**

Appeals (also called proofs) are the means by which you prove or establish the argument you are making. First discussed by Aristotle in the fourth century BCE, pathos, ethos, logos, and mythos are considered the traditional appeals by most scholars today. Modern speakers can use other types of appeals grounded less in the logical and more in the psychological, such as need, harmony, gain, and commitment.

See pages 400–403.

14.4 What Are the Parts of An Argument?

Objective 14.4: **DISCUSS THE PARTS OF AN ARGUMENT**

An argument has three main parts: a claim, evidence, and warrants.

- The *claim* of an argument is the assertion you are making and will be a claim of fact, value, or policy.
- The support materials you have gathered become *evidence*, or the information that proves your claim.
- The *warrants* are assumptions that act as links between the evidence and the claim. Warrants are authorative, motivational, or substantive.

See pages 404–405.

14.5 What Are the Different Types of Arguments?

Objective 14.5: **EXPLAIN THE DIFFERENT TYPES OF ARGUMENTS**

The types of arguments are:

- *Argument by deduction*, or a series of general statements that together prove the claim
- *Argument by induction*, or a series of specific cases that lead to a general statement that something is likely
- *Argument by analogy*, or concluding something will be accurate for one case if it is true for another similar case
- *Argument by cause*, or demonstrating how one event or factor causes another
- *Argument by authority*, or supporting a claim via the ethos of testimony offered by others who are regarded as highly credible.

See pages 406–409.

14.6 How Do You Develop and Research a Persuasive Topic?

Objective 14.6: **EXPLAIN HOW TO DEVELOP AND RESEARCH A PERSUASIVE TOPIC**

- Get to know the audience and situation.
- Create a persuasive idea bank.
- Select and narrow your persuasive topic.
- Confirm the best type of persuasive speech.
- Identify your specific purpose.
- Identify your central idea.
- Create a working outline.
- Conduct your research.

See pages 410–415.

14.7 How Do You Outline and Organize a Persuasive Speech?

Objective 14.7: **DISCUSS HOW TO OUTLINE AND ORGANIZE A PERSUASIVE SPEECH**

- Start with basic, effective outlining.
- Commit to an appropriate persuasive strategy.
- Construct main points.
- Organize support materials. Decide which appeals to use, which types of arguments best fit your speech, and how to arrange the arguments.
- Compose your introduction and conclusion.

See pages 416–429.

14.8 How Do You Present or Evaluate a Persuasive Speech?

Objective 14.8: **EXPLORE HOW TO PRESENT OR EVALUATE A PERSUASIVE SPEECH**

- Put your speech on its feet. Language, delivery, and presentation aids (if any) should be crafted based on how they can help an audience change their attitudes, values, beliefs, and/or behaviors.
- Evaluate the speech. Evaluate the message for how clearly and accurately it persuades. Watch for fallacies or faulty arguments. Evaluate the presentation for techniques that inspire an audience to listen.

See pages 430–433.

Key Terms

persuasion (396)
persuasive speaking (396)
coercion (396)
speech to convince (396)
speech to stimulate (396)
speech to actuate (396)
proposition of fact (397)
proposition of value (397)
proposition of policy (397)
appeals (400)
pathos (400)
ethos (401)
mythos (401)
logos (401)
reasoning (401)
cognitive dissonance theory (402)
expectancy-outcome values theory (403)
elaboration likelihood model (ELM) (403)
central processing (403)
peripheral processing (403)
argument (404)
claim (404)
evidence (404)
warrants (405)
argument by deduction (406)
syllogism (406)
argument by induction (408)
argument by analogy (409)
argument by cause (409)
argument by authority (409)
target audience (410)
fallacy (431)
non sequitur (432)
hasty generalization (432)
faulty use of authority (432)
post hoc ergo propter hoc (432)
ad hominem (432)
appeal to tradition (432)
ad populum (432)
slippery slope (432)

Improve Your Communication

What kinds of topics are persuasive?

For a topic to be persuasive, it must be debatable. In other words, it must be something that people can reasonably have differing opinions on. A debatable topic has more than one side to it (such as the abortion issue). It is not something generally agreed on or accepted as fact by most people (for instance, traditional cars produce carbon dioxide). It is best to select a topic you can be passionate about or interested in. Here are a few examples to help you start brainstorming:

- Are hybrid vehicles better than nonhybrids?
- Should states implement voter ID requirements?
- Should all citizens be required to participate in community service?
- Can we reverse the effects of global warming?
- Should all students face mandatory drug testing?
- Is the No Child Left Behind Act working?
- Are 12-hour shifts for nurses safe?
- How should the United States prevent illegal immigration?
- Is the death penalty effective?
- Is homeschooling better than public schooling?
- Is online education effective?
- Are cell phones dangerous?
- Should the United States institute bilingual education?
- Should all employers offer birth control through health insurance?

What should you do if your audience resists your claim?

Trying to convince your audience to make big changes or serious moral decisions is difficult at best. It might be better to ask them to take a small step toward a big change rather than a momentous one. For example, asking your audience to walk to work once a week might be more successful than persuading them to give up their cars. Speeches arguing for abortion rights in cases of rape or incest might work better than those arguing for pro-choice views in general. If the audience verbally resists, stay calm, relaxed, and resolute; consider their points of view; and ask them simply to allow you to present your point of view. Keep in mind that they have a right to disagree with you.

Apply Your Knowledge

1. What is the difference between speeches to convince, to stimulate, or to actuate? Give an example of each.

2. Give an example of a speech using one of the strategies best suited for persuasion—problem–solution, comparative, Monroe's motivated sequence, and causal.

3. Other than those in your text, find examples for five of the fallacies.

Other Resources

Persuasive Topics

- www.ereadingworksheets.com/writing/persuasive-essay-topics

Tips on Persuasive Speaking

Weston, Anthony. *A Rulebook for Arguments*. Indianapolis: Hackett, 2009. Print.

Heinrichs, Jay. *Thank You for Arguing: What Aristotle, Lincoln, and Homer Simpson Can Teach Us about the Art of Persuasion*. New York: Three Rivers, 2013. Print.

- blog.ted.com/2012/10/31/how-to-give-more-persuasive-presentations-a-qa-with-nancy-duarte

Glossary

accommodation A conflict management strategy that occurs when one person cooperates at the highest level and lets others have their way in relationship to the conflict. (Chapter 7)

adaptors Gestures that satisfy a personal need and are often learned early in life. (Chapter 4)

ad hominem The fallacy of attacking the person instead of challenging the argument. (Chapter 14)

ad populum The fallacy of arguing that a claim is accurate because many people believe it or do it. (Chapter 14)

affect display Gestures that communicate emotion. (Chapter 4)

affection exchange theory A theory suggesting that people's use of affectionate behavior (hugging, kissing, holding hands, and listening) contributes to their survival and promotes bonding with those they consider potential intimate partners. (Chapter 5)

affective conflict A type of conflict that involves interpersonal disagreement prejudices, antagonism, emotional tensions, trust or respect issues, attitudes, personality or power clashes, and other interpersonal struggles unrelated to a task or procedure. (Chapter 7)

affective style The communication style that tends to be more process-oriented. (Chapter 3)

all-channel networks Group communication arrangements in which communication is open between and among all members. (Chapter 8)

ambushing Listening carefully for the purpose of attacking the other person. (Chapter 5)

analogy The way of using support material to help explain through comparing and contrasting. (Chapter 11)

appeals The means by which you prove or establish the argument you are making in a persuasive argument. (Chapter 14)

appeal to tradition The fallacy of assuming something is best or correct because it is traditional. (Chapter 14)

appreciative listening Listening for recreation or enjoyment. (Chapter 5)

arbitrary The principle that the relationship between a word and what it stands for is random, subjective, or coincidental. (Chapter 3)

arbitration The conflict resolution process of having a third party make a decision that the disagreeing sides must adhere to. (Chapter 7)

argument A reason or a series of reasons a person gives to support an assertion in a persuasive speech. (Chapter 14)

argument by analogy Reasoning that something will be accurate for one case if it is true for another similar one. (Chapter 14)

argument by authority Reasoning that locates its power in the ethos of the testimony of others to support a claim. (Chapter 14)

argument by cause Reasoning that attempts to demonstrate a relationship between two events or factors in which one of the events or factors causes the other. (Chapter 14)

argument by deduction Reasoning that constructs a series of general statements (known as premises) that together prove correct the claim/conclusion. (Chapter 14)

argument by induction Reasoning that argues from specific cases to a general statement suggesting something is likely based on the specific cases. (Chapter 14)

articulation How completely and clearly a person utters a word. (Chapter 4)

asynchronous engagements Individual interactions occurring with a time delay or not in real time. (Chapter 2)

attending The phase of the listening process when a person pays attention to a given sound or equivalent stimulus. (Chapter 5)

attitudes Learned persistent psychological responses, predispositions, or inclinations to act one way or feel a particular way toward something. (Chapter 10)

attraction theory A theory suggesting that a person forms relationships on the basis of interpersonal attraction or that one person is drawn to another for particular reasons. (Chapter 6)

attractiveness Nonverbal cues related to looks and personality, as perceived by others. (Chapter 4)

attribution How a person explains the cause of her or his own behavior or others' behavior. (Chapter 2)

audience analysis A systematic investigation of unique audience characteristics such as attitudes, beliefs, and values. (Chapter 10)

audience centered Speeches created and delivered while identifying and considering the unique characteristics and viewpoints of their audiences. (Chapter 10)

audio clips Recordings of sound only, used as presentation aids in a speech. (Chapter 12)

authoritarian leaders A leader who assumes and maintains control over the group. (Chapter 8)

authority rule A decision-making result where decisions are made by a designated leader or person who has power over the situation. (Chapter 9)

avoidance A conflict management strategy that occurs when one person simply avoids the issue and doesn't pursue any resolution, or an "I lose–You lose" tactic. (Chapter 7)

avoiding The stage of relationship deterioration in which a person starts to physically and emotionally avoid the other person. (Chapter 6)

background A communicator's identity and life experiences. (Chapter 1)

bar graphs Visuals consisting of vertical or horizontal bars that represent sets of data. (Chapter 12)

beliefs Those things a person accepts as plausible based on interpretation and judgment, such as believing in a religion or philosophy. (Chapter 10)

belongingness theory A theory stating that humans have a strong fundamental motivation (not a want) for closeness and social belongingness. (Chapter 6)

biased attributions The errors people make when they evaluate others or their behaviors. (Chapter 7)

blatant plagiarism Plagiarism that occurs when either speakers take an entire speech or document and present it as their own or when a speaker takes parts of information from other sources and links the parts together, creating an entire speech out of someone else's words. (Chapter 10)

body-to-body communication A type of communication that occurs when the individuals participating in the interaction are co-present (physically in the same space), stressing the use of the entire body as a channel for sending a message. (Chapter 1)

bonding The stage of relationship development in which people often enter into a public ritual such as announcing commitments or engagements, getting married or holding commitment ceremonies, having children, creating business partnerships, and even, as friends, getting the same tattoo or sharing living space. (Chapter 6)

brainstorming The process of creative thinking that jumps from one word or concept to another to generate a lot of ideas. (Chapters 9, 10)

brainwriting A form of brainstorming that replaces the calling out of ideas with the private recording of an individual's ideas and adds cross-fertilization back into the process. (Chapter 9)

causal strategy An organizational strategy used when public speakers want their audience to understand the cause and effect or consequences of something. (Chapter 11)

central idea The concise, single sentence summarizing and/or previewing what a speaker will say during a speech; also called a thesis statement. (Chapter 10)

central processing Being motivated to listen and think critically about a message. (Chapter 14)

chain networks Group communication arrangements in which members interact with the person above and below them in rank. (Chapter 8)

channel The pathway or conduit for getting the message across to the receiver. (Chapter 1)

charts Visual summaries of complex or large quantities of information. (Chapter 12)

chronemics The study of how people use, structure, perceive, react to, and interpret time. (Chapter 4)

chronological strategy An organizational strategy used when a person needs to move through steps in a process or develop a timeline when arranging a speech. (Chapter 11)

circumscribing The stage of relationship deterioration in which communication becomes more superficial as the people in the relationship pull apart. (Chapter 6)

claim The assertion made in an argument. (Chapter 14)

clichés Overused words or phrases that have lost their effect. (Chapter 3)

co-cultures Diverse smaller groups within a culture, distinguished by such factors as age, gender, sexual orientation, race, mental or physical abilities, religion, political affiliation, education, occupation, economic status, and other group affiliations or activities, that often have beliefs, values, attitudes, norms, language, and behaviors different from the larger culture. (Chapter 1)

coercion Forcing somebody, via threats or intimidation, to do something against his or her will. (Chapter 14)

cognitive dissonance The discomfort one feels from experiencing conflicting beliefs, ideas, values, or emotions. (Chapter 2)

cognitive dissonance theory Leon Festinger's theory emphasizing the human need to be in a harmonious state (consonant state) and that conflicting attitudes, values, beliefs, ideas, or behaviors can cause an inharmonious feeling (dissonant state). (Chapter 14)

cohesion The state of joining and working together as a unit, coupled with the wish to remain part of the unit. (Chapter 8)

collaboration An assertive conflict management strategy that focuses on discovering the most mutually acceptable solution, or an "I win a little–You win a little" solution. (Chapter 7)

collective identity A shared sense that each individual belongs to the group and is responsible for the group goal. (Chapter 8)

common ground The overlap within the communicators' identities and life experiences. (Chapter 1)

communication The intentional or unintentional process of using verbal and nonverbal interaction to share information and construct meaning. (Chapter 1)

communication apprehension Fears and anxiety a person may have when engaging in communicative interactions with one or more other persons. (Chapter 1)

communicators Individuals equally responsible for creating meaning through simultaneous messages. (Chapter 1)

comparative strategy An organizational strategy that uses the practice of compare and contrast to arrange a speech. (Chapter 11)

comparison Using support material to point out similarities between two or more ideas, things, factors, or issues. (Chapter 11)

competition A conflict management strategy that uses the outcome tactic of "I win–You lose" and occurs when one person is very assertive about achieving his or her goal without the help of others or their perspectives. (Chapter 7)

compromise A conflict management strategy that focuses on discovering the most mutually acceptable solution, or an "I win a little–You win a little" solution. (Chapter 7)

confirmation bias The tendency to screen, notice, search for, interpret, and/or remember perceptions based on what you believe; this bias can significantly influence perception. (Chapter 2)

confirming messages Verbal and nonverbal messages that communicate empathy, worth, regard, and respect for each other. (Chapter 6)

conflict An expressed struggle between at least two interdependent parties who perceive incompatible goals, scarce resources, and interference from others in achieving their goals. (Chapter 7)

conflict management The process of managing and limiting the negative effects of conflict while capitalizing on its positive aspects. (Chapter 7)

conflict situation A situation in which at least two people appear to be at an impasse or in an incompatible state. (Chapter 7)

connotative meaning The emotional and personal reaction a person might have to a word. (Chapter 3)

consensus The entire group agrees or consents to a particular decision or solution. (Chapter 9)

contempt Negative communication that attacks or tears down the partner's self-worth with the intention of insulting or psychologically abusing her/him; one of Gottman's Four Horsemen of the Apocalypse behaviors. (Chapter 7)

context The physical, relational, and psychological environments in which communication takes place. (Chapter 1)

contrast Using support material to point out differences between two or more ideas, things, factors, or issues. (Chapter 11)

conversation style How individuals uniquely exchange their thoughts, opinions, and feelings. (Chapter 3)

counterfeit questions Questions used to mask a message. (Chapter 5)

creativity The ability to "think outside the box" or to imagine new and original ideas, things, and solutions. (Chapter 9)

critical listening Listening carefully to a message in order to judge it as acceptable or not. (Chapter 5)

critical thinking The careful, deliberate determination of whether one should accept, reject, or suspend judgment about a claim and the degree of confidence with which one accepts or rejects it. (Chapter 5)

criticism Negative communication that attacks or complains about a relational partner's personality or character rather than his/her behavior that bothers the other partner; one of Gottman's Four Horsemen of the Apocalypse behaviors. (Chapter 7)

culture The system or learned patterns of beliefs, values, attitudes, norms, and behaviors shared by a large group of people and handed down from generation to generation. (Chapter 1)

deception The practice of deliberately making someone believe an untruth. (Chapter 2)

DECIDE model Thomas Harris and John Sherblom's approach to decision making and problem solving that has six steps: defining the goal, examining issues preventing success, considering the alternatives, initiating a decision, developing a plan, and evaluating the results. (Chapter 9)

decision making The process of deciding what to do or distinguishing between alternatives. (Chapter 9)

defensive listening A type of listening in which individuals take comments as critical or hostile attacks. (Chapter 5)

defensiveness Negative behavior that occurs when a person starts to see himself/herself as the victim and deny responsibility; one of Gottman's Four Horsemen of the Apocalypse behaviors. (Chapter 7)

democratic leaders Leaders who involve group members in decision-making and/or creative processes. (Chapter 8)

denotative meaning The commonly accepted meaning of a word within a culture or co-culture, often the meaning found in a dictionary. (Chapter 3)

designated leader A leader chosen by election or appointment when the group is formed. (Chapter 8)

design principles The arrangement and placement of various elements (color, text, line, images, space, etc.) in a visual presentation aid for optimum effect. (Chapter 12)

dialect The way a particular group of people pronounces and uses language. (Chapter 4)

differentiating The stage of relationship deterioration in which people begin to drift apart (increase interpersonal space) and view each other as individuals again. (Chapter 6)

direct style A conversation style in which the verbal message straightforwardly reveals the intent, need, want, and desire. (Chapter 3)

disconfirming messages Verbal and nonverbal messages that deny validation of the other person. (Chapter 6)

discrimination Unfair actions against or treatment of people one is prejudiced toward. (Chapter 2)

display rules Rules dictated by a social situation and the culture that tell people what they can or cannot, should or should not, and must or must not do in certain contexts. (Chapter 4)

dominating (or monopolizing) listening Listening for moments that allow a person to turn the focus back on himself/herself. (Chapter 5)

drawings Maps, sketches, diagrams, plans, or other nonphotographic representations of places, concepts, people, animals, or objects used as presentation aids in speeches. (Chapter 12)

elaborate style A communication style that stresses rich, expressive language. (Chapter 3)

elaboration likelihood model (ELM) A model arguing that people will process a message by one of two ways: central processing or peripheral processing. (Chapter 14)

emblems Gestures that are speech independent and culturally learned, with direct verbal translations. (Chapter 4)

emergent leader A group member who evolves as the leader during the early stages of the group's formation. (Chapter 8)

emotional intelligence A person's ability to recognize and manage his/her own emotions and others' emotions within relationships. (Chapter 6)

empathic listening Listening for the purpose of giving emotional support to another person. (Chapter 5)

enunciation The ability to use distinctiveness and clarity while saying linked whole words. (Chapter 4)

environmental barriers External noise or conditions within the speech location that interrupt the listener's ability to concentrate, such as movement, heat, cold, or hard seats. (Chapter 5)

equity theory A theory suggesting that relational partners must both feel that the rewards and costs of their relationship are balanced. (Chapter 6)

ethical communicator A person who sets and follows a high moral standard of norms, beliefs, behaviors, attitudes, values, and actions in all of his or her body-to-body or mediated interactions. (Chapter 1)

ethics A set of standards that guide a person to good and honorable behavior and help others see that person in a positive manner. (Chapter 1)

ethnicity Traits that stem from a person's national and religious affiliations. (Chapter 10)

ethnocentrism The assumption that an individual's own culture or co-cultural group is superior. (Chapter 1)

ethos Aristotle's appeal related to credibility and a speaker's character. (Chapter 14)

euphemisms Mild or indirect words or expressions substituted for harsher, more blunt ones, to make the meaning more palatable. (Chapter 3)

evidence The support materials or information proving a claim. (Chapter 14)

examples Specific instances or cases that embody or illustrate points in a person's speech. (Chapter 11)

expectancy-outcome values theory A theory suggesting that people will evaluate the cost, benefit, or value related to making a change in an attitude, value, belief, or behavior to decide if it is worthwhile or not. (Chapter 14)

expectancy violation theory A theory by Judee Burgoon that explains how unusual behavior will increase uncertainty and be regarded as positive or negative by those receiving the message. (Chapter 4)

experimenting The stage of relationship development in which people explore, look for common ground, and learn about each other. (Chapter 6)

expert opinion A decision-making result occurring when one member has superior knowledge about the issues and that person is given the power to make the decision. (Chapter 9)

expert testimony Testimony from a person the audience recognizes as an expert or specialist on a particular topic. (Chapter 11)

extemporaneous speaking A method of delivery in which a person plans out, rehearses, and delivers the speech from an outline consisting of key words, phrases, and delivery notes. (Chapter 12)

external noise Any barrier to effective listening that originates outside of the communication partners' body and minds. (Chapter 5)

facial expressions The use of facial muscles to convey internal thoughts or feelings. (Chapter 4)

facial primacy The tendency to give more communicative weight to the face than any other channel. (Chapter 4)

fallacy An unintentional or intentional faulty argument or error in logic. (Chapter 14)

faulty use of authority The fallacy of using information or testimony from someone who is not a legitimate authority on the subject. (Chapter 14)

feedback The verbal and nonverbal responses an individual has to another person's verbal or nonverbal message. (Chapter 1)

femininity A cultural construct that uses such qualifiers as nurturing, emotional, beautiful, gentle, sweet, timid, and submissive. (Chapter 6)

figurative analogy An analogy that compares and contrasts two essentially different things. (Chapter 11)

fillers Sounds, words, or phrases that serve no purpose, do not help communicators understand each other, and may become distracting. (Chapter 3)

flaming Hostile and insulting behavior during Internet interaction. (Chapter 7)

flowcharts Presentation aid charts that diagram step-by-step development through a procedure, relationship, or process. (Chapter 12)

formal networks Small group networks that form specific interaction patterns when a group has a defined identity and goal. (Chapter 8)

Four Horsemen of the Apocalypse The four negative partner-response behaviors (criticism, contempt, defensiveness, and stonewalling) noted by John Gottman that have the potential to set off a "cascade" of events leading to ending the relationship. (Chapter 7)

fundamental attribution error An error that occurs when an individual overestimates a person's disposition or personality as the cause of his or her behavior and underestimates external factors such as situation. (Chapter 2)

gatekeeper Someone in the group who has the power to control communication access between members and to regulate content and delivery of specific messages. (Chapter 8)

gender A social construction or classification of what it means to be female or male in a specific culture at a particular time. (Chapter 6)

gender identity Private perceptions or how individuals view themselves related to feminine and masculine traits. (Chapter 6)

general purpose The unrestricted aim of a person's speech, which can fall into three different categories: to inform, to persuade, and to accentuate a special occasion. (Chapter 10)

gestures The movements of a part of the body to communicate. (Chapter 4)

glass ceiling The transparent barrier in the workplace that allows professional women to look higher and see possibilities for advancements but prevents them from attaining higher positions. (Chapter 8)

graphs Visual representations of numerical information that demonstrate relationships or differences between two or more variables, used as presentation aids. (Chapter 12)

group interaction role Any member role that helps create and maintain a positive climate and interpersonal relationships. (Chapter 8)

group task role Any member role in which a person's behavior will assist the group with completing tasks and the group goal. (Chapter 8)

groupthink The willingness to conform to what the group thinks rather than engaging in critical decision making or thinking. (Chapter 8)

gunnysacking The behavior of storing up a complaint and bringing it up as a surprise during a disagreement, in order to provoke. (Chapter 7)

haptics The study of touch behavior. (Chapter 4)

hasty generalization The fallacy of drawing a general conclusion without sufficient supporting materials. (Chapter 14)

hearing The physiological process that happens when sound waves strike the eardrum and spark a chain reaction that ends with the brain registering the sound. (Chapter 5)

heterogeneous groups Groups with a membership that is diverse in culture and/or co-culture. (Chapter 9)

hidden agenda An undisclosed motive or objective that negatively influences the group goal or others' personal goals. (Chapter 8)

homogeneous groups Groups made up of like-minded members who are similar in culture and/or gender. (Chapter 9)

honorific style A communication style that emphasizes a person's status in life. (Chapter 3)

hybrid engagements Engagements that occur when part of the interaction is in real time and a subset is not. (Chapter 9)

hypothetical examples Examples based on potential outcomes of imagined scenarios that gain power from future possibilities. (Chapter 11)

idea bank A list of general words and phrases that could be speech topics. (Chapter 10)

identification Kenneth Burke's notion of the human need and willingness to understand as much as possible the feelings, thoughts, motives, interests, attitudes, values, behaviors, and lives of others. (Chapter 2)

identity Individuality made up of a person's beliefs, values, and attitudes. (Chapter 10)

idioms Phrases that have meanings different from what the individual words mean and can be culturally specific. (Chapter 3)

illustrators Gestures that are dependent and closely linked to what is being said. (Chapter 4)

implied leader A type of leader that emerges when other group members defer to the member because of her or his rank, expertise, or other characteristics. (Chapter 8)

impression formation The tactics or approaches a person uses to form an impression of others. (Chapter 2)

impression management The process of selecting which aspects of one's self to disclose, hide, or fake in order to create an impression on those one interacts with. (Chapter 2)

impromptu speaking A method of delivery that has very little, if any, preparation or rehearsal. (Chapter 12)

indirect style A conversation style in which a verbal message's intent, need, want, and desire is less obvious or obscured. (Chapter 3)

informal networks Small group networks that form out of friendship, common interest, work situations, or proximity and are not controlled by the larger organization. (Chapter 8)

informative listening Listening to gain insight or comprehension. (Chapter 5)

informative speaking Speaking to give the audience completely new knowledge, skills, or understanding about a topic or increase the audience's current knowledge, skills, or understanding. (Chapter 13)

initiating A stage of relationship development in which a person forms quick impressions (right or wrong) about the other person after initial contact is made. (Chapter 6)

instrumental style Communication style that uses verbal language as a means to be goal-oriented. (Chapter 3)

integrating The stage of relationship development in which people become even more familiar with each other and might finish each other's sentences or have a special language. (Chapter 6)

intensifying The stage of relationship growth in which, if there is enough common ground and interest, a person seeks more intimacy, starts to share more private information, and waits for the other person to reciprocate. (Chapter 6)

interactional model Developed by Wilber Schramm, the model of communication that strengthened our understanding of communication by adding a feedback loop highlighting interaction and a setting, or context, for the interaction. (Chapter 1)

interaction appearance theory Kelly Abada, Mark Knapp, and Katheryn Theune's theory suggesting a person will change his/her original impressions of someone the more he/she interacts with that person. (Chapter 2)

intercultural competence The willingness to work toward understanding others and communicating effectively with them. (Chapter 2)

interdependence A state in which each member of a small group is connected or interacting with the others in some significant way and all members depend on each other for assistance, support, success, and ultimately, the survival of the group. (Chapter 8)

internal noise Any barrier to effective listening that originates within the body or mind of the listener. (Chapter 5)

internal previews Links that serve as mini-introductions and look like detailed signposts, telling the audience what is next in a speech. (Chapter 11)

internal reviews Links that serve as mini-conclusions, summarizing what has just been covered in the previous section of a speech. (Chapter 11)

interpersonal attraction A relationship or process in which one person is drawn to another person for particular reasons. (Chapter 6)

interpersonal communication The verbal and nonverbal interaction between individuals, usually two, who are in some sort of significant relationship developing over time. (Chapters 1, 6)

interpreting The third phase in the process of perception, in which a person attaches meaning to what he or she has learned in the first two phases about a person, place, event, or object. (Chapter 2)

intimacy The state of closeness evolving from physical, emotional, intellectual, and behavioral contact with one who is significant in your life. (Chapter 6)

intimate partner violence (IPV) The actual or threatened physical, sexual, psychological, or emotional abuse by a current or former intimate partner. (Chapter 7)

intrapersonal communication Communication with oneself. (Chapter 1)

jealousy The emotional resentment toward or suspicious fear of unfaithfulness of others, which feeds feelings of hurt, fear, anger, and mistrust. (Chapter 6)

Johari Window model Joseph Luft and Harri Ingham's self-awareness and disclosure model, symbolically represented as a window with four panes (or quadrants) that signify information about an individual that falls in one of these categories: (1) known to individual and others, (2) known to others but not that individual, (3) known to that individual only, or (4) unknown to that individual or anyone else. (Chapter 6)

kinesics The study of the body in motion. (Chapter 4)

kitchen sinking The behavior of rehashing old arguments or bringing up totally unrelated issues during a new argument. (Chapter 7)

ladder of abstraction The concept developed by Samuel Hayakawa noting the abstraction level of a word on a continuum of abstraction or specificity. (Chapter 3)

laissez-faire leaders Leaders who give group members complete freedom with the process necessary to reach the goal. (Chapter 8)

language A systematic, rule-governed set of symbols (words) that have meaning for a particular group of people. (Chapter 3)

lay testimony Testimony from an ordinary person other than the speaker who bears witness to his or her own experiences and beliefs. (Chapter 11)

leakage and deception cues Nonverbal cues that can reveal deception or the true feelings of the messenger. (Chapter 4)

linear model The earliest and most simplistic model of communication, developed by Claude Shannon and Warren Weaver, representing communication as a process that injects or inoculates the message from the sender into the receiver. (Chapter 1)

line graphs Presentation aid graphs that contain numerical points plotted on a horizontal axis for one variable and on the vertical axis for another; the points are then connected to make a line. (Chapter 12)

linguistic barriers Barriers to listening that occur when the verbal and/or nonverbal messages from the speaker are unfamiliar to or misunderstood by the listener. (Chapter 5)

linguistic determinism The "firmer" version of the Sapir-Whorf hypothesis that suggests that language limits and determines our knowledge, thoughts, and perceptions. (Chapter 3)

linguistic relativity The "softer" version of the Sapir-Whorf hypothesis that suggests that language affects or shapes our thoughts, experiences, behaviors, or perceptions but is not as constraining as determinism. (Chapter 3)

links Words, phrases, or sentences used to make logical connections between parts of a speech. (Chapter 11)

listening The conscious learned act of paying attention, assigning meaning, and responding to a verbal and/or nonverbal message. (Chapter 5)

literal analogy An analogy that compares and contrasts two like things. (Chapter 11)

literal listening Paying attention to and interpreting only the denotative verbal message. (Chapter 5)

logos Aristotle's appeal related to logical reasoning. (Chapter 14)

main points The main ideas or claims covered in a speech. (Chapter 11)

majority rule A decision-making result in which a decision is made or a solution is selected with a majority vote—one vote more than half of the group—or a plurality. (Chapter 9)

manuscript speaking A method of delivery in which a speaker reads word for word from a copy of the speech. (Chapter 12)

masculinity A cultural construct that uses such qualifiers as unemotional, strong, brave, fearless, self-reliant, aggressive, successful, and determined. (Chapter 6)

Maslow's hierarchy of needs A theory developed by Abraham Maslow suggesting that individuals have five hierarchical levels of needs (physiological, safety, social, self-esteem, and self-actualization needs). (Chapter 10)

mass communication Communicating with a mass audience via electronic or print media. (Chapter 1)

mediated communication Interaction that takes place across time and space via some sort of media or technological channel to facilitate the interaction. (Chapter 1)

mediated presentations Presentations that use technology as a channel outside of the speaker or audience to exchange a message. (Chapter 12)

mediation A conflict resolution method that brings in a neutral party to help facilitate the resolution process. (Chapter 7)

memorized speaking A method of delivery in which a speaker commits the full text of a speech to memory. (Chapter 12)

message The verbal and nonverbal elements encoded (conveyed) and decoded (interpreted) which create the meaning in communication. (Chapter 1)

metacommunication Communication about how you want your verbal message interpreted. (Chapter 4)

minority rule A decision-making result in which a small fraction of a larger group makes the decision for the larger organization. (Chapter 9)

models Three-dimensional representations sometimes used as presentation aids. (Chapter 12)

Monroe's motivated sequence Alan Monroe's five-stage problem–solution strategy that bases a speech on what motivates the audience, in order to convince the audience that the speaker has the solution to their needs. (Chapter 11)

multimedia The combination of multiple presentation aids (still images, graphs, text, sound, and video) into one choreographed production. (Chapter 12)

multitasking The behavior of attending to multiple things at once that can negatively influence a person's listening skills. (Chapter 5)

MUSE model A model of conflict resolution that has four steps: Meet, Understand, Solve, and Employ. (Chapter 7)

mythos Aristotle's appeal related to sense of one's history in the larger culture and the need to be a member of that culture. (Chapter 14)

no-citation plagiarism A form of plagiarism that occurs when speakers fail to give source credit to a specific part of their speech that has been taken from another source. (Chapter 10)

noise Anything that can interfere with the message being sent or received. (Chapters 1, 5)

Nominal Group Technique A highly structured creative five-step process for generating ideas, possibilities, or solutions, created by Andre Delecq and Andrew Van de Ven. (Chapter 9)

non sequitur A fallacy that occurs when an argument's conclusion is not connected to the premises. (Chapter 14)

nonverbal communication The intentional or unintentional transmission of a message or a portion of a message without the use of words that are spoken, written, or signed. (Chapter 4)

nonverbal cues All nonlinguistical objects, observables, or behaviors that have meaning during an encounter. (Chapter 4)

norm of reciprocity A norm dictating that a person is obligated to return a behavior with a similar behavior. (Chapter 6)

norms Informal (usually unwritten or implicit) guidelines for appropriate actions and behaviors. (Chapter 8)

objective The part of a specific purpose that describes the outcome or behavior a speaker wants the audience to experience or adopt. (Chapter 10)

oculesics The study of eye behavior. (Chapter 4)

olfactics The study of smell as a nonverbal message. (Chapter 4)

organizational charts Presentation aid charts that illustrate the structure or the chain of command in an organization. (Chapter 12)

organizing A phase in the process of perception in which a person mentally arranges sensory information into more manageable patterns. (Chapter 2)

overattribution Assigning too much of a person's behavior to one or two characteristics. (Chapter 2)

passivity syndrome A negative listening issue that occurs when communicators believe that the person initiating the message is entirely responsible for the effectiveness of the message. (Chapter 5)

pathos Aristotle's appeal related to eliciting the audience's emotions. (Chapter 14)

perception The ability to translate information into insight or awareness about something, usually people, places, events, or objects. (Chapter 2)

perception checking The ability to critically evaluate one's perceptions of others. (Chapter 2)

peripheral processing Not paying close attention to an argument; or superficially accepting an argument. (Chapter 14)

personal groups The groups that predominately provide members with affection, safety, solidarity, and socialization. (Chapter 8)

personal space The space around the body that a person perceives as his/her own. (Chapter 4)

personal style A communication style that stresses equality and being personal. (Chapter 3)

personal testimony Testimony from a person's own experience or point of view. (Chapter 11)

personal traits Demographics that include age, gender, sexual orientation, household type, education, occupation, income, and disabilities, which help provide insight into what is important to an audience. (Chapter 10)

persuasion A deliberate attempt by a speaker to create, reinforce, or change the attitudes, beliefs, values, and/or behaviors of the listener. (Chapter 14)

persuasive speaking Speaking with the general purpose to persuade. (Chapter 14)

phonology The accepted methods for combining sound or making sound patterns to create words. (Chapter 3)

photographs Two-dimensional representations of places, concepts, people, animals, or objects, sometimes used as presentation aids. (Chapter 12)

physiological barriers Bodily conditions that prevent or constrain a person's ability to process information. (Chapter 5)

pictographs Bar graphs that use pictures instead of bars to represent sets of data, sometimes used as presentation aids. (Chapter 12)

pie graphs Circular graphs with sections representing a percentage of a given quantity, sometimes used as presentation aids. (Chapter 12)

pitch How high or low a person's voice is in frequency, determined by how fast or slow the vocal cords vibrate. (Chapter 4)

plagiarism Intentional or accidental use without proper credit of all or a portion of the words, ideas, or illustrations created by someone else. (Chapter 10)

population A large group of individuals. (Chapter 11)

post hoc ergo propter hoc The fallacy of assuming that because one event comes after another, the first event caused the second. (Chapter 14)

posture The positioning of the body or how a person carries his/her body. (Chapter 4)

power The ability to produce intended effects and the ability to influence the behavior of another person. (Chapter 6)

pragmatics How language is used in everyday interactions, or how one person says something to another in a particular situation within a certain context. (Chapter 3)

prejudice Opinions formed about a person or cultural group based on little or no knowledge and illogical feelings. (Chapter 2)

presentation aids Two- or three-dimensional visual items, video footage, audio recordings, and/or multimedia segments that support and enhance a person's speech. (Chapter 12)

prestige testimony Testimony that draws its effectiveness from the status of the person testifying. (Chapter 11)

primacy effect This type of impression formation indicates that individuals are more likely to remember things at the beginning of a list or at the first encounter. (Chapter 2)

principal of consistency The desire to keep things harmonious, which can be a barrier to perception. (Chapter 2)

problem–solution strategy An organizational strategy used when a speaker wants to show the audience how to solve a problem. (Chapter 11)

problem solving The process of finding (a) solution(s) to an obstacle or concern. (Chapter 9)

procedural conflict Disagreement over how to achieve a goal and resolution. (Chapter 7)

process of perception A conscious or unconscious process consisting of three phases: selecting, organizing, and interpreting. (Chapter 2)

profanity Obscene, rude, or abusive language. (Chapter 3)

professional group Groups offering members the ability to increase their knowledge and to complete a task in a professional setting. (Chapter 8)

pronunciation The standard or commonly accepted way to make a word sound. (Chapter 4)

propinquity effect Suggests that people tend to have interpersonal relationships with those they have more exposure to. (Chapter 6)

proposition of fact The persuasive proposition that seeks to prove something factual and answers the question "What is accurate or not?" (Chapter 14)

proposition of policy The persuasive proposition that seeks to prove a need for a new or different policy or answers "What procedures, plans, or courses of action need to be terminated and/or implemented?" (Chapter 14)

proposition of value The persuasive proposition that seeks to make a value judgment and answers "What has worth or importance? What is good, wise, ethical, or beautiful?" (Chapter 14)

proxemics The study of personal space as communication. (Chapter 4)

pseudo conflict Conflict that occurs when people think there is a problem or disagreement, while there really isn't. (Chapter 7)

pseudolistening Pretending to listen. (Chapter 5)

psychological barriers Emotional conditions or a mental state that prevents a person from focusing on and absorbing a message. (Chapter 5)

psychological traits A person's needs and motivations. (Chapter 10)

public groups Groups that offer a mechanism to support and help others or engage in public discourse. (Chapter 8)

public speaking Communicating as an individual speaker to a large audience. (Chapter 1)

quorum The minimum number of members (usually 50 percent plus 1) that must be present before business can take place at a meeting. (Chapter 9)

race The biological differences of humankind, often noticeable in physical markers such as color and texture of hair, color of skin and eyes, shape of facial features, and bodily build and proportions. (Chapter 10)

rate The speed at which a person speaks. (Chapter 4)

reasoning The rational thinking humans do to reach conclusions or to justify beliefs or acts. (Chapter 14)

receiver The person or persons receiving the message. (Chapter 1)

receiving The physiological process of hearing. (Chapter 5)

recency effect This type of impression formation implies that the most recent (or last) impression of someone will be remembered the best. (Chapter 2)

reflected appraisal The process of understanding self through symbolic interaction. (Chapter 2)

regulators Gestures that control conversation flow. (Chapter 4)

relational dialectics theory Leslie Baxter and Barbara Montgomery's theory suggesting that relationships are not linear, are characterized by change, and are full of contradictions—or dialectics—that interact with each other in a "both/and" manner. (Chapter 6)

relational maintenance behaviors theory A theory suggesting that people tend to use specific behaviors to effectively maintain relationships. (Chapter 6)

relationship The state of connectedness an individual has with a person or persons that is revealed in how that individual behaves toward and feels about the person(s). (Chapter 6)

remembering The final stage of the listening process, in which the listener retains the information heard. (Chapter 5)

responding The phase of the listening process in which a person gives feedback or a reply to the messages processed. (Chapter 5)

response typology A system for understanding how people respond to conflict (exit, voice, neglect, and loyalty) according to the dimensions of constructive/destructive and active/passive. (Chapter 7)

rules theory A theory claiming that interaction is more successful when the relational partners share the same rules, norms, or standards. (Chapter 6)

schemes The techniques of manipulating word order to create distinctive language. (Chapter 12)

selecting The moment in the process of perception when some factor grabs a person's attention and forces that person to focus on certain stimuli and ignore others. (Chapter 2)

selective attention The conscious or unconscious tendency to pay attention and expose oneself to a small scope of sensory information that satisfies or supports belief. (Chapter 2)

selective listening Tuning into only a part of the message or listening to only what one wants to hear. (Chapter 5)

self-awareness A person's heightened capacity for self-reflection and the ability to recognize who he/she is as a separate individual. (Chapter 2)

self-centered role Any member role in which a person only focuses on his/her own needs. (Chapter 8)

self-concept The knowledge a person has of himself/herself. (Chapter 2)

self-disclosure The communicative process of revealing oneself to another person. (Chapter 6)

self-esteem The personal value (positive or negative), or self-worth, a person holds of himself/herself. (Chapter 2)

self-fulfilling prophecy A prediction an individual or someone else makes about that individual, which directly or indirectly causes the prediction to come true. (Chapter 2)

self-monitoring The internal process that individuals engage in to pay close attention to social interactions so they can adapt to a particular situation. (Chapter 2)

self-serving bias The tendency to attribute one's successes internally while attributing failures externally. (Chapter 2)

semantics The process of understanding the meaning of words. (Chapter 3)

sender The person who initiates and is responsible for the feelings, ideas, or thoughts conveyed via a message. (Chapter 1)

signposts Words or phrases that signal to the audience where they are in a speech with regard to related thoughts and/or what is important to remember. (Chapter 11)

slang Typically informal language restricted to a particular context or group. (Chapter 3)

slippery slope The fallacy of arguing that a small event sets off a chain reaction to disaster. (Chapter 14)

small group A group of three to approximately seven interdependent people united over time as a cohesive unit with a common goal. (Chapter 8)

small group communication Interaction in a group of 3 to 12 people united over time for a common purpose. (Chapter 1)

social comparison theory Leon Festinger's theory that suggests individuals are driven to evaluate themselves by comparing looks, attitudes, values, beliefs, and abilities to others in a social group. (Chapter 2)

social exchange theory A theory suggesting that if individuals put time and effort into something, they generally want something of equal or better quality in return (the costs-rewards) (Chapter 6).

social interaction Any type of relationship that is based on communicative interaction between people. (Chapter 1)

social loafing Occurs when people exert less effort as group members than they would working alone. (Chapter 8)

social penetration theory Irwin Altman and Dalmas Taylor's theory that over time and as a relationship develops, one partner penetrates deeper into the personal information and the identity of the other, metaphorically like peeling an onion. (Chapter 6)

social traits Relate to how the audience is affected by or identifies with other groups of people. (Chapter 10)

spatial strategy An organizational strategy recognizing space as a way to arrange a speech. (Chapter 11)

specific purpose A single statement that combines a speech's general purpose, audience, and objective. (Chapter 10)

speech anxiety The uneasiness and fearfulness a person might feel when preparing or giving a speech. (Chapter 10)

speech to actuate A persuasive speech that asks the audience to take action. (Chapter 14)

speech to convince A persuasive speech that aims to create a new or change an existing attitude, belief, value, or behavior. (Chapter 14)

speech to describe An informative speech that describes an object, a person, an animal, or an event. (Chapter 13)

speech to explain An informative speech that clarifies a concept or issue. (Chapter 13)

speech to instruct An informative speech that teaches or demonstrates a process. (Chapter 13)

speech to report An informative speech that is an oral report or briefing. (Chapter 13)

speech to stimulate A persuasive speech that aims to overcome apathy or reinforce an existing attitude, belief, value, or behavior. (Chapter 14)

stagnating The stage of relationship deterioration in which the relationship still persists but the individuals are not interdependent. (Chapter 6)

statistics Numerical facts or data that are summarized, organized, and tabulated to present significant information about a given population (people, items, ideas, etc.). (Chapter 11)

stereotype An oversimplified and generalized prejudgment applied to an individual or group based on group belongingness or cultural patterns. (Chapter 2)

stereotyping The false or oversimplified generalizing applied to individuals based on group characteristics. (Chapter 10)

sticky floor phenomenon Factors that keep women in low-level, support roles in the workplace and that prevent them from seeking or gaining promotion or career development. (Chapter 8)

stonewalling Negative behavior characterized by withdrawal from an interaction or, potentially, a relationship to avoid conflict; one of Gottman's Four Horsemen of the Apocalypse behaviors. (Chapter 7)

subpoints The support materials that relate back to the main points of a speech. (Chapter 11)

substantive conflict Disagreement over issues related to the decision-making process. (Chapter 7)

superficial listening Paying attention to superficial things rather than the complex message. (Chapter 5)

support materials Information that explains, elaborates, or validates a speech topic. (Chapter 11)

syllogism The classical form of deductive reasoning, featuring major and minor premises and a conclusion. (Chapter 14)

symbol A representation (such as language) that stands for, represents, or suggests something else. (Chapter 3)

synchronous engagements Interactions that occur in real time. (Chapter 2)

synergy The process of mixing the strengths of individual group members together to form something stronger, better, and more effective. (Chapter 8)

syntactics The rules for determining word order, placement, and sequencing. (Chapter 3)

tables Visual representations of numbers or words arranged in rows, columns, or lists, sometimes used as presentation aids. (Chapter 12)

target audience The primary group of people that a speaker is aiming to persuade or engage. (Chapter 14)

terminating The stage of relationship deterioration in which the relationship is ended, such as a break-up, divorce, or ending of a partnership or job. (Chapter 6)

territoriality The behavior people display toward the space and objects that they permanently or temporarily claim as their own and will often defend. (Chapter 4)

testimony Firsthand knowledge or opinions, either your own or from others. (Chapter 11)

topical strategy An organizational strategy used when there is a strong inherent or traditional division of subtopics within the main topic of a speech. (Chapter 11)

transactional model Developed by Paul Watzlawick, Janet Beavin Bavelas, and Don Jackson, the communication model that emphasizes the simultaneous negotiation of meaning between communicators as they respond to each other and the context. (Chapter 1)

transitions Words or phrases in a speech that signal movement from one point to another as well as how the points relate to each other. (Chapter 11)

trigger words Verbal expressions that arouse emotions and create intense psychological noise in the listener. (Chapter 3)

tropes Techniques used to embellish or enhance ordinary words to create distinctive language. (Chapter 12)

Tuckman's group development model A model that explains group formation in five stages: forming, storming, norming, performing, and terminating/reforming. (Chapter 8)

two-thirds vote A decision-making result requiring two-thirds of the membership to vote in favor. (Chapter 9)

uncertainty reduction theory A theory asserting that people will engage in interaction as a means to reduce uncertainty and ambiguity. (Chapter 6)

understanding A phase in the listening process that occurs when a person applies literal and emotional meaning to a sound or equivalent stimulus. (Chapter 5)

understated style A communication style that stresses modest language, understatement, pauses, and silence. (Chapter 3)

values What a person views as having worth or sees as right or wrong, important or unimportant, desirable or undesirable, which in turn shapes beliefs. (Chapter 10)

verbal communication The act of sending and receiving messages via language (words). (Chapter 3)

video clips Any footage from television, movies, or any other type of video, sometimes used as presentation aids. (Chapter 12)

virtual small groups Small groups that may never, or rarely, meet in person and interact primarily through electronic media. (Chapter 8)

vocal variety The fluctuation or adjustment of vocal cues. (Chapter 4)

warrants Assumptions that act as links between the evidence and the claim in an argument. (Chapter 14)

wheel networks Group communication arrangements that require a gatekeeper, who takes on the role as the collector and transmitter of information. (Chapter 8)

Notes

Preface

1. Joseph P. Lash, *Helen and Teacher: The Story of Helen Keller and Anne Sullivan Macy* (Lawrence: Merloyd Lawrence Book: Delacorte, 1980), 515, print.

Chapter 1

1. National Association of Colleges and Employers, "Job Outlook: The Candidate Skills/Qualities Employers Want, the Influence of Attributes," *Job Outlook 2015*, NACE, 12 Nov. 2014, web, 29 July 2015; American Association of Retired Persons, "What Skills Are Employers Looking For?" *AARP Work Search*, AARP, n.d., web, 29 July 2015; Marcel M. Robles, "Executive Perceptions of the Top 10 Soft Skills Needed in Today's Workplace," *Business Communication Quarterly* 75.4 (2012): 453–65, *Business Source Complete*, web, 29 July 2015.

2. George Gordon Coulton, *From St. Francis to Dante: Translations from the Chronicle of the Franciscan Salimbene, 1221–1288* (London: Nutt, 1907), 242, print.

3. Sarah Penn, "Overcoming the Barriers to Using Kangaroo Care in Neonatal Settings," *Nursing Children and Young People* 27.5 (2015): 22–27, *CINAHL with Full Text*, web, 6 July 2015.

4. Julianne Holt-Lunstad, Timothy B. Smith, and J. Bradley Layton, "Social Relationships and Mortality Risk: A Meta-Analytic Review," *Plos Medicine* 7.7 (2010): e1000316, *MEDLINE*, web, 6 July 2015.

5. John D. Rockefeller, Jr., "I Believe" credo from July 8, 1941, radio broadcast, box 76, folder 272, series Z, personal collection (FA335), New York: Office of the Messrs., Rockefeller Records (OMR), Rockefeller Archive Center, 2009, print.

6. Claude E. Shannon and Warren Weaver, *The Mathematical Theory of Communication*, 5th ed. (Urbana: U of Illinois P, 1972), print. 6–24.

7. Wilbur Schramm and Donald F. Roberts, *The Process and Effects of Mass Communication*, 2nd ed. (Urbana: U of Illinois P, 1971), print. 22–34.

8. Paul Watzlawick, Janet Beavin Bavelas, and Don D. Jackson, *Pragmatics of Human Communication*, 2nd ed. (New York: Norton, 2011), print. 29–52.

9. Abraham H. Maslow, *The Psychology of Science: A Reconnaissance* (New York: Harper, 1966), 2, print.

10. Publius Syrus, *The Moral Sayings of Publius Syrus, A Roman Slave*, trans. Darius Lyman, Jr. (Cleveland: L. E. Barnard, 1856), 43, print.

11. Lepoldina Fortunati, "Is Body-to-Body Communication Still the Prototype?" *The Information Society* 22 (2005): 53–61, print.

12. National Communication Association, "NCA Credo for Ethical Communication," NCA, Nov. 1999, web, 6 July 2015.

13. Nel Noddings, *Caring: A Feminine Approach to Ethics and Moral Education* (Berkley: U of California P, 1984), print; Carol Gilligan, *In a Different Voice: Psychological Theory and Women's Development* (Cambridge: Harvard UP, 1998), print.

14. Maha Ghosananda, *Step by Step: Meditations on Wisdom and Compassion*, ed. Jane Sharada Mahoney and Philip Edmonds (Berkeley: Parallax Press, 1992), 53, print.

15. Ben Agger, *Oversharing: Presentations of Self in the Internet* (New York: Routledge, 2012), print; Jennifer Kane, *Social Media Etiquette for Business: 100 Ways to Communicate with Grace and Class* (Amazon Digital Services, 2014), Kindle file; Leonard Kim, *The Etiquette of Social Media: How to Connect and Respond to Others in the World of Social Media* (CreateSpace, 2014), Kindle file; Rebecca Black, *Electronic Etiquette: Cell Phones, Netiquette, Social Media . . . Oh My* (Etiquette Now! Publishing, 2002), Kindle file.

16. Maya Angelou, *Wouldn't Take Nothing for My Journey Now* (New York: Random, 1993), 124, print.
17. Geert Hofstede, *Cultural Consequences: Comparing Values, Behaviors, Institutions, and Organizations Across Nations,* 2nd ed. (Thousand Oaks: SAGE), 2001, print; Geert Hofstede, Gert Jan Hofstede, and Michael Minkov, *Cultures and Organizations: Software of the Mind,* 3rd ed. (New York: McGraw, 2010), print; Edward T. Hall, *The Hidden Dimension* (New York: Anchor, 1990), print; Edward T. Hall, *The Silent Language* (New York: Anchor, 1973), print.

Chapter 2

1. Timothy A. Judge and Daniel M. Cable, "When It Comes to Pay, Do the Thin Win? The Effect of Weight on Pay for Men and Women," *Journal of Applied Psychology* 96.1 (2011): 95–112, *Business Source Complete,* web, July 7, 2015; Timothy A. Judge and Daniel M. Cable, "The Effect of Physical Height on Workplace Success and Income," *Journal of Applied Psychology* 89.3 (2004): 428–41; Alauddin Majumder, "Does Obesity Matter for Wages? Evidence from the United States," *Economic Papers* 32.2 (2013): 200–17, *Business Source Complete,* web, 7 July 2015.
2. Ziva Kunda, *Social Cognition: Making Sense of People* (Cambridge: Bradford, 2000), 83–85, 557, print.
3. Susan Fiske and Shelley E. Taylor, *Social Cognition: From Brains to Culture,* 2nd ed. (Thousand Oaks: SAGE, 2013), 104, 121, 346, print.
4. Susan Fiske and Shelley E. Taylor, *Social Cognition: From Brains to Culture,* 2nd ed. (Thousand Oaks: SAGE, 2013), 345–46, print.
5. U.S. Department of Education, National Center for Education Statistics (NCES), *Student Reports of Bullying and Cyber-Bullying: Results From the 2011 School Crime Supplement to the National Crime Victimization Survey,* NCES 2013–329, by Melissa Cidade and Deborah Lessne, Synergy Enterprises, Incorporated (SEI), NCES, April 2015, web, 17 June 2015.
6. Julia T. Wood, *Gendered Lives: Communication, Gender, and Culture,* 11th ed. (Stamford: Cengage, 2015), 113–15, print.
7. Nancy K. Baym, *Personal Connections in the Digital Age* (Malden: Polity, 2010), 7–8, 99–121, print.
8. Nancy K. Baym, *Personal Connections in the Digital Age* (Malden: Polity, 2010), 115–19, print.
9. Nancy K. Baym, *Personal Connections in the Digital Age* (Malden: Polity, 2010), 81, print.
10. Richard L. Draft and Robert H. Lengel, "Information Richness: A New Approach to Managerial Behavior and Organizational Design," *Research in Organizational Behavior* 6 (1984): 191–233, print.
11. Benjamin Franklin, *Poor Richard's Almanack* (Waterloo: The U.S.C. Publishing Co., 1914), 50, print.
12. Morris Rosenberg, *Society and the Adolescent Self-Image* (Middletown: Wesleyan UP, 1989), 325–27, print.
13. Charles Cooley, *Human Nature and the Social Order* (New York: Scribner's, 1902), print; Wayne E. Hensley, "A Theory of the Valenced Other: The Intersection of the Looking-Glass-Self and Social Penetration," *Social Behavior and Personality* 24.3 (1996): 293–308, print.
14. Leon Festinger, "A Theory of Social Comparison Processes," *Human Relations* 7 (1954): 117–40, print.
15. Thomas A. Wills, "Downward Comparison Principles in Social Psychology," *Psychological Bulletin* 90.2 (1981): 245–71, *PsycARTICLES,* web, 1 Mar. 2015; Rebecca L. Collins, "For Better or Worse: The Impact of Upward Social Comparison on Self-Evaluations," *Psychological Bulletin* 119.1 (1996): 51–69,

PsycARTICLES, web, 1 Mar. 2015; Joanne V. Wood, "Theory and Research Concerning Social Comparisons of Personal Attributes," *Psychological Bulletin* 106.2 (1989): 231–48, *PsycARTICLES*, web, 1 Mar. 2015.

16. Thomas Shelley Duval and Paul J. Silvia, "Self-Awareness, Probability of Improvement, and the Self-Serving Bias," *Journal of Personality and Social Psychology* 82.1 (2002): 49–61, print.

17. Erving Goffman, *The Presentation of Self in Everyday Life* (Garden City: Doubleday Anchor, 1959), 252–53, print.

18. Mark Snyder, "Self-Monitoring of Expression Behavior," *Journal of Personality and Social Psychology* 30.4 (1974): 526–37, print.

19. Mark Snyder, "Self-Monitoring of Expression Behavior," *Journal of Personality and Social Psychology* 30.4 (1974): 526–37, print.

20. Solomon E. Asch, "Forming Impressions of Personality," *Journal of Abnormal Psychology* 41 (1946): 258–90, *MEDLINE*, web, 12 June 2015.

21. Jérôme, "Letter 107: To Laeta," *The Principal Works of St. Jérôme*, trans. W.H. Fremantle (Oxford: James Parker and Co., 1893), 191, print.

22. Lee Ross, "The Intuitive Psychologist and His Shortcomings: Distortions in the Attribution Process," *Advances in Experimental Social Psychology*, ed. L. Berkowitz, vol. 5 (New York: Academic, 1977), 173–220, print.

23. Robert Rosenthal and Lenore Jacobson, *Pygmalion in the Classroom: Teacher Expectation and Pupils' Intellectual Development* (Norwalk: Crown House, 1992), print.

24. Elisha Y. Babad, Jacinto Inbar, and Robert Rosenthal, "Pygmalion, Galatea, and the Golem: Investigations of Biased and Unbiased Teachers," *Journal of Educational Psychology* 74.4 (1982): 459–74, *PsycARTICLES*, web, 8 July 2015.

25. Leon Festinger, *A Theory of Cognitive Dissonance* (Stanford: Stanford UP, 1957), print.

26. Stephen R. Covey, *The 7 Habits of Highly Effective People: Powerful Lessons in Personal Change* (New York: Free Press, 2004), 18, print.

27. Jennifer Guthrie and Adrianne Kunkel, "Tell Me Sweet (And Not-So-Sweet) Little Lies: Deception in Romantic Relationships," *Communication Studies* 64.2 (2013): 141–57, *Communication & Mass Media Complete*, web, 22 Feb. 2015.

28. Nancy K. Baym, *Personal Connections in the Digital Age* (Malden: Polity, 2010), 115–18, print.

29. Kelly Fudge Albada, Mark L. Knapp, and Katheryn E. Theune, "Interaction Appearance Theory: Changing Perceptions of Physical Attractiveness Through Social Interaction," *Communication Theory (10503293)* 12.1 (2002): 8, *Communication & Mass Media Complete*, web, 8 July 2015.

30. Kenneth Burke, *A Rhetoric of Motives* (Berkeley: U of California P, 1969), viii, print.

31. Stephen W. Littlejohn and Karen A. Foss, *Theories of Human Communication*, 9th ed. (Belmont: Thomson, 2008), 91, print.

32. University of Pennsylvania, "The Language of Personality," *World Well-Being Project*, web, 8 July 2015, <http://www.wwbp.org/personality_wc.html>.

33. Michal Kosinski, David Stillwell, and Thore Graepel, "Private Traits and Attributes Are Predictable from Digital Records of Human Behavior," *Proceedings of the National Academy of Sciences of the United States of America* 110.15 (2013): 5802–05, *Academic Search Complete*, web, 8 July 2015.

Chapter 3

1. Ludwig Wittgenstein, *Tractatus Logico-Philosophicus,* ed. C. K. Ogden (New York: Harcourt, 1922), 149, print.

2. M. Paul Lewis, Gary F. Simons, and Charles D. Fennig, eds., *Ethnologue: Languages of the World,* 18th ed., SIL International, 2015, web, 9 June 2015.

3. Joseph Campbell, *Flight of the Wild Gander* (New York: HarperPerennial, 1990), 143, print.

4. Charles K. Ogden and Ivor A. Richards, *The Meaning of Meaning*, 8th ed. (New York: Harcourt, 1949), print.

5. "Bat," entry 1, def. 2, *Longman Dictionary of American English*, 4th ed., 2007, print.

6. "Bat," entry 1, def. 1, *Longman Dictionary of American English*, 4th ed., 2007, print.

7. S. I. Hayakawa and Alan R. Hayakawa, *Language in Thought and Action*, 5th ed. (San Diego: Harcourt, 1990), 84–86, print.

8. Dell Hymes, "Models of the Interaction of Language and Social Life," *Directions in Sociolinguistics: The Ethnography of Communication*, eds. John Gumperz and Dell Hymes (New York: Holt, 1972), 3–47, print; Gerry Philipsen, "A Theory of Speech Codes," *Developing Communication Theories*, eds. Gerry Philipsen and Terrance L. Albrecht (Albany: SUNY P, 1997), 119–56, print.

9. Pew Research Center, "Cell Phone Activities 2012," Pew Research Center, 25 Nov. 2012, web, 5 Mar. 2015.

10. Pew Research Center, "5 Facts about Online Video, for YouTube's 10th Birthday," Pew Research Center, 12 Feb. 2015, web, 15 Mar. 2015.

11. Clay Shirky, *Here Comes Everybody: The Power of Organizing Without Organizations* (New York: Penguin, 2008), 165, print.

12. American Dialect Society, "'Hashtag' Is the 2012 Word of the Year," ADS, 4 Jan. 2013, web, 9 July 2015.

13. Benjamin L. Whorf, "The Relation of Habitual Thought and Behavior to Language," *Language Thought and Reality*, ed. John B. Carroll (Cambridge: MIT P, 1956), 134–59, print.

14. Maya Hickman, "Linguistic Relativity and Linguistic Determinism: Some New Directions," *Linguistics* 38.2 (2000): 409–34, print.

15. William B. Gudykunst and Stella Ting-Toomey, *Culture and Interpersonal Communication* (Newbury Park: SAGE, 1988), 99–116, print; Stella Ting-Toomey, *Communicating Across Cultures* (New York: Guilford, 1999), 103–12, print; Judith N. Martin and Thomas K. Nakayama, *Experiencing Intercultural Communication*, 4th ed. (New York: McGraw, 2001), 146–47, print; Myron W. Lustig and Jolene Koester, *Interpersonal Competence: Interpersonal Communication Across Cultures*, 7th ed. (Boston: Pearson, 2013), 216–21, print; Min-Sun Kim, "Cross-Cultural Comparisons of the Perceived Importance of Conversational Constraints," *Human Communication Research* 21.1 (1994): 128–51, *Communication & Mass Media Complete*, web, 13 July 2015.

16. William B. Gudykunst and Stella Ting-Toomey, *Culture and Interpersonal Communication* (Newbury Park: SAGE, 1988), 99–116, print; Stella Ting-Toomey, *Communicating Across Cultures* (New York: Guilford, 1999), 103–06, print.; Stella Ting-Toomey and Leeva C. Chung, *Understanding Intercultural Communication* (New York: Oxford UP, 2012), 125–26, print.; James W. Neuliep, *Intercultural Communication: A Contextual Approach* (Los Angeles: SAGE, 2012), 249–50, print.

17. William B. Gudykunst and Stella Ting-Toomey, *Culture and Interpersonal Communication* (Newbury Park: SAGE, 1988), 99–116, print; Stella Ting-Toomey, *Communicating Across Cultures* (New York: Guilford, 1999), 103–06, print; Stella Ting-Toomey and Leeva C. Chung, *Understanding Intercultural Communication* (New York: Oxford UP, 2012), 125–26, print; James W. Neuliep, *Intercultural*

Communication: A Contextual Approach (Los Angeles: SAGE, 2012), 249–50, print.

18. William B. Gudykunst and Stella Ting-Toomey, *Culture and Interpersonal Communication* (Newbury Park: SAGE, 1988), 105–08, print; James W. Neuliep, *Intercultural Communication: A Contextual Approach* (Los Angeles: SAGE, 2012), 251–52, print.

19. William B. Gudykunst and Stella Ting-Toomey, *Culture and Interpersonal Communication* (Newbury Park: SAGE, 1988), 105–08, print.

20. Donal Carbaugh and Saila Poutiainen, "By Way of Introduction: An American and Finnish Dialogue," *Among US: Essays on Identity, Belonging, and Intercultural Competence*, 2nd ed., eds. Myron W. Lustig and Jolene Koester (Boston: Pearson, 2006), 82–93, print.

21. Howard Giles, Nikolas Coupland, and John Wiemann, "'Talk Is Cheap. . . ' but 'My Word Is My Bond': Beliefs About Talk," *Sociolinguistics Today: International Perspectives*, 218–43 (London: Routledge, 1992), *MLA International Bibliography*, web, 13 July 2015.

22. Stella Ting-Toomey, *Communicating Across Cultures* (New York: Guilford, 1999), 111–13, print.

23. Kathryn Dindia, "Men Are from North Dakota, Women Are from South Dakota," *Sex Differences and Similarities in Communication*, 2nd ed., eds. Kathryn Dindia and Daniel Canary (New York: Erlbaum, 2006), 3–20, print.

24. Nicholas Palomares, "Exploring Gender-Based Language Use: Effects of Gender Identity Salience on References to Emotion and Tentative Language in Intra- and Intergroup Contexts," *Human Communication Research* 34.2 (2008): 263–86, print.

25. Julia T. Wood and Kathryn Dindia, "What's the Difference? A Dialogue about Differences and Similarities between Women and Men," *Sex Differences in Communication*, eds. Daniel Canary and Kathryn Dindia (New Jersey: Erlbaum, 1998), 19–39, print.

26. Anthony Mulac, "The Gender-Linked Language Effect: Do Language Differences Really Make a Difference?" *Sex Differences and Similarities in Communication*, 2nd ed., eds. Kathryn Dindia and Daniel Canary (New York: Erlbaum, 2006), 219–39, print.

27. John Gastil, "Generic Pronouns and Sexist Language: The Oxymoronic Character of Masculine Generics," *Sex Roles* 23.11/12 (1990): 629–43, *SocINDEX with Full Text*, web, 13 July 2015; Megan M. Miller and Lori E. James, "Is the Generic Pronoun He Still Comprehended As Excluding Women?" *American Journal of Psychology* 122.4 (2009): 483–96, *Academic Search Complete*, web, 13 July 2015.

28. Francis Bacon, *Meditationes Sacræ* (London, 1597), *Essayes* (New York: Da Capo Press, 1968), The English Experiences: Its Record in Early Printed Books Published in Facsimile 1, 13, print.

Chapter 4

1. Neha Gupta, "Effective Body Language in Organizations," *IUP Journal of Soft Skills* 7.1 (2013): 35–44, *Business Source Complete*, web, 3 Mar. 2014; Albert Mehrabian, *Nonverbal Communication* (Piscataway: Aldine Transaction, 2009), 182, print; Judee Burgoon and Gregory Hoobler, "Nonverbal Signals," *The Handbook of Interpersonal Communication*, 3rd ed., eds. Mark L. Knapp and John A. Daly (Thousand Oaks: SAGE, 2002), 246, print.

2. Robert G. Harper, Arthur N. Wiens, and Joseph D. Metarazzo, *Nonverbal Communication: The State of the Art* (New York: Wiley, 1978), 80, 100–05, print.

3. Gordon Wiseman and Larry Baker, *Speech— Interpersonal Communication*, 2nd ed. (New York: Chandler, 1974), print; Virginia Peck Richmond, James C. McCroskey, and

Mark L. Hickson III, *Nonverbal Behavior in Interpersonal Relations,* 7th ed. (Boston: Allyn, 2012), 5, print.

4. Paul Ekman and Wallace V. Friesen, "Nonverbal Leakage and Clues to Deception," *Psychiatry* 32.1 (1969): 88–106, print.

5. Judee Burgoon, "Truth, Lies, and Virtual Worlds," The National Communication Association's Carroll C. Arnold Distinguished Lecture, 2005 NCA National Conference, Boston, MA, 17 Nov. 2005, Keynote Address; Laura K. Guerrero and Kory Floyd, *Nonverbal Communication in Close Relationships* (Mahwah: Erlbaum, 2006), 181, Kindle file.

6. Laura K. Guerrero and Kory Floyd, *Nonverbal Communication in Close Relationships* (Mahwah: Erlbaum, 2006), 173–80, Kindle file.

7. Paul Ekman, "Body Position, Facial Expression, and Verbal Behavior during Interviews," *Journal of Abnormal Social Psychology* 43 (1964): 295–301, print.

8. Jean Paul Friedrich Richter, *Levana: Or, the Doctrine of Education,* trans. A.H. Liverpool (London: Bell, 1891), 309, print.

9. Ray Lee Birdwhistell, *Introduction to Kinesics: An Annotation System for Analysis of Body Motion and Gesture* (Louisville: U of Louisville, 1952), print.

10. Nele Dael, Marcello Mortillaro, and Klaus R. Scherer, "Emotion Expression in Body Action and Posture," *Emotion* 12.5 (2012): 1085–101, *PsycARTICLES*, web, 3 Mar. 2014.

11. Pablo Briñol, Richard E. Petty, and Benjamin Wagner, "Body Posture Effects on Self-Evaluation: A Self-Validation Approach," *European Journal of Social Psychology* 39.6 (2009): 1053–64, print.

12. Paul Ekman and Wallace V. Friesen, "The Repertoire of Nonverbal Behavior: Categories, Origins, Usage, and Coding," *Semiotica* 1 (1969): 49–98, print.

13. Paul Ekman, "Communication through Nonverbal Behavior: A Source of Information about an Interpersonal Relationship," *Affect, Cognition, and Personality*, eds. S. S. Tomkins and C. E. Izard (New York: Springer, 1965), 390–442, print.

14. Rick Chillot, "Louder Than Words," *Psychology Today* 46.2 (2013): 52, *MasterFILE Premier*, web, 3 Mar. 2013; Carol Sjostrom Miller, "The World According to Babies," *Parents* 82.3 (2007): 118, *MasterFILE Premier*, web, 14 July 2015.

15. Richard Heslin and Aari Alper, "Nonverbal Intimacy in Airport Arrival and Departure," *Personality and Social Psychology Bulletin* 6 (1980): 248–52, print; David B. Givens, *Love Signals: A Practical Field Guide to the Body Language of Courtship* (New York: St. Martin's, 2005), print.

16. Stanley E. Jones, and Elaine Yarborough, "A Naturalistic Study of the Meanings of Touch," *Communication Monographs* 52.1 (1985): 19–56, *Communication & Mass Media Complete*, web, 14 July 2015.

17. Michael Argyle, *Bodily Communication* (New York: International UP, 1975), 211, print; Laura K. Guerrero and Kory Floyd, *Nonverbal Communication in Close Relationships* (Mahwah: Erlbaum, 2006), 174, Kindle file.

18. Paul Ekman and Wallace V. Friesen, "Head and Body Cues in the Judgement of Emotions: A Reformation," *Perception and Motor Skills* 24 (1967): 711–24, print.

19. Paul Ekman and Wallace V. Friesen, "The Repertoire of Nonverbal Behavior: Categories, Origins, Usage, and Coding," *Semiotica* 1 (1969): 49–98, print; Paul Ekman and Wallace V. Friesen, "A New Pan-cultural Expression of Emotion," *Motivation and Emotion* 10.2 (1986), 159–68, print.

20. Irenäus Eibl-Ebesfeldt, "Similarities and Differences between Cultures in Expression Movement," *Nonverbal Communication*, ed. Robert A. Hinde (Cambridge: Cambridge UP, 1972), 297–314, print; Paul Ekman, *Emotions*

Revealed: Recognizing Faces and Feelings to Improve Communication and Emotional Life (New York: Time Books, 2003).

21. Paul Ekman and Wallace V. Friesen, *Unmasking the Face* (Englewood Cliffs: Prentice, 1975), print; Paul Ekman and Wallace V. Friesen, "The Repertoire of Nonverbal Behavior: Categories, Origins, Usage, and Coding," *Semiotica* 1 (1969) 49–98, print.

22. T. Joel Wade and Sara Bieltz, "The Differential Effect of Skin Color on Attractiveness, Personality Evaluation, and Perceived Life Success of African Americans," *Journal of Black Psychology* 31.3 (2005): 215–36, *ERIC*, web, 3 Mar. 2014; Michael B. Lewis, "Who Is the Fairest of Them All? Race, Attractiveness and Skin Color Sexual Dimorphism," *Personality & Individual Differences* 50.2 (2011): 159–62, *Academic Search Complete*, web, 3 Mar. 2014; Bernhard Fink, et al., "Facial Symmetry and Judgements of Attractiveness, Health and Personality," *Personality & Individual Differences* 41.3 (2006): 491–99, *Academic Search Complete*, web, 3 Mar. 2014.

23. Blackwell Publishing Ltd., "Personality Traits Influence Perceived Attractiveness," *ScienceDaily*, 30 Nov. 2007, www.science daily.com/releases/2007/11/071129145852 .htm; Lihi Segal-Caspi, Sonia Roccas, and Lilach Sagiv, "Don't Judge a Book by Its Cover, Revisited: Perceived and Reported Traits and Values of Attractive Women," *Psychological Science* 23.10 (2012): 1112–16, *Business Source Complete*, web, 3 Mar. 2014.

24. Mark L. Hickson III and Don W. Stacks, *NVC, Nonverbal Communication: Studies and Applications* (Dubuque: Brown, 1993), print; Peter H. Bloch and Marsha L. Richins, "Attractiveness, Adornments, and Exchange," *Psychology & Marketing* 10.6 (1993), 467–70, print; Bethia J. Best and Paul E. Spector, "The Effects of Applicant Attractiveness, Managerial Attributes and Gender on Executive Employment Decisions," (1984), *ERIC*, web, 2 Mar. 2014; "Looking Good Pays Off," *Hispanic* 22.4 (2009): 9, *MAS Ultra-School Edition*, web, 2 Mar. 2014; Melissa Ann Lavin and Thomas F. Cash, "Effects of Exposure to Information about Appearance Stereotyping and Discrimination on Women's Body Images," *International Journal of Eating Disorders* 29.1 (2001): 51–58, *Academic Search Complete*, web, 2 Mar. 2014; Nicole Bode, "Put on a Happy Face," *Psychology Today* 34.1 (2001): 18, *Business Source Complete*, web, 2 Mar. 2014.

25. James McCroskey and Thomas A. McCain, "The Measurement of Interpersonal Attraction," *Speech Monographs* 41 (1974): 261–66, print.

26. Linda L. McCroskey, James C. McCroskey, and Virginia P. Richmond, "Analysis and Improvement of the Measurement of Interpersonal Attraction and Homophily," *Communication Quarterly* 54.1 (2006): 1–31, print.

27. Diane DiResta, "Vocal Fry Can Hurt Your Presentation and Job Interview," *Knockout Presentations Blog*, DiResta Communications, Inc., 5 Nov. 2014, web, 1 Mar. 2015.

28. Francesca Sbardella, "Inhabited Silence: Sound Constructions of Monastic Spatiality," *Etnográfica: Revista Do Centro De Estudos De Antropologia Social* 17.3 (2013): 515–34, *Academic Search Complete*, web, 8 Mar. 2014.

29. Cheng Chuan-chuan and Charles Tardy, "A Cross-Cultural Study of Silence in Marital Conflict," *China Media Research* 5.2 (2009): 35–44, *Communication & Mass Media Complete*, web, 8 Mar. 2014.

30. William B. Gudykunst, Stella Ting-Toomey, Tsukasa Nishida, eds., *Communication in Personal Relationships Across Cultures* (Thousand Oaks: SAGE, 1996), 8, 115, print; Keith Basso, "To Give Up on Words: Silence in Western Apache Culture," *Southern*

Journal of Anthropology 26 (1970): 213–30; Stella Ting-Toomey, *Communicating Across Cultures* (New York: Guilford, 1999), 110–11, print; Elizabeth Molina-Markham, "Finding the 'Sense of the Meeting': Decision Making Through Silence Among Quakers," *Western Journal of Communication* 78.2 (2014): 155–74, *Academic Search Complete*, web, 8 Mar. 2014.

31. Elisabeth Noelle-Neumann, *The Spiral of Silence: A Theory of Public Opinion* (Chicago: U Chicago P, 1984), print.

32. "Taste and Smell," *University of Connecticut Health Center*, UCONN Health Center, n.d., web, 3 Mar. 2014.

33. "Taste and Smell," *University of Connecticut Health Center*, UCONN Health Center, n.d., web, 3 Mar. 2014.

34. Jobie E. Riley, "The Olfactory Factor in Nonverbal Communication," *Communication* 8.1 (1979): 159, *Communication & Mass Media Complete*, web, 3 Mar. 2014.

35. "Taste and Smell," *University of Connecticut Health Center*, UCONN Health Center, n.d., web, 3 Mar. 2014.

36. Carole Counihan and Penny Van Esterik, eds., *Food and Culture: A Reader,* 2nd ed. (New York: Routledge, 2008), print.

37. Tom Bruneau, "Chronemics: The Study of Time in Human Interaction," *Communication* 6.2 (1977): 1–30, *Communication & Mass Media Complete*, web, 3 Mar. 2014.

38. Edward T. Hall, *The Dance of Life: The Other Dimension of Time* (Garden City: Anchor, 1983), 3, print.

39. Edward T. Hall, *The Dance of Life: The Other Dimension of Time* (Garden City: Anchor, 1983), 41–54, print; Edward T. Hall and Mildred Reed Hall, *Understanding Cultural Differences* (Yarmouth: Intercultural P, 1990), 13–15, print.

40. Mark Knapp, *Nonverbal Communication in Human Interaction* (New York: Holt, 1978), print.

41. Judee K. Burgoon, Laura K. Guerrero, and Valerie Manusov, "Nonverbal Signals," *The SAGE Handbook of Interpersonal Communication*, 4th ed., eds. Mark L. Knapp and John A. Daly (Los Angeles: SAGE, 2011), 239–80, print.

42. Michael Argyle, *Bodily Communication*, 2nd ed. (New York: Routledge, 2013), 184–87, Kindle file.

43. Irwin Altman, *The Environment and Social Behavior: Privacy, Personal Space, Territory, Crowding* (Monterey: Brooks, 1975), print.

44. Edward T. Hall, *The Slient Language* (New York: Anchor, 1990).

45. Michael Argyle, "Diversity Tip Sheet" by the Diversity Council, *Bodily Communication* (New York: International UP, 1975), 73–101, print; Edward T. Hall and Mildred Reed Hall, *Understanding Cultural Differences* (Yarmouth: Intercultural P, 1990), print; Edward T. Hall, *The Dance of Life: The Other Dimension of Time* (Garden City: Anchor, 1983), print.

46. Virginia Peck, James C. McCroskey, and Mark L. Hickson III, *Nonverbal Behavior in Interpersonal Relations,* 7th ed. (Boston: Allyn, 2012), 209–10, print.

47. Virginia Peck Richmond, James C. McCroskey, and Mark L. Hickson III, *Nonverbal Behavior in Interpersonal Relations,* 7th ed. (Boston: Allyn, 2012), 208–31, print; Barbara Westbrook Eakins and Rollin Gene Eakins, *Sex Differences in Human Communication* (Boston: Houghton, 1978), print; David W. Addington, "The Relationship of Selected Vocal Characteristics to Personality Perception," *Speech Monographs* 35.4 (1968), *ERIC*, web, 15 July 2015; Matthew Hertenstein and Dacher Keltner, "Gender and the Communication of Emotion Via Touch," *Sex Roles* 64.1/2 (2011): 70–80, *SocINDEX with Full Text*, web, 15 July 2015; Petra Schmid, et al., "Gender Effects in Information Processing on a Nonverbal Decoding Task," *Sex Roles* 65.1/2 (2011): 102–07,

SocINDEX with Full Text, web, 15 July 2015; Judith A. Hall, "How Big Are Nonverbal Sex Differences? The Case of Smiling and Nonverbal Sensitivity," *Sex Differences and Similarities in Communication*, 2nd ed., eds. Kathryn Dindia and Daniel Canary (New York: Erlbaum, 2006), 59–81, print; Tobias Knöfler and Margarete Imhof, "Does Sexual Orientation Have an Impact on Nonverbal Behavior in Interpersonal Communication?" *Journal of Nonverbal Behavior* 31.3 (2007): 189–204, *Communication & Mass Media Complete*, web, 15 July 2015.

48. Virginia Peck Richmond, James C. McCroskey, and Mark L. Hickson III, *Nonverbal Behavior in Interpersonal Relations*, 7th ed. (Boston: Allyn, 2012), 223, print; T. Nguyen, R. Heslin, and M. L. Nguyen, "The Meanings of Touch: Sex Differences," *The Journal of Communication* 25.3 (1975): 92–103, *MEDLINE*, web, 15 July 2015.

49. Judee K. Burgoon, "A Communication Model of Personal Space Violation: Explication and an Initial Test," *Human Communication Research* 4 (1978): 129–42, print.

Chapter 5

1. Rachel Naomi Remen, *Kitchen Table Wisdom: Stories That Heal* (New York: Berkley, 2006), 143, print

2. Rebecca Z. Shafir, *The Zen of Listening* (Wheaton: Quest Books, 2003), Kindle file.

3. Alvin Toffler, *Future Shock* (New York: Bantam, 1970), print; David Shenk, *Data Smog: Surviving the Information Glut* (San Francisco: Harper, 1997), print.

4. National Institute on Deafness and Other Communication Disorders, "Quick Statistics"(Bethesda: National Institutes for Health), 20 Apr. 2015, web, 6 Aug. 2015.

5. International Listening Association, "What Is ILA?" (Belle Plaine: ILA), n.d., web, 20 July 2015.

6. Andrew D. Wolvin and Carolyn Gwynn Coakley, "A Survey of the Status of Listening Training in Some Fortune 500 Corporations," *Communication Education* 40.2 (1991): 152–64, *ERIC*, web, 23 July 2015; Larry Barker, et al., "An Investigation of Proportional Time Spent in Various Communication Activities by College Students," *Journal of Applied Communications Research* 8.2 (1980): 101–09, *Communication & Mass Media Complete*, web, 23 July 2015; Laura Janusik, Lynn Fullenkamp, and Lauren Partese, "Listening Facts and References," International Listening Association, n.d. web, 23 July 2015; Richard Emanuel, et al., "How College Students Spend Their Time Communicating," *International Journal of Listening* 22.1 (2008): 13–28, *Communication & Mass Media Complete*, web, 23 July 2015.

7. Laura A. Janusik and Andrew D. Wolvin, "24 Hours in a Day: A Listening Update to the Time Studies," *International Journal of Listening* 23.2 (2009): 104–20, *Communication & Mass Media Complete*, web, 15 Mar. 2014.

8. Kevin Sharer, "Why I'm a Listener: Amgen CEO Kevin Sharer," *McKinsey Quarterly* 2 (2012): 61–65, *Business Source Complete*, web, 6 Aug. 2015.

9. Walter Lippmann, "The Indispensable Opposition," *Atlantic Monthly* 164.5 (1939): 188, print.

10. Irene Hansen Savarese, "Practicing Active Listening Can Improve Your Relationship," *GoodTherapy.org*, GoodTherapy.org, 15 May 2013, web, 15 Mar. 2015.

11. Kory Floyd, "Empathic Listening as an Expression of Interpersonal Affection," *International Journal of Listening* 28.1 (2014): 1–12, *Communication & Mass Media Complete*, web, 17 Mar. 2014; Graham D. Bodie, "Listening as Positive Communication," *The Positive Side of Interpersonal Communication*, eds. Thomas J. Socha and Margaret J. Pitts (New York: Lang, 2012), 109–25, print.

12. Jonathan Eyre, "A Word in Your Ear," *Builders Merchants Journal* (2014): 16–17, *Business Source Complete*, web, 24 July 2015; Rick Bommelje, "Listening Pays!" *Leader to Leader* 2013.70 (2013): 18–25, *Business Source Complete*, web, 24 July 2015; Robin T. Peterson, "An Exploratory Study of Listening Practice Relative to Memory Testing and Lecture in Business Administration Courses," *Business Communication Quarterly* 70.3 (2007): 285–300, *Business Source Complete*, web, 16 Mar. 2014; S. A. Welch and William T. Mickelson, "A Listening Competence Comparison of Working Professionals," *International Journal of Listening* 27.2 (2013): 85–99, *Communication & Mass Media Complete*, web, 16 Mar. 2014; Scott D. Johnson and Curt Bechler, "Examining the Relationship Between Listening Effectiveness," *Small Group Research* 29.4 (1998): 452, *Business Source Complete*, web, 16 Mar. 2014.

13. U.S. Department of Labor, "What Work Requires of Schools," 15 Dec. 2009, web, 15 Mar. 2014.

14. Judy Edworthy and Hannah Waring, "The Effects of Music Tempo and Loudness Level on Treadmill Exercise," *Ergonomics* 49.15 (2006): 1597–610, print.

15. Linda Eve Diamond, *Rule #1: Stop Talking! A Guide to Listening* (Silicon Valley: Happy About, 2007), 3–5, print.

16. Kenneth Burke, *A Rhetoric of Motives* (Berkeley: U of California P, 1969), viii, print.

17. Brooke Noel Moore and Richard Parker, *Critical Thinking*, 4th ed. (Mountain View: Mayfield, 1995), 4, print.

18. Carl Sagan, *The Demon-Haunted World: Science as a Candle in the Dark* (New York: Random, 1996), 209–17, print.

19. George B. Ray and Christopher J. Zahn, "Regional Speech Rates in the United States: A Preliminary Analysis," *Communication Research Reports* 7.1 (1990): 34–37, *Communication & Mass Media Complete*, web, 24 July 2015; Florence Wolff and Nadine C. Marsnik, *Perceptive Listening* (Fort Worth: Harcourt, 1992), 66, print.

20. Kittie W. Watson, Larry L. Barker, and James B. Weaver III, "The Listening Styles Profile (LSP-16): Development and Validation of an Instrument to Assess Four Listening Styles," *International Journal of Listening* 9 (1995): 1–13, *Communication & Mass Media Complete*, web, 16 Mar. 2014; Graham D. Bodie, Debra L. Worthington, and Christopher C. Gearhart, "The Listening Styles Profile-Revised (LSP-R): A Scale Revision and Evidence for Validity," *Communication Quarterly* 61.1 (2013): 72–90, *Communication & Mass Media Complete*, web, 16 Mar. 2014.

21. Graham D. Bodie and Debra L. Worthington, "Revisiting the Listening Styles Profile (LSP-16): A Confirmatory Factor Analytic Approach to Scale Validation and Reliability Estimation," *International Journal of Listening* 24.2 (2010): 69–88, *Academic Search Complete*, web, 17 Mar. 2014; Graham D. Bodie, Debra L. Worthington, and Christopher C. Gearhart, "The Listening Styles Profile-Revised (LSP-R): A Scale Revision and Evidence for Validity," *Communication Quarterly* 61.1 (2013): 72–90, *Academic Search Complete*, web, 17 Mar. 2014.

22. John Stauffer, et al., "The Attention Factor in Recalling Network Television News," *Journal of Communication* 33.1 (1983): 29–37, *ERIC*, web, 19 June 2015.

23. Brenda Ueland, *Strength to Your Sword Arm: Selected Writings* (Duluth: Holy Cow! Press, 1993), 205, print.

Chapter 6

1. Julianne Holt-Lunstad, Timothy B. Smith, and J. Bradley Layton, "Social Relationships and Mortality: A Meta-Analysis," *PLoS*

Medicine, 27 July 2010, web, 8 June 2014; Paula R. Pietromonaco, Bert Uchino, and Christine Dunkel Schetter, "Close Relationship Processes and Health: Implications of Attachment Theory for Health and Disease," *Health Psychology* 32.5 (2013): 499–513, *PsycARTICLES*, web, 8 June 2014; Bert N. Uchino, "Understanding the Links Between Social Support and Physical Health: A Life-Span Perspective with Emphasis on the Separability of Perceived and Received Support," *Perspectives on Psychological Science (Wiley-Blackwell)* 4.3 (2009): 236–55, *Academic Search Complete,* web, 8 June 2014; Lisa. F. Berkman, Thomas Glass, Ian Brissette, and Teresa E. Seeman, "From Social Integration to Health: Durkheim in the New Millennium," *Social Science & Medicine* 51 (2000), 843–57, *MEDLINE*, web, 10 Aug. 2015; Sheldon Cohen, "Social Relationships and Health," *American Psychologist* 59 (2004), 676–84; Po-Ju Chang, Linda Wray, and Yeqiang Lin, "Social Relationships, Leisure Activity, and Health in Older Adults," *Health Psychology* 33.6 (2014): 516–23, *PsycARTICLES*, web, 8 June 2014.

2. Sandra Petronio, *Boundaries of Privacy: Dialectics of Disclosure* (Albany: SUNY, 2002), 6, print.

3. William W. Wilmot, *Relational Communication* (New York: McGraw, 1995), 28, print.

4. Kathleen M. Galvin, Carma L. Bylund, and Bernard J. Bromel, *Family Communication: Cohesion and Change* (Boston: Allyn, 2012), 8, print.

5. Shmuel Shulman, et al., "Parental Divorce and Young Adult Children's Romantic Relationships: Resolution of the Divorce Experience," *American Journal of Orthopsychiatry* 71.4 (2001): 473–78, *PsycARTICLES*, web, 9 June 2014; Geraldine K. Piorkowski, *Adult Children of Divorce: Confused Love Seekers* (Westport: Praeger, 2008), *eBook Academic Collection (EBSCOhost)*, web, 9 June 2014; Naomi Ben-Ami and Amy J. L. Baker, "The Long-Term Correlates of Childhood Exposure to Parental Alienation on Adult Self-Sufficiency and Well-Being," *American Journal of Family Therapy* 40.2 (2012): 169–83. *Consumer Health Complete–EBSCOhost*, web, 9 June 2014; Martha Putallaz, Philip R. Costanzo, and Tovah P. Klein, "Parental Childhood Social Experiences and Their Effects on Children's Relationships," *Understanding Relationship Processes, Vol. 2: Learning about Relationships*, Steve Duck, ed. (New York: SAGE, 1993), 63–117, print.

6. Carl Jung, *Modern Man in Search of a Soul*, trans. W.S. Dell and Cary F. Baynes (New York: Harcourt, Brace and Co., 1933), 49, print.

7. Robert J. Sternberg, "A Triangular Theory of Love," *Psychological Review* 93.2 (1986): 119–35, *PsycARTICLES*, web, 13 June 2014.

8. Scott F. Madey and Lindsey Rodgers, "The Effect of Attachment and Sternberg's Triangular Theory of Love on Relationship Satisfaction," *Individual Differences Research* 7.2 (2009): 82, *Academic Search Complete*, web, 13 June 2014.

9. Martha Bailey and Amy J. Kaufman, *Polygamy in the Monogamous World: Multicultural Challenges for Western Law and Policy* (Santa Barbara: Praeger, 2010), *eBook Academic Collection (EBSCOhost)*, web, 12 June 2014.

10. Emily C. Cook, Cheryl Buehler, and Robert Henson, "Parents and Peers as Social Influences to Deter Antisocial Behavior," *Journal of Youth & Adolescence* 38.9 (2009): 1242, *SocINDEX with Full Text*, web, 13 June 2014.

11. Emily C. Cook, Cheryl Buehler, and Robert Henson, "Parents and Peers as Social Influences to Deter Antisocial Behavior," *Journal of Youth & Adolescence* 38.9 (2009): 1241, *SocINDEX with Full Text*,

web, 13 June 2014; Marianne Helsen, Wilma Vollebergh, and Wim Meeus, "Social Support from Parents and Friends and Emotional Problems in Adolescence," *Journal of Youth and Adolescence* 29.3 (2000): 319–35, *ERIC*, web, 13 June 2014.

12. Scott D. Gest, Sandra A. Graham-Bermann, and Willard W. Hartup, "Peer Experience: Common and Unique Features of Number of Friendships, Social Network Centrality, and Sociometric Status," *Social Development* 10.1 (2001): 23–40, *ERIC*, web, 13 June 2014; Willard W. Hartup, "The Company They Keep: Friendships and Their Developmental Significance," *Child Development* 67.1 (1996): 1–13, *Academic Search Complete*, web, 13 June 2014; L. Alan Sroufe, "Attachment and Development: A Prospective, Longitudinal Study from Birth to Adulthood," *Attachment & Human Development* 7.4 (2005): 349–67, *Academic Search Complete*, web, 13 June 2014.

13. Amy Whyte, "Friendly Advice on Friendships," *Workforce* 94.5 (2015): 10, *Business Source Complete*, web, 25 July 2015; Patricia M. Sias and Daniel J. Cahill, "From Coworkers to Friends: The Development of Peer Friendships in the Workplace," *Western Journal of Communication* 62.3 (1998): 273–99, *Communication & Mass Media Complete*, web, 11 June 2014.

14. Brené Brown, "Want to Be Happy? Stop Trying to Be Perfect," *CNN.com*, Cable News Network, 1 Nov. 2010, web, 10 July 2014.

15. Roy F. Baumeister and Mark R. Leary, "The Need to Belong: Desire for Interpersonal Attachments as a Fundamental Human Motivation," *Psychological Bulletin* 117.3 (1995): 497, *Business Source Premier*, web, 13 June 2014.

16. Michael E. Roloff, *Interpersonal Communication: The Social Exchange Approach* (Thousand Oaks: SAGE, 1981), print; George C. Homans, *Social Behavior: Its Elementary Forms* (New York: Harcourt, 1974), print; John W. Thilbaut and Harold H. Kelley, *The Social Psychology of Groups* (New York: Wiley, 1959), print.

17. Christopher R. Agnew and Justin J. Lehmiller, "Social Exchange," *Encyclopedia of Social Psychology*, eds. Kathleen D. Vohs, Roy F. Baumeister, and SAGE Publications (Thousand Oaks: SAGE, 2007), 895–96, *eBook Collection (EBSCOhost)*, web, 12 June 2014.

18. Robert L. Burgess and Ted L. Huston, *Social Exchange in Developing Relationships* (New York, Academic, 1979), print.

19. Narissra Maria Punyanunt-Carter, "Using Equity Theory to Examine Relationship Maintenance and Satisfaction in Father-Daughter Relationships," *Human Communication* 11.2 (2008): 161–76, *Communication & Mass Media Complete*, web, 23 July 2014.

20. Ted L. Huston and George Levinger, "Interpersonal Attraction and Relationships," *Annual Review of Psychology* 29.1 (1978): 115, *Business Source Complete*, web, 12 June 2014.

21. James McCroskey and Thomas A. McCain, "The Measurement of Interpersonal Attraction," *Speech Monographs* 41 (1974): 261–66, print; Linda L. McCroskey, James C. McCroskey, and Virginia P. Richmond, "Analysis and Improvement of the Measurement of Interpersonal Attraction and Homophily," *Communication Quarterly* 54.1 (2006): 1–31, print.

22. Leon Festinger, Stanley Schachter, and Kurt Back, *Social Pressure in Informal Groups: A Study of Human Factors in Housing* (Stanford: Stanford UP, 1950), 33–59, print.

23. Brant R. Burleson, Adrianne W. Kunkel, and Jennifer D. Birch, "Thoughts about Talk in Romantic Relationships: Similarity Makes for Attraction (and Happiness, Too)," *Communication Quarterly* 42.3 (1994): 259–73, *Communication &*

Mass Media Complete, web, 12 June 2014; Brent R. Burleson, Wendy Samter, and Anne E. Lucchetti, "Similarity in Communication Values as a Predictor of Friendship Choices: Studies of Friends and Best Friends," *Southern Communication Journal* 57 (1992): 260–76, *Communication & Mass Media Complete*, web, 12 June 2014.

24. Elaine Hatfield and Richard L. Rapson, "Similarity and Attraction in Close Relationships," *Communication Monographs* 59.2 (1992): 209–12, *Communication & Mass Media Complete*, web, 12 June 2014.

25. Elaine Hatfield and Susan Sprecher, *Mirror, Mirror: The Importance of Looks in Everyday Life* (New York: SUNY, 1986), 114, print.

26. Jack McKillip and Sharon L. Riedel, "External Validity of Matching on Physical Attractiveness for Same and Opposite Sex Couples," *Journal of Applied Social Psychology* 13.4 (1983): 328–37, *SocINDEX*, web, 12 June 2014; Gregory L. White, "Physical Attractiveness and Courtship Progress," *Journal of Personality & Social Psychology* 39.4 (1980): 660–68, *SocINDEX*, web, 12 June 2014; Erich Goode, "Gender and Courtship Entitlement: Responses to Personal Ads," *Sex Roles* 34.3/4 (1996): 141–69, *SocINDEX with Full Text*, web, 12 June 2014.

27. Mark L. Knapp, Anita L. Vangelisti, and John P. Caughlin, *Interpersonal Communication and Human Relationships* (Boston: Pearson, 2013), 33–47; Mark L. Knapp, *Social Intercourse: From Greeting to Goodbye* (Needham Heights: Allyn, 1978), print.

28. Irwin Altman and Dalmas A. Taylor, *Social Penetration* (New York: Holt, 1973), print.

29. Joseph Luft, *Of Human Interaction* (Palo Alto: National Press, 1969), 177, print.

30. Daniel Goleman, *Emotional Intelligence: Why It Can Matter More Than IQ* (New York: Bantam, 2005), print; John D. Mayer, Marc A. Brackett, and Peter Salovey, *Emotional Intelligence: Key Readings on Mayer and Salovey Model* (Port Chester: Dude Publishing, 2004), print; Howard Gardner, *Frames of Mind: The Theory of Multiple Intelligences* (New York: Basic, 2011), print.

31. Charles R. Berger, "Producing Messages Under Uncertainty," *Message Production: Advances in Communication,* ed. John O. Greene (Mahwah: Erlbaum, 1997), 221–24, print; Charles R. Berger and Richard J. Calabrese, "Some Explorations in Initial Interaction and Beyond: Toward a Developmental Theory of Interpersonal Communication," *Human Communication Research* 1 (1975): 99–112, *Communication & Mass Media Complete*, web, 12 June 2014.

32. Richard West and Lynn H. Turner, *Introducing Communication Theory: Analysis and Application* (New York: McGraw, 2014), 144, print.

33. Sharon B. Shimanoff, *Communication Rules: Theory and Research* (Beverly Hills: SAGE, 1980), 57, print.

34. Sharon B. Shimanoff, "Group Interaction via Communication Rules, "*Small Group Communication: A Reader,* eds. Robert S. Cathcart and Larry A. Samovar (Dubuque: Brown, 1992), 250–62, print.

35. Guo-Ming Chen, "The Impact of New Media on Intercultural Communication in Global Context," *China Media Research* 8.2 (2012): 1–10, print.

36. "Japan," *The Hofstede Centre: Strategy, Culture, Change,* Item national, n.d., web, 25 July 2015.

37. "United States," *The Hofstede Centre: Strategy, Culture, Change,* Item national, n.d., web, 25 July 2015.

38. Geert Hofstede and Gert Jan Hofstede, *Cultures and Organizations: Software of the Mind* (New York: McGraw, 2005), 53–54, print.

39. Min-Sun Kim, *Non-Western Perspectives on Human Communication* (Thousand Oaks: SAGE, 2002), 38, print.

40. Min-Sun Kim, *Non-Western Perspectives on Human Communication* (Thousand Oaks: SAGE, 2002), 134–35, print.
41. Min-Sun Kim, *Non-Western Perspectives on Human Communication* (Thousand Oaks: SAGE, 2002), 38–39, print.
42. Min-Sun Kim, *Non-Western Perspectives on Human Communication* (Thousand Oaks: SAGE, 2002), 134–36, print.
43. Much of the content of this table is based on William B. Gudykunst and Yuko Matsumoto, "Cross-Cultural Variability of Communication in Personal Relationships," *Communication in Personal Relationships Across Cultures*, eds. William B. Gudykunst, Stella Ting-Toomey, and Tsukasa Nishida (Thousand Oaks: SAGE, 1996), 19–56, print.
44. Robert S. Tokunaga, "High-Speed Internet Access to the Other: The Influence of Cultural Orientations on Self-Disclosures in Offline and Online Relationships," *Journal of Intercultural Communication Research* 38.3 (2009): 133–47, *Communication & Mass Media Complete*, web, 14 June 2014.
45. Diana Ivy, *GenderSpeak: Personal Effectiveness in Gender Communication* (Boston: Pearson, 2012), 27, print.
46. Diane Holmberg and Karen L. Blair, "Sexual Desire, Communication, Satisfaction, and Preferences of Men and Women in Same-Sex Versus Mixed-Sex Relationships," *Journal of Sex Research* 46.1 (2009): 57, *MasterFILE Premier*, web, 14 June 2014; Helen Fisher, "Intimacy: His & Hers," *O, The Oprah Magazine* 10.10 (2009): 138, *MasterFILE Premier*, web, 23 June 2014; Letitia Anne Peplau, "Human Sexuality: How Do Men and Women Differ?" *Current Directions in Psychological Science (Wiley-Blackwell)* 12.2 (2003): 37–40, *Academic Search Complete*, web, 14 June 2014; Geoffery Greif, *Buddy System: Understanding Men's Friendships* (New York: Oxford UP, 2008), print; Diana Ivy, *GenderSpeak: Personal Effectiveness in Gender Communication* (Boston: Pearson, 2014), 215–73, print; Rowland Miller, *Intimate Relationships* (New York: McGraw, 2012), 212–304, print; Scott Swan, "Covert Intimacy: Closeness in Men's Friendships," *Gender in Intimate Relationships: A Microstructural Approach*, eds. Barbara J. Risman and Pepper Schwartz (Belmont: Wadsworth, 1991), 71–86, print; Paul Perrin, et al., "Aligning Mars and Venus: The Social Construction and Instability of Gender Differences in Romantic Relationships," *Sex Roles* 64.9/10 (2011): 613–28, *SocINDEX*, web, 23 June 2014; Iboro F. A. Ottu, "Psychosocial Health Indexing in Marriage: A Pilot Study of Empathic-Accuracy, Personal-Relational Dialectics, and Gender in Relationship Maintenance Among Ibibio Couples," *IFE Psychologia* 20.1 (2012): 294–322, *Academic Search Elite*, web, 24 June 2014.
47. J.K. Rowling, *Harry Potter and the Order of the Phoenix* (New York: Scholastic, 2003), 834, print.
48. Richard West and Lynn H. Turner, *Introducing Communication Theory: Analysis and Application* (New York: McGraw, 2014), 198–214, print; Barbara M. Montgomery and Leslie Baxter, *Dialectical Approaches to Studying Personal Relationships* (New York: Taylor & Francis, 2008), print; Leslie A. Baxter and Barbara M. Montgomery, *Dialogues and Dialectics* (New York: Guilford, 1996), print.
49. Andrew M. Ledbetter, Heather M. Stassen-Ferrara, and Megan M. Dowd, "Comparing Equity and Self-Expansion Theory Approaches to Relational Maintenance," *Personal Relationships* 20.1 (2013): 38–51, *Academic Search Complete*, web, 23 July 2014; Amie M. Gordon, et al., "To Have and to Hold: Gratitude Promotes Relationship Maintenance in Intimate Bonds," *Journal of Personality and*

Social Psychology 103.2 (2012): 257–74, *PsycARTICLES*, web, 25 July 2015; Laura Stafford and Dan J. Canary, "Equity and Interdependence as Predictors of Relational Maintenance Strategies," *Journal of Family Communication* 6 (2006): 227–54.

50. Erin Bryant, "Real Lies, White Lies and Gray Lies: Towards a Typology of Deception," *Kaleidoscope: A Graduate Journal of Qualitative Communication Research* 7 (2008): 23–48, *Communication & Mass Media Complete*, web, 24 June 2014.

51. William R. Cupach and Brian H. Spitzberg, *The Dark Side of Interpersonal Communication* (Hillsdale: Erlbaum, 1994), 184–91, print.

52. René M. Dailey, "Confirmation in Parent–Adolescent Relationships and Adolescent Openness: Toward Extending Confirmation Theory," *Communication Monographs* 73.4 (2006): 434–58, *Communication & Mass Media Complete*, web, 24 June 2014.

53. Norah E. Dunbar and Gordon Abra, "Observations of Dyadic Power in Interpersonal Interaction," *Communication Monographs* 77.4 (2010): 657–84, *Communication & Mass Media Complete*, web, 24 June 2014.

54. Leslie A. Baxter, "Gender Differences in the Heterosexual Relationship Rules Embedded in Break-Up Accounts," *Journal of Social & Personal Relationships* 3.3 (1986): 289–306, *SocINDEX*, web, 23 June 2014.

55. For a more detailed discussion of family communication rules, see Kathleen M. Galvin, Carma L. Bylund, and Bernard J. Bromel, *Family Communication: Cohesion and Change* (Boston: Allyn, 2012), 82–95, print.

56. Michael Argyle and Monika Henderson, "The Rules of Friendship," *Journal of Social & Personal Relationships* 1.2 (1984): 211–37, *SocINDEX with Full Text*, web, 23 June 2014.

57. Walter Scott, "Walter Scott's Personality Parade," *Parade* 20 July 2014: 2, print.

Chapter 7

1. Joyce L. Hocker and William W. Wilmot, *Interpersonal Conflict* (New York: McGraw, 2014), 4, print.

2. William Wilmot, *Relational Communication* (New York: McGraw, 1995), 95, print.

3. Rowland Miller, *Intimate Relationships* (New York: McGraw, 2012), 351–52, print; Dan Farrell and Caryl E. Rusbult, "Exploring the Exit, Voice, Loyalty, and Neglect Typology: The Influence of Job Satisfaction, Quality of Alternatives, and Investment Size," *Employee Responsibilities & Rights Journal* 5.3 (1992): 201–18, *SocINDEX with Full Text*, web, 28 June 2014.

4. Albert O. Hirschman, *Exit, Voice, and Loyalty: Responses to Decline in Firms, Organizations, and States* (Cambridge: Harvard UP, 1970), print; Caryl E. Rusbult, Isabella M. Zembrodt, and Lawanna K. Gunn, "Exit, Voice, Loyalty, and Neglect: Responses to Dissatisfaction in Romantic Involvements," *Journal of Personality and Social Psychology* 43.6 (1982): 1230–42, *PsycARTICLES*, web, 28 June 2014.

5. Rebecca E. Burnett, "Substantive Conflict in a Cooperative Context: A Way to Improve the Collaborative Planning of Workplace Documents," *Technical Communication* 38.4 (1991): 532–39, *ERIC*, web, 19 July 2015.

6. Steven A. Beebe and John T. Masterson, *Communicating in Small Groups: Principles and Practices* (Boston: Allyn, 2012), 176, print.

7. Shelley D. Lane, *Interpersonal Communication: Competence and Context* (Boston: Pearson, 2008), 314, print.

8. John Mordechai Gottman, *The Mathematics of Marriage: Dynamic Nonlinear Models* (Cambridge: MIT Press, 2002), 296–310, *eBook Academic Collection (EBSCOhost)*, web, 29 June 2014; John M. Gottman, *What Predicts Divorce? The Relationship between Marriage Processes and Marital Outcomes* (Hillsdale: Erlbaum, 1994), 110–11, print.

9. John M. Gottman, *The Marriage Clinic: A Scientifically Based Marital Therapy* (New York: Norton, 1999), 46, print.

10. Ralph H. Kilmann and Kenneth W. Thomas, "Developing a Forced-Choice Measure of Conflict-Handling Behavior: The 'Mode' Instrument," *Educational and Psychological Measurement* 37.2 (1977): 309–25, print; Robert R. Blake and Jane S. Mouton, *The Managerial Grid III: The Key to Leadership Excellence* (Houston: Gulf, 1985), print; M. Afzalur Rahim, "A Measure of Styles of Handling Interpersonal Conflict," *Academy of Management Journal* 26.2 (1983): 368–76, *Business Source Complete*, web, 1 July 2014.

11. United States Census Bureau, "USA QuickFacts," *U.S. Census Bureau*, U.S. Department of Commerce, 8 July 2014, web, 10 July 2014.

12. Stella Ting-Toomey and John G. Oetzel, *Managing Intercultural Conflict Effectively* (Thousand Oaks: SAGE, 2001), 70–71, *eBook Academic Collection (EBSCOhost)*, web, 30 June 2014.

13. Stella Ting-Toomey and Leeva C. Chung, *Understanding Intercultural Communication* (New York: Oxford, 2012), 184, print; Stella Ting-Toomey and John G. Oetzel, *Managing Intercultural Conflict Effectively* (Thousand Oaks: SAGE, 2001), 63–171, *eBook Academic Collection (EBSCOhost)*, web, 30 June 2014; Stella Ting-Toomey, *Communicating Across Cultures* (New York: Guilford, 1999), 202–04, print; Michael W. Morris and Kaiping Peng, "Culture and Cause: American and Chinese Attributions for Social and Physical Events," *Journal of Personality & Social Psychology* 67.6 (1994): 949–71, *Business Source Complete*, web, 30 June 2014; Antonia Calvo-Salguero, José-María Salinas Martínez-de-Lecea, and María del Carmen Aguilar-Luzón, "Gender and Work–Family Conflict: Testing the Rational Model and the Gender Role Expectations Model in the Spanish Cultural Context," *International Journal of Psychology: Journal International De Psychologie* 47.2 (2012): 118–32, *MEDLINE*, web, 1 July 2014; Min-Sun Kim, *Non-Western Perspectives on Human Communication* (Thousand Oaks: SAGE, 2002), 57–68, print.

14. Mark Davis, Sal Capobianco, and Linda Kraus, "Gender Differences in Responding to Conflict in the Workplace: Evidence from a Large Sample of Working Adults," *Sex Roles* 63.7/8 (2010): 500–14, *SocINDEX with Full Text*, web, 1 July 2014; John M. Gottman, *What Predicts Divorce? The Relationship between Marriage Processes and Marital Outcomes* (Hillsdale: Erlbaum, 1994), 110–11, print; Katherine Miller, *Organizational Communication: Approaches and Processes* (Belmont: Thomson, 2006), 206, print; Michael Gurian, *Leadership and the Sexes: Using Gender Science to Create Success in Business* (San Francisco: Jossey-Bass, 2008), 114–15, print; Barbara Dolinska and Dariusz Dolinski, "To Command or to Ask? Gender and Effectiveness of 'Tough' Vs 'Soft' Compliance-Gaining Strategies," *Social Influence* 1.1 (2006): 48–57, *SocINDEX with Full Text*, web, 3 July 2014.

15. Mark Davis, Sal Capobianco, and Linda Kraus, "Gender Differences in Responding to Conflict in the Workplace: Evidence from a Large Sample of Working Adults," *Sex Roles* 63.7/8 (2010): 500–14, *SocINDEX with Full Text*, web, 1 July 2014; Elizabeth Mears and Melissa Neevel, "'You Are Being Unfair': Emotional Trigger Phrases and Conflict," *University of Wisconsin–La Crosse Journal of Undergraduate Research* XI (2008): 491–504, web, 3 July 2014.

16. Mark Davis, Sal Capobianco, and Linda Kraus, "Gender Differences in Responding to Conflict in the Workplace: Evidence from a Large Sample of Working Adults," *Sex Roles* 63.7/8 (2010): 500–14, *SocINDEX with Full Text*, web, 1 July 2014.

17. R. A. Mackey and B. A. O'Brien, "Marital Conflict Management: Gender and Ethnic

Differences," *Social Work* 43.2 (1998): 128–41, *CINAHL with Full Text*, web, 1 July 2014.

18. John Mordechai Gottman, et al., "Observing Gay, Lesbian and Heterosexual Couples' Relationships: Mathematical Modeling of Conflict Interaction," *Journal of Homosexuality* 45.1 (2003): 65–91, *Academic Search Complete*, web, 1 July 2014.

19. Division of Violence Prevention, National Center for Injury Prevention and Control, "Intimate Partner Violence," Centers for Disease Control and Prevention, 2015, web, 6 July 2015.

20. Division of Violence Prevention, National Center for Injury Prevention and Control, "Understanding Intimate Partner Violence: Fact Sheet," Centers for Disease Control and Prevention, 2012, web, 6 July 2015.

21. Ronald Reagan, "Address at Commencement Exercises at Eureka College in Illinois, May 9, 1982," *Public Papers of the President of the United States: Ronald Reagan: 1982 (in Two Books), Book I—January 1 to July 2, 1982* (Washington: U.S. Government Printing Office, 1983), 581, print.

22. George R. Bach and Peter Wyden, *The Intimate Enemy: How to Fight Fair in Love and Marriage* (New York: Avon, 1983), 18–19, print; Laura K. Guerrero, Peter A. Andersen, and Walid A. Afifi, *Close Encounters: Communication in Relationships* (Los Angeles: SAGE, 2011), 343, print.

23. Roger Fisher, William Ury, and Bruce Patton, *Getting to Yes: Negotiating Agreement without Giving In* (New York: Penguin, 2011), print.

24. John M. Gottman, *The Marriage Clinic: A Scientifically Based Marital Therapy* (New York: Norton, 1999), 218–33, print.

25. United States, Dept. of Health and Human Services, Office on Women's Health (OWH), "Violence Against Women," *WomensHealth.gov*, OWH, 18 May 2011, web, 6 July 2015.

Chapter 8

1. The Henry Ford, *Annual Report 2004,* The Henry Ford, 2004, 2, web, 6 April 2015.

2. Katherine Adams and Gloria J. Galanes, *Communicating in Groups: Applications and Skills* (Boston: McGraw, 2009), 12–13, print.

3. J. Dan Rothwell, *In Mixed Company: Communicating in Small Groups and Teams* (Belmont: Thomson, 2007), 179–81, print.

4. Irving R. Janis, *Group Think: Psychological Studies of Policy Decisions and Fiascoes* (Boston: Wadsworth, 1982), 7, print.

5. Some of the most discussed are: Stewart L. Tubbs, *A Systems Approach to Small Group Interaction* (New York: McGraw, 1995), print; B. Aubrey Fisher, "Decision Emergence: Phases in Group Decision Making, *Speech Monographs* 37.4 (1970): 53–66, print; Marshall S. Pool, "Decision Development in Small Groups I: A Comparison of Two Models," *Communication Monographs* 48 (1981): 4, print; J. E. McGrath, "Time, Interaction, and Performance (TIP): A Theory of Groups," *Small Group Research* 22.2 (1991): 147–74, print.

6. Bruce W. Tuckman and Mary Ann C. Jensen, "Stages of Small-Group Development Revisited," *Group and Organizational Studies* 2 (1997): 419–27, print.

7. Cal W. Downs and Allyson D. Adrian, *Assessing Organizational Communication* (New York: Guilford, 2004), 59, 173–74, print; Lorenzo Sierra, "Tell It to the Grapevine," *Communication World* 19.4 (2002): 28, *Communication & Mass Media Complete*, web, 13 July 2014; "Executives Evaluate the Importance of Grapevine Communication," *Communication World* 11.3 (1994): 17, *Communication & Mass Media Complete*, web, 13 July 2014.

8. Fred C. Lunenburg, "Network Patterns and Analysis: Underused Sources to Improve Communication Effectiveness," *National Forum of Educational Administration and Supervision Journal* 28.4 (2011): 1–7, print;

Nancy Katz, David Lazer, Holly Arrow, and Noshir Contractor, "The Network Perspective on Small Groups: Theory and Research," *Theories of Small Groups,* eds. Marshall Scott Poole and Andrea B. Hollingshead (Thousand Oaks: SAGE, 2005), 289–92, print; B. Aubrey Fisher, *Small Group Decision Making,* 2nd ed. (New York: McGraw, 1980), 76–87, print.

9. Peter G. Northouse, *Leadership Theory and Practice,* 7th ed. (Los Angeles: SAGE, 2016), 1–18, print; Rafaela Martínez Méndez, José Gerardo Serafín Vera Muñoz, and María Antonieta Monserrat Vera Muñoz, "Leadership Styles and Organizational Effectiveness in Small Construction Businesses in Puebla, Mexico," *Global Journal of Business Research (GJBR)* 7.5 (2013): 47–56, *Business Source Complete,* web, 13 July 2014; M. Sean Limon and Betty H. La France, "Communication Traits and Leadership Emergence: Examining the Impact of Argumentativeness, Communication Apprehension, and Verbal Aggressiveness in Work Groups," *Southern Communication Journal* 70.2 (2005): 123–33, *Communication & Mass Media Complete,* web, 13 July 2014; Fred E. Fiedler, "Leadership Effectiveness," *American Behavioral Scientist* 24.5 (1981): 619, *Business Source Complete,* web, 13 July 2014; Anneloes M. L. Raes, et al., "Top Management Team and Middle Managers," *Small Group Research* 38.3 (2007): 360–86, *Professional Development Collection,* web, 7 Aug. 2015.

10. Peter G. Northouse, *Leadership Theory and Practice,* 7th ed. (Los Angeles: SAGE, 2016), 6, print; Gail T. Fairhurst, "Discursive Leadership: A Communication Alternative to Leadership Psychology," *Management Communication Quarterly* 21.4 (2008): 510–21, *Business Source Complete,* web, 13 July 2014.

11. Peter G. Northouse, *Leadership Theory and Practice,* 7th ed. (Los Angeles: SAGE, 2016), 19–42, print; Rafaela Martínez Méndez, José Gerardo Serafín Vera Muñoz, and María Antonieta Monserrat Vera Muñoz, "Leadership Styles and Organizational Effectiveness in Small Construction Businesses in Puebla, Mexico," *Global Journal of Business Research (GJBR)* 7.5 (2013): 47–56, *Business Source Complete,* web, 13 July 2014.

12. Peter G. Northouse, *Leadership Theory and Practice,* 7th ed. (Los Angeles: SAGE, 2016), 71–92, print; Kurt Lewin, Ron Lippit, and R. K. White, "Patterns of Aggressive Behavior in Experimentally Created Social Climates," *Journal of Social Psychology* 10: 271–301, print; Rafaela Martínez Méndez, José Gerardo Serafín Vera Muñoz, and María Antonieta Monserrat Vera Muñoz, "Leadership Styles and Organizational Effectiveness in Small Construction Businesses in Puebla, Mexico," *Global Journal of Business Research (GJBR)* 7.5 (2013): 47–56, *Business Source Complete,* web, 13 July 2014.

13. Peter G. Northouse, *Leadership Theory and Practice,* 7th ed. (Los Angeles: SAGE, 2016), 93–114, print; Paul Hersey, Kenneth H. Blanchard, and Dewey E. Johnson, *Management of Organizational Behavior* (Englewood Cliffs: Prentice, 2012), print; Rafaela Martínez Méndez, José Gerardo Serafín Vera Muñoz, and María Antonieta Monserrat Vera Muñoz, "Leadership Styles and Organizational Effectiveness in Small Construction Businesses in Puebla, Mexico," *Global Journal of Business Research (GJBR)* 7.5 (2013): 47–56, *Business Source Complete,* web, 13 July 2014.

14. Sandra M. Ketrow, "Communication Role Specialization and Perceptions of Leadership," *Small Group Research* 22.4 (1991): 492, *Business Source Complete,* web, 7 Aug. 2015; Kenneth D. Benne and Paul Sheats, "Functional Roles of Group Members," *Group Facilitation: A Research & Applications Journal* 8 (2007): 30–35, *Business Source Complete,*

web, 7 Aug. 2015; Thomas E. Harris and John C. Sherblom, *Small Group and Team Communication*, 5th ed. (Boston: Allyn, 2011), 46–47, 154, print.

15. Rita Salvi and Hiromasa Tanaka, *Intercultural Interactions in Business and Management* (Bern: Lang, 2011), 31, *eBook Academic Collection (EBSCOhost)*, web, 12 July 2014.

16. Jolanta Aritz and Robyn C. Walker, "Leadership Styles in Multicultural Groups: Americans and East Asians Working Together," *International Journal of Business Communication* 5.1 (2014): 87–88, print; Peter G. Northouse, *Leadership Theory and Practice,* 7th ed. (Los Angeles: SAGE, 2016), 431–66, print.

17. Min-Sun Kim, *Non-Western Perspectives on Human Communication* (Thousand Oaks: SAGE, 2002), 32, print.

18. Institute of Education Sciences, "Undergraduate Enrollment," *National Center for Education Statistics*, U.S. Department of Education, May 2015, web, 7 Aug. 2015.

19. United States Department of Labor, Bureau of Labor Statistics, "Women in the Labor Force: A Databook," *Bureau of Labor Statistics, BLS Reports*, U.S. Bureau of Labor Statistics, 2, web, 25 Aug. 2015.

20. Executive Office of the President of the United States, "Eleven Facts about American Families and Work," *WhiteHouse.gov*, The White House, Oct. 2014, 4, web, 25 Aug. 2015.

21. Larissa Myaskovsky, Emily Unikel, and Mary Amanda Dew, "Effects of Gender Diversity on Performance and Interpersonal Behavior in Small Work Groups," *Sex Roles* 52.9/10 (2005): 645–57, *SocINDEX with Full Text*, web, 9 July 2014.

22. Diana K. Ivy, *GenderSpeak: Personal Effectiveness in Gender Communication* (Boston: Pearson, 2012), 318–19, print.

23. Diana K. Ivy, *GenderSpeak: Personal Effectiveness in Gender Communication* (Boston: Pearson, 2012), 321, print.

24. Mia Hamm, *Go for the Goal: A Champion's Guide to Winning in Soccer and Life* (New York: Harper, 1999), print, 3–4.

25. Nancy L. Harper and Lawrence R. Askling, "Group Communication and Quality of Task Solution in a Media Production Organization," *Communication Monographs* 47.2 (1980): 77–100, *Communication & Mass Media Complete*, web, 11 July 2014.

Chapter 9

1. Thomas E. Harris and John C. Sherblom, *Small Group and Team Communication* (Boston: Allyn, 2011), 143, print.

2. John Dewey, *How We Think* (Boston: Heath, 1910), print.

3. Thomas E. Harris and John C. Sherblom, *Small Group and Team Communication* (Boston: Allyn, 2011), 154, print.

4. Thomas E. Harris and John C. Sherblom, *Small Group and Team Communication* (Boston: Allyn, 2011), 166, print.

5. Alex F. Osborn, *Applied Imagination: Principles and Procedures of Creative Thinking* (New York: Scribner, 1957), 80, print.

6. Alex F. Osborn, *Applied Imagination: Principles and Procedures of Creative Thinking* (New York: Scribner, 1957), 182, print.

7. Andrew H. Van de Ven and Andre L. Delbecq, "The Nominal Group as a Research Instrument for Exploratory Health Studies," *American Journal of Public Health* 62.3 (1972): 337–42, print.

8. Nicolas Michinov, "Is Electronic Brainstorming or Brainwriting the Best Way to Improve Creative Performance in Groups? An Overlooked Comparison of Two Idea-Generation Techniques," *Journal of Applied Social Psychology* 42.S1 (2012): E222–43, *SocINDEX with Full Text*, web, 26 July 2014.

9. Milam Aiken, et al., "The Use of Two Electronic Idea Generation Techniques in Strategy Planning Meetings," *Journal of Business Communication* 34.4 (1997): 370–82, *Communication & Mass Media Complete*, web, 26 July 2014.

10. Poppy Lauretta McLeod, Sharon Alisa Lobel, and Taylor H. Cox, Jr., "Ethnic Diversity and Creativity in Small Groups," *Small Group Research* 27.2 (1996): 248–64, print; Taylor H. Cox, Jr., and Stacy Blake, "Managing Cultural Diversity: Implications for Organizational Competiveness," *Academy of Management Executive* 5.3 (1991): 45–56, print.

11. Poppy Lauretta McLeod, Sharon Alisa Lobel, and Taylor H. Cox, Jr., "Ethnic Diversity and Creativity in Small Groups," *Small Group Research* 27.2 (1996): 248–64, print; Taylor H. Cox, Jr., and Stacy Blake, "Managing Cultural Diversity: Implications for Organizational Competiveness," *Academy of Management Executive* 5.3 (1991): 45–56, print; Nancy J. Adler and Allison Gundersen, *International Dimensions of Organizational Behavior*, 5th ed. (Mason: Thomson, 2008), 135, 138–40, Kindle file.

12. Abraham Sagie and Zeynep Aycan, "A Cross-Cultural Analysis of Participative Decision-Making in Organizations," *Human Relations* 56.4 (2003): 453–73, print; Nancy J. Adler and Allison Gundersen, *International Dimensions of Organizational Behavior*, 5th ed. (Mason: Thomson, 2008), 135, Kindle file.

13. Nancy J. Adler and Allison Gundersen, *International Dimensions of Organizational Behavior*, 5th ed. (Mason: Thomson, 2008), 145–47, Kindle file.

14. Nancy J. Adler and Allison Gundersen, *International Dimensions of Organizational Behavior*, 5th ed. (Mason: Thomson, 2008), 50, Kindle file; Niles G. Noorderhaven, Jos Benders, and Arjan B. Keizer, "Comprehensiveness versus Pragmatism: Consensus at the Japanese–Dutch Interface," *Journal of Management Studies* 44.8 (2007): 1350, *Business Source Complete*, web, 27 Aug. 2015.

15. Table created from information collected from the following articles and book: Do-Yeon Kim and Junsu Park, "Cultural Differences in Risk: The Group Facilitation Effect," *Judgment and Decision Making* 5.5 (2010): n. pag., web, 31 July 2014; Abraham Sagie and Zeynep Aycan, "A Cross-Cultural Analysis of Participative Decision-Making in Organizations," *Human Relations* 56.4 (2003): 453–73, print; Robert K. Conyne, et al., "Cultural Similarities and Differences in Group Work: Pilot Study of a U.S.–Chinese Group Comparison," *Group Dynamics: Theory, Research, and Practice* 3.1 (1999): 40–50, *PsycARTICLES*, web, 31 July 2014; Nancy J. Adler and Allison Gundersen, *International Dimensions of Organizational Behavior*, 5th ed. (Mason: Thomson, 2008), Kindle file.

16. "Supreme Court Nominee Sonia Sotomayor's Speech at Berkeley Law in 2001," News Archive: 2009 Archive, *Berkeley Law*, UC Berkeley School of Law, 6 May 2009, web, 17 Sept. 2014.

17. Rebecca Hannagan and Christopher Larimer, "Does Gender Composition Affect Group Decision Outcomes? Evidence from a Laboratory Experiment," *Political Behavior* 32.1 (2010): 51, *Academic Search Complete*, web, 4 Aug. 2014.

18. Renee A. Meyers, et al., "Sex Differences and Group Argument: A Theoretical Framework and Empirical Investigation," *Communication Studies* 48.1 (1997): 19, *Communication & Mass Media Complete*, web, 4 Aug. 2014.

19. Carole Kennedy, "Gender Differences in Committee Decision-Making: Process and Outputs in an Experimental Setting," *Women & Politics* 25.3 (2003): 27–45, *Academic Search Elite*, web, 4 Aug. 2014.

20. Do-Yeon Kim and Junsu Park, "Cultural Differences in Risk: The Group Facilitation

Effect," *Judgment and Decision Making* 5.5 (2010): n. pag., web, 31 July 2014.

21. Jeffrey W. Lucas and Michael J. Lovaglia, "Leadership Status, Gender, Group Size, and Emotion in Face-to-Face Groups," *Sociological Perspectives* 41.3 (1998): 617–37, *Business Source Complete*, web, 4 Aug. 2014.

22. Erina L. MacGeorge, et al., "Sex Differences in Goals for Supportive Interactions," *Communication Studies* 56.1 (2005): 23–46, *Communication & Mass Media Complete*, web, 4 Aug. 2014.

23. Frederick J. Klopfer and Thomas Moran, "Influences of Sex Composition, Decision Rule, and Decision Consequences in Small Group Policy Making," *Sex Roles* 4.6 (1978): 907–15, *SocINDEX with Full Text*, web, 4 Aug. 2014.

24. Allen Brown and Tara Mistry, "Group Work with 'Mixed Membership' Groups: Issues of Race and Gender," *A Quarter Century of Classics (1978–2004): Capturing the Theory, Practice, and Spirit of Social Work with Groups*, eds. Andrew Malekoff and Roselle Kurland (Binghamton: Haworth, 2005), 133–48, print.

25. Global Workplace Analytics, "Latest Telecommuting Statistics," *Global Workplace Analytics: Making the Case for Space*, Global Workplace Analytics, Sept. 2013, web, 19 Nov. 2014.

26. "Study: Virtual Work Force a Competitive Advantage," *Hypergrid Business: News*, Hypergrid Business, 13 June 2011, web, 20 Nov. 2014.

27. "Making Group Contracts," *University of Waterloo: Centre for Teaching Excellence* (University of Waterloo, n.d.), web, 7 Aug 2015.

Chapter 10

1. Norman Katlov, *The Fabulous Fanny: The Story of Fanny Brice* (New York: Knopf, 1953), 71, print.

2. United States Census Bureau, "Current Population Survey, 2010 Annual Social and Economic Supplement," *U.S. Census Bureau*, U.S. Department of Commerce, Nov. 2010, web, 4 Dec. 2012.

3. Lynne C. Lancaster and David Stillman, *When Generations Collide* (New York: Harper, 2002), 18–32, print.

4. Abraham Maslow, *Motivation and Personality* (New York: Harper, 1954), 80–106, print. Near the end of his life, Maslow reconsidered the five levels of need and began to articulate eight levels (physiological, safety, social, self-esteem, cognitive, aesthetic, self-actualization, and transcendence). Most introductions to Maslow's hierarchy still use the original five levels, as this book does. See the following publications published after Maslow's death for more on the eight levels: Abraham H. Maslow, "Critique of Self-Actualization Theory," *Future Visions: The Unpublished Papers of Abraham Maslow*, ed. Edward L. Hoffman (Thousand Oaks: SAGE, 1996), 26–32, print; Abraham H. Maslow, "The Farther Reaches of Human Nature," *Journal of Transpersonal Psychology* 1.1 (1969): 1–9, print; A. H. Maslow, *The Farther Reaches of Human Nature* (New York: Viking, 1971), print; Mark E. Koltko-Rivera, "Rediscovering the Later Version of Maslow's Hierarchy of Needs: Self-Transcendence and Opportunities for Theory, Research, and Unification," *Review of General Psychology* 10.4 (2006): 302–17, print.

Chapter 11

1. Aristotle, "Rhetorica," trans. W. Rhys Roberts, *The Basic Works of Aristotle*, ed. Richard McKeon (New York: Random, 1941), print.

2. Alan H. Monroe, *Principles and Types of Speeches* (Chicago: Scott, 1935), print.

3. "Quintilian," *Forty Thousand Quotations: Prose and Poetical*, comp. Charles Noel Douglas (New York: Halcyon House, 1917), *Bartleby.com*, 2012, web, 9 July 2014.

Chapter 12

1. Although commonly attributed to Aristotle, this quotation originates from Will Durant's summation of Aristotle's ideas in *Ethics*, book II, chapter 4, and book I, chapter 7. See Will Durant, *The Story of Philosophy: The Lives and Opinions of the World's Greatest Philosophers* (New York: Pocket, 1991), 76, print.
2. Based on Edward J. Corbett and Robert J. Connors, *Classical Rhetoric for the Modern Student*, 4th ed. (New York: Oxford UP, 1999), 396–409, print.
3. Based on Edward J. Corbett and Robert J. Connors, *Classical Rhetoric for the Modern Student*, 4th ed. (New York: Oxford UP, 1999), 380–95, print.
4. Nancy Duarte, *Slide:ology: The Art and Science of Creating Great Presentations* (Sebastopol: O'Reilly, 2008), 83, print.
5. Nancy Duarte, *Slide:ology: The Art and Science of Creating Great Presentations* (Sebastopol: O'Reilly, 2008), 13, print.

Chapter 13

1. United Nations, "'If Information and Knowledge Are Central to Democracy, They Are Conditions for Development,' Says Secretary-General" (New York: United Nations, 23 June 1997), web.

Chapter 14

1. Ludwig Wittgenstein, *On Certainty*, trans. Denis Paul and G. E. M. Anscombe, ed. G. E. M. Anscombe and G.H. von Wright (New York: Harper, 1969), print.
2. Aristotle wrote in his *Rhetoric* about persuasion and determined that you persuade others by three main appeals (pathos, ethos, and logos). In the *Poetics*, Aristotle introduced the concept of mythos, and other scholars—such as Michael, Suzanne, and Randall Osborn—reference it as another appeal. See Aristotle, "Rhetorica," trans. W. Rhys Roberts, *The Basic Works of Aristotle*, ed. Richard McKeon (New York: Random, 1941), print, and Aristotle, *The Poetics of Aristotle*, trans. by Preston H. Epps (Chapel Hill: U of North Carolina P, 1942), print.
3. Abraham Maslow, *Motivation and Personality* (New York: Harper, 1954), 80–106, print. Near the end of his life, Maslow reconsidered the five levels of need and began to articulate eight levels (physiological, safety, social, self-esteem, cognitive, aesthetic, self-actualization, and transcendence). Most introductions to Maslow's hierarchy still use the original five levels, as this book does; see Chapter 10, note 4, for more research on the eight levels.
4. Leon Festinger, *A Theory of Cognitive Dissonance* (Stanford: Stanford UP, 1957), print.
5. Martin Fishbein and Icek Ajzen, *Belief, Attitude, Intention, and Behavior: An Introduction to Theory and Research* (Reading: Addison, 1975), 6, print.
6. Richard E. Petty and John T. Cacioppo, *Communication and Persuasion: Central and Peripheral Routes to Attitude Change* (New York: Springer, 1986), print.
7. Stephen Edelston Toulmin, *The Uses of Argument* (New York: Cambridge UP, 1958), 94–145, print.
8. Edward J. Corbett and Robert J. Connors, *Classical Rhetoric for the Modern Student*, 4th ed. (New York: Oxford UP, 1999), 62–71, print; Stephen Toulmin, Richard Rieke, and Allan Janik, *An Introduction to Reasoning*, 2nd ed. (New York: Macmillan, 1984), 129–97, print.

Index

A

Abdulazeez, Muhammad Youssef, 75
About.com, 279
Abstract, nonverbal communication as an, 93
Abstraction, degree of, 71
Abstract words, 71
Accentuation, 99
Accidental touch, 105
Accommodation in conflict management, 193, 194
Accuracy of support materials, 307
Action model of communication, 10. *See also* Linear model of communication
Action-oriented listening, 143
Actual items, 350
Actuate, speech to, 396, 412, 418
Adam, Salimbene di, 6
Adams, Katherine, 210
Adaptors, 103
Ad hominem, 432
Adler, Nancy, 246, 247
Ad populum, 432
Advisory groups, 215
Affect, touch as, 105
Affect display, 103
Affective conflict, 188
Affective exchange theory, 135
Affective style of communication, 78
AFLAC duck, 140
African Americans, conflict and, 199
Agenda, 230, 253
  hidden, 213
Agenda setters, 225
Albada, Kelly, 60
Alliteration, 339
All-channel networks, 219, 227
Altman, Irwin, 163
Ambiguity, in nonverbal community, 93
Ambushing, 142
American Dialect Society, 74

American Psychological Association (APA)
  citations for outline, 314
  source page for outline and, 308
American Sign Language, 68
Analogy, 305
  argument by, 409
  figurative, 305
  literal, 305
Analytical listening, 143
Angelou, Maya, 26
Anger, 106
Annan, Kofi, 368
Anxiety
  controlling, 34
  speech, 265
  symptoms of, 19
Appeals in persuasive speaking, 400–403
  balanced, 401
  to commitment, 403
  defined, 400
  to ethos, 401
  to gain, 403
  to harmony, 402
  to know, 402
  to logos, 401
  to mythos, 401
  to pathos, 400
  to tradition, 432
Appearance, 108
Appraisal, reflected, 48
Appreciative listening, 138
Apprehension, managing your, 19, 34
Appropriateness, 84
Arbitrary, nonverbal communication as, 93
Arbitration, 202, 245
Arguments in persuasive speaking, 404–409
  by analogy, 409
  by authority, 409
  by cause, 409
  claims in, 404, 405
  by deduction, 406–407
  defined, 404
  ethical, 407
  evidence in, 404
  faulty, 409

by induction, 408
  warrants in, 405
Aristotle, 400, 401
Arranged marriages, 154
The Art and Science of Creating Great Presentations (Duarte), 358
Articulation, 112
Asch, Solomon, 54
Asian cultures, cooperative leadership in, 227
Askling, Lawrence R., 234
Assertiveness, 192
Assonance, 339
Assurances, 176
Asynchronous engagements, 44, 45, 254, 255, 346, 347
Attackers, 225
Attending in listening, 133
Attention getter
  in informative speaking, 381
  in introduction, 321
  in persuasive speaking, 421
Attention seekers, 225
Attentive listening, 253
Attitudes
  attraction and, 108, 109, 158
  in audience analysis, 268
  gender bias and, 229
Attraction, 158–159
  attitude, 108, 109, 158
  attractiveness and, 158, 159
  background, 108, 109, 158
  complementarity and, 158, 159
  interpersonal, 108, 109, 158–159
  physical, 108, 109, 158
  proximity and, 158
  similarity and, 158
  social, 108, 109, 158
  task, 109, 158
  theory, 158
  types of, 109
Attraction theory, 158
Attractiveness, 108, 158, 159
  types of, 108
Attribution, 49, 56
  biased, 196
Audience analysis, 268–273, 277
  attitudes in, 268
  beliefs in, 269

R

Race, 273
Reagan, Ronald, 200
Realism, 271
Reasoning, 401
Receiver
  in the interactional model, 13
  in the linear model, 10, 11
Receiving in listening, 133
Recency effect, 55
Reciprocity, 162
  norm of, 162
Recorded mediated presentations, 347, 349
Recorders, 225
Reference works, 300
Reflected appraisal, 48
Reforming stage of group development, 217
Regulation, 99
Regulators, 103
Reinforcement, 121
Relational conflict, 188
Relational dialectics theory, 174, 175
Relational environment in communication, 12
Relational listening, 143
Relational maintenance, stages of, 160–161
Relational maintenance behaviors theory, 176
Relationships. *See also* Interpersonal relationships
  defined, 152
  health and, 6
  identity and, 6
  listening in building, 135
  rules theory of, 169
  social interactions and, 6
Relaxed posture, 101
Remembering in listening, 133
Remen, Rachel Naomi, 129
Repetition, 99, 339
Reports, 367, 372, 379
Research
  for informative speaking, 375
  for persuasive speech, 415
Resolution method, commitment to, 202

Respectful disclosure, 163
Responding in listening, 133
Response typology, 187
Responsible, being, 24
Responsible decisions, 243
Restraint cultures, 29
Rewards, 157
Rhetorical questions, 339
Rhythm, 359
Richards, Ivor A., 69
Rich media, 45
Richmond, Virginia, 108, 120
Richter, Jean Paul, 100
Rieke, Richard, 431
Ritual, touch as, 105
Robinson, Mary, 75
Rockefeller, John D., Jr., 7
Role constructs, 41
Roles in impression management, 51
Romantic relationships, 154
  gender differences in, 173
  rules for, 178
Rosenberg, Morris, 47
Rosenberg Self-Esteem Scale (RSES), 47
Rowling, J. K., 174
Rule #1: Stop Talking! A Guide to Listening (Diamond), 136
Rules
  in governing self-disclosure, 162
  in shaping relationships, 169
  in small groups, 212
  for social networking language, 73
Rules theory, 169
Rusbult, Caryl, 187
Rushing, 161

S

Sadness, 106
Safety, with presentation aids, 351
Safety needs, 272
St. Jérôme, 55
Same sex couples, conflict and, 199
Sapir, Edward, 75
Sapir-Whorf hypothesis, 75
Schemas, organizing perception by, 41

Schemes, 339
School grapevines, 218
Schramm, Wilber, 12
Scripts, organizing perception by, 41
Secondary territory, 117
Secretary's Commission on Achieving Necessary Skills (SCANS), 136
Selective attention, 60
Selective listening, 142
Selective perception, 40
Self, management of, 50–51
Self-actualization needs, 272
Self-awareness, 46, 164–165
Self-centered roles, 224, 225
Self-concept, 46, 47
Self-disclosure
  assessing levels of, 167
  defined, 162
  as gradual, 162
  influence on relationship development, 162–167
  as intentional, 162
  as reciprocal, 162
  as risky business, 166
  rules in governing, 162
  as varying, 162
Self-esteem, 47, 272
Self-fulfilling prophecy, 49, 57
Self-monitoring, 24, 51
Self-Monitoring Scale, 52–53
Self-presentation, 50
Self-serving bias, 49, 56
Semantics, 72
Semantic triangle, 69
Sender
  in the interactional model, 13
  in the linear model, 10, 11
Senses
  appealing to, in speech, 338
  listening with your, 133
Sentences, using full, in outlines, 309
Shafir, Rebecca Z., 130
Shakespeare, William, 100
Shannon, Claude, 10
Sharer, Kevin, 134
Sheats, Paul, 224
Sherblom, John, 238, 240
Shimanoff, Susan, 169

Credits

CHAPTER 1

Photos: CO Vstock Llc/Getty Images; **4** Mark Edward Atkinson/AGE Fotostock; **7** Ellen Isaacs/Alamy; **7** Pressmaster/Shutterstock; **7** Triangle Images/Photodisc/Getty Images; **7** Lane Oatey/Blue Jean Images/Getty Images; **8** Caiaimage/Sam Edwards/Getty Images; **10** Mikeledray/Shutterstock; **11** Tongro Images/Alamy; **11** Itanistock /Alamy; **13** TongRo Images/Alamy; **13** Itanistock/Alamy; **13** TongRo Images/Alamy; **13** itanistock/Alamy; **14** Contrastwerkstatt/Fotolia; **15** TongRo Images/Alamy; **15** itanistock/Alamy; **16** Af archive/Alamy; **17** Wavebreakmedia/Shutterstock; **17** Monkey Business Images/Shutterstock; **17** Monkey Business Images/Shutterstock; **17** Elena11/Shutterstock; **17** Frank Chmura/Alamy; **18** Steve Debenport/Getty Images; **20** Johoo/Fotolia; **21** Caiaimage/Caiaimage/Robert Daly/Getty Images; **21** Monkey Business Images/Shutterstock; **22** Jakob Helbig/Cultura/Getty Images; **026** Alexander Tamargo/Getty Images;

Text: 5 National Association of Colleges and Employers, "Job Outlook: The Candidate Skills/Qualities Employers Want, the Influence of Attributes," Job Outlook 2015, NACE, 12 Nov. 2014, web, 29 July 2015; American Association of Retired Persons, "What Skills Are Employers Looking For?" AARP Work Search. AARP, n.d., web, 29 July 2015; Marcel M. Robles, "Executive Perceptions of the Top 10 Soft Skills Needed in Today's Workplace," Business Communication Quarterly 75.4 (2012): 453-465, Business Source Complete, web, 29 July 2015.; **6** George Gordon Coulton, From St Francis to Dante: Translations from the Chronicle of the Franciscan Salimbene (1221-1288) (London: Nutt, 1907), 242, Print; **7** Rockefeller, Jr., John D. "I Believe" credo from July 8, 1941 radio broadcast. Box 76, Folder 272, Series Z, Personal collection (FA335). New York: Office of the Messrs. Rockefeller Records (OMR), Rockefeller Archive Center, 2009. Print; **18** Maslow, Abraham H. The Psychology of Science: A Reconnaissance. New York: Harper & Row, 1966. Print. 2; **20** Roman author Publilius Syrus wrote in Fortunati. Lepoldina. "Is the Body-to-Body Communication Still the Prototype?; **23** National Communication Association. "NCA Credo for Ethical Communication." Washington D.C.: NCA, Nov. 1999. Web. 6 July 2015. Reprinted with permission from the National Communication Association. All Rights Reserved; **24** Maha Ghosananda. Step by Step: Meditations on Wisdom and Compassion. Ed. Jane Sharada Mahoney and Philip Edmonds. Berkeley: Parallax Press, 1992. 53. Print; **27** Angelou, Maya. Wouldn't Take Nothing for My Journey Now. New York: Random House, 1993. Print. 124.

CHAPTER 2

Photos: CO Ashley Cooper/Terra/Corbis; **38** Graham Corbett/DK Images; **38** Graham Corbett/DK Images; **38** Chronicle/Alamy; **42** Sam Edwards/Ojo Images/Getty Images; **45** WavebreakmediaMicro/Fotolia; **45** Tatyana Gladskih/Fotolia; **46** Shmel/Fotolia; **48** DK Images; **48** Ra2 studio/Fotolia; **48** JG Photography/Alamy; **48** Africa Studio/Fotolia; **48** Sabphoto/Shutterstock; **48** Hugo Felix/Shutterstock; **50** Pascal Broze/Onoky/Getty Images; **51** Purestock/Getty Images; **51** Michaeljung/Fotolia; **54** Luis Louro/Shutterstock; **58** Ariel Skelley/Getty Images; **61** Radius Images/Getty Images;

Text: 12 Franklin, Benjamin. Poor Richard's Almanack. Waterloo: The U.S.C. Publishing Co., 1914. Print. 50; **13** Rosenberg, Morris. Society and The Adolescent Self-Image. Middletown: Wesleyan UP, 1989. Print. 325-32; **16** Erving Goffman, The presentation of self in everyday life (Garden City, N.Y. : Doubleday, 1959); **18–19** Copyright (c) 1974 by the American Psychological Association. Reproduced with permission. The official citation that should be used in referencing this material is Synder, Mark. "Self-Monitoring of Expression Behavior." Journal of Personality and Social Psychology 30.4 (1974): 526-537. No further reproduction or distribution is permitted without written permission from the American Psychological Association; **21** St. Jerome. Translated by W.H. Fremantle, G. Lewis and W.G. Martley. From Nicene and Post-Nicene Fathers, Second Series, Vol. 6. Edited by Philip Schaff and Henry Wace. (Buffalo, NY: Christian Literature Publishing Co., 1893.) Revised and edited for New Advent by Kevin Knight. http://www.newadvent.org/fathers/3001107.htm; **23** Stephen R. Covey, The 7 Habits of Highly Effective People: Powerful Lessons in Personal Change (New York: Free Press, 2004), 18, print.

CHAPTER 3

Photos: CO Aso Fujita/AmanaimagesRF/Getty Images; **68** Furo_Felix/Fotolia; **69** Frank Greenaway/Natural History Museum, London/DK Images; **69** Bettman/Corbis; **70** DK Images; **70** Dave King/DK Images; **71** Dave King/DK Images; **71** Eric Isselee/DK Images; **71** Theo Malings/DK Images; **71** Ivonne Wierink/Fotolia; 71 Geoff Dann/Peter Griffiths/DK Images; **74** Karolina Webb/Alamy; **76** Frank and Helena/Cultura/Getty Images; **78** Budimir Jevtic/Fotolia; **79** Ira Berger/Alamy; **80** Stuart Jenner/Shutterstock; **82** Dimitri Otis/Getty Images; **88** Hill Street Studios/Blend Images/Getty Images

Text: 67 Ludwig Wittgenstein, Tractatus Logico-Philosophicus, ed. C. K. Ogden (New York: Harcourt, 1922), 149, Print; **68** Campbell, Joseph. Flight of the Wild Gander. New York: HarperPerennial, 1990; **69** Ford-Brown, DK Guide to Public Speaking (now in its 2nd ed); **70** PEARSON EDUCATION, LONGMAN DICTIONARY OF AMERICAN ENGLISH, 4TH EDITION, 4th Ed., ©2008. Reprinted and Electronically reproduced by permission of Pearson Education, Inc., New York, NY; **70** PEARSON EDUCATION, LONGMAN DICTIONARY OF AMERICAN ENGLISH, 4TH EDITION, 4th Ed., ©2008. Reprinted and Electronically reproduced by permission of Pearson Education, Inc., New York, NY.; **73** Pew Research Center; **74** Clay Shirky, Here Comes Everybody: The Power of Organizing Without Organizations. New York: Penguin, 2008. 165. Print.; **74** American Dialect Society; **79** Giles, Howard, Nikolas Coupland, and John Wiemann. "'Talk Is Cheap...' But 'My Word Is My Bond': Beliefs About Talk." Sociolinguistics Today: International Perspectives. 218-243. London: Routledge, 1992. MLA International Bibliography. Web. 13 July 2015; **80** Dindia, Kathryn. "Men are From North Dakota, Women are From South Dakota." Sex Differences and Similarities in Communication. 2nd Ed. Eds. Kathryn Dindia and Daniel Canary. New York: Lawrence Erlbaum Associates, 2006. 3-20. Print; **81** Wood, Julia T. and Kathryn Dindia. "What the difference? A Dialogue About Differences and Similarities between Women and Men. Sex Differences in Communication. Eds. Daniel Canary and Kathryn Dindia. New Jersey: Erlbaum, 1998, 19-39. Print. (This Wood quote in on page 32-33.); **88** Wallace Bacon

CHAPTER 4

Photos: CO Chris Hackett/Getty Images; **92** Mike Kemp/Rubberball/Getty Images ; **93** Mike Kemp/Getty Images; **94** Susan Chiang/Getty Images; **95** Denise Hager/Catchlight Visual Services/Alamy; **96** Luca Bertolli/123RF; ; **96** Jokatoons/Fotolia; **96** Yurkina Alexandra/Shutterstock; **96** Maxi_m/Shutterstock; **98** Bettmann/Corbis; **100** Robbie Jack/Corbis Entertainment/Corbis; **101** Pete Souza/The White House/Rapport Syndication/Newscom; **102** Aaron Rutten/Shutterstock; **102** Winston Link/Shutterstock; **102** Praisaeng/Fotolia; **102** Byheaven/Fotolia; **103** Comstock/Getty Images; **103** Pathdoc/Fotolia; **105** Steve Debenport/E+/Getty Images; **106** Xin wang/Fotolia; **108** William87/Fotolia; **110** Johan Larson/Fotolia; **114** Muratortasil/Fotolia; **116** Michaeljung/Shutterstock; **118** PhotosIndia/Getty Images ; **120** KidStock/Blend Images/Getty Images; **122** Syda Productions/Fotolia

Text: 100 Ulysses, in Shakespeare's Troilus and Cressida IV.5. 54–57; **100** Richter, Jean Paul Friedrich. Levana; Or, The Doctrine of Education. Trans. A.H. Liverpool. London: George Bell and Sons, 1891. 309. Print.; **103** Based on Ekman, Paul and Wallace V. Friesen. "The Repertoire of Nonverbal Behavior: Categories, Origins, Usage, and Coding." Semiotica, 1 (1969) 49-98. Print ; **115** Hall, Edward T. The Dance of Life: The Other Dimension of Time. Garden City N.Y.: Anchor/Doubleday, 1983. 3. Print ; **117** Altman, Irwin. The Environment and Social Behavior: Privacy, Personal Space, Territory, Crowding. Monterey: Brooks/Cole, 1975. Print; **119** Burgoon, Judee K., Laura K. Guerrero, and Valerie Manusov. "Nonverbal Signals." The Sage Handbook of Interpersonal Communication. 4th ed. Eds. Mark L. Knapp and John A. Daly. Los Angeles: Sage, 2011. Print; **121** Richmond, Virginia Peck, James C. McCroskey, and Mark L. Hickson, III. Nonverbal Behavior in Interpersonal Relations. 7th ed. Boston: Allyn & Bacon, 2012. 208-231.. Print.; Eakins, Barbara Westbrook, and Rollin Gene Eakins. Sex differences in Human Communication. Boston: Hoghton-Mifflin, 1978. Print.; Addington, David W. The Relationship Of Selected Vocal Characteristics To Personality Perception. n.p.: Speech Monographs, 1968. ERIC. Web. 15 July 2015.; Hertenstein, Matthew, and Dacher Keltner. "Gender And The Communication Of Emotion Via Touch." Sex Roles 64.1/2 (2011): 70-80. SocINDEX with Full Text. Web. 15 July 2015.; Schmid, Petra, et al. "Gender Effects In Information Processi

CHAPTER 5

Photos: CO David Schultz/Mint Images/Glow Images; **130** Severin Schweiger/Getty Images; **131** Monkey Business Images/Shutterstock; **131** Rido/Fotolia; **131** Rawpixel/Fotolia; **131** Micromonkey/Fotolia; **132** Yeko Photo Studio/Shutterstock; **134** Hill Street Studios/Blend Images/Getty Images; **138** Uniquely India/Getty Images; **140** Lulu/Fotolia; **144** Youngoggo/Fotolia; **146** Danijel Levicki/Fotolia; **149** Sergey Nivens/Fotolia

Text: 129 Rachel Naomi Remen, Kitchen Table Wisdom: Stories that Heal (New York: Berkley, 2006), 143, Print.; **130** Rebecca Z. Shafir, The Zen of Listening (Wheaton: Quest Books, 2003).; **131** United States. Department of Health & Human Services.; **134** Kevin Sharer, "Why I'm a Listener: Amgen CEO Kevin Sharer," McKinsey Quarterly 2 (2012): 61–65, Business Source Complete, web, 6 Aug. 2015; **135** Lippmann, Walter. "The Indispensable Opposition." Atlantic Monthly 164.5 (1939): 188; **136** United States. Department of Labor. "What Work Requires of Schools." DOL, 15 Dec. 2009 Web. 15 Mar. 2014; **137** Linda Eve Diamond, Rule #1: Stop Talking! A Guide to Listening (Silicon Valley: Happy About, 2007), 4-5, Print; **139** Brooke Noel Moore; Richard Parker, Critical thinking, Mountain View, Calif : Mayfield Pub. Co, ©1992; **139** Sagan, Carl. The Demon-Haunted World: Science as a Candle in the Dark. New York: Random, 1996. 209–217. Print; **143** Watson, Kittie W., Larry L. Barker, and James B. Weaver III. "The Listening Styles Profile (LSP-16): Development And Validation Of An Instrument To Assess Four Listening Styles." International Journal Of Listening 9.(1995): 1-13. Communication & Mass Media Complete. Web. 16 Mar. 2014; **143** Bodie, Graham D., and Debra L. Worthington. "Revisiting The Listening Styles Profile (LSP-16): A Confirmatory Factor Analytic Approach To Scale Validation And Reliability Estimation." International Journal Of Listening 24.2 (2010): 69-88. Academic Search Complete. Web. 17 Mar. 2014.; Bodie, Graham D., Debra L. Worthington, and Christopher C. Gearhart. "The Listening Styles Profile-Revised (LSP-R): A Scale Revision And Evidence For Validity." Communication Quarterly 61.1 (2013): 72-90. Academic Search Complete. Web. 17 Mar. 2014; **148** Karl Menninger, in Ueland, Brenda. Strength To Your Sword Arm: Selected Writings. Duluth: Holy Cow! Press; New York: Distributed by Talman Co., 1993. 203 Print.

CHAPTER 6

Photos: CO Jane Burton/Nature Picture Library/Corbis; **152** Caiaimage/Caiaimage/Robert Daly/Getty Images; **152** Monkey Business Images/Shutterstock; **154** Antonioguillem/Fotolia; **156** Image Source/Getty Images; **162** Mangostock/Fotolia; **168** Bikeriderlondon/Shutterstock; **172** Juanmonino/E+/Getty Images; **174** Peopleimages/E+/Getty Images; **178** Eric Audras/PhotoAlto/Getty Images; **179** Alex Segre/Moment/Getty Images; **182-183** Monkey Business Images/Shutterstock

Text: 153 Galvin, Kathleen M. , Carma L. Bylund, and Bernard J. Bromel's Family Communication: Cohesion and Change. Boston: Allyn and Bacon, 2012. 8. Print; **153** Jung, Carl. Modern Man in Search of a Soul. Trans. W.S. Dell and Cary F. Baynes. New York: Harcourt, Brace and Co., 1933. Print. 49; **154** Sternberg, Robert J. "A Triangular Theory of Love." Psychological Review 93.2 (1986): 119-135. PsycARTICLES. Web. 13 June 2014; **154** Madey, Scott F., and Lindsey Rodgers. "The Effect Of Attachment And Sternberg's Triangular Theory Of Love On Relationship Satisfaction."Individual Differences Research 7.2 (2009): 82. Academic Search Complete. Web. 13 June 2014; **156** Brown, Brené. "Want to Be Happy? Stop Trying to Be Perfect." CNN.com. Cable News Network, 1 Nov. 2010. Web. 10 July 2014; **159** Hatfield, Elaine and Susan Sprecher. Mirror, Mirror: The Importance of Looks in Everyday life. New York: SUNY, 1986. 114. Print ; **169** Shimanoff, Sharon B., Communication Rules: Theory and Research. Beverly Hills: Sage, 1980. 57. Print; **171** The content of this table is adapted from Gudykunst, William B. and Yuko Matsumoto. "Cross-Cultural Varibility of Communication in Personal Relationships." Communication in Personal Relationships Across Cultures. Eds. William B. Gudykunst, Stella Ting-Toomey, and Tsukasa Nishida. Thousand Oaks: Sage, 1996. 19-56. Print.; **172** Diana Ivy, GenderSpeak: Personal Effectiveness in Gender Communication (Boston: Pearson, 2012), 27, print; **173** Holmberg, DianeBlair, Karen L. "Sexual Desire, Communication, Satisfaction, And Preferences Of Men And Women In Same-Sex Versus Mixed-Sex Relationships." Journal Of Sex Research 46.1 (2009): 57. MasterFILE Premier. Web. 14 June 2014.; Fisher, Helen. "Intimacy: His & Hers." O, The Oprah Magazine 10.10 (2009): 138. MasterFILE Premier. Web. 23 June 2014.; Peplau, Letitia Anne. "Human Sexuality: How Do Men And Women Differ?." Current Directions In Psychological

Science (Wiley-Blackwell) 12.2 (2003): 37-40. Academic Search Complete. Web. 14 June 2014.; Greif, Geoffery. Buddy Syste: Understanding Men's Friendships. New York: Oxford UP, 2008. Print.;Ivy, Diana. Gender Speak: Personal Effect; **174** Rowling, J.K. Harry Potter and the Order of the Phoenix. New York: Scholastic Inc., 2003. Print. 834; **178** Baxter, Leslie A. "Gender Differences In The Heterosexual Relationship Rules Embedded In Break-Up Accounts."Journal Of Social & Personal Relationships 3.3 (1986): 289-306. SocINDEX. Web. 23 June 2014; **179** Galvin, Kathleen M. , Carma L. Bylund, and Bernard J. Bromel's Family Communication: Cohesion nd Change. Boston: Allyn and Bacon, 2012. 82-95. Print; **179** Argyle, Michael, and Monika Henderson. "The Rules Of Friendship." Journal Of Social & Personal Relationships 1.2 (1984): 211-237. SocINDEX with Full Text. Web. 23 June 2014; **182** http://www.unh.edu/emotional_intelligence/; **183** Scott, Walter. "Walter Scott's Personality Parade." Parade 20 July 2014: 2. Print.

CHAPTER 7

Photos: CO Daniel Grill/Getty Images; **186** Image Source/Getty Images; **188** Holger Ehlers/Alamy; **190** Image Source/Getty Images; **192** 2A Images/Getty Images; **193** Jet Sky/Fotolia; **193** Martin Barraud/Getty Images; **193** Minerva Studio/Fotolia LLC; **193** Vadymvdrobot/Fotolia; **193** Antonio Guillem Fernández/Alamy; **196** Myrleen Pearson/Alamy; **198** Hero Images/Getty Images; **200** Juice Images/Cultura/Getty Images; **202** Dmitrimaruta/Fotolia; **206** Mats Bergstrom/Shutterstock

Text: 186 Hocker, Joyce L. and William W. Wilmot. Interpersonal Conflict. New York: McGraw-Hill, 2014. 13. Print ; **196** Wilmot, William. Relational Communication. New York: McGraw-Hill, 1995. 95. Print ; **197** Ting-Toomey, Stella and Leeva C. Chung. Understanding Intercultural Communication. New York: Oxford, 2012. 184. Print.; Ting-Toomey, Stella, and John G. Oetzel. Managing Intercultural Conflict Effectively. Thousand Oaks, Calif: SAGE Publications, 2001. 63-171. eBook Academic Collection (EBSCOhost). Web. 30 June 2014.; Ting-Toomey, Stella. Communicating Across Cultures. New York: Guilford, 1999. 202-204. Print.; Morris, Michael W., and Kaiping Peng. "Culture And Cause: American And Chinese Attributions For Social And Physical Events." Journal Of Personality & Social Psychology 67.6 (1994): 949-971. Business Source

Complete. Web; **198** Davis, Mark, Sal Capobianco, and Linda Kraus. "Gender Differences In Responding To Conflict In The Workplace: Evidence From A Large Sample Of Working Adults." Sex Roles 63.7/8 (2010): 500-514. SocINDEX with Full Text. Web. 1 July 2014; **198** Davis, Mark, Sal Capobianco, and Linda Kraus. "Gender Differences In Responding To Conflict In The Workplace: Evidence From A Large Sample Of Working Adults." Sex Roles 63.7/8 (2010): 500-514. SocINDEX with Full Text. Web. 1 July 2014; **199** Mackey, RA, and BA O'Brien. "Marital Conflict Management: Gender And Ethnic Differences." Social Work 43.2 (1998): 128-141. CINAHL with Full Text. Web. 1 July 2014; **199** Gottman, John Mordechai, et al. "Observing Gay, Lesbian And Heterosexual Couples' Relationships: Mathematical Modeling Of Conflict Interaction." Journal Of Homosexuality 45.1 (2003): 65-91. Academic Search Complete. Web. 1 July 2014; **200** Ronald Reagan, "Address at Commencement Exercises at Eureka College in Illinois, May 9, 1982," Public Papers of the President of the United States: Ronald Reagan: 1982 (in Two Books), Book I—January 1 to July 2, 1982 (Washington: U.S. Government Printing Office, 1983), 581, print.; **207** http://www.womenshealth.gov/violence-against-women/types-of-violence/domestic-intimate-partner-violence.html

CHAPTER 8

Photos: CO Marco Simoni/Glow Images; **210** Robert Daly/Caiaimage/OJO+/Getty Images; **210** Monkey Business Images/Shutterstock; **216** Alandawson/Alamy; **216-217** Kali9/E+/Getty Images; **218** Zerbor/Shutterstock; **219** Silhouette Lover/Shutterstock; **219** Silhouette Lover/Shutterstock; **220** Fuse/Getty Images; **223** Monkey Business Images/Shutterstock; **223** Monkey Business Images/Shutterstock; **223** Altrendo images/Stockbyte/Getty Images; **223** Monkey Business Images/Shutterstock; **226** Lynn Gail/Robert Harding World Imagery/Alamy; **228** Jake Lyell/Alamy; **230** Mint Images/Shutterstock;

Text: 208 The Henry Ford. Annual Report 2004. The Henry Ford, 2004. 2. Web. 6 April 2015. https://www.thehenryford.org/images/AnnualReport04.pdf. Their copyright verbiage, if it helps: https://www.thehenryford.org/copyright.aspx.; **210** Adams, Katherine and Gloria J. Galanes. Communicating in Groups: Applications and Skills. Boston: McGraw-Hill, 2009. Print.; **222** Lewin, Kurt, Ron Lippit, and R. K. White. "Patterns of aggressive behavior in experimentally created social climates." Journal of Social Psychology 10: 271–301. Print.; **229** These first six bullets were either outlined in the literature review of the following article or what they discovered in their study.. So, some of these were finding from other studies cited in this article: Myaskovsky, Larissa, Emily Unikel, and Mary Amanda Dew. "Effects Of Gender Diversity On Performance And Interpersonal Behavior In Small Work Groups." Sex Roles 52.9/10 (205): 645-657. SocINDEX with Full Text. Web. 9 July 2014.; **229** Ivy, Diana K. GenderSpeak: Personal Effectiveness in Gender Communication. Boston: Pearson, 2012. 318-319. Print.; **229** Ivy, Diana K. GenderSpeak: Personal Effectiveness in Gender Communication. Boston: Pearson, 2012. 321. Print.; **230** Hamm, Mia. Go for the Goal: A Champion's Guide to Winning in Soccer and Life. New York: Harper Collins, 1999. Print. 3-4; **234** Harper, Nancy L., and Lawrence R. Askling. "Group Communication And Quality Of Task Solution In A Media Production Organization." Communication Monographs 47.2 (1980): 77-100. Communication & Mass Media Complete. Web. 11 July 2014

CHAPTER 9

Photos: CO John Fedele/Blend Images/Getty Images; **236** Joggie Botma/Shutterstock; **238** Hero Images/Getty Images; **240** Hero Images/Getty Images; **242** Sam Edwards/Caiaimage/OJO+/Getty Images; **246** Andy Roberts/Caiaimage/Getty Images; **250** Zuma Press/ Alamy; **252** Blue Jean Images/ Alamy; **259** Micromonkey/Fotolia

Text: 240 Harris, Thomas E. and John C. Sherblom. Small Group and Team Communication. Boston: Allyn & Bacon, 2011. 166. Print.; **241** Van de Ven, Andrew H. and Andre L. Delbecq. "The nominal group as a research instrument for exploratory health studies". American Journal of Public Health 1972; 62: 337–342; **246** Adler, Nancy J. and Allison Gundersen. International Dimensions of Organizational Behavior. 5th ed. Mason: Thomson South-Western, 2008. 135: 138-140; **247** Adler, Nancy J. and Allison Gundersen. International Dimensions of Organizational Behavior. 5th ed. Mason: Thomson South-Western, 2008. 135: 145-147; **248-249** Table created from information collected from the following articles and book: Kim, Do-Yeon and Junsu Park. "Cultural Differences in Risk: The Group Facilitation Effect." Judgment and Decision Making 5.5 (2010): n. pag. Web. 31 July 2014.; Sagie, Abraham and Zeynep Aycan. "A Cross-Cultural Analysis of Participative Decision-making in

organizations." Human Relations 56.4 (2003): 453-473. Print.; Conyne, Robert K., et al. "Cultural Similarities and Differences In Group Work: Pilot Study Of A U.S.–Chinese Group Comparison." Group Dynamics: Theory, Research, And Practice 3.1 (1999): 40-50. PsycARTICLES. Web. 31 July 2014.; Adler, Nancy J. and Allison Gundersen. International Dimensions ; **250** "Supreme Court Nominee Sonia Sotomayor's Speech at Berkeley Law in 2001." News Archive: 2009 Archive. Berkeley Law. UC Berkeley School of Law, 6 May 2009. Web. 17 Sept. 2014; **250** Hannagan, Rebecca, and Christopher Larimer. "Does Gender Composition Affect Group Decision Outcomes? Evidence From A Laboratory Experiment." Political Behavior 32.1 (2010): 51. Academic Search Complete. Web. 4 Aug. 2014; **250** Hannagan, Rebecca, and Christopher Larimer. "Does Gender Composition Affect Group Decision Outcomes? Evidence From A Laboratory Experiment." Political Behavior 32.1 (2010): 51. Academic Search Complete. Web. 4 Aug. 2014; **251** Brown, Allen and Tara Mistry. "Group Work with 'Mixed Membership" Groups: Issues of Race and Gender." A Quarter Century of Classics (1978-2004): Capturing the Theory, Practice, and Spirit of Social Work with Groups. Eds. Andrew Malekoff and Roselle Kurland. Binghamton: Haworth, 205. 133-148. Print

CHAPTER 10

Photos: CO Marc Romanelli/Blend Images/Getty Images; **264** Robert Daly/Caiaimage/OJO+/Getty Images; **264** Monkey Business Images/Shutterstock; **266** Miscellaneoustock/Alamy; **268** Rawpixel/ Fotolia; **270** Skynesher/E+/Getty Images; **271** Jack Hollingsworth/DigitalVision/Getty Images; **274** Hero Images/Getty Images; **276** Ke Yu/E+/Getty Images; **278** Avantgarde/Fotolia; **282-283** Blend Images/ Hill Street Studios/Brand X Pictures/Getty Images; **282-283** Blend Images/Hill Street Studios/Brand X Pictures/Getty Images; **288-289** Kunal Mehta/ Shutterstock; **291** Kasto/Fotolia

Text: 269 Norman Katlov, The Fabulous Fanny: The Story of Fanny Brice (New York: Knopf, 1953), 71, Print.; **271** Lancaster, Lynne C., and David Stillman. When Generations Collide. New York: Harper, 2002. 18–32. Print; **272** Maslow, Abraham. Motivation and Personality. New York: Harper, 1954. 80–106. Print.

CHAPTER 11

Photos: 292 Antoine Arraou/PhotoAlto Agency RF Collections/Getty Images; **294** James Hardy/

PhotoAlto Agency RF Collections/Getty Images; **302** Andrey Popov/Fotolia; **306** Anthony Lee/ OJO Images/Getty Images; **308** Aycatcher/Fotolia; 316 Room the Agency/Alamy; **320** Wavebreakmedia/ Shutterstock

Text: 300 Judy Strauss and Raymond Frost, E-marketing, (Upper Saddle River, NJ Prentice Hall. 2nd ed. 2009).; **301** Dr. Lyle Petersen, the director of the Division of Vector-borne Infectious Diseases, Centers for Disease Control and Prevention on August 23, 2012.; **303** Neil Shea, Africa's Last Frontier, Ethiopia's Omo Valley is still a place ruled by ritual and revenge. But change is coming, from upriver. Published: March 2010; **303** Aristotle. "Rhetorica." Trans. W. Rhys Roberts. The Basic Works of Aristotle. Ed. Richard McKeon. New York: Random, 1941. Print; **315** The American Society for the Prevention of Cruelty to Animals. "Pet Statistics." ASPCA.org. ASPCA, 2012. Web. 10 Oct. 2012; **323** Monroe, Alan H. Principles and Types of Speeches. Chicago: Scott, 1935. Print; **325** "Quintilian."Forty Thousand Quotations: Prose and Poetical. Comp. Charles Noel Douglas. New York: Halcyon House, 1917; Bartleby. com, 2012. Web. 9 July 2014

CHAPTER 12

Photos: 322 Mtkang/Shutterstock; **332** Lorraine Harris/Moment/Getty Images; **334** Sumaya Hisham/ Demotix/Corbis News/Corbis; **340** Laura Doss/ Fuse/Getty Images; **342** Myrleen Pearson/Alamy; **346** Neyro/Fotolia; **346** Pearson Education; **350** Image Source/Stockbyte/Getty Images; **351** Fuse/Getty Images; **351** Eric Isselee/Fotolia; **351** Eric Isselee/Fotolia; **351** Eric Isselee/Fotolia; **355** Ifeelstock/Fotolia; **356** Vgajic/E+/Getty Images

Text: 332 President Barack Obama, at the December 10, 2013, memorial service for Nelson Mandela; **332** Although commonly attributed to Aristotle, this quotation originates from Will Durant's summation of Aristotle's ideas in Ethics, book II, chapter 4, and book I, chapter 7. See Will Durant, The Story of Philosophy: The Lives and Opinions of the World's Greatest Philosophers (New York: Pocket, 1991), 76, Print; **334** The Declaration of Independence: A Transcription, In Congress, July 4, 1776; **337** Based on Edward J. Corbett and Robert J. Connors, Classical Rhetoric for the Modern Student, 4th ed. (New York: Oxford UP, 1999), 62–71, Print; **337** William Shakespeare, The

Merchant of Venice, 3:1; **337** Based on Edward J. Corbett and Robert J. Connors, Classical Rhetoric for the Modern Student, 4th ed. (New York: Oxford UP, 1999), 62–71, Print; **337** Hillary Rodham Clinton, US election: Full text of Hillary Clinton's speech in Denver, 2008 DNC speech; **337** Winston Churchill, Churchill: The Power of Words, (Da Capo Press, 2012); **337** John F. Kennedy, Profiles In Courage, (New York, Harper & Row ©1964); **337** Benjamin Franklin (Franklin, circa 18th century); **356** Nancy Duarte, Slide:ology: The Art and Science of Creating Great Presentations, (Sebastopol: O'Reilly, 2008), 83, 222. Print.

CHAPTER 13

Photos: 364 Alexa Miller/Photodisc/Getty Images; **366** Image Source/Getty Images; **368** Mark Lewis/ Photographer's Choice RF/Getty Images; **370** Hero Images/Getty Images; **376** Hero Images/Alamy; **380** Sam72/Shutterstock; **388** Fuse/Getty Images

Text: 366 United Nations, "'If Information and Knowledge Are Central to Democracy, They Are Conditions for Development,' Says Secretary-General" (New York: United Nations, 23 June 1997), Web; **381** Muir, J. (1901). Our national parks. New York, NY: Houghton Mifflin.

CHAPTER 14

Photos: 391 Steve Debenport/E+/Getty Images; **394** Radius Images/Getty Images; **396** Ghislain & Marie David de Lossy/Cultura/Getty Images; **398** Photka/Fotolia; **400** Jamie Rose/Aurora Photos/ Alamy; **404** Grove Pashley/Photodisc/Getty Images; **406** Barry Fackler/Moment Open/Getty Images; **410** Blend Images/Hill Street Studios/Alamy; **416** Ingolf Hatz/Cultura/Getty Images; **420** Hero Images/Getty Images; **430** Stokkete/Shutterstock; **437** Paul Bradbury/Caiaimage/OJO+/Getty Images

Text: 392 Ludwig Wittgenstein, On Certainty, trans. Denis Paul and G. E. M. Anscombe, ed. G. E. M. Anscombe and G.H. von Wright (New York: Harper, 1969), Print; **398** President George W. Bush, Statement by the President in His Address to the Nation, September 11, 2001; **421, 422** Female student, 20, Pittsburg, quoted by Schwarz, Alan. "In Their Own Words: 'Study Drugs.'" New York Times. New York Times, 9 June 2012. Web. 6 Mar. 2013; **423** Substance Abuse & Mental Health Services Administration in Feb. 10, 2013 article.